Multilingual Youth Practice Communication

With an eye to the playful, reflexive, self-conscious ways in which global youth engage with each other online, this volume analyzes user-generated data from these interactions to show how communication technologies and multilingual resources are deployed to project local as well as translocal orientations. With examples from a range of multilingual settings, each author explores how youth exploit the creative, heteroglossic potential of their linguistic repertoires, from rudimentary attempts to engage with others in a second language to hybrid multilingual practices. Often, their linguistic, orthographic, and stylistic choices challenge linguistic purity and prescriptive correctness, yet, in other cases, their utterances constitute language policing, linking "standardness" or "correctness" to piety, trans-local affiliation, or national belonging. Written for advanced undergraduates, postgraduates, and researchers in linguistics, applied linguistics, education, and media and communication studies, this volume is a timely and readymade resource for researching online multilingualism with a range of methodologies and perspectives.

CECELIA CUTLER is Professor of Linguistics at the City University of New York, Lehman College and the Graduate Center. Her sociolinguistic research explores language and identity among adolescents, language attitudes towards Spanish and dialects of English, digital language practices, and changes in New York City English. She is author of *White Hip Hoppers, Language and Identity in Post-Modern America* (2014) and co-editor of *Language Contact in Africa and the African Diaspora in the Americas* (2017).

UNN RØYNELAND is Professor of Scandinavian Linguistics and Deputy Director of MultiLing, Center for Multilingualism in Society across the Lifespan, at the Department of Linguistics and Scandinavian Studies at the University of Oslo. Her sociolinguistic research investigates linguistic practices among adolescents in multilingual Oslo, enregisterment of new speech styles, language attitudes, dialect acquisition among immigrants, language policy and planning, and digital language practices. She is co-editor of *Language Standardisation: Theory and Practice* (2016), and *Reality Rhymes – Recognition of Rap in Multicultural Norway* (2016).

Multilingual Youth Practices in Computer Mediated Communication

Edited by

Cecelia Cutler

City University of New York

Unn Røyneland

University of Oslo

CAMBRIDGE
UNIVERSITY PRESS

University Printing House, Cambridge CB2 8BS, United Kingdom

One Liberty Plaza, 20th Floor, New York, NY 10006, USA

477 Williamstown Road, Port Melbourne, VIC 3207, Australia

314-321, 3rd Floor, Plot 3, Splendor Forum, Jasola District Centre, New Delhi - 110025, India

79 Anson Road, #06-04/06, Singapore 079906

Cambridge University Press is part of the University of Cambridge.

It furthers the University's mission by disseminating knowledge in the pursuit of education, learning and research at the highest international levels of excellence.

www.cambridge.org
Information on this title: www.cambridge.org/9781107464544
DOI: 10.1017/9781316135570

© Cambridge University Press 2018

This publication is in copyright. Subject to statutory exception and to the provisions of relevant collective licensing agreements, no reproduction of any part may take place without the written permission of Cambridge University Press.

First published 2018
First paperback edition 2021

A catalogue record for this publication is available from the British Library

ISBN 978-1-107-09173-3 Hardback
ISBN 978-1-107-46454-4 Paperback

Cambridge University Press has no responsibility for the persistence or accuracy of URLs for external or third-party internet websites referred to in this publication, and does not guarantee that any content on such websites is, or will remain, accurate or appropriate.

Contents

Figures

Tables

Notes on the Contributors

ZANNIE BOCK is Associate Professor in the Linguistics Department at the University of the Western Cape. Her current publications include work on narrative and discourse analysis, with a focus on racializing discourses among university students, emerging styles in youth instant messaging chats and the ways in which affect and stance are encoded in texts. Earlier publications include discourse analyses of testimonies given before South Africa's Truth and Reconciliation Commission. She also has a long-standing interest in adult education, curricula and materials development and is the project co-ordinator and co-editor of the first southern African textbook in the field, *Language, Society and Communication: An Introduction* (2014).

CECELIA CUTLER is Professor of Linguistics at Lehman College and the Graduate Center of the City University of New York. Her work explores how people project identity and stance through linguistic style choices. Currently, she is working on a collaborative NSF-funded, corpus-building project on language variation in New York City (with Christina Tortora, Michael Newman and Bill Haddican). Her monograph, *White Hip Hoppers, Language and Identity in Post-Modern America* appeared in 2014 and her co-edited volume, *Language Contact in Africa and the African Diaspora in the Americas* appeared in 2017.

NAUSHEENA DALWAI is currently Lecturer in the English Department of the Al Kharj Armed Forces Military Hospital Nursing Institute in Al Kharj, Saudi Arabia. She completed her undergraduate, Honours and Masters degrees at the University of the Western Cape, South Africa. The topic of her Masters thesis was "Social Networking Among UWC Students: Instant Messaging Genres and Registers." Her research interests include discourse analysis, and social media texting styles, norms, and registers.

ANA DEUMERT is a Professor at the University of Cape Town. Her research program is located within the broad field of African sociolinguistics and has a strong transdisciplinary focus. She has worked on the history of Afrikaans (*The Dynamics of Cape Dutch*, 2004), co-authored *Introducing*

Sociolinguistics (with Rajend Mesthrie, Joan Swann and William Leap, 2009) and the *Dictionary of Sociolinguistics* (with Joan Swann, Rajend Mesthrie and Theresa Lillis, 2004). Her latest book looks at mobile communication from a global perspective (*Sociolinguistics and Mobile Communication*, 2014). Her current work explores the use of language in global political movements. She is co-editor of *IMPACT – Studies in Language and Society* (with Kristine Horner), co-editor of *Cambridge Approaches to Language Contact* (with Salikoko Mufwene) and co-editor of *Edinburgh Sociolinguistics* (with Paul Kerswill). She is a recipient of the Humboldt Research Award (2016) and is an NRF-rated scientist.

CÉCILE EVERS lectures in anthropology at the University of California, Riverside. Central themes in her research include the cultural citizenship of French Muslim youth, their language practices, and their religious trajectories. She is currently working on a postdoctoral research project entitled "Alienated from home: orthodox Muslim young women retreat from Marseille to the Muslim world." This project examines how young Muslim women from Marseille are relocating to their parents' home countries, and sometimes other countries in the Muslim world, in their search for cultural belonging and spiritual fulfillment.

MATT GARLEY is Assistant Professor in the Department of English at York College of the City University of New York, as well as a member of the doctoral faculty in the linguistics program at the Graduate Center of the City University of New York. In his research, he uses both qualitative and quantitative (corpus) methods to investigate the properties of varieties of English, the linguistics of hip hop culture, the linguistics of computer-mediated communication, and writing systems. His present research project involves aspects of language contact and linguistic change in Latinx hip hop culture in the US. His work has appeared in *Discourse, Context, and Media*, as well as in edited volumes.

LARS HINRICHS is Associate Professor of English language and linguistics at the University of Texas at Austin. His doctoral work (PhD 2006, Freiburg, Germany) was a discourse analysis of Creole-English code-switching in Jamaican e-mails. In other work, he has investigated sociophonetic aspects of speech in the Jamaican-Canadian community, the effect of prescriptivism on morphosyntactic alternation in standard English corpora, and variation and change in Texas English. His work has appeared in journals such as *Language, English Language and Linguistics, English World-Wide* and others.

JAMIE SHINHEE LEE is Associate Professor of Linguistics at the University of Michigan-Dearborn and editor of *World Englishes in Pop*

Culture (with Yamuna Kachru, 2006) and *English in Asian Popular Culture* (with Andrew Moody, 2012). Her research interests include world Englishes, language and popular culture, globalization and education policy, bilingualism, and Korean pragmatics/discourse analysis. Her articles have appeared in *Asian Englishes, Critical Discourse Studies, Critical Inquiry in Language Studies, English Today, English World-Wide, Journal of Creative Communications, Journal of Pragmatics, Language in Society, Language Research, World Englishes* as well as in several edited collections.

KRISTIN VOLD LEXANDER is Postdoctoral Fellow at MultiLing, Centre for Multilingualism in Society across the Lifespan at the Department of Linguistics and Scandinavian Studies, University of Oslo. Her research focuses on digital media and multilingualism, and she has worked with digital literacy practices in African languages and orthographies in the Senegalese context. Currently, she studies language use and mediated communication in Norwegian-Senegalese families in Norway. Her work has appeared in *Journal of Sociolinguistics, New Media and Society*, and *Journal des Africanistes*, as well as in edited volumes.

UNN RØYNELAND is Professor of Scandinavian Languages and Deputy Director at MultiLing, Center for Multilingualism in Society across the Lifespan at the Department of Linguistics and Scandinavian Studies, University of Oslo. Her research interests include language and dialect contact, new dialect formation, dialect leveling and youth language. Central themes of her current research are the emergence and enregisterment of multiethnolectal speech styles among adolescents in multilingual Oslo, language attitudes, ideologies and language, and identity. Her work has appeared in the *International Journal of Bilingualism*, the *International Journal of the Sociology of Language*, as well as several edited volumes.

CHRISTOPHER STROUD is Senior Professor of Linguistics and Director for the Centre for Multilingualism and Diversities Research (CMDR) at the University of the Western Cape. He is also Professor of Transnational Bilingualism at Stockholm University. His current research focuses on practices and ideologies of multilingualism in socially and politically transforming economies in Southern Africa. In this context, he is exploring the notion of *linguistic citizenship* as a way of rethinking the role of language in brokering diversity in contemporary polities in a decolonial framework. His work has appeared in *Journal of Sociolinguistics, The International Journal of Bilingualism, International Journal of Bilingualism and Bilingual Education, Language Policy, International Journal of the Sociology of Language, Linguistic Landscape, Journal of Multilingual and*

Multicultural Development, Journal of Linguistic Anthropology, as well as several edited volumes.

KARL SWINEHART is Assistant Professor of Comparative Humanities, University of Louisville. His research concerns multilingualism and language contact in popular culture, with a particular interest in the role of state and non-state institutions in the formation of linguistic registers. His current research among indigenous language media professionals and educators in Bolivia addresses relationships between institutions, linguistic practice, and social change. His work has appeared in the *Journal of Linguistic Anthropology, Language and Communication, Language in Society*, and *Social Text*.

Preface

What can people do with multiple languages that they cannot do with one? What kinds of practices does multilingualism enable and how does it shape communication in the digital sphere among young people? These questions have motivated the volume *Multilingual Youth Practices in Computer Mediated Communication* (CMC). Inspired by some of the work now emerging in sociolinguistics on the multilingual digital practices of people in a globalizing world, it aims a spotlight on the multilingual practices of young people who have taken up the affordances of digital communication more fervently than any other age group. More specifically, it examines how the "digital generation" in different parts of the world makes use of multilingual repertoires and the social meanings they attach to various linguistic features in their digital communications with others. The volume assembles the work of twelve scholars from sociolinguistics and linguistic anthropology to understand the multilingual digital practices that young people engage in and what these hybrid interactions help them to achieve. With data from youth in South Africa, Senegal, Norway, the USA, France, Germany, the Jamaican and Andean diasporas, and global fans of K-pop, the authors explore how young people make strategic use of their linguistic resources, and the pragmatic and social functions of alternating codes as resources for self-presentation and identity performance, to mark urbanity and cosmopolitanism or to signal alignments with certain groups as opposed to others. The contributions also illustrate how multilingualism takes many forms and serves many functions, from rudimentary attempts to engage with another community to hybrid practices that illustrate a high degree of metapragmatic and metalinguistic awareness of multiple codes.

Acknowledgements

We gratefully acknowledge the support of MultiLing, The Center for Multilingualism in Society across the Lifespan at the Department of Linguistics and Scandinavian Studies (University of Oslo) for its generous support in bringing Cecelia Cutler to MultiLing as a visiting researcher in 2014, for funding a workshop for the contributing authors at MultiLing in 2014, and for subsequent working meetings between the editors, Cecelia Cutler and Unn Røyneland, at MultiLing in 2015, and New York in 2016. These were invaluable opportunities for us to share ideas and move the project forward. We also thank the Professional Staff Congress of the City University of New York for funding the research that went into Cecelia Cutler's chapter. Lastly, we wish to express our gratitude to Kristin Myklestu, research assistant at MultiLing, for her careful work reading and correcting all the chapters and merging the reference lists, and Carmen Lee for her valuable reviewer comments, and to Helen Barton of Cambridge University Press for her constant encouragement and guidance throughout the development and production of the volume.

Part I

From Offline to Online

Multilingual Practices across Settings

1 Multilingualism in the Digital Sphere

The Diverse Practices of Youth Online

Cecelia Cutler and Unn Røyneland

What can people do with multiple languages that they cannot do with one? What kinds of practices does multilingualism enable and how does it shape communication in the digital sphere among young people? These questions have motivated the volume *Multilingual Youth Practices in Computer Mediated Communication* (CMC). This volume was inspired by some of the work now emerging in sociolinguistics on the multilingual digital practices of people in a globalizing world (e.g. Androutsopoulos 2015; Barton and Lee 2013; Danet and Herring 2007a; Deumert 2014a; Spilioti and Georgakopoulou 2015; Jones et al. 2015; Lee 2017; Thurlow and Mroczek 2011a). In contrast with these volumes, however, the present work aims a spotlight on the multilingual practices of young people who have taken up the affordances of digital communication more fervently than any other age group (Beheshti and Large 2013; Buckingham and Willett 2013). More specifically, we examine how the "digital generation" in different parts of the world makes use of multilingual repertoires and the social meanings they attach to various linguistic features in their digital communications with others.

The purpose of the volume is not to make definitive claims about multilingual CMC practices among young people, but rather to describe the state of the art based on what a select group of researchers have observed in particular settings around the world. In the process, we hope to document where the field is at this moment in time, and provide a window onto the nature of the debates and unanswered questions that exist within it pertaining to multilingual youth practices in CMC. This book assembles the work of twelve scholars from sociolinguistics and linguistic anthropology to understand the multilingual digital practices that young people engage in and what these hybrid interactions help them to achieve. With data from youth in South Africa, Senegal, Norway, the US, France, Germany, the Jamaican and Andean diasporas, and global fans of K-pop[1], the authors explore how young people use their multilingual repertoires when interacting with one another online.

[1] K-pop is a pop cultural genre originating in South Korea.

Following Deumert (2014a), the chapters place a great deal of emphasis on the playful, creative, reflexive, and self-conscious ways that many young people interact with one another in digital spaces. This contrasts with the focus on language as a bounded entity and the systematic, rule-governed aspects of language production that typifies what Eckert (2012: 87) calls "first" and "second" wave sociolinguistic studies. This "third wave" approach opens up the field of inquiry to speaker-generated, creative, spontaneous data in contrast to strictly researcher-driven forms of data (Blommaert and Rampton 2012). Our approach also contrasts with approaches to CMC organized by genre (e.g. Baron 2008; Crystal 2006), and the analysis of specific linguistic variables via "coding and counting methods" (Androutsopoulos 2011: 277). Nor do we focus on the distribution of languages, or language choice within websites or across linguistic settings (e.g. Danet and Herring 2007a). Rather, we explore how communication technologies are "locally appropriated to enact a variety of discourse genres" (Androutsopoulos 2006: 421), and what kinds of social and semiotic work multilingual practices accomplish in online discourse.

Increasingly, scholars are turning to examinations of how people interact across languages, geographical boundaries, diasporas, and in far-flung places around the world as opposed to geographically bounded speech communities. And as Lee (2017) points out, despite the dominance of English in the Internet Age, the presence of other languages is rising and even monolingual web users find that using more than one language can be an important resource for interacting with others or doing things online (Danet and Herring 2003; Wright 2004). Furthermore, recent work has shown that CMC offers people the ability to interact in minority languages or varieties that have no written standard, opening up new possible meanings and domains of use for hitherto marginalized codes (e.g. Deumert and Masinyana 2008; Deumert and Lexander 2013).

This volume aims its sights on individuals who live in specific places around the world, but reach beyond the confines of the local to "hang out" and "share" with others, in many cases with others whom they have never met or physically interacted with. Often, they are drawn together by a common interest (e.g. K-pop, indigenous Aymara rap music, or becoming a more pious Muslim); in other instances, they are interacting with intimate friends, lovers, or family in proximal geographical locations. The point is that digital interaction brings people into common virtual spaces and helps overcome the physical separation between them – whether great or small (Androutsopoulos 2014; Deumert 2014a).

Multilinguals make strategic use of their linguistic resources, and the pragmatic and social functions and alternating codes are important resource for self-presentation and identity performance (chapters in this volume by Hinrichs,

Bock, Dalwai and Stroud, Swinehart, and Røyneland). Some use international languages like English, French, Arabic, or Spanish to mark urbanity and cosmopolitanism or to signal alignments with certain groups as opposed to others (chapters in this volume by Evers, Garley, Lexander, and Cutler). The physical distances and language boundaries that separate individuals can be bridged by various forms of polylinguistic practices or the ways in which speakers use features associated with different "languages" – even when they know very little of them (Lee this volume). Thus, we observe how multilingualism takes many forms and serves many functions, from rudimentary attempts to engage with another community to hybrid practices that illustrate a high degree of metapragmatic and metalinguistic awareness of multiple codes. Using another language allows people to project local as well as translocal orientations, signal shifts in frame, mitigate face-threatening acts, and engage in humorous, sarcastic play, etc. (Androutsopoulos 2007; Jonsson and Muhonen 2014). There is also great subversive and transgressive potential in the freedom that writing and interacting in more than one language affords and young people exploit this potential in their hybrid linguistic and orthographic practices, flouting spelling rules, contesting standard language ideologies, and "talking back" to colonial languages (Deumert and Lexander 2013; hooks 1989).

What Do We Mean by "Multilingualism"?

Before venturing any further, we need a working definition of multilingualism, both in terms of individual and societal multilingualism. There are very strict and specific psycholinguistic definitions, such as the one proposed by Bloomfield (1933) who posited that a bilingual should possess "native-like control of two or more languages" ("perfect bilinguals"). On the other hand, there are rather loose definitions like: Anyone who possesses a minimum of competence in one of the four language skills: listening comprehension, speaking, reading, writing (Macnamara 1967: 59). Others, such as Weinreich (1953) and Grosjean (1997; 2008; 2010) propose definitions that are based on language use rather than language competence: A bi-/multilingual is a person who uses, or can use, more than one language in daily life or in particular situations. Linguists' definitions have been shifting in recent years towards these more inclusive interpretations, so as to include all people who function in more than one language regardless of proficiency. Multilinguals exist on a continuum, with varying levels of proficiency in terms of speaking, oral comprehension, reading, and writing: It is common for people to be able to read in a second language, but not speak it or, alternatively, to be able to speak and understand a language, but lack literacy skills. With respect to CMC, people may use languages online that they do not use in "body-to-body" interaction (Deumert

2014a: 9, 12) so multilingual CMC practices are not exclusive to highly competent multilinguals.[2] Framing individual multilingualism in an open and inclusive way acknowledges the variable language competencies of individuals and the achievement that functioning in a second or other language entails. It also makes us as researchers more attuned to what people can do with their linguistic repertoires and what sorts of multilingual communicative practices they engage in in CMC contexts.

Societal multilingualism pertains to the ways in which languages are dealt with at the institutional level, which is contingent in many ways upon the status and relationship between languages in a given society; this involves attitudes towards languages, potential determinants of language choice, the symbolic practices, and the correlations between language use and social factors such as ethnicity, religion, and class (Sridhar 1996: 47). Societal multilingualism does not entail that all individual group members are multilingual; some countries such as Canada have an official policy of French-English bilingualism, yet many Canadians are monolingual. In other settings, there may be an official policy of monolingualism while most people speak at least two languages.

Thus, we consider multilingual practices among individuals with varying levels of language proficiency, but also individuals living in societies with different types of multilingualism (i.e. Germany vs. South Africa vs. Bolivia). In some instances, we observe people interacting with others who share norms of societal multilingualism (e.g. educated young people in Dakar who routinely mingle French and Wolof in Lexander's chapter); in other cases, we observe individuals interacting who have very different patterns of individual and societal multilingualism (e.g. Malaysian vs. Korean youth in Lee's chapter on K-pop fans). As noted above, just because someone uses more than one language in their CMC interactions does not entail that they use more than one language in their everyday communication. Without ethnographic corroboration, we simply cannot know this about all subjects. The important point is that it is very common for people to employ their multilingual repertoires in CMC, raising questions about the degree to which CMC affords people more opportunities to engage in multilingual practices, and what new practices are emerging as a result (cf. Lee 2017). Other questions include whether CMC practices are helping to revitalize dying, minority, and/or endangered languages and dialects by establishing written norms and creating new domains for their use. Does online multilingual interaction trigger shifts in language attitudes and ideologies? Additionally, we ask whether multilingual practices are transforming the way ordinary people view language itself and whether

[2] e.g. Deumert (2014a) notes how people tend to orient towards bodies, not only to faces, thus motivating the use of the term "body-to-body" over "face-to-face."

these practices contribute to a less delineated, more unified conception of a "language repertoire."

An important point we wish to make is that multilingualism in CMC can refer to many different phenomena: it can be the *gestalt* co-existence of many languages on different websites or channels in their entirety (e.g. Internet Relay Chat, Flickr, blogger.com, which are "massively multilingual") (Androutsopoulos 2013b: 671–672). These can be viewed as multilingual or heteroglossic discourse spaces held together by their spatial co-existence in product and reception rather than their dialogic orientation to each other. In other words, there is a qualitative difference between the juxtaposition of codes within static, non-dialogic websites and interactive modalities that involve participants' code choices and the multilingual practices that emerge in dialogic exchanges between individuals as showcased in this volume. Following Androutsopoulos (2013b), we can imagine a model that orders various forms of interaction in CMC from the least to the most interactive and "speech-like," bearing in mind that the code choices made by specific individuals in a corpus of comments or microblogs are not necessarily sequentially related to one another.

What Do We Mean by Computer Mediated Communication?

This volume embraces a broad definition of *Computer Mediated Communication* (CMC), including any communicative transactions that occur through the use of two or more electronic devices such as mobile phones, tablets, PCs, etc. The older, umbrella term for this was *Electronically Mediated Communication* or EMC, which comprised both the study of CMC as well as the communicative technologies themselves (computers, PDAs, mobile phones, etc.). *New Media* is another commonly used term in studies of online discourse (e.g. Danesi 2015; Tannen and Trester 2013; Thurlow and Mrozcek 2011a). Whereas CMC entails some form of interaction or transaction, *New Media* usually pertains to online content that is available on-demand and visible to anyone in any place with internet access and that offers the possibility of interactive user feedback and creative participation (i.e. online newspapers, websites, blogs, online games, etc.). Thus, we can think of New Media as the content itself and CMC as online engagement – oftentimes, but not always – in response to New Media content.

Very commonly, CMC entails communication between two or more individuals posting comments, links, tweets, and sending messages asynchronously or synchronously with their mobile phones or tablets. The various analyses of multilingual CMC practices in the volume focus on real-time generation of new, unregulated interaction. We view these as forms of CMC because of their transactional nature. Furthermore, we claim that including these stylized, reflexive, self-conscious forms of language use within the larger scope of routine unselfconscious language practices gives a much richer and empirically more sound understanding of multilingual language practices than strictly examining speech data (Blommaert and Rampton 2012).

What Can the Organization of the Chapters Reveal?

This volume could have been organized in several possible ways. Several chapters feature practices associated with popular music fandom and/or hip-hop culture (Cutler, Garley, Lee, Røyneland, and Swinehart). The ease of creating and sharing music video content (e.g. YouTube) and participating in online forms of fandom (microblogs, Facebook and Twitter) have created a core set of practices among young people. However, these practices do not characterize all the contributions in the volume, the remainder of which are rather heterogeneous in terms of their interactional purposes and functions. Hence, we have chosen to organize the chapters in terms of the type of data collected by the authors – online vs. blended online and offline data (Androutsopoulos 2013a; Spilioti 2011).

Among CMC scholars, there has been a tendency to view data collection methods on a continuum from screen-based (analyses of user-generated online data, but no systematic online observation) to user-based (data prompted by researchers who are in direct contact with users about their practices, but no online data) (Androutsopoulos 2013a: 241). In between these two poles, researchers may have differing degrees of contact with users and rely on different types of data: only online data, blended data (offline and online), or only offline data.

The data and methods in the present volume do not fit neatly into this model given that the authors are coming from a more sociolinguistic perspective in which contact with the community is the starting point. The chapters in the volume illustrate a number of different approaches reflecting the disciplinary backgrounds and interests of the authors. Early work on CMC was carried out mainly by scholars in media studies and communication rather than sociolinguistics (e.g. Herring 1996). Over the years, media and communication scholars have increasingly moved *offline* to enrich their investigations of online CMC phenomena. In contrast, most of the contributors in the present volume are sociolinguists and linguistic anthropologists by training who have moved *online* to further their ethnographic, fieldwork-based research in variationist sociolinguistics, dialectology, language ideologies, discourse analysis, and other fields. The merger of scholars from these various fields has generated greater interest in contextually rich data that combines online ethnographic approaches with analysis of offline communicative practices. Building on the model above, but with the important caveat that our investigations generally begin offline and move online, we have organized the ten chapters into two sections as shown below:

Part 1 Evers (Chapter 2), Bock, Dalwai, and Stroud (Chapter 3), Lexander (Chapter 4), Garley (Chapter 5)
Part 2 Strictly Online: Multilingual Practices in Texting, Blogging, and Commenting Deumert (Chapter 6), Cutler (Chapter 7), Røyneland (Chapter 8), Swinehart (Chapter 9), Hinrichs (Chapter 10), Lee (Chapter 11)

Part 1 is made up of chapters that explore youth identities through offline and online multilingual practices. Part 2 consists of chapters that stem from long-term researcher engagement in various communities but which analyze how the concerns and interests of community members are played out online.

What Kinds of Data are Showcased in the Volume and How Is It Useful for Sociolinguists?

A significant tendency within recent youth language research has been the focus on particular speech styles developing in urban multicultural communities. These heteroglossic linguistic practices, dubbed "multiethnolectal youth language" (Nortier 2008; Quist and Svendsen 2010), "polylingual languaging" (Jørgensen 2008) or "late modern urban youth style" (Madsen, Møller, and Jørgensen 2010) may involve overt evaluative language use such as commentary, crossing, and stylization (Rampton 2014; Coupland 2007). Studies of these aspects of enregisterment and, indeed, any analysis of youth language can be complemented substantially by including analyses of multilingual practices in CMC because they allow us to examine self-generated video, music, and speech as well as appropriations and recontextualizations of media material in local codes for local audiences (Cutler and Røyneland 2015; Deumert 2014a; Lexander 2011a, b; Terkourafi 2010; Swinehart 2012a). Importantly, these recontextualizations can be a key way in which various registers, local dialects, and speech varieties become culturally noticed or enregistered (Agha 2005).

Most of the data analyzed in the volume are written, but strongly oral and visual in style. This "digital orality" (Soffer 2012) entails a great deal of non-standard writing, including deliberate misspellings, the use of initialisms, rebus spellings, and onomatopoeia (Crystal 2006; Danet 2001). It includes personal texts and SMS messages between friends and family members (chapters by Bock, Dalwai and Stroud, Lexander, and Evers), posts on an online forum (Garley), YouTube video content and comments (chapters by Swinehart, Røyneland, and Cutler), Facebook updates and posts (Evers), blogs (Hinrichs), and micro-blogging (Lee). The degree of orality in each of these genres is slightly different (more or less speech-like), as is the directionality (synchronous/asynchronous, one-to-one vs. one-to-many, many-to-many) and purpose of the communication (flirting, greeting a friend, expressing opinions, performing fandom, etc.). As is true of speech data, digital writing contains all kinds of hybrid language use, mixing, polylanguaging, metalinguistic and metapragmatic commentary, and language policing. We can observe and identify emerging sociolinguistic, discourse, and pragmatic norms and see how these norms are negotiated, played with, and contested. Multilingual CMC data can help us understand how users construct their ethnolinguistic identities and alignments and how they maintain boundaries and define who is part of the group and who is not.

The data in the volume are also characterized by a wealth of language play, crossing (Blommaert and Rampton 2012), and the enregisterment of ways of talking and of languages and styles (Stæhr 2014), all of which show that these forms of data are increasingly playing a role in the spread of language attitudes and ideologies as well as the spread of multilingual practices themselves. The value of this kind of data for sociolinguists is that it is spontaneous and user-generated and avoids some of the problems associated with the Observer's Paradox, since in most cases the CMC data were created without the involvement of the researcher. As such, it gives us a snapshot of users' social worlds and written online practices. This kind of data can therefore greatly complement traditional ethnographic and sociolinguistic methods by showing us how individuals interact across more than one event, and across various modalities and channels both online and off. However, this does not imply that CMC data are strictly "complementary"; these data are of course valuable and interesting in their own right and are in no way inferior to "traditional" forms of sociolinguistic data, but as sociolinguists, we deem it necessary to make this claim explicit given the preference for speech data in the field.

Of course, there are things you cannot do with written CMC data; the most obvious is fine-grained phonetic analysis, since there is no speech signal (see discussion in De Decker and Nycz 2011 regarding speech data in YouTube). However, there is a lot of "dialectal" and phonemic writing that can give us clues to a people's ways of speaking, their language attitudes, or stances they wish to project. As noted earlier, CMC data are not necessarily well suited to "coding and counting methods" (Androutsopoulos 2011) and lend themselves more to qualitative approaches in which even a single token may have social significance and quite nuanced, socially-situated meanings. Thus, this kind of data does not allow for quantitative analysis of sound changes or intra-speaker phonological variation because written CMC data are not categorically representative of how people talk, although it is in many ways more speech-like and relaxed than formal writing (Deumert 2014a; McWhorter 2013).

One additional type of multilingual practice includes the use of two or more languages across different modes and platforms at the same time. Though not explored in this volume, it is common for youth who engage in online gaming (e.g. in Scandinavia) to talk in English, then Skype at the same time with their peers in the home language (e.g. Norwegian or Danish), send SMS in the home language and chat on Facebook in both English and the home language (for other examples see Jonsson and Muhonen 2014; Kytölä and Westinen 2015; Leppänen et al. 2009; Stæhr 2015). Switching modes and languages – speaking and writing in more than one language at the same time on different platforms – is undoubtedly common practice for many people and deserves future investigation.

How Do the authors Conceptualize Multilingualism and the Juxtaposition of Different Codes in Their Data?

The authors embrace a range of concepts to describe the mixing of codes that reflect developments in sociolinguistics challenging the boundedness of distinct languages. Generally, they adopt a more fluid conception of linguistic repertoires as sets of resources that may come from disparate sources (Agha 2008; García 2009). Though no one goes so far as to wholly reject the idea that discrete languages can be identified, most are focused on the social meanings and indexical references of various codes rather than the boundaries between them. This allows for a more socially informed analysis of how multilingual digital interaction allows people to challenge, play with, and reevaluate the social-indexical values of speech-forms (Agha 2008). While only one author (Hinrichs) deploys code switching explicitly as an analytical frame implying the boundedness of specific codes, others refer to "mixed codes," "mixed vernaculars," or "code mixing" (Bock, Dalwai, and Stroud, Deumert, Swinehart, Lexander, and Cutler). Several authors use the term heteroglossia (Bakhtin 1981) to describe the co-existence, combination, alternation, and juxtaposition of contrasting codes within a discourse (Hinrichs, Lexander, Garley, Cutler, and Røyneland). Swinehart uses the term "voicing effects" for the use of different registers within a stretch of Spanish, whereas Cutler uses "polyphony" for similar blending of voices, accents, and codes. In using these terms, the authors still rely on the idea that multiple codes are being used, but are not necessarily invested in identifying specific codes within an interaction. The two exceptions are Lexander, who engages in quantitative analysis of which codes are used by her multilingual Senegalese informants, and Hinrichs, whose analysis of Jamaican bloggers hinges on a conception of code switching.

What Do We Mean by "Multilingual CMC Practices?"

Gee (2015) describes practices as the concrete, situated interactions people perform with particular mediational means in order to enact membership in social groups. However, in reference to the digital realm, Jones et al. (2015: 2) observe that it is difficult to speak of the "practice of social networking" or "video gaming" without considering how such practices are performed by real people in real situations. Tagging, for instance, can have different functions and meanings on Twitter versus Flickr (Barton 2015), and most digital practices are "nested" within offline, non-digital practices such as shopping, gardening, dieting, story-sharing (Jones et al. 2015: 3).

Jones et al. (2015: 3) define digital practices as "'assemblages' of actions involving tools associated with digital technologies, which have come to be recognized by specific groups of people as ways of attaining particular social goals, enacting specific social identities, and reproducing certain sets of social relationships." In other words, digital practices are simply new ways to connect with other people, telling them who we are, and signaling where we fit in the social order. By making possible new ways of behaving and being, digital practices alter how people engage in "traditional" non-digital practices like writing letters, shopping for shoes, choosing a restaurant or house hunting (Jones et al. 2015). Thus, we may read not only a newspaper article online, but also the comments of other readers and follow hyperlinks to related content. In some ways, our online practices duplicate or replace older offline practices (we have digital address books, we maintain digital correspondence with friends and colleagues, and send e-vites for parties). Yet in other ways, digital practices depart from our offline practices: celebrities and even heads of state tweet messages to millions of followers; homeowners swap houses with strangers thousands of miles away; polyglots perform their linguistic prowess on YouTube for a global audience, and obscure individuals achieve overnight fame and lucrative corporate deals on the basis of their online activities (Leland 2012; Squires 2014; Tolson 2010).

Within studies of multilingual CMC, the analytical focus on which language dominates within a platform or how users code-switch in interaction has shifted; we are now examining how people act differently given the affordances offered by the chance to engage with others in different languages in CMC and what kinds of "translingual" practices emerge from these new opportunities (Lee 2017: 126). The emphasis in this volume is on the "communicative practices across groups and communities" rather than within a specific geographically defined group (Lee 2017: 126). Androutsopoulos (2013c: 4) has dubbed the term "networked multilingualism" as a cover term for these kinds of practices which include everything language users do with the entire range of linguistic resources constrained by mediation of written language, access to network resources, and orientation to networked audiences. Networked multilingualism encompasses how language resources are "appropriated, combined, juxtaposed and displayed to a networked audience 'for fun' and 'for show' . . . in playful and poetic ways, which both replicate and transcend ordinary conversational practices" (Androutsopoulos 2013c: 7).

Following Blommaert and Rampton (2012: 16), we believe that a focus on multilingual practices allows us to observe how polylingual, heteroglossic, translingual norms are "being manufactured, interrogated or altered" and to identify the "social, cultural and/or political stakes" involved. Multilingual CMC practices entail the use of more than one language, register, or style either at the individual level (e.g. within a stretch of discourse written or uttered by a single person) or between speakers in a larger set of data such as a set of comments posted in response to a video or newspaper article. Rather than strictly attuning to the switching itself or the distribution of one language versus another, we are interested in how individuals use their full linguistic repertoires (languages, styles, registers, etc.) in communicating with each other and what these interactions can tell us about evolving linguistic norms and ideologies.

The multilingual CMC practices analyzed in this volume include multilingual texting and SMS messaging among friends (Bock, Dalwai, and Stroud and Lexander), posting metalinguistic and metapragmatic commentary on YouTube (Cutler, Røyneland, and Swinehart), teaching and learning a resistance vernacular (Deumert), posting, linking, and commenting in multiple languages and scripts on Facebook (Evers), ritualized use of emblematic Korean on fan microblogs (Lee), blending orthographies in online hip-hop fora (Garley), and blogging by and for a Jamaican diasporic community (Hinrichs).

What Do We Mean by "Youth" and What are the Ethical Considerations of Studying Youth Practices Online?

Who is considered "young" has changed considerably over the centuries and differs from one society to another. Antonio Gramsci (1891–1937), the Italian political theorist, described the human life cycle as consisting of just two periods: pre-puberty (childhood) and post-puberty (adulthood). In his view, childhood ended with the onset of puberty, marking one's entrance into adulthood and adult responsibilities (Gramsci 1994). However, in late modern, industrialized, middle-class society, definitions of what part of life constitutes youth have continually expanded to include a larger segment of individuals as people live longer and affluence allows for the postponement of adulthood (Danesi 2003). For example, US-based institutions including the Society for Adolescent Medicine and the MacArthur Foundation view people as old as 34 as part of the adolescent generation. Few people in contemporary Europe or North America would consider 14-year-olds to be adults, but in other parts of the world, 14-year-olds can legally marry. In general, many people living in developing economies and/or people with limited financial resources and social capital take on "adult" responsibilities at a younger age than more affluent individuals or those living in more affluent societies, although this simplistic division may cut across national and class boundaries.

As our volume brings together data from a wide range of countries and cultures, we have chosen to define youth rather loosely, encompassing people in their teens to about age 30. However, when it comes to digital interaction, we do not always know the exact age of most of the people we observe because we do not always have access to their personal information. As Jones and Schieffelin (2009) point out, we never actually know the true identity of anyone who communicates online. Iorio (2009: 129) uses the term "demographically lean" to refer to this kind of data in contrast to social media spaces like Facebook where users are encouraged to represent themselves accurately. Much online writing between strangers is anonymous, with few clues as to a person's identity aside from their usernames or the use of particular registers and stylistic features. In the absence of "offline" ethnographic data about a given individual, we can only speculate about the age range of the young people who created the content we analyze in the volume.

We are interested in young people in part because they are the most likely to be engaging in online/digital/computer-mediated practices of any group. A study by the Pew Research Center (2016a) showed that in all 40 countries tracked across all continents, so-called developed and developing economies, people from 18 to 34 were more likely to own a smartphone and use the internet than adults over the age of 34. In the US, 18–29-year-olds have the highest rates of internet and smartphone use than any group, and roughly three-quarters of Americans own a smartphone (Pew Research 2016a)[3]. Eurostat's survey on Information Communications Technology (ICT) usage in households and by individuals in 28 European countries shows that a far higher proportion of young people made use of a computer and the internet on a daily basis than the rest of the population.[4] This is also true of China, and the so-called "developing" world (Pew Research 2016b). Smartphone use is highest among the 18–29-year-olds in South Africa compared with any other group (Vermeulen 2011). The Pew Research Center (2016b) also reports that in a number of African countries, including South Africa, Nigeria, Senegal,

[3] According to the Pew Research Center (2016a), in the USA, the average teen sends and receives five times more text messages a day than a typical adult. On average, a teen in the USA typically sends or receives 50 text messages a day, while the average adult sends or receives 10. Fully 31 percent of teens send more than 100 texts a day and 15 percent send more than 200 a day, while just 8 percent and 5 percent of adults send that many, respectively.

[4] Across the 28 European countries surveyed, four out of every five, or 80 percent, of young people aged 16–29 used a computer on a daily basis in 2014, nearly 20 percentage points higher than among the whole population (63 percent). In 2014, over half (51 percent) of the population used a mobile device such as a portable computer (includes laptops and tablets) or a handheld device connected to the internet when away from home or work and this proportion reached four-fifths (80 percent) of all young people aged 16–29 (EuroStat 2016).

Ghana, Uganda, Tanzania, and Kenya, 18–34-year-olds were statistically more likely to send text messages and take pictures with their cell phones than people aged 35 and older. Worldwide, 18–34-year-olds are also the most active users of social media (Pew Research 2016c).

In sum, people under the age of 34 are on average more likely to own a smartphone, check their phones, send text messages, use social media, and use their smartphones to access the internet than people aged 35 and over. Consequently, they play a disproportionately large role in the development of written norms and in the creation of online multilingual practices than older people, making them an important demographic to study.

Internet and cellphone technology allow for a great deal more contact with people who speak other languages than ever before. Thus, young people who are the most active users of smartphone technology, the internet, and social media are also more likely to encounter digital opportunities to read and interact with others using more than one language than any other age group. Furthermore, due to the fact that youth is a "liminal stage" in life, young people are perhaps more likely to use their multilingual and multistylistic repertoires in playful, experimental ways although these practices are clearly not limited to young people (Deumert 2014a; Rampton 2011). Androutsopoulos (2015) notes that playfulness and performance are considered key dimensions of convivial social practice in social media and that poetic and playful uses of language characterize multilingual talk online. They are also central dimensions of metrolingualism, polylanguaging and language crossing (Boyd 2011; Papacharissi 2011; Otsuji and Pennycook 2010).

As noted above, one of the challenges in working with CMC data is that we often lack information about users' ages, ethnicities, educational levels, and national origins because data are not always readily apparent, nor do all users represent themselves the same way as they do offline. However, it is also possible to glean a great deal of information from a close reading of the usernames, writing styles, the use of grammatical gender marking, and the comments themselves (providing that these data are indeed indicative of a person's real identity). Thus, we can often speculate about the approximate age, gender, language proficiency, country of origin, interests, and ideologies of a portion of the individuals who post comments, blogs, text messages, and Facebook pages, enabling us to make generalizations about how young people engage with one another online and the nature of their multilingual CMC practices.

The inability to know users' exact ages raises important ethical considerations, particularly as it pertains to the use of data from potentially underage individuals who may not be aware of the ramifications of posting data about themselves or comments online. Research carried out by the project *EU Kids*

Online of 25,000 children (9–16-year-olds) in 25 European countries, show that age restrictions are only partially effective (Livingstone, Ólafsson and Staksrud 2013: 308–311). For instance, more than one third of 9–12-year-olds have a social network site profile (like Facebook), even though the network in most countries sets a minimum age of 13 to join. A quarter of 9–16-year-olds on social networking sites across Europe have their profile set to "public." Staksrud (2016) shows that teenagers publish sensitive photos of themselves online, considering these private while in reality they can be publicly accessible. Sharing one's information online has become much more common since the early days of the internet (Berezkina 2016). We are currently witnessing the evolution of norms regarding the use of online, digital data for research purposes. Traditionally, the degree to which data were of a public or private nature guided ethical considerations regarding informed consent; where a reasonable expectation of privacy exists, researchers were and are expected to obtain consent. However, as Bolander and Locher (2014) point out, the division between public and private is becoming increasingly blurred and should be conceived of as gradable rather than absolute (Bolander and Locher 2014: 17). Furthermore, it is entirely possible for a media text to combine public and private aspects; "[digital texts] may be public in the sense that they are within the public space and can be read by a large and anonymous audience, while at the same time discussing topics which we think of as 'private' and using language which is associated with informal and private conversations" (Landert and Jucker 2011: 1423). The fact that online data is public and possible to retrieve via different sorts of scraping tools, should, of course, not misguide us into thinking that it is freely available for download. By comparison, it would for instance be considered highly unethical to make clandestine recordings of people's conversations in public space even if we have the technology to do so. Regardless of where an oral conversation is taking place, informed consent is expected to be obtained – also from third parties. This poses a considerable challenge to online data collection – and to our conceptualizations of what is private and public, and for whom.

The Association of Internet Researchers has published two documents with guidelines for conducting research in computer-mediated settings (Ess 2002; Markham and Buchanan 2012) as well as a wiki (AOIR ethics wiki 2002).[5] The emphasis in these documents is on guidelines as opposed to rules, given the need for flexibility and the fact that technologies and practices are constantly evolving (Bolander and Locher 2014: 17). These guidelines include several principles for scholars doing research online (Markham and Buchanan 2012: 4–5): weighing the vulnerability of the subjects with the obligation to minimize

[5] Recommendations from the AOIR ethics working committee can be viewed at: www.aoir.org /reports/ethics.pdf

harm, following human research guidelines, and consulting with experts and colleagues about how best to resolve ethical issues as they arise at different stages of the research.

The guidelines suggest, rather than dictate, a path how best to present data from young subjects, prompting each contributing author to consider whether or not to include online usernames or substitute pseudonyms and how best to protect their subjects' privacy. Some have elected to obscure usernames even when the data are from quite "public" spaces like YouTube and despite the fact that, in many cases, the user's online identity can be reconstructed by entering a string in a search engine. Others treat usernames as public data and include some analysis of the names people choose to represent themselves online.

Online Affordances: What Does CMC Allow Young People To Do?

What do multilingual CMC practices allow individuals to do? What are they able to do in CMC beyond what they can do in "body-to-body" interactions? Affordances in CMC are usually understood as the range of what forms of communication are made possible by digital technologies as opposed to practices, which are what people do with digital options (Androutsopoulos 2015). Building on this, we briefly discuss the forms of social and psychological connections that are made possible by CMC as they pertain to this volume. One obvious affordance of CMC practices is the possibility of engaging in culture from a distance or connecting with co-ethnics or like-minded people in far-flung places. Platforms like Skype and Viber allow immigrants to experience a degree of connectedness to their families and friends in the homeland – never before possible. Regardless of whether people live near or far from their families, social media is a vital way in which they keep tabs on one another (Deumert 2014a). Several chapters in the volume illustrate this. Swinehart and Hinrichs write about the Bolivian and Jamaican diasporas and how young people use YouTube and blogs to connect with others from their respective communities. Multilingual practices like code switching between Jamaican Patois, Standard Jamaican, and stylized Rasta talk index local Jamaican repertoires and recreate a sense of collective identity. A similar pattern has emerged in response to Aymara rap, which draws youth in the Andean diaspora together around a linguistically defined cultural object – the Aymara language. K-pop is a global phenomenon with fans in every continent. Lee illustrates how fans engage in K-pop fandom through the practice of micro-blogging and using emblematic Korean in a low stakes environment to express kinship with their fellow fans.

A second possibility afforded in these kinds of online encounters includes imagining another identity, networking, dreaming about being someone or somewhere else, or identifying with others (Evers, Lee). Evers describes how social media, SMS, and online phone calling allow young Muslim women in Marseilles to use their multilingual repertoires to express their disaffection with life in France and fantasize about life in the Gulf with others who feel the same way. The digital networks that they access through mastery of Modern Standard Arabic and Standard French offer them possibilities to relocate and find work abroad.

The long-distance communicative possibilities illustrated by the CMC practices of diasporic Andean and Jamaican youth, K-pop fans and disaffected Muslim girls in France contrast with the more local motivations of socialization and negotiation of belonging in the remaining chapters. Contributing to online hip-hop forums, German fans socialize each other into the use of an English hip-hop leave-taking expression – *peace* – while experimenting with various ways to write it (Garley). Multilingual SMS messaging gives young people in Senegal (Lexander) and South Africa (Bock, Dalwai and Stroud) a way to enhance local ties and challenge the hegemonic status of colonial languages through the blending and manipulation of local and colonial languages and registers. Deumert also focuses on the highly local practice of teaching and learning how to use an historical South African register – Tsotstitaal – to bespeak the modern experience.

Another local set of CMC affordances centers around negotiating group belonging and challenging ideologies of language and identity. Immigrant youth in Norway (Røyneland) and Mexican-American youth in the USA (Cutler) find in YouTube a space where they can express and navigate belonging in societies that do not fully accept them. The fact that these youth use elements from a multiethnolectal repertoire in the case of Norway, and Spanish in the US, is often used against them in YouTube discussions, but youth themselves deploy these linguistic resources in conjunction with other local registers to legitimize their bi-/multicultural identities.

Technology: How Does Technology Shape the Data? The practices?

How different are multilingual CMC practices in different parts of the world? How does access to high-speed digital networks and the newest gadgets shape practices? How are practices different when these resources are not available? The chapters in our volume explore digital practices in economically and socially diverse settings where people have differential access to technology and bandwidth and the kind of data each author examines very much reflects current distribution of digital resources around the world.

Deumert (2014a) argues that a particular discourse in the North sees the internet as the great hope, a new public sphere, a space of participation and creativity, yet more than half of the world's population is still excluded from this space. She observes that the digital has a particular shape in different parts of the world and that we should not see the South as lagging behind the North or as playing catch-up. Rather, the experience of modernity – including digital modernity – is just different, and thus we need to start thinking more about alternative versions of the world rather than keeping with the idea that there is one version everyone aspires to.

The following chart illustrates the huge differences in internet use as a percentage of the population (Figure 1.1): Among the countries featured in this volume, Norway is way on top with internet penetration in 97 percent of households. The remaining countries include South Korea at 90 percent, Germany and France at 85–87 percent, the USA at 75 percent, South Africa at just over 50 percent, Bolivia and Jamaica at around 45 percent, and Senegal at just above 20 percent. Large disparities are also found within continents where we see gaps between relatively more prosperous countries like South Africa or Argentina with much higher rates than some of their neighbors.

There are large disparities in smartphone ownership among adults in the US (72 percent), Europe (60 percent) and the Middle East (57 percent) versus Latin America (43 percent) Asia/Pacific (37 percent) and Africa (19 percent), indicating by extension the kinds of practices people can engage in on the go

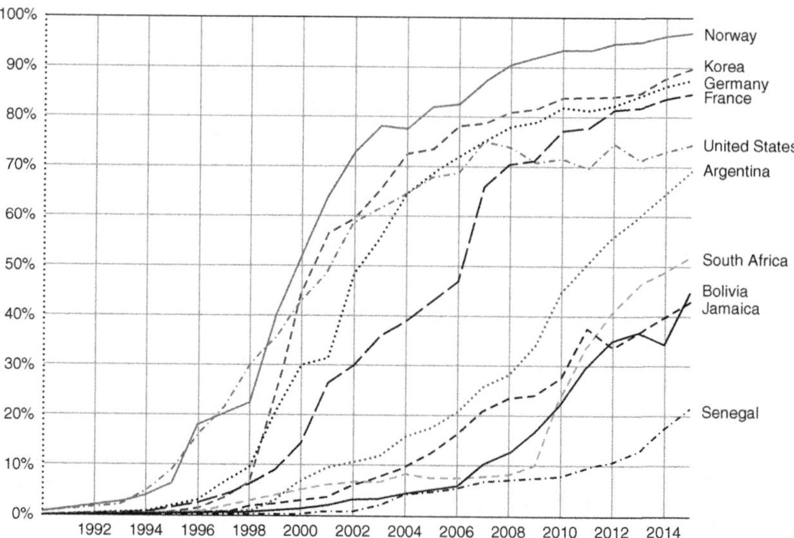

Figure 1.1 Internet use as a percentage of the population (Google Public Data, World Development Indicator)

(Pew Research 2016a). Smartphones enable users to replicate pre-digital practices like navigating with a map, listening to the radio, watching TV, shooting photos and movies, recording sounds, setting alarms, etc. Now they increasingly duplicate many of the practices associated with desktop/laptop computers: sending emails and text/SMS messages, video conferencing, streaming content, and sharing digital content with other users/followers. As new platforms appear on the market, new practices emerge, giving people an increasing number of ways to engage in, and interact with, others digitally.

In Africa, the most common devices are not smartphones, but older types of phones and those who access social media do so exclusively on their phones because they lack access to broadband and computers. As a result of these fundamental differences, SMS is perhaps only one truly global social media application (Deumert 2016), although Twitter and Facebook have made significant inroads in the past five years because they allow easy access via phones. Yet, contrary to what one might assume, the poor in the developing world as well as immigrants and refugees are often some of the most prevalent users of cellphone technology, which is a lifeline to support networks of friends and family (Deumert 2014a; Graham 2015; Sabaté i Dalmau 2012).

Access to various social media platforms is also highly related to socioeconomic conditions. Jenkins (2006: 274) describes YouTube "as a key site for the production and distribution of grassroots media," but many people in countries like South Africa and Senegal cannot access it because they do not have an internet connection at home and do not own internet enabled smartphones. People in Norway, Germany, the US, and Korea, in contrast, are extremely likely to have broadband internet and smartphone access allowing for access to all forms of social media, streaming audio, video, as well as SMS at home and wherever they go. Thus, social media and other forms of digital networking are much more a part of everyday practice in some places as opposed to others.

As can be gathered from the foregoing discussion, the practices described in this volume are shaped by monetary, technological, and infrastructural disparities. The differences in access described above also illustrate how difficult it is to make sweeping generalizations with respect to data coming from one platform. For example, Hinrichs, Lee, and Swinehart write about young people who converge in particular digital spaces from many different places in the world with very different rates of access to the internet. We know very little about their individual circumstances and the kinds of digital access they have and can only extrapolate based on rates of internet penetration and smartphone use for the countries from which they are writing.

We can make more conclusive generalizations about the kinds of practices young people engage in based on the kinds of technological affordances that characterize the societies in which they live. Young people whose digital communication is limited to SMS tend to use local languages in interaction with one (or more) colonial language to interact with local friends and family. This pattern characterizes the chapters by Bock, Dalwai, and Stroud, and Lexander on South African and Senegalese youth who interact in locally relevant languages (English, Kaaps, Afrikaans, and Zulu in South Africa; French, Wolof, and English in Senegal).

In contrast, the young devout Muslim women described in Evers' chapter have extensive international networks in France, North Africa, and the Gulf States and interact via Skype, Viber, Facebook, and SMS in Modern Standard Arabic, Gulf Arabic dialects, and French. Three of the chapters deal exclusively with data from YouTube (Røyneland, Cutler, and Swinehart), a platform that allows for multilingual interaction, but often tends to generate interest among those who can understand the language of the video. Consequently, most of the comments in their respective chapters are in Spanish (Cutler, Swinehart) and Norwegian (Røyneland).

The German hip-hop forum described in Garley's chapter is similarly dominated by German with significant influence from American hip-hop orthography and lexis as is typical of global hip hop (Alim et al. 2009; Cutler 2014; Pennycook 2007a; Terkourafi 2010). The diasporic blogs written by Jamaicans described by Hinrichs allow for highly nuanced heteroglossic mixing of varieties (Patois, AAVE, and Rasta talk) in ways that reflect the collective language ideologies and practices of diasporic Jamaicans. At the extreme end of multilingual practice are the young K-pop fans described by Lee who are keen to use the little Korean they know to connect with other K-pop performers and fans. The micro-blogging interface provides a low-stakes platform for practicing and performing a language one is learning (i.e. Korean). In sum, the chapters show how access to various digital platforms, mediated by local digital infrastructure (primarily bandwidth) and monetary resources, shape the nature of young people's multilingual practices.

At the same time, these practices are constantly evolving: With the introduction of Twitter across the African continent in 2011, young people have for the first time been able to engage with people in neighboring countries and explore a common identity. Similarly, we see how diaspora communities around the world are increasingly connecting with each other in ways that reflect their sense of common identity as well as their local situatedness (see Heyd and Honkanen 2015; Lee 2017).

Language Status: Can You Do Anything in Any Language in CMC?

The work in this volume illustrates how international languages like English, French, and Arabic have different meanings for different people (e.g. bilinguals in post-colonial societies, minority language speakers, hip-hop fans, etc.), and that they are utilized in different ways and for diverse reasons by various individuals. In contrast, indigenous, minority, and non-native languages, previously limited to oral communication or to second languages classrooms, are entering written communication and may fulfill unique functions in CMC. In order to explore these developments in specific contexts, we now turn to a brief, non-sequential overview of each chapter, how it illustrates what multilingual youth do with specific languages in CMC, what social meanings the youth attach to different languages, and how they deploy languages in their repertoires in CMC.

Digital varieties of English in Africa show higher frequencies of abbreviations than those reported for the USA and the UK. As an international language, English is seen as belonging to everyone and can thus be a site for contestation and play. As Lexander points out in Chapter 4, each language has a special resonance and fulfills a different function in CMC: English is also starting to challenge French in Senegal as the language that represents communication with the outside world. Wolof and other indigenous codes, previously only used in the oral domain, have entered the written realm, and are mixed with French, English, Arabic, and Spanish in the text messages of young people.

Mixing languages is conventional practice in CMC in many contexts, signaling stances and orientations to the local social order. In Chapter 3, Bock, Dalwai, and Stroud write that in Cape Town, South Africa, young people mix Afrikaans, isiXhosa, Kaaps, and English in their texts; Afrikaans, as the language of the former apartheid regime, is associated with "white" political conservatism, but local (spoken) varieties of Afrikaans, such as Kaaps and mixed English-Afrikaans carry strongly positive values of colored identity, community solidarity, and local belonging. Similarly, complex attitudes exist in relation to isiXhosa. While varieties based on the codified standard are often perceived as pure, correct, and carriers of the culture, young black urban speakers tend to stigmatize this deep Xhosa as rural and old-fashioned. For them, urban mixed varieties, while commonly seen as "slang" or "incorrect," also index cool, sophisticated urbanity.

The social meanings of particular codes are rooted in historical events and carried on in the collective memory of the community. Deumert (Chapter 6) explores the revival of Afrikaans-based Tsotsitaal online, a linguistically hybrid code which evokes a particular time and place in South Africa's history (1950s Sophiatown). The term *tsotsi* refers to a small-scale criminal, and *taal* is Afrikaans for "language" so Tsotsitaal literally means thug language or language of criminals; however, it also evokes streetwise urbanity, resistance to oppression, youth, and masculinity, and is linked to "performative displays of linguistic virtuosity." Afrikaans-based Tsotsitaal is fairly common on Facebook and Twitter, yet writing in Tsotsitaal online is not habitual practice and is thus experienced self-consciously as marked, as exploring a different and unfamiliar voice.

In other instances, a code can fulfill an aspirational function linked to fandom. Although many global K-pop oriented youth contribute to fan sites mainly in English, Lee's exploration of global K-pop micro-blogs in Chapter 11 illustrates how young fans attempt to use rudimentary and often incorrect Korean kinship terms and short popular Korean informal expressions to establish solidarity, "linguistic fellowship," and "imagined closeness" with K-pop artists. For K-pop fans who have very little proficiency in Korean the Korean language serves as a connector – a relationship-building device and tool for social bonding.

The interplay between global hip-hop English and local languages characteristic of so many settings (e.g. Alim et al. 2009; Cutler 2014; Pennycook 2007a; Terkourafi 2010) is illustrated in Garley's piece (Chapter 5) which explores how German hip-hop youth engage in intensive linguistic borrowing from English and stylization of English borrowings in ways that involve the complex application of morphological, phonological, and orthographic knowledge from multiple linguistic systems. In the German-language internet hip-hop discussion forum MZEE.com, participants' use of variant orthography is a marker of sociocultural identity while also signaling engagement in both global and local subcultural hip-hop practices.

For diasporic Jamaicans, described by Hinrichs in Chapter 10, blogs written in Patois, and Standard Jamaican English serve as important points of contact for sharing information, opinions, folk knowledge, nostalgia, group belonging, and national identity, yet, online writers may also engage in double-voicing using the "Rasta" voice in a humorous way to align with a worldview about black oppression pervading every aspect of life. In Chapter 9, Swinehart shows how posting Aymara rap songs on YouTube serves a similar function for indigenous Andeans, and Aymaras from the city of El Alto for communicating with their counterparts abroad, with other hip-hop artists and fans through the musical genre of hip hop. Swinehart also shows how YouTube provides a space where non-indigenous advocates for indigenous cultural and political rights, and migrants from the Andean republics of Bolivia, Peru, and Ecuador to countries like Argentina, Spain, and the USA can encounter contemporary indigenous Andean cultural production like Wayna Rap, and engage with other speakers of indigenous Andean languages. Among the Mexican heritage bilinguals in the USA described by Cutler in Chapter 7, Spanish at times symbolizes ethnic authenticity and ties to the homeland (Mexico) and in others, an anti-colonial, anti-racist stance vis-à-vis the US. However, it is also common for YouTube comments to contain some mixing with English and hybrid, highly inventive forms of orthography that index knowledge of English and American (US) culture and stances of belonging.

Despite the fact that hip-hop youth with an immigrant origin rap in Norwegian, they are rejected by some for not using the "right" kind of Norwegian. Røyneland's contribution (Chapter 8) explores how young people in Norway navigate and negotiate linguistic ownership, identity and belonging on YouTube. Following a rap video posted by a Norwegian-Chilean-Peruvian rapper "Pumba," some YouTubers contest while others affirm and align with the rapper's claim to a mixed identity and to be part of a new multicultural Norway. Moreover, as Evers shows in her in-depth ethnographic study in chapter 2, young Muslim women in Marseille with cultural ties to North Africa make special efforts to learn Modern Standard Arabic (MSA) and use Standard Parisian French (as opposed to the local Marseillais dialect or immigrant "project" Marseillais French they grew up with) as important symbolic resources (along with adopting Muslim dress, i.e. jilbab, hijab, etc.) for signaling an ideological commitment to greater religious piety; using MSA and Gulf Arabic on social media are thus vital resources for connecting with the larger Muslim community or *ummah* outside of France and particularly the Arab Gulf states (Saudi Arabia, Oman, etc.) where many of them aspire to live one day.

The chapters collectively show that for many (but not all) young people around the world, the ordinary everyday way to interact is to draw on a large variety of linguistic resources at many levels: within a turn, at the lexical level, but also within and across morpheme boundaries using hybrid orthographies. In fact, using a single code or standard written norms in CMC is often highly marked except in very particular circumstances. Code choice is also highly indexical; former colonial languages have the expected social and academic resonances in post-colonial settings, but in CMC, playing with them and mixing them can be a resource for challenging their current or former hegemonic status or for signaling global cosmopolitan alignments.

Using standard orthography is also unusual (although not necessarily for every language); CMC is a place where standard written norms are flouted (McSweeney 2016) and where writers have a great deal of freedom to be funny and creative (Deumert 2014a). This kind of play, however, may be more rampant in some languages than others, as alluded to earlier (e.g. English in post-colonial settings versus indigenous ones like Zulu or Wolof or institutionalized standard languages like MSA in Islamic communities).

Overarching Generalization about Multilingual Youth Practices in CMC

This volume, following in a now robust tradition of CMC research, focuses quite squarely on the affordances of text-based communication (Androutsopoulos 2013a) using discourse analytic methods. Rather than exploring the distribution of languages or language variation in CMC, the object of investigation is focused on the creative, identity-constructing, and metapragmatic dimensions of personal expression and interpersonal communication. Now that the field has moved beyond the question of whether online/digital communication is more like speech or writing (McSweeney 2016), we can engage in a more nuanced understanding of digital writing as something unique and distinct unto itself with elements of orality and standard writing, but not simply a blending of the two. Rather than simply an impoverished or informal, speech-like form of written communication, digital online writing is presented as a new form with its own evolving written and visual conventions for expressing affect, stance, and illocutionary force (Sebba 2007; Thompson and Filik 2016; Darics 2013; Iorio 2009; Diego and Lage 2013; Soffer 2012; Sabaté i Dalmau 2012). This is not to say that the speech-like norms that are emerging online go uncontested. In the absence of official policies and institutional control online, individuals often feel the urge to engage in their own "folk linguistic policing" and linguicism (Back and Zepeda 2013; Heyd 2014).

The studies in this volume illustrate how global youth engage in a range of visual affective textual practices with the added dimension of multilingualism. The mixing of languages in digital writing often reflects oral practices (Deumert, Bock, Dalwai and Stroud, Evers, Lexander, Cutler, and Hinrichs), but it can also reflect users' attempts to test out their language skills in a low-stakes environment (Lee, Evers) or assert linguistic rights (Cutler, Røyneland). The written mode also gives writers a much larger range of orthographic and graphemic options, allowing them to experiment with different interlingual variants (Garley, Lexander, Evers, Cutler). Thus, it is possible to see digital writing, not just as a unique form of expression, but also one that gives writers a whole range of written *and* oral resources from any and all languages in their repertoires. A key dimension of these practices is their creativity and playfulness (e.g. Deumert 2014a; Jones and Schieffelin 2009), drawing on insider knowledge about language variation and ideologies of language. It is in these interactions that we observe how speakers reevaluate the indexical values of speech forms (Agha 2008), instilling them with new meanings, but also at times discussing, policing, and contesting these practices (Cutler, Røyneland, and Swinehart). Thus, observing the multilingual practices of global youth is a window into how speech styles, dialects, and languages are being reevaluated at the local and the global level, reflecting ongoing social shifts in the indexical values of these various codes (Lexander, Evers, Lee, Deumert, and Bock, Dalwai and Stroud).

The chapters in the volume illustrate how speakers themselves often freely mix language forms and writing systems as if their repertoires were consolidated and unified rather than compartmentalized. Thus, online multilingual communication appears to be contributing to the blurring of boundaries between languages as young people routinely draw from their multilingual competencies to construct heteroglossic, polylingual, and polyphonous utterances (Agha 2008; Jørgensen et. al. 2015). One final question is whether CMC is paving the way for local, indigenous, and minority language literacy practices (Lexander 2011a, b) versus ever-greater linguistic homogenization (Belling and de Bres 2014; Berezkina 2016). While we do not have a definitive answer to this question, the studies presented here illustrate that multilingual interaction is quite common and increasingly part of the way youth around the world communicate with each other. We see that young people are actively writing in minority, indigenous, or marginalized youth languages with a mainly oral tradition (e.g. Wolof, isiXhosa, Kaaps, Tsostitaal, Iscamtho, Aymara). But we also know that despite these highly heteroglossic practices, it is also increasingly common for people to use English in their daily CMC interactions (Belling and de Bres 2014; Durham 2003; Wodak and Wright 2004; Wright 2004) so the effects of the digital dominance of English on multilingualism and minority/indigenous languages in CMC will need to be examined for many years to come before we know the answer.

2 Alienated at Home

The Role of Online Media as Young Orthodox Muslim Women Beat a Retreat from Marseille

Cécile Evers

Introduction

Went down the harbour and stood upon the quay,
Saw the fish swimming as if they were free:
Only ten feet away, my dear, only ten feet away.

Written by W.H. Auden (1967) in 1939, these three verses describe the plight of European Jews who, for lack of the right papers or a dearth of departing ships, could not leave for safer shores during World War II. The port city of Marseille was, during France's non-occupied years of 1939–1942, one such point of frozen departures. Auden, who was not Jewish, emigrated to the United States himself that same year. Nevertheless, he appears to have sympathized – perhaps as a queer Englishman living abroad (Roberts 2005) – with Jewish fugitives' sentiment of feeling alienated while at home.

Roughly three-quarters of a century later, the atmosphere in Marseille is again weighing heavily on its human margins. Only now those seeking refuge are a pious generation of young Muslim men and women who, while born in Marseille, are made to feel unduly foreign in their hometown. Such youth, born in Marseille's northern housing projects (*Quartiers Nord*) to parents from Muslim countries in North, West, and East Africa, report sensing rejection from Marseille's non-Muslim inhabitants in both conspicuous and more subtle ways. The forms of discrimination they enumerate include harassment, hate speech, and being barred from the public school system, rental housing, and the job market (in spite of high school and university degrees). It is, moreover, precisely the same visual signs which such orthodox youth use to signal belonging to their community, from the floor- and wrist-length outfits (e.g. *'abāyah, jilbāb*) and accessories like the *ḥijāb* or gloves worn by young women, to the beards, short pants, and caps donned by young men, that are to most non-Muslim people in Marseille cause for suspicion, fear, and, not uncommonly, loathing.[1]

This chapter gathers narrative and behavioral accounts of how youth, and especially young orthodox women, are dealing with the disjuncture between their commitment to a pious lifestyle, on the one hand, and the largely secular social environment that obtains in Marseille, on the other. I argue that the main result of this disconnect is that young Muslims from Marseille, and young women in particular, have come to conceptualize Islamic piety in terms of their relocation to the Muslim World. Further, I show how computer-mediated forms of communication, including Facebook, Whatsapp, and Skype, have enabled such youth, first, to cultivate a feeling that they belong to a community of pious peers intent on retreating from Marseille, and, second, to coordinate friendships and vital contacts in the places to which they plan to move.

Data and Fieldwork

The accounts and analyses I present are the result of prolonged ethnographic engagement with several youth peer groups in northern Marseille between 2012 and 2013.[2] During that period, I partook in daily activities alongside youth, ranging from school and mosque attendance, to leisure activities, to family events, and also conducted interviews with them and their acquaintances. I met many of these young adults through their participation in Modern Standard Arabic (henceforth MSA) classrooms, whether in religious institutions or public schools, and my position with regards to them has tended to mix the roles of outsider and insider. Born to a French mother but raised in the United States, I have typically been viewed by my participants as someone largely on the periphery of French culture. This outsider status has often been helpful in my research, particularly in light of French Muslims' awareness of widespread French ambivalence towards them and their customs. I also suspect that I was welcomed in Muslim community settings – ones that might otherwise have been difficult to access – thanks to my position as an MSA teacher, my experience traveling in the Arab World, and also to my Muslim husband. Additionally, while my on-site research came to an end in late 2013, many of my participants and I have continued to interact, over Facebook, Skype, and

[1] With regards to Arabic orthographic conventions, I use the MSA transcription standards of the American Library Association-Library of Congress. A left-facing apostrophe is used to indicate the letter *'ayn* (ع) and a right-facing one is used for the letter *hamzah* (ء). Terms in MSA, along with French, are italicized within the body of the text. The sole exception are words familiar to general readership (e.g., Sunni, Koran, Muslim, Mecca, Medina, Wahhabi, Salafi, Sharia, arrondissement), for which I use English conventions.

[2] This research and its analysis were made possible by generous grants from the Wenner Gren Foundation (2012–13) and the Spencer Foundation/National Academy of Education (2014–15).

Whatsapp, from 2013 to present. Some of these more recent interactions have also made their way into this analysis.

One of the main questions guiding the larger project of which this is a part inquired into the diversity or convergence in the experiences of those who profess Islam in Marseille. This question was prompted by the observation of a nationwide tendency, over the past 20 years of Republican political debate over the French national identity, for popular media and French State surveys (e.g. INSEE/INED 2010) to group youth, whose parents hail from France's African ex-colonies, into the broad category of "Muslim." Not surprisingly, my ethnographic research demonstrated that even just within the circumscribed area of Marseille's northern housing projects, people practiced Islam quite differently. These nuances were not lost on residents of the projects themselves, who could easily name a handful of local Muslim "types" and their corresponding lifestyle choices. Here, my concern is primarily with a particular Islamic "figure of personhood," a term that Agha (2011: 172) defines as a social type that has been linked to a set of performable behaviors by a given population. Specifically, I discuss how a particular set of my research participants qualified themselves as "pious Muslims" or "Sunnis." By these labels, they meant that they observed the instituted model within Islam according to which one undertakes, not only the behaviors obligatory under Sharia (*Sharīʻah*), but also a series of actions imitating the Prophet and believed to bestow additional spiritual benefits (Asad 1986; Gleave 2010). Even for the young men and women who identified as "orthodox Muslims" or "Sunnis," however, there remained a measure of fluidity as to how piety was conceptualized. Some of these orthodox youth performed piety by doing social activism on behalf of Marseille's Muslim community. Others, meanwhile, thought they exhibited piety best by relocating from Marseille. In these pages, I only discuss the cases of young women who yearned to leave Marseille. It nevertheless remains an important fact that youth who oriented away from Marseille were in some measure responding, via this stance, to the existence of other youth who instead enacted piety by affiliating with Marseille.

Organization of the Chapter

The chapter is organized into two main sections. In the first (One Ideology of Piety: *al-Barāʻ* or Disavowal), I discuss accounts given by several young women of how Marseille's non-Muslim inhabitants make them feel as though they do not belong. I focus on a Facebook conversation in which a group of young women analogize the social alienation they feel in Marseille to the religious persecution Prophet Mohammed faced in the seventh century. In a continuation of this analogy, I illustrate how these young women have decided to imitate the Prophet's *hijrah*, or the migration he undertook to escape persecution, and have come to conceive of piety in terms of a relocation from Marseille to the Muslim World. Computer-mediated forms of communication, furthermore, provide them with a handy means of disseminating among friends this particular strategy for coping with alienation. I also argue that this concept of piety – requiring self-removal from non-Muslim lands – shows "interdiscursive" links (Silverstein 2005) to texts penned by twentieth-century Saudi proponents of Wahhabism. These Wahhabi scholars defined piety in terms of *al-Walā'* and *al-Barā'*, or loyalty to Muslims and dissociation from non-Muslims, respectively (Wagemakers 2012a, b).

In the second section (Online Practices of Piety: Exemplifying *al-Barā'*), I provide additional social media examples illustrating how young orthodox women from Marseille employ language online in ways that reinforce this Wahhabi notion of piety. Concretely, in their Facebook and Voice over Internet Protocol (VoIP) conversations, these young women position different places and language varieties in their environment in accordance with the ideological binary they uphold, that between the pious and the non-Muslim impious. Following the logic of *al-Barā',* which requires the faithful to relinquish ties to French disbelievers, they categorize Marseille itself, together with the French vernacular often spoken by diasporic youth from Marseille's northerly housing projects, as vulgar and excessively local. Dialectal varieties of Arabic heavily mixed with French, similarly, are thought to project a European affiliation that contrasts with these young women's own project to migrate to the Muslim World. Varieties they associate with the Islamic heartlands, by contrast, including MSA and less-mixed Arabian peninsular varieties of Arabic, are revered for their religious significance, purity, and their potential to strengthen relations with people in the Muslim World (*al-Walā'*). These young women also value and aspire to speak Standard French, interestingly. They cite the language's ability to index propriety, but also its utility as a tool for international communication. I argue that this nexus of language ideologies illustrates a form of the fractally recursive reasoning discussed by Irvine and Gal (2000), where phenomena at various social levels (e.g. language varieties, places, people) are grouped into binary categories, in this case into those of *al-Barā'* and *al-Walā'*.

This chapter, as such, contributes to recent research on how online users adopt certain linguistic practices in conjunction with the language ideologies they hold (Barton and Lee 2013). To wit, the second and third sections below show a strong link between the specific notions of piety these young women have developed, the language ideological stances they evince, and the way in which they use language in their computer-mediated interactions. Moreover, it is when electronically mediated texts are set side-by-side with more traditional forms of ethnographic data, like fieldnotes and interviews, that these links rise to the fore. It would therefore appear, to echo Androutsopoulos (2008), that the process of reconstructing the social meaning of internet texts relies greatly upon previous insights we have into our participants' unique lives and perspectives, often gained through ethnographic inquiry in the field. That said, occasionally the inductive process functions in the inverse direction as well; namely, online texts may also help deepen one's considerations during fieldwork. Thus, in my own research I was frequently led by developing content on youth's Facebook feeds, whether imagery or commentary, to confirm or reject an interpretation I had made of their behavior while in other "live" social settings. Furthermore, were it not for my concurrent online friendship with these young women, perhaps I would not have become aware of the centrality of such media in their ability to form social networks in the Muslim World. Adopting an ethnographic approach for this research, I believe, has yielded a fuller picture of the variety of ways that young orthodox women marshal to communicate about their experiences of being Muslim in Marseille.

One Ideology of Piety: *al-Barāʿ* or Disavowal

Like other school days, I stepped onto the 25 bus line at Bougainville, the northernmost end of the metro line. As I looked for a seat, I noticed Kalima, a young woman I had met only two weeks earlier at an "only Muslim sisters" dinner (*dîner pour les sœurs*) to celebrate our mutual friend Sana's wedding.[3] I told her I was going to my teaching job at the private Muslim school a bit further north, in the 15th arrondissement, and asked where she was headed. Kalima explained that she was on her way to a café to meet with a young man who had previously lived in London. She hoped he could tell her what it was like in case she decided to move there. Kalima scanned northern Marseille through the bus window, and mused, "In London, I can be myself, I think." I wanted to know what about Marseille, the city where she was raised and went to school, made her want to leave. She replied: "I'm too sensitive. It's difficult to live here with the stares ... I'm French on my mom's side but born in Algeria, and everyone calls me 'foreigner.'"[4] Looking at Kalima momentarily from the perspective of the non-Muslim Marseillais people on the bus, I imagined they might indeed wonder at her use of fashion gloves in April and the large gray *ʿabāyah,* or floor-grazing dress, on this willowy 21-year-old. Her way of speaking about Marseille, describing alienation and the sense of a truer home elsewhere, was nevertheless familiar to me from other

3 To protect my research participants, I have replaced their real names with pseudonyms throughout this chapter.

4 "Je suis très sensible. C'est difficile de vivre ici avec les regards. Je suis française du côté de ma mère (mais née en Algérie) mais tout le monde me dit étrangère... À Londres, je peux être moi-même, je crois" (April 9, 2013).

conversations I had held with other young women from the self-identified Sunni, or orthodox, community in Marseille.

What are the circumstances leading young women like Kalima to feel alienated from Marseille? Why did these young women not speak of Marseille as "home," but rather set their sights on creating new homes in places like the Gulf States, North Africa, and the United Kingdom? Alongside these questions, it is interesting to trace the paths of reasoning inspiring these young women to choose migration as the preferred way of handling their estrangement from Marseille. Facebook conversations conducted between several of my female acquaintances from Marseille show how these young women relied on the prescriptions found in particular religious texts – dictating how devout Muslims should deal with oppressive circumstances – in deciding to move away from the West. The circulation of such religious discourses about living in the Muslim World, via media like Facebook as well as personal ties, coupled with the dream of living in a place where it was imaginable to fulfill their personal, spiritual, educational, and professional goals, proved strong incentives indeed for these young women. Their decisions often remained fraught with uncertainty in a practical sense, however, seeing as many of these young women lacked financial autonomy from their parents and had often developed only tenuous contacts in the places on which they had set their sights, whether London, Algiers, or Doha.

On her Facebook page, a young Marseillaise named Qailah writes about wanting to break with the social dislocation she experiences in Marseille. Making comparisons between her lack of religious freedom locally and how the Prophet Mohammed reacted when faced with religious persecution in Mecca, she settles upon relocation as the answer to her troubles. That Qailah identifies relocation to the Muslim World as the desirable course of action for a contemporary Muslim living in the West illustrates her engagement, both with the history of Islam's Prophet, but also, significantly, with ideals of piety developed by Wahhabi scholars in twentieth-century Saudi Arabia. The distinguishing mark of the pious believer, in these writings, was his or her willingness to practice "Disavowal" (*al-Barā'*) and distance themself from non-Muslim places, practices, and people in the name of God (Wagemakers 2012a). A detailed description of Qailah's transition towards a pious lifestyle, given below, highlights the different understandings of piety through which Qailah passed before settling on the *al-Barā'* concept of piety requiring movement away and dissociation from non-Muslims.

Over the course of the 2012–2013 school year, I spent time with Qailah in MSA classes offered by a private religious institute in downtown Marseille. In her early twenties, Qailah was raised in an Algerian Kabyle household in one of northern Marseille's housing projects. Between our first encounter and now, I have observed Qailah transition from, first, being a non-practicing Muslim with curiosity about the faith to, second, devoting herself to social activism on behalf of Marseille's Muslim community to, third, restricting her sphere of contacts as she undertook a piously motivated retreat from Marseille. The first of these phases was exemplified by her behavior at the beginning of the school year. When I first met her, other priorities seemed to come before Islam. Qailah had, for instance, signed up for the Institute's MSA class and another in Islamic jurisprudence (*fiqh*). She only attended, however, when class times did not interfere with the coursework she needed to finish for her master's in social work. In keeping with her nominally Muslim background, she likewise joined the other students at prayer times only occasionally and wore loose sweatpants and long sweaters, with her brown hair uncovered, throughout the first months of class. Qailah's classmates were also amused by her use of Marseille's "project accent" (*accent de quartier*) in this Islamic setting.[5] Indeed, for the pious Muslims in attendance, the sounds and turns-of-phrase associated with the vernacular speech of Marseille's projects cued hyper-local associations that were quite opposed to the kind of Islamic cosmopolitanism they themselves tried to cultivate, mainly by adhering to more standard forms of French and Arabic.

By late in the fall of 2012, Qailah's demeanor began to show novel facets. In a first instance, she began keeping a tight prayer schedule. This was accompanied by her adoption of the sporty head-to-knee-length veil known as a *jilbāb,* which she wore over long skirts and tennis shoes. Qailah additionally took to conducting *da'wāh,*[6] or the Islamic social activism and missionizing encouraged in the Koran. When, for example, one of the institute's founders organized a meeting to enlist volunteers from among the students to collect aid money for the Palestinian cause and the war in Syria, Qailah was among the first to step forward and offer her services. She likewise became the director of Marseille's branch of a France-wide Muslim charity association. Via the Facebook page she managed for the charity, Qailah coordinated all manner of social and financial assistance to Muslim families and (mainly divorced) "sisters" in need throughout Marseille, ranging from soliciting blankets, clothes, and monies, to finding safe housing and distributing free meals. Her posts on behalf of the charity read much like this one, which she put up in November of 2012.

[5] The French variety spoken in Marseille's northern Projects demonstrates linguistic syncretism of the interference type (Woolard 1999) between the French regional dialect local to Marseille and dialectal Arabic. In it, youth overlay Marseille's working-class vernacular with phonology from Algerian and other varieties of Arabic, also borrowing lexis and discourse markers (Evers 2016). The variety that results conveys an auditory impression of having an "Arabic accent" in Marseille's vernacular. Space does not allow for further discussion of this "project speech" here; it is simply flagged as a variety that serves as an ideological counterpoint to the type of French spoken by orthodox youth.

[6] MSA for teachings and doings in the name of Islamic unity (Canard 1999), though often synonymous with Islamic outreach and social activism.

> *"Salâm 3alaykoum wa rahmatou Allah wa barakâtouh* ('Peace be upon you and the mercy and blessings of God as well"). Are you familiar with the principle of marauding? It involves a group vigil during the evening and overnight as we roam the area looking for homeless people. (. . .) During our marauds we distribute meals, drinks, warm clothes/covers/blankets, and smiles![7]

This post also warrants linguistic attention, insofar as it suggests Qailah had passed from using language associated with youth from Marseille's projects to observing the local ideological preference among devout Muslims for hewing to the Arabic and French linguistic standards. Qailah opens with an elaborate Muslim greeting in MSA and then continues in a quasi-academic register of French, using standard turns of phrase like *il s'agit de* ("it involves") and such diction as *sillonnant* ("traverse," "roam").[8]

Four years have passed since these initial forays of Qailah's into Marseille's Islamic milieu. Today, Qailah no longer runs the charity as before and has closed its Facebook page. I gained some insight into these changes when, in September of 2015, I received a phone call from another member of our old MSA class. He filled me in on how our classmates were doing, reporting with enthusiasm that Qailah had married – a local Shaykh from a Comorian background. Shifting downwards in tone, he let me know that he only ever encounters Qailah by accident now, since she no longer feels comfortable joining in the reunions for the MSA class. He explained that when not long ago he crossed Qailah in the street, he did not in fact recognize her because she was covering her face and body. These recent developments in Qailah's Islamic practice are further clarified by the Facebook post I examine below. The post dates from January of 2014, when Qailah's charity page was still up but she no longer used it, as before, to make weekly requests for donations. The post suggests that she had by this time begun adhering to a new notion of Islamic piety, one less based in conducting Islamic social activism on Marseille's local front, and oriented instead towards breaking away from the West and settling in the Muslim World. It was apparent that Qailah's aversion towards Marseille

[7] "Connaissez-vous le principe des maraudes? Il s'agit d'une mission de veille sociale en soirée et durant la nuit sillonnant le territoire à la rencontre de personnes sans domicile fixe. (. . ..) Lors de nos maraudes, nous distribuons des repas, boissons, et des vêtements chauds/couettes/couvertures et des sourires!" (November 15, 2013).

[8] It is worth noting, here, that although Qailah's Arabic greeting is one typically associated with religious settings and hence with MSA, Qailah renders it in what Palfreyman and Khalil (2007: 48) term "common romanized Arabic," meaning the romanized transliteration of Arabic. Her use of this orthography, typically associated with youth fora online, rather than the more religiously associated Arabic script, perhaps proceeds from her desire to connect with her charity's young Facebook users. She also transliterates the long "a" of *salām* in French fashion as "*â*" and the nominative case ending plus possessive suffix of *barakāt* ("blessings"), typically *barakātuhu* in MSA, using the dialectal Arabic possessive suffix /-uh/. These inconsistencies in Qailah's use of MSA speak to her ongoing transition towards assuming both a pious lifestyle and the language ideologies associated with such an existence.

was initially borne of her own negative experiences with the city's inhabitants. What subsequently nurtured this stance, however, was Qailah becoming familiar with a distinct religious ideology enjoining relocation upon the devout.

Thus, on a morning in January of 2014, Qailah posted on her charity's Facebook page for the first time in several months. She implored her charity's followers in French: "May Allah help us to leave this country. France is going from bad to worse. Mayday!!!!!!!!!!!!"[9] Her post inspired affirmative replies of *"wallahi"* (MSA, "by God") and *"amin"* (MSA, "amen") from several group members. Then a friend, pressing Qailah, inquired further, "To go where?"[10] Yet another protested, "But France is our home! Let those who don't like us leave France! ☺"[11] This last sentiment seemed not to resonate with the majority of commentators on Qailah's post, none of whom liked the comment. The next post, however, was met with five likes. This female friend supported Qailah's desire to leave and spoke, specifically, of her desire to conduct a religious emigration or *hijrah* to distance herself from the French:

> Salam wa3leyki oukhty. Naam Allahuma amin (MSA, "Peace be with you as well, my sister. Yes O God amen"). May Allah ease our hijra quickly because I hate them [the French] more and more and I cannot take it here anymore.[12]

This young woman marks herself, both linguistically and in content, as being a member of the orthodox Muslim community in Marseille. Linguistically, she alternates between MSA and Standard French. She uses religious phraseology drawn from the Koran (e.g. *Allahuma,* MSA, "O God"), MSA lexis written in a francisized orthography of MSA (e.g. <u>ou</u>khty "sister"/naam "yes"), and examples of the romanized orthography of MSA (e.g. wa<u>3</u>leyki "and upon you"), an orthography typically associated with how Arab youth communicate online and via SMS. She distinguishes herself from an Arab youth, however, insofar as she both appeals to Allah to facilitate her relocation to a Muslim country and conveys this message mainly in Standard French.

The comments made by Kalima at the beginning of this section, in Qailah's post, and in this response by Qailah's friend all attest to the spread, among young orthodox-identified women from Marseille, of a specific way of speaking about their lives in Marseille. Specifically, these orthodox young women's discourse evinces a reconceptualization of Marseille as a place of temporary exile, rather than their home. Examples of this discourse about Marseille abounded among my female research participants. A female university student

9 "Qu'Allah nous aide à quitter ce pays. La France, c'est de pire en pire. Au secours!!!!!!!!!!!" (January 23, 2014, 7:34 a.m.)

10 "Pr aller où?" (January 23, 2014, 9:35 a.m.)

11 "Mais on est chez nous en France! Et ceux qui nous aiment pas, c'est à eux de quitter la France! ☺" (January 23, 2014, 10:35 a.m.)

12 "Salam wa3leyki oukhty. Naam Allahuma amin. Qu'Allah nous facilite rapidement la hijra parce que je les déteste de plus en plus et je ne tiens plus ici." (January 23, 2014, 5:06 p.m.)

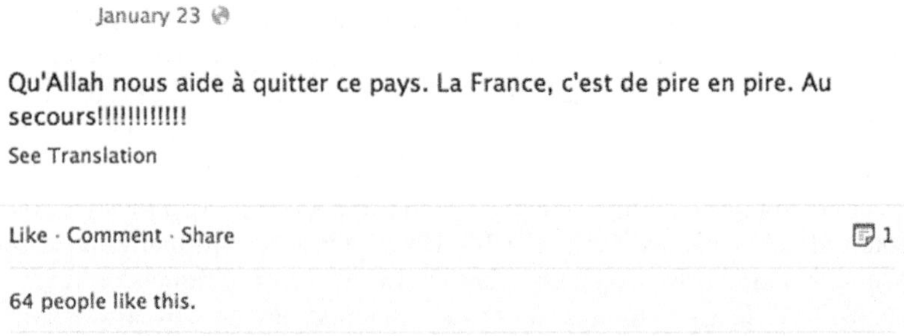

January 23

Qu'Allah nous aide à quitter ce pays. La France, c'est de pire en pire. Au secours!!!!!!!!!!!

See Translation

Like · Comment · Share 1

64 people like this.

Figure 2.1 Qailah's initial Facebook post (January 23, 2014)

named Bushrah, for instance, often joked with her girlfriends about being *apatride*, or country-less, despite her status as a French citizen and local of Marseille. Another young woman named Radya, in turn, pointed out that whereas in Marseille she felt disoriented, "when I go to Algeria, I don't experience country shock."[13] Some time into my research, it occurred to me that perhaps my participants' avowals of feeling at home somewhere other than France were in fact a way they had found to reappropriate non-Muslims' perception of them as belonging elsewhere. Indeed, it was for them a daily experience to have strangers yell at them to "go home!" (*rentrez chez vous!*) as they were walking with friends downtown or making their way to the university. Whether or not these young women were effectively reappropriating others' perspective of them in speaking thus about Marseille, it was nevertheless the case that they elaborated certain emic discourses justifying that their true homes lay in the Muslim World.

A follow-up post by Qailah to the same Facebook conversation discussed above showcases the principal discursive mode via which young orthodox women from Marseille naturalized their transposition of home from Marseille to the Muslim World. In this post, Qailah draws upon the mode of historical analogy to encourage her friends to seek out new homes in the Muslim World. Hence, at 8:29 p.m. on the evening of January 23, Qailah chimed back in to the Facebook conversation she had begun that morning. She cited only Verse 97 of the 4th *Sūrah* (*Al-Nisā'*) from a French translation of the Koran:

> The angels will ask those whom they claim back while steeped in sin: "What were you doing?" "We were oppressed in the land," they will reply. They will say: "Was not the earth of God spacious enough for you to fly for refuge?" Hell shall be their home: an evil fate.[14]

[13] "Je me sens pas depaysée quand je pars en Algérie" (September 19, 2012).

[14] This English version of Qailah's French translation comes from Dawood's (2000: 93) translation and exegesis of the Koran. Qailah's French original reads: "Ceux qui ont fait du tort à eux mêmes, les Anges enlèveront leurs âmes en disant: 'Où en étiez-vous?' (à propos de votre

This Verse describes the oppressive conditions facing early Muslims in Mecca during the seventh century, along with the varying responses to this oppression chosen by the Prophet Mohammed's followers. More specifically, before 622 CE, Mohammed and his Muslim followers had experienced a decade of severe religious persecution at the hands of their own tribe, the Quraysh, in their hometown of Mecca. Thus, on September 24, 622 CE, Mohammed took flight with dozens of his followers to the city of Medina. This migration, known as the *hijrah* in MSA, was in fact only undertaken by a small number of those who had professed Islam by that time. The majority of the Quraysh elected to remain in Mecca instead, afraid of losing their material comforts or still wavering between Mohammed's monotheistic message and their traditional paganism (Saleh 2010). The concept of a hierarchy of moral excellence among Muslims dates back to this early period, when those in the community were evaluated according to *sābiqah*, or one's precedence in converting to Islam, and whether one had been among the first to accompany the Prophet in the dangerous *hijrah* journey north (Afsaruddin 2010). Indeed, as the Verse cited by Qailah states, those who stayed behind in Mecca angered God's angels and earned themselves an eternal home in Hell. The *muhājirūna*, or emigrants, by contrast, were valued both for standing by the Prophet during the *hijrah* and for relinquishing kinship ties to their Meccan brethren in favor of a new allegiance: loyalty to the *Ummah* or Islamic community (Rubin 2010).

By invoking this Verse, Qailah maps parallels between how Mohammed reacted when he was forsaken by residents of his native Mecca, on the one hand, and how she and her devout Muslim friends must behave in response to their current oppressive circumstances in Marseille. Just as the morally superior Muslims of yore were those who chose to "fly for refuge" with their Prophet to Medina, so, too, must contemporary Muslims leave Marseille behind in search of their true home. The morning after posting Verse 97, Qailah made yet another follow-up post in which she further clarified her reading of the Verse: "At the risk of losing authenticity, our residence [in France] must be provisional, temporary. . . " (January 24, 2014, 8:51 a.m.). Here, Qailah makes clear reference to the existence of a moral hierarchy among Muslims in Marseille, or in France more broadly. She appears to support the idea that, just as piety belonged only to those who conducted *hijrah* and stood by the Prophet, so must Muslims in Marseille lift themselves from their circumstances in order to be pious. For Qailah and her orthodox friends, many of whom currently face difficulty in relocating, oftentimes the main way they can demonstrate the authenticity of their piety is by conveying a sincere intent to relocate from

religion) – 'Nous étions impuissants sur terre,' dirent-ils. Alors les Anges diront: 'La terre d'Allah n'était-elle pas assez vaste pour vous permettre d'émigrer?' Voilà bien ceux dont le refuge et [*sic*] l'Enfer. Et quelle mauvaise destination! (Sourate 4 verset 97)."

the West. As shown in this section, one of the primary ways these young women indicate this intent is by discursively recasting their continued residence in Marseille in terms of a life of pious exile. Using these historical analogies as a touchstone, these young women speak about Marseille as though it were a stopover to be abided *en route* to their true homes, which they articulate to lie in the Muslim World.

It is worth pointing out, furthermore, that several of the points Qailah touches on throughout this protracted Facebook conversation – her contempt for France, the utmost piety of the first Muslims who followed the Prophet, and the need to relocate – suggest that in her formulations she is also drawing interdiscursively upon, not a Salafi interpretation of Sunni Islam per se, but the form of Salafism better known to the public as Wahhabism (*al-Wahabiyyah*).[15] As per Silverstein (2005: 9), interdiscursivity takes place when an individual on a certain occasion creates a text, spoken or written, that reveals their "retrospective or recuperative relationship to either another discursive event (in what I term a manifestation of 'token'-interdiscursivity) or to an internalized notion of a type or genre of discursive event (in what I term 'type'-interdiscursivity)." Whereas the Salafi movement centers on the principle that special moral distinctions are bestowed upon the Prophet and the next two generations that followed him, twentieth-century Wahhabi scholars theorized piety as depending upon the duplex practice of *al-Walā'* and *al-Barā'*.[16] Practices corresponding to *al-Walā'*, defined as showing loyalty only to Muslims, and *al-Barā'*, meaning the disavowal of anything related to disbelief (*kufr*) and disbelievers (*kuffār*), included not greeting non-Muslims or celebrating their holidays, not showing attachment to non-Islamic people, places, and things, and refusing to live in or visit the West unnecessarily. To indulge in such practices was to risk being ex-communicated from the community of believers (Wagemakers 2012a). The first interdiscursive link of Qailah's, as such, is the way in which she sequentially retraces the original reasoning of Salafism through her Facebook comments. In citing a Koranic verse speaking of disbelievers in the seventh century and then warning against Muslims in Marseille displaying the same inauthenticity, she recreates the parallel upon which Salafi philosophy was founded: that between the moral Muslims of yore and those of today. The second indication of interdiscursivity lies in her advocacy for relocation. Her insistence on

[15] Despite some terminological confusions over which thinkers, precisely, considered themselves proponents of Salafism (cf. Lauzière 2010), Salafism is here understood in Wagemakers' (2012b) sense as the movement proper to twentieth-century purists who used textual analysis of *Ḥadīth* to strictly imitate Islam's pious predecessors (or *salaf*) in as many domains of life as possible.

[16] These include thinkers like the Saudis 'Abd al-'Azziz b. al-Baz (d. 1999) and Muhammad b. Salih al-'Uthaymin (d. 2001), both of whom were influenced by the earlier writings of Muhammad b. 'Abd al-Wahhab (1703–1792).

leaving Marseille, or planning to, channels an ideology of piety resembling Wahhabi scholars' insistence on *al-Barā'*, or the "disavowal of non-Muslim conditions."

Qailah likely became familiar with this mode of reasoning through reading, during her classes at the institute, or through her contact with other young women also seeking a way to address their feelings of alienation. It is worth noting, in this regard, that within Marseille the ideology of piety as relocation is something I have only encountered among young women. It may be the case that young Muslim women, given their relatively more visible styles of dress compared to young Muslim men, are more liable to feel unloved and alienated by Marseillais society and are hence more likely to seek redress through stringent religious solutions to their predicament. In sum, this section has described how my personal and online engagements with young orthodox women revealed a growing subculture of piety centered on the desire to renounce Marseille in favor of living in the Muslim World. In the next section, I analyze several images and texts from social media to further illustrate the importance of such online networks in solidifying this particular understanding of piety, namely, as warranting relocation and other forms of disavowal.

Online Practices of Piety: Exemplifying *al-Barā'*

In this section, I examine three examples of social media engagement by young orthodox women to document how the disavowal of non-Muslims, or the ideology of piety known as *al-Barā'* ("disavowal of non-Muslims"), is in effect practiced. The first example, drawn from conversations with Radya, presents how this young woman has taken concrete steps to depart from Marseille. A social media network she has developed is shown to play a pivotal role in increasing the practicality of her move to Doha, Qatar. The other two examples, gathered from two young women who do not have the means to leave Marseille but nevertheless yearn to, demonstrate how they practice disavowal from within Marseille, in part via social media. All three cases point to the centrality of social media as young women either, network in preparation for their departure or, alternatively, seek to communicate their commitment to disavowing Marseille to their peers while still living in Marseille.

Radya, who turned 20 this year but was 17 when I met her, occasionally attended the same private institute where Qailah was taking MSA classes. A couple of months into the 2012–2013 class year, however, Radya stopped visiting the institute in Marseille altogether, preferring to spend her time mostly at home, an apartment in a housing project on the outskirts of Aix-en-Provence. When I asked her why she stopped attending classes, Radya replied, "I never go outside. What for? I'd rather stay home and speak to interesting people."[17] Since her junior year of high school, Radya had in fact begun leading an unusual life for a French-born 17-year-old.[18] Inspired by visits to her mother's family outside Algiers, back in Marseille Radya began wearing the *ḥijāb* and removing it before entering school premises. She likewise became increasingly disenchanted with the French public curriculum and, after finding her history and geography teacher's treatment of the French–Algerian War rather perfunctory, took to skipping classes. Shortly after this episode, at the outset of her baccalaureate year, Radya left high school altogether and enrolled in distance learning.

The "interesting people" with whom she conversed at home during this period were three women, two from Qatar and another from Saudi Arabia, whom she had met while shopping in a boutique in Aix. Radya had surprised the tourists in the boutique with her cosmopolitan allure, as she chatted facilely about the latest trends from the New York-based online magazine *Fashion Week*, and in an Algerian that sounded markedly un-Algerian in accent.[19] When I inquired further with Radya as to what had made her Algerian accent seem unusual to these women, she explained how she tried to maintain a pure Algerian, which to her meant one that was untainted by non-Arab influences and approximated MSA as much as possible. During her yearly trips to Algeria to visit family, Radya had observed a difference between how people from the capital spoke Algerian, namely with many contributions from French and Berber, and how people from her family's province of Batna spoke Algerian, "with accents from there [Batna] but *only* in Arabic words. ... Their dialect is more [standardly] Arabic."[20] In an interesting turn of events, Radya has since her encounter with these women four years ago become very interested in learning from them how to speak Saudi and Qatari (*Khalījī*) Arabic. It is these varieties, she now believes, that display the greatest linguistic proximity to the speech forms from the Arabian Peninsula that participated in shaping MSA during and in the centuries following the Prophet's lifetime (Suleiman 2012). Intent on fashioning herself into a "true Arab" (*une vraie Arabe)*, as she calls people from the Arabian Peninsula, Radya spends her afternoons and evenings conversing and texting in Saudi and *Khalījī*. This she does via several Voice over Internet Protocol

17 "Je sors jamais dehors. Pour quoi faire? Je préfère rester à la maison et parler avec des gens intéressants" (November 2, 2012).

18 Radya's father was born in Marseille to a Moroccan father and a *pied-noir* (or French) mother. Her mother was born in Algeria, of Arab heritage, and speaks to Radya in Algerian.

19 I use the label Algerian to refer to Algerian Arabic. This is in keeping with the movement within Arabic linguistics to consider the so-called "dialects" of Arabic as languages in their own right.

20 "Mais à Batna, ils parlent arabe avec des accents de chez eux, mais c'est *que* des mots en arabe. Leur dialecte c'est plus de l'arabe."

(VoIP) applications, notably Skype, BlackBerry Messenger, and Viber, both with her girlfriends in Abha (Saudi Arabia) and Doha (Qatar), as well as with their friends and relatives.

In the fall of 2014, Radya was able to arrange an initial trip to Doha to visit her friends there. She returned with stories of what life was like for young Muslims "in the real Muslim lands" (*dans les vraies terres musulmanes*): the courtesy of strangers, modesty in the streets, and the ease with which her friend's family hosted her for two months. Now back in Marseille, Radya has discontinued her distance learning and given up on her baccalaureate. Based on assurances from the well-to-do family in Doha that they can easily find her employment in the fashion sector in Doha, Radya bides her time sketching designs for modern *'abāyah*s (head-to-toe dresses) and awaiting the day when she can leave Marseille to settle "back home" (*chez moi*), as she refers to Doha. Akin to Yang's (2009: 156) description of online communities as fora allowing the Chinese to express and affirm their "utopian impulses," Radya has used and continues to use VoIP applications as networking devices to further define many of her hunches, whether about Marseille's depravity or the Arabian Peninsula's paradisiacal offerings for young Muslims.

VoIP correspondence also provides Radya with a handy way of learning Gulf Arabic (*Khalījī*), an item that is high on her list of preparations to make before leaving for Doha. In the example I discuss below, I argue that VoIP applications have been a venue for Radya to formulate a local Gulf persona for herself, and that, in so doing, they have facilitated her impending resettlement to Doha. Figure 2.2 depicts a BlackBerry Messenger conversation between Radya and her friend Maha, who is a Saudi young woman from Abha. Here, Radya and Maha resume a previous joke about how Maha is counting on Radya – now the recognized world traveler – to reserve her a ticket to Japan. Maha pleads in Saudi, "Just don't let me go back to Saudi Arabia. Reserve for Japan instead." Radya laughs and says "of course" (*min 'uyūnī*), using a generic expression that literally means "from my eyes." Maha then sends kisses of appreciation and finishes with "bless your eyes" (*tuslim 'uyūnij).* Although Maha usually sticks to Saudi Arabic, in this instance she opts to address Radya with the *Khalījī* possessive suffix *-j* rather than the Saudi *-sh* or *-s* or MSA *-k*. When I inquired with Radya via Whatsapp as to why Maha had chosen the *Khalījī* rather than the Saudi or MSA suffix, she laughed and explained in French that Maha has grown accustomed to Radya using the Gulf dialect in her speech: "Every time Maha uses the Saudi way, I say 'lol,' so now she just addresses me using the way I prefer."[21] In a Whatsapp text to me later that afternoon, Radya clarified in English: "usually in saudia they

[21] "Chaque fois que Maha utilise la façon saoudienne je dis LOL, donc maintenant elle m'addresse de la façon que je préfère" (May 24, 2015).

don't use ج [j] but she seen that i am speaking like this... yeah coz when she use ك [k] i always answer with ههه [hhh] ج [j]!"

This text conversation is telling because it illustrates how, by 2015, Radya had clearly taken to playing the role of a *Khalījīyyah* (or woman from the Gulf) with her acquaintances, even when they come from elsewhere and are less familiar with *Khalījī* speech. Moreover, unlike the female university students from the United Arab Emirates studied by Palfreyman and Khalil (2007), who preferred the "common romanized Arabic" orthography in their

Figure 2.2 Radya's BlackBerry Messenger conversation with her Saudi friend Maha

online conversations, Radya and Maha employ the Arabic script to exchange with one another. This choice of the Arabic script, typically associated with Arab culture and the history of Islam, harks back to Radya's intent to speak in varieties, like "pure" Algerian or *Khalījī* (Gulf Arabic), that she believes will align her with the pious purity and linguistic past of MSA. In sum, Radya's VoIP interactions with people in the Gulf help her to both learn varieties like *Khalījī,* through which she presents herself to her acquaintances as a pious person affiliated with the geographic nucleus of Islam, and set up relationships with people in the region who are likely to facilitate her actual departure.

Whereas Radya leans on social media to network for her relocation and develops the kind of Gulf-based pious persona she imagines for her life in Doha, other orthodox young women from Marseille nurture the same dream but currently lack the means to undertake their *hijrah*, or religious emigration. Manal was a 24-year old university graduate when I met her in 2013. Born near Marseille to two Arab Algerian parents, Manal grew up with little religious education. Friends at Marseille's local university helped her in that regard, and she began practicing and wearing the veil in 2010, later switching to the more modest *jilbāb*. Since her graduation, Manal's main source of income has been a low-paying retail position. She nevertheless holds out for a more prosperous future and the means to relocate permanently to Algeria. Though she was not born there, she refers to it as "my country" (*mon pays*) and returns often via the ferry between Marseille and Algiers. Manal, like Radya, grew up with both French and Algerian spoken in her household. As part of her pious ethic, she, too, would like to improve her MSA. For lack of time, however, she instead dedicates herself to making her French as polished as possible, with the understanding that to speak Standard French and not Marseille's iconic youth vernacular is yet another way of disaligning with the city.

One of the French-language fora she participates in online is a private Facebook group for women entitled "*Hijrah* to Algeria." There one can listen to clips in which religious scholars speak in French about the meaning and necessity of conducting *hijrah*, particularly from European countries, and read French-language articles about why a young Muslim woman does not need a *maḥram*, or male escort, in order to conduct *hijrah* to the Muslim World. French-born women who have moved to varying locales in Algeria also contribute posts on a weekly basis dealing with the novelties and difficulties of creating new lives in these places. Topics discussed include where to send their children to school, best places to grocery shop and get a gym membership, and which religious resources are locally available. The page also addresses more practical concerns, like how to obtain Algerian papers and work permits as a French-born person. Manal occasionally reposts interesting articles from this forum on her Facebook page, such as the promotion for a magazine issue shown in Figure 2.3. Posted in March of 2015, the image depicts the cover of an Islamic magazine published in France called *Faith* (*Imān*). This issue in particular features the title "Desire to leave. . . . Special Issue on *hijrah*" and a photo of a Muslim woman beside a suitcase on a desert landscape. Below this, lyrical French captions read: "Once upon a time, emigration"; "The reason behind *hijrah*"; "Why stay? Why leave?"; "Travelers in this lifetime"; "They left"; and "*En route* to a new life."

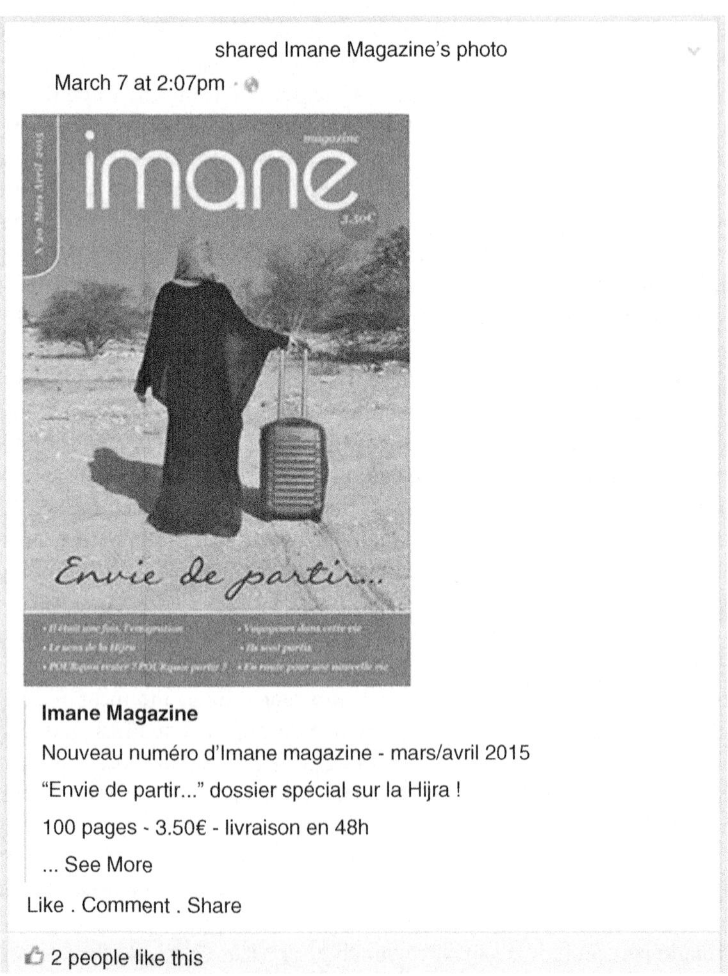

Figure 2.3 *Faith* (*Imān*) Magazine

These examples of Manal's engagement with Facebook reveal its duplex utility for her. On the one hand, her Facebook page serves as a platform through which to convey to her friends and acquaintances her plans to relocate and, thus, her commitment to this understanding of Islamic piety. On the other, Facebook also allows her to tap into online social networks like the *Hijra en Algérie* group and hence glean information about the technicalities involved in *hijrah*. Judging from the posts made by recent emigrants to Algeria and the number and specificity of comments that accrue to each post, this Facebook group no doubt aids young French Muslim women in working out the logistical details of their moves to Algeria. Most recently, for example, a "sister" posted about her positive experiences newly living in the capital, Algiers. She writes that "since I began living in Algeria, I have really advanced in the knowledge of our religion. I have started reading and writing the [Modern Standard] Arabic language ... I have also been able to enroll my children in a private Muslim school run by the Saudi Arabian Embassy."[22] Several sisters who presumably live in France followed up with her in the comments section, pleading with her to provide more information about her children's school. One wrote: "*Salam alaykoum* (MSA, 'peace be upon you') would it be possible for the sister [who posted] to contact me *min fadlikum* (MSA, 'please') I have some questions concerning the private school."[23]

The two previous examples demonstrated how social media proved particularly useful for both Radya and Manal, whether to broadcast the imminence of their departure from Marseille, or to network with individuals living in the Muslim World. This final example illustrates the use of social media to exhibit young women's disavowal of Marseille and France, much in the same vein as Qailah's "Mayday!" post. Expressing fatigue and disgust with life in Marseille is, in effect, the other side of the coin of departure. Thus, in 2012–2013, I met an orthodox young woman named Bushrah who was studying for her BA in Arabic and Arab civilizations at the local university. After my subsequent departure from Marseille, we became friends on Facebook. I was intrigued by the trajectory of one of her posts in particular. In November of 2014, Bushrah changed her profile picture to the image depicted in Figure 2.4. The image captures a cartoon drawing of a man who, as he steps back with both hands up, claims in a mix of French and MSA: "No one loves me. I do not love anyone. *Al-ḥamdulilleh* (thanks be to God)." In choosing this image, along with its accompanying text and content, Bushrah conveyed

[22] "Depuis que je vis en Algérie, j'ai beaucoup avancé dans l'apprentissage de notre religion, je commence à lire et à écrire la langue Arabe. . . . J'ai d'ailleurs pu scolariser mes enfants dans une école privée islamique dirigée par l'ambassade d'Arabie Saoudite d'Algérie." (November 13, 2015).

[23] "*Salam alaykoum* serait-il possible que la sœur me contacte *min fadlikum* j'aurai des questions concernant l'école privé" [*sic*] (November 13, 2015).

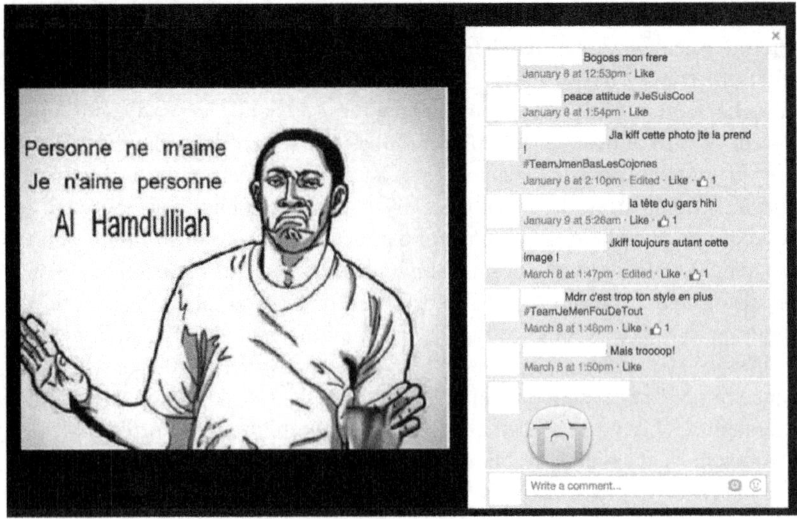

Figure 2.4 Bushrah's Profile Picture

to her Facebook friends a strong sense of apathy towards the nature of social relationships in France. Initially, her change of picture solicited no replies and only a few "likes" from friends. However, when several months later, on January 8, Bushrah added the hash-tags *#JeSuisCool* (#ImChill) and *#TeamJeMenFouDeTout* (#TeamIDoNotGiveACrapAboutaThing) to her profile picture, friends contributed a torrent of comments. Importantly, January 8, 2015 was the day after the shootings at the *Charlie Hebdo Magazine* headquarters.

Bushrah's addition of two hash-tags, one claiming that she "is chill" and the other that she "does not give a crap," at this moment of crisis in French society effectively transformed her apathetic attitude to a clearly anti-French stance, one on a par, for instance, with the pro-Muslim "I am *not* Charlie Hebdo" campaign that circulated on some of my research participants' Facebook pages in the days after the shooting. Contributing to her anti-French stance here, additionally, is a voicing contrast Bushrah sets up through a change in linguistic footing. The cartoon's text, on the one hand, alternates between a more standard form of written French, which insists on the formal non-contracted *personne ne m'aime* ("no one loves me"),[24] and the MSA formula *Al-ḥamdulilleh*. These linguistic varieties are consistent with the language practices and aspirations of Muslim orthodox youth in Marseille, as described in the cases of Qailah and

[24] The more informal counterpart, common in speech, would be *personne m'aime,* without the negative particle *ne*.

Manal. If the text and image represent the voice of the pious French Muslim youth, then the hash-tags, by contrast, "style" (Hill 1999; Cutler 1999) the voice of the non-Muslim French person. What reveals Bushrah's hash-tags to be an instance of voicing the other is her resort to profanity (e.g. *je m'en fous,* "I do not give a crap/fuck"), a language practice otherwise very negatively viewed within her peer group. One of Bushrah's best girlfriends described their group's avoidance of profane language thus: "One mustn't say bad words or speak loudly in the street. We have to be respectful, say sorry, and smile when insulted. One can never be vulgar."[25] Bushrah's deployment of profanity, thus, reveals that she is assuming the voice of the non-Muslim French "other," also indicated by her use of French slang borrowed from English in the hash-tags (e.g. *cool, team*). As Cutler (1999) has proposed in her article on how an adolescent white male adopts African American Vernacular features in his speech, or Barrett (1999) has described in his article on how African American drag queens employ a register of "white women speech" in their performances, embedding speech associated with an out-group in one's own talk can act as a metacomment on those who are in fact thought to speak in such a way. Here, Bushrah animates the voice of the non-Muslim French youth to cue her skeptical stance on the degree of "team commitment" such youth display. Via her hash-tags, Bushrah suggests that these are the kinds of comments non-Muslim French youth make when French Muslim youth face troubles in their midst. Not only is she cynically returning the favor of not showing solidarity, but, by using their type of speech to do so, Bushrah signals that her move to dissociate herself from the French victims is an echo of previous moves made by the French to disalign with people like her.

Some of Bushrah's friends found this cynicism amusing, as was the case of one friend who likened Bushrah's attitude to that of the Japanese cartoon character Calimero: "*Mdrrr, #SoumyModeCaliméro ACTIVÉE!*" (Lol, #SoumyCalimeroMode ACTIVATED). Calimero is a black chicken who complains of being unfairly treated in his family of yellow chickens and hence goes about life with a rather negative, defensive outlook. Other friends, by contrast, were disappointed by Bushrah's transition from apathy, as connoted by the original image and text, to her outright declaration of disregard for the French victims, as purveyed by her hash-tags. One writes "Moi je t'aiiiiiime" ("Me, I loooooove you"); another, "Oui moi aussi je t'aime Bushry" ("Yeah, I love you too Bushry"); then a third young woman adds a large emoticon with tears running down its face. These three female friends seem to be urging Bushrah away from this ideology of piety as disavowal of the French and towards a less combative stance vis-à-vis the

[25] "Il faut pas dire de mots grossiers, ni parler fort dans la rue. On doit être respectueux, dire pardon, sourire quand on nous insulte. Il faut jamais être grossier" (October 29, 2012).

French. Indeed, as I intimated in the introduction, some orthodox-identified youth from Marseille were proponents of an ideology of piety requiring affiliation with Marseille, one that contrasted starkly with the ideology of piety as disavowal being incarnated here by Bushrah.

Via these three examples, it becomes apparent that social media provide useful spaces for all manner of ideological positioning. In Radya and Manal's case, VoIP applications and Facebook furnished useful contacts for their impending moves away from Marseille. Bushrah's case, in turn, crystallized the efficacy of media like Facebook in broadcasting an ideological stance, like disavowal of France, to a larger audience. The *al-Barā'* or disavowal stance I have been analyzing throughout this chapter was found, furthermore, to have clear language ideological coordinates. It becomes of particular importance, as such, to account for these fractally recursive links (Irvine and Gal 2000), between ideologies of piety and ideologies of language, when interpreting how youth engage one another linguistically through online media. Without knowing, for instance, that Radya puts Gulf Arabic on a pedestal based on an etymological link she draws between it and MSA, which she considers the utmost religious language, her use of *Khalījī* could not be recognized as a display of piety in hopes of relocation. Likewise, in the absence of familiarity with the ideology, prevalent in Marseille's orthodox community, by which one's adherence to standard varieties of French and Arabic is performative of piety, Bushrah's change of footing, from her own voice to styling the other's voice, could not be read as a cynical gesture.

Concluding Remarks

This chapter has examined how ideological discourses and personal circumstances have come together, across linked face-to-face and social media speech events, to give shape to the particular figure of personhood youth in Marseille subsumed under the label of being orthodox or "Sunni." In the context of an increasing incompatibility between how the non-Muslim French imagine their homes and how the practicing Muslim French imagine theirs, being an orthodox youth has increasingly meant thinking about substituting another home for Marseille. Gender, too, appears to be of paramount importance in determining which youth come to understand piety in terms of relocation and which do not. Pious young women are more likely to struggle to visibly fit into their surroundings and to be excluded from French institutions, like secondary schools, that have a direct bearing on their ability to later integrate with the French workforce. Imagining a future for oneself in a country where one does not meet the job market's barriers to entry is a daunting task indeed. Radya, for example, was unable to find an alternative to French school and thus found herself alone in her apartment year-round aged 17. The prospect of moving forward again as she learns about Doha and prepares a life there has been a source of great excitement for her. In a Skype conversation at the close of 2014, for instance, Radya articulated her enthusiasm at finding a new home, whether in London or Doha, with obvious emotion: "Let me tell you something. I hope, well, I hope to be stable. And I'll be stable in whatever it will be, in one of these places, and I would be very very very happy if you would come visit."[26] It stands to reason that, given their relatively more abject circumstances, young orthodox women may find greater appeal in ideas like those found in the Wahhabi scholarship on piety, such as the disavowal of the West (*al-Barā'*) and relocating to the Muslim World. Whether such young women ultimately come to enact their piety by planning to set off from Marseille is surely due to a mix of factors, however, including financial, biographical, and quite centrally, social ones. Insofar as social media can limit or expand participation in peer groups, expose one to new role models (e.g. religious leaders, authors), and direct one's gaze to new websites, I imagine online media will continue to play a key role in mediating youth's migratory trajectories.

Lastly, I find that Hage's (2005: 470–471) remarks on types of mobility capture the dynamics described here in a particularly elegant and concise way. Hage explains what he calls "existential mobility" as the shared human desire to feel like we are "going places" in our lives. He writes, moreover, that "migratory physical mobility is only contemplated when people experience a crisis in their sense of existential mobility." As such, the young female proponents of *hijrah* that I have presented can be said to be experiencing a crisis in their existential mobility that has made physical migration seem the only way forward. In the interim, that is, between the moment when young women feel irreversibly alienated and when they actually leave Marseille, online media play a vital role in allowing them to enjoy a modicum of "existential mobility." For instance, as Radya chatted about the Gulf with her friends in Doha through BlackBerry Messenger or Manal scoped out pleasant Algerian cities on the Facebook group "*Hijrah* to Algeria," these young women were able to feel as though they were in the throes of planning to leave Marseille. Such exchanges granted them the sense that they were moving forward, conducting a virtual *hijrah*, as it were, even as they continued living in Marseille's housing projects. One Muslim sister spoke to the mental importance of this planning phase for French women conducting *hijrah* in a follow-up post to the posts by Qailah analyzed in the first section of the chapter. This woman urged her fellow French sisters to start planning: "A piece of advice for all of you: make a project, get organized, and prepare

[26] "Je vais te dire une chose. J'éspère, fin, j'éspère être stable… Et je serai stable dans quoique ce soit, dans un de ces endroits … Je serais très très très contente que tu viennes là-bas" (December 31, 2014).

your departure. (...) I am myself ethnically French, but believe me, this country is no longer mine, and of this I am reminded every day by the French themselves. So come up with some plans. If your intention is in keeping with Allah, Allah will ease your hijra... "[27] This young woman's comments about feeling disoriented within France – despite her Frenchness – connect to one of the larger points made in this chapter. It emerges from the young women's stories I have presented that the ongoing apprehensions the French exhibit towards French Muslims, and especially young orthodox women, have deleterious effects on their ability to imagine futures for themselves in their French places of origin. Indeed, as is apparent from these young women's discourses on piety, their language preferences, and their online practices, home has since become a moving target for them.

[27] "Un conseil pour tous: faites un projet, organisez vous, et préparez le départ... Je suis moi même française de souche, et croyez moi ce pays n'ai [sic] plus le mien, et ça c'est les français eux mêmes qui nous le font comprendre chaque jour. Alors donnez vous des objectifs, et si votre intention est pour Allah, Allah vous facilitera votre hijra..." (January 24, 2014).

3 Cool Mobilities

Youth Style and Mobile Telephony in Contemporary South Africa

Zannie Bock, Nausheena Dalwai, and Christopher Stroud

The popularity of social media as sites for identity performance and friendship maintenance is well documented and much has been written on the rapidly evolving practices and texting styles of digital communication (see, for example, Herring et al. 2013; Thurlow and Mroczek 2011b; Jones et al. 2015). While the international literature points to a range of features that are often cited as typical or characteristic of digital communication (e.g. emoticons, abbreviations, shortenings), the focus of research in recent years has been increasingly on the diversity and creativity inherent in many youth texting styles and instant messaging registers. Thurlow and Poff (2013), for example, argue that their research shows considerable variation on almost every aspect of texting across different contexts, and other recent scholarship points to the fluid and flexible nature of many of these analytical categories as new hybrid genres and creative styles of texting emerge in response to local contexts and conditions (Deumert 2014a).

These texting practices take place within a context of considerable innovation in mobile phone technology, from the earliest "black and white" phones to the smartphone generation, along with increasingly sophisticated applications. Yet little research has explored the impact of changing technologies on texting styles. Similarly, minimal scholarship has reflected on the materiality of the phone and the meanings that this has for its users.[1] This chapter aims to address these gaps by exploring the role of phone, affordance, and application in the texting styles of young students at a higher education institution in South Africa. We use our analysis to make the argument that the changing technologies and their associated affordances provide new resources for

[1] A notable exception to this is Carrington (2015: 158), who points out how mobile phones are "impacting on the ways in which young people conceptualize their engagements with the everyday and develop and deploy a range of identity and textual practices." She argues that her participant Rosie's phone "clearly mediated her everyday life and the ways in which she understood and interacted with her world" (2015: 162).

styling identity among our participants, and that what shapes the selection and combination of both linguistic features of texting as well as choice of mobile technologies is a fluid and complex interplay of factors, driven by the participant's changing identities and ideologies as well as a strong element of affect and an appreciation of what is symbolically valued and socially "cool."

First, however, we offer a brief overview of changing mobile technologies, and introduce our research context and data. We then explore two primary foci in our data: first, the significant shift in the participants' choice of technology (phone and application) over a five-year period; and second, the relative continuity of the linguistic and semiotic elements they mobilize for their chats during this time. Based on our consideration of the relationship between these dimensions, we argue that the shifting trends and patterns we note are affected by a range of competing factors which interact in complex and creative ways.

Central to our account of both the shifting preferences of users and the creativity and diversity of texting practices is a view of style as an "assemblage of design choices" (Coupland 2007). We further argue that our conception of style needs to be expanded to take into account the materiality of the phone as well as the users' interpersonal affect and subjectivity. To help us make this argument, we refer to research which explores the human/technology interface and proposes that "there is no social that is not also material, and no material that is not social" (Orlikowski 2007: 1437).

Changing Technologies: National Trends

In Africa, mobile phones are the preferred medium for telecommunications, with subscriptions showing a phenomenal increase over the past one and a half decades (ITU 2015). This growth has been fueled in part by young people who use them as their primary means for social networking and instant messaging. This dramatically expanding uptake is paralleled by rapid global developments in the technologies themselves, especially with regard to design and technological affordances.

In South Africa, there has been a steady shift of make and model over the years. The most popular instant messaging application to first rise to prominence was Mxit, which was developed by a South African based company in 2004. In the ensuing years, it grew to become the largest social network in Africa as well as enjoying a presence in Asia, Europe, and the United States. In 2011, a report by Fuseware and World Wide Worx indicated that Mxit had approximately ten million active users in South Africa (Wronski and Goldstuck 2011) and close to 37 million users worldwide in the same year

(SouthAfrica.info 2011). This was also the year in which its popularity peaked. From this point on, it experienced a significant decline as more and more users switched over to smartphones and began using applications such as BlackBerry Messenger (BBM) and WhatsApp. These applications allowed users to send voice and image files, features which were not initially available on Mxit. BlackBerry packages, which included the signature instant messaging application, BBM, and unlimited internet access, were the most affordable of the smartphone options available locally and therefore the most popular amongst South African users. Interestingly, although later versions of Mxit were upgraded to run on smartphones and to allow for the exchange of image, video, and sound files, this did not save it from going out of grace with users.

However, BlackBerry's popularity was also short lived. In April 2011, Vodacom (one of the three primary service providers in the country) had around one million BlackBerry devices on its network (Mybroadband 2012). By comparison, they only had 150,000 subscribers with iPhones and 100,000 with Android devices. By September 2013, Vodacom had 3,100,000 BlackBerry devices on its network, but by March 2014, this had declined to 3,030,000 (Mybroadband 2014). In May 2014, Vodacom's CEO admitted that the demand for BlackBerry devices had "plummeted" but that they had seen a "big upswing" in the number of Android devices on the Vodacom network (Mybroadband 2014). This shift was facilitated by the increasingly cheaper packages available for Android phones in the country. As the demand for Android phones grew, WhatsApp (launched internationally in 2008) became increasingly the application of choice. As Deumert (2014a) notes, affordability is a very significant constraining factor in choice of phone and application in (South) Africa.

It would be reasonable to expect that these rapid technological developments and shifts in user preference would impact on the texting styles and practices of young people. For example, we could assume that the wider range of emoticons (or multimodal options like voice notes) available on smartphones would lead to an increase in their use for texting. We could also assume that developments in predictive texting technology might mediate users' texting styles. Because this function "suggests" words to the user based on the first letters typed and the context of other words, it could well result in more standard and monolingual forms being selected. In this chapter, we explore this possibility, as well as the extent to which the national trends referred to above are visible among our community of users. Specifically, we ask, do we find evidence of shifts in choice of phone and application? And if yes, to what extent do these changing affordances seem to impact on the texting styles of our users, or are other factors shaping these practices?

Research Context and Data

Our data are taken from undergraduate students at the University of the Western Cape (UWC) and their mobile phone use. UWC has historically served students from more marginal educational and social backgrounds as it is, in South Africa, what is termed a "historically black" university. While the student body of over 19,000 includes students from all over South Africa and, increasingly, African countries to the north, it still comprises predominantly students drawn from two provinces in South Africa: the Western Cape (in which the university is situated) and the Eastern Cape. As such, the student population reflects the historic social demographics of these regions, as well as the varied linguistic repertoires of the participants.

According to university enrolment statistics for 2012, of the 19,217 registered students, 43 percent described themselves (on their registration forms) as English speaking, 13 percent as Afrikaans speaking, 6 percent as bilingual in English and Afrikaans, and 38 percent as speakers of various African languages. The figures above have hardly changed over the years and are thus a good indication of the linguistic profile of UWC students at the time of research. It is worth bearing in mind that most students would probably describe themselves as bi- or multilingual, even if they only indicated one language as a home language. Thus, this registration statistic does not reflect the multilingual nature of the student body. As the vast majority are able to converse in more than one of these languages, translanguaging is the norm, with different varieties expressing different social values and facets of youth identity.

The data for this chapter include a focus group interview (held in 2014) and a corpus of chats collected over five years (2010–2014). The focus group interview was semi-structured and open-ended and aimed to establish insider views on the mobile technologies used by participants, reasons for their shift from one application to another, and what they perceive as typical norms and styles for texting.

The chats are drawn from assignments given to first-year students in our department each year as a part of their introduction to language and communication. The assessment rubric asks students to collect, transcribe, and analyze one of their own instant messaging chats in order to answer the question: "What does your data show about how languages are used in new ways in contemporary communication in South Africa?" With a first-year class of about one thousand students each year, the potential data pool was huge. However, our corpus consists of 398 chats and includes all those we could photocopy before tutors returned the scripts to students and those left uncollected at the end of term. We also only worked with chats which had consent forms attached. From this corpus, a further subset of 245 chats was selected for detailed qualitative analysis.

The data were transcribed by first-year students as part of their major assignment. Accuracy of transcription was ensured as far as possible by conducting a tutorial on transcription methodology. Additionally, we worked on the data with student tutors who are themselves users of social media as well as speakers of the local mixed varieties and so relied on their insider knowledge and intuitions with respect to the authenticity of the data that were selected for detailed analysis (Dalwai 2010, 2015; Thompson 2013). We used quantitative methods to establish trends within the total corpus, such as the shifting choice of application over the years. We then used qualitative methods (e.g.discourse analysis) to analyze the changing styles (genres and registers) in the corpus (see Bock 2013).

Shifting Technological Preferences

As noted above, national figures indicate how user preferences have changed dramatically in recent years, from predominantly Mxit in 2010, to BBM and increasingly WhatsApp in 2014. Our data clearly supports this trend. Table 3.1 summarizes the choice of application among UWC first-year users for the total chat corpus and indicates the decline of Mxit and the growth in popularity of BBM and increasingly WhatsApp. Raw figures are given in brackets.

According to Dalwai (2010), the popularity of Mxit among the youth at UWC in 2010 was due to it being mobile phone-based and therefore more affordable than computer-based applications, and because it could run on the pre-smartphone generation of internet-enabled phones. It was also cheaper to use than the alternative at the time, short message service (SMS), as it did not include a character limit per message (see also Chigona and Chigona 2008). A further reason was that it gave users access to a virtual community of friends and networks and enjoyed a "coolness" factor that afforded the "right" kind of social status and visibility (see also Beger, Hoveyda, and Sinha 2011). However, as noted above, the popularity of Mxit began to wane in 2011 as newer applications gained popularity.

Table 3.1 *Percentage of chats in each application in total chat corpus*

Application	2010 (140)	2011 (60)	2012 (47)	2013 (75)	2014 (76)
Mxit	82.1% (115)	83.3% (50)	53.2% (25)	28% (21)	6.6% (5)
BBM		3.3% (2)	27.7% (13)	36% (27)	39.5% (30)
WhatsApp			14.9% (7)	28% (21)	44.7% (34)
SMS	17.9% (25)	11.6% (7)	2.1% (1)		
Facebook		1.6% (1)	2.1% (1)	8% (6)	9.2% (7)

This clear shift in our data prompted us to ask: Do these technological shifts impact on the texting styles of our participants, and if so, how? For example, is there an increase in the use of monolingual (as opposed to mixed) varieties or standard orthographies (as opposed to textese[2]) between 2010 and 2014, and to what extent could this be driven by technological innovations such as the increasingly sophisticated predictive texting affordances? While the older phones, like the Nokia, had predictive texting functions, these were not intuitive like the contemporary versions which are attuned to a user's personal style and "remember" preferred spellings and forms. The older versions did not therefore allow for abbreviated spellings or language mixing. As a result, participants in this study report finding these early versions "irritating" and switching them off as soon as they bought a new phone.

Changing Affordances and Texting Styles

As part of the larger project, we conducted qualitative analyses of the texting styles of our participants from both a genre and register perspective (see Bock 2013; Thompson 2013; Dalwai 2015). In this chapter, however, we focus on only two aspects of linguistic style, namely, the choice of language variety, as well as the extent to which our participants use standard orthographic forms as opposed to abbreviated textese. Interestingly, and contrary to our expectations, our data do not show any sustained pattern with respect to an increase in monolingual varieties over the five-year period (2010–2014) with 63 percent of the corpus making use of multilingual varieties. Similarly, the use of textese was pervasive and consistent, with almost 100 percent of the chats each year using textese as opposed to standard spellings. It should be noted, of course, that these figures only reflect the data in our corpus, which are dependent on what students chose to submit for their essay. In other words, our data do not describe the range of practices that students may in fact be using on a daily basis. Having said this, the *lack* of a clear shift in the choice of codes and orthographic norms in this five-year period, despite the clear shift in choice of phone and application during the same period, raised for us the question: What then is driving our participants' stylistic choices?

To answer this question, we turn to our qualitative analysis which suggests that while the developing technologies and affordances certainly may provide additional resources for styling, they are by no means the primary driver of

[2] By 'textese', we refer to the global shorthand for chatting on various social media (Thurlow 2003, Thurlow and Poff 2013) which includes "typical features" such as accent stylisations (e.g. *inie* for "in die," the Afrikaans for "in the"), clippings (*hav* for "have"), number homophones (*2* for "to"), non-conventional spellings (*u* for "you") and contractions (*gna* for "gonna") as well as the use of paralinguistic features such as emoticons and excessive punctuation.

choice. Consider, for example, the following chat between two female friends on BBM in 2013. What is interesting about this chat is that even though both participants are using the same application, they come across as making quite distinct choices in their texting styles: X uses the local variety of mixed Afrikaans English, *Kaaps*, and unconventional spellings of global textese, while Y uses a relatively standard variety of English and conventional orthographic forms.

Chat 1: Females (X, Y), BBM, 2013

1. X: Elo skat. Hoe gaanit?
   [Hello sweetheart. How're you doing?]
2. Y: Hey there. Its going well thanks and with you?
3. X: Eks oryt, jus vri busi wit werk…dit maak n mens moeg jng…hws ur clsses?
   [I'm alright, just very busy with work…it makes one tired man…how're your classes?]
4. Y: Shame man. I hope you fit in some time to rest hey. My classes are okay, they are manageable but I'm also just as tired and busy too (thumbs down emoticon)
5. X: Ja maar anyway, spk agn ne skat? 🙂 c u.
   [Yes but anyway, speak again okay sweetheart? (smiley face) see you.]
6. Y: Okay, keep well doll 🙂 😚 (smiley face, kiss face).

The mixing of styles in this chat is evidence, we would argue, that texting is primarily a matter of choice and social normativity. While the choice of a more standard variety by Y may signal her lesser proficiency in the local variety, Kaaps (which she obviously understands but may not easily produce), it may also reflect an aspiration towards the more "educated middle-class" values carried by Standard English (Anthonissen 2013). Even so, Y's style includes typical markers of South African English, namely "shame man" and "hey" in turn 4. The former is an expression of sympathy and the latter an interrogative marker. Thus both their stylistic choices index local belonging, albeit in different ways.

As noted above, the majority of chats in this corpus are multilingual in nature. As standard English is the medium of instruction at UWC and the language of prestige both in the province and the country, it is unsurprising that English features as the predominant language in the data. It is, however, frequently mixed with other languages, as illustrated in Chat 1 and by the following three turns from Chat 2, which takes place on Mxit between two male friends in 2011. The mixing of isiXhosa and English is evident in phrases such as *kule wikend*, where *wikend* is a borrowing from English "weekend." Further, the chat includes features of typical of textese, such as spellings which reflect spoken contractions (e.g. *uzoyenza* for *uzakuyenza* "you will be doing"), number-letter homophones (*mfe2*, for *mfethu* "brother"), and global norms, such as *den*, for "then." Here, once again, participants use a variety of linguistic forms to style identities which index a mix of global and local situatedness.

Chat 2: Males, Mxit, 2011

8. Y: Akonto uzoyenza kule wikend?
[Akonto uzakuyenza kule wikend?]
[Anything special that you will be doing this weekend?]
9. X: Nha mfe2 ndzawbona
[No mfethu ndizakubona]
[No my brother I will see]
10. Y: K den ndzawjikela apho kuwe emzini.
[Okay then ndizakujikela apho kuwe emzini]
[Okay then I will come around this weekend at your place]

Given South Africa's history of racial segregation, the participants' linguistic repertoires generally reflect their social and racial identities. For example, while standard Afrikaans, as the language of the former apartheid regime, is associated with "white" political conservatism, local (spoken) varieties of Afrikaans, such as the Kaaps in Chat 1, although commonly viewed as "inferior" to the standard, carry strongly positive values of "coloured identity," community solidarity, and local belonging (McCormick 2002).[3] Similarly complex attitudes exist in relation to isiXhosa. While varieties based on the codified standard are often perceived as "pure," "correct," and "carriers of the culture," young black urban speakers tend to stigmatize this "deep Xhosa" as "rural" and "old-fashioned." For them, the urban mixed varieties, while commonly seen as "slang" or "incorrect," index "cool urban sophistication" (Dyers 2009).

Thus the creative blending of these linguistic elements enables our participants to style for themselves complex identities which include an aspiration for urban middle-class lifestyles and global mobility, together with a display of local solidarity and community situatedness. Our analysis of the total data set indicates that these stylistic patterns permeate the data, despite the shift from

[3] The term "coloured"' in South Africa is used to refer to people of complex heritage arising out of a history of colonialism and slavery. During the apartheid era, South Africans were classified into the following racial categories: "White," "Coloured," and "Native" by the Population Registration Act of 1950. "Asian," as a fourth category, was added later. During the years of opposition to apartheid which followed, these labels were rejected by the opposition movements which chose to refer to all oppressed people in South Africa as "black." Although the term, "coloured," is now much more acceptable as an identity marker, notions of coloured identity and the use of this term are still contested. The participants in this study, however, overwhelmingly use the term for self-identification and point to the English-Afrikaans code mixing in their data as linguistic indices of their "coloured" identities.

Mxit to smartphone applications. This suggests, we would argue, that these stylistic choices are articulations of social and identity considerations rather than the outcome of technological innovation.

Further support for this position can be found in the international literature. Bieswanger (2013: 466) contends that styles of texting depend on a range of use and user-related factors such as communicative purpose, writer intention, participant gender, and age, as well as choice of genre, language, and script. Baron (2013) identifies gender-based differences in the openings and closings and length of chats in her data, as well as in the use of emoticons. Spilioti (2011) shows how the interactional context (such as the time of day and questions of face) shapes the ways in which her participants close off their chats. And according to Deumert and Lexander (2013), texting styles are influenced by regional norms and ideologies. For example, African digital varieties of English show higher frequencies of abbreviations than those reported for the USA and UK, which Deumert and Lexander interpret as users "speaking back" to the ex-colonial language.

Yet further evidence comes from our focus group data which point clearly to the role of participant identities and ideologies in the shaping of style. As the focus group comprised second- and third-year students between the ages of 20 and 23 years, they were old enough to have used a range of different instant messaging applications (Mxit, BBM, WhatsApp) but still young enough to be "typical" users of instant messaging applications. Three of the participants with pseudonyms, Mahmood (M), Tasneem (T), and Brandon (B) and the facilitator (also an author), Nausheena (N), were well known to each other. The other two participants, Billie (Bi) and Kiara (K) did not know each other or the other members of the group before the interview.

Their comments indicate their awareness of conventionalized norms and genres of chatting. For example, they argue about whether one must always greet or not, or whether *g2g* ("got to go") suffices for "goodbye," with their differences reflecting individual notions of politeness or appropriateness. Tasneem, for example, indicates she usually always greets (it's "rude" not to) but dislikes it when a person who wants a favor from her first goes through the ritual of asking, *hey, how you doing, what you doing?* This, she explains is because "you know this person is only chatting to you coz they want something from you." She would rather they didn't "waste [her] time" and got straight to the point. However, she also indicates that when she chats with her best friend, she does not always greet or close, as their chats become one long interaction interspersed throughout the day, a comment which points to the shaping role of the interactional context as well (see Spilioti 2011 for a similar finding).

Brandon claims that although he always says goodbye, he never uses *g2g* or *chat later* as "that's Mxit language," and he is at pains to distance himself from this style of writing. It is clear that for most of the participants in this group, textese is now associated with Mxit, laziness, and bad education. For example, Brandon says it irritates him when someone writes "even" as *evan*, as both words have four letters and so take the same "energy," so why didn't they just "write it correctly in the first place." And Tasneem and Mahmood agree this style "messes up your brain" and has a deleterious effect on your writing. (Participant Y's insistence on standard English in Chat 1 could also be read as further evidence of this attitude.) However, they all admit to still using "a lot of emoticons" and agree that the one Mxit word that never "died" is *mwah*, the South African textese version of "kiss."

Thus, even though textese *is* the dominant style in the chat corpus, the focus group appears to strongly resist it. Their stance can perhaps be explained by the fact that most of them are slightly older than the first-year chat corpus (20–23 years as opposed to 18 or 19 years) and so this shift may be due to changing identities and ideologies. As they have developed from teenagers to young adults and progressed with their education, their styles of texting have similarly changed. (See Ling and Baron 2013 for a similar trend of teens outgrowing abbreviated styles of texting.) Although they acknowledge that the predictive texting function of smartphones is one reason for their reported shift to more standard texting forms, their reasons focus more on notions of "correctness" and what is appropriate for someone with their level of education than on the affordance per se. They have therefore made the conscious decision to stop using textese completely, or as frequently as they used to, a choice which is facilitated by the fact that their Android phones have the predictive text option available by default.

We find further support for our argument that texting styles are significantly affected by considerations of self-presentation in the following quotation from Mahmood. In the context of the discussion about whether you need to greet every time you chat or whether you can "just jump straight in," he defends his choice of unusual greetings by saying that he likes his style of chatting to reflect his "personality" as a "bubbly person," an indication that for him, texting is an expression of personal style:

M: And **it also has to do with your personality** also, I think that's just how a person is. Like if I'm like – for me if **I'm a bubbly person** right? So . . . when I, when I chat, **I'd like to express the way I feel or the way I am** right now over Mxit or instant messaging towards the next person

Given the above, we would argue that the notion of *style* offers purchase in getting to grips with the UWC population's shifting preferences. Here we are working with a conception of style as referring to "short-lived fashion and to adoptive ways of dressing and behaving" (Coupland 2007: 30), an "assemblage of design choices" (2007: 1) which individuals may combine in creative and relatively distinct ways "to signal [their] uniqueness while still being recognized as affiliated with a particular group or groups" (Stroud and Wee 2012: 4–5). From this perspective, style is "oriented towards consumption" and has "agentive possibility for social identification" (Coupland 2007: 30). Thus, the texting styles of our participants form part of the repertoire of design choices on which participants draw when crafting identities for self-presentation.

However, our data further suggest that our notion of style needs to be expanded to take into account the materiality of the phone and the interpersonal affect of the user. We develop these arguments in the following sections with a consideration of the phone as a "lifestyle accessory" and "extension of self." Here we refer to Turkle's (2005; 2007) work on "evocative objects" in which she argues that in contemporary life, there is an increasing tendency for objects (or technologies) to be invested with meanings and values and to act as "companions to our emotional lives" (2007: 5). We further argue, following Suchman's (2005) notion of "affiliative object," that style can also be seen as that which references a particular "constitution of objects and subjects ... enacted within culturally and historically specific fields" (Suchman 2005: 395).

The Phone as Lifestyle Accessory

In this section, we argue that the exercise of style is not restricted to variability in texting, but also found in conjunction with choice of mobile phone itself. We focus on data which suggest that the materiality of the phone together with associated technologies are clearly resources in the styling of desirable interpersonal selves. Over and above being able to run the latest instant messaging applications and keeping up with technological advances (internet access, inbuilt cameras, etc), the make, model, color, size and special features are also significant.

Thurlow and Poff (2013: 177) allude to the significance of the materiality of the phone as an articulation of style when they argue that "the act of texting has cachet" and "(t)exting (and mobile phones) carries cultural capital in and of itself – as a lifestyle accessory and a ludic resource." Although their focus is on texting rather than the materiality of the phone, they make the point that "buying into the cachet of texting means drawing on – or rejecting altogether – symbolic resources such as ringtones, keypad covers, and popularized linguistic markers like initialisms, clippings and letter-number homophones" (2013: 177). The phone, we would argue, has significance in the lives of our participants as a fashion accessory, worn like a prosthetic extension on their bodies, part of the bricolage of elements that constitute their style. As such it is imbued with the same desire and affect that drives the consumption of style in contemporary life. Thurlow and Mroczek (2011b: xxv) allude to this view with their apt description of social media "as prosthetic extensions of people's abilities and lives, rather like the hearing aid and the paper clip" (2011: xxv).

Our participant commentaries make the point very clearly that the phone, together with its associated applications, has cachet. When asked why they prefer the new smartphone application to Mxit, they are at first vague, referring to the "longer log in" and slower processing speed of Mxit as disadvantages. However, as the interview proceeds, what emerges in this data is a clear consensus that the shift was due to "the bandwagon effect" – that is, the persuasive power of peer-group pressure to determine what an individual aspires to and appreciates as desirable.

The participants in the focus group recollect using Mxit on their first phones: "Yor [wow], Mxit was then the shit, yoh," Mahmood says, and Tasneem agrees, "Yor it was so cool." However, none of them now admit to using Mxit and explain their shift to first BBM and increasingly WhatsApp as primarily due to the "bandwagon effect" or keeping up with the changing trends in phone and application. In the two extracts which follow, Kiara recalls getting her first smartphone in "grade 10 or 11" because she also "wanted to be cool," and Brandon describes his desire for a smartphone as a function of "the bandwagon effect":

K: Like at that time everyone had like BBM and stuff and I was like so sad because I was still on Mxit and stuff and I wanted a BlackBerry. So I think ja I got it like around there and **I was like you know wanted to be like cool and BBM and stuff** ja.

B: But I wanted to shift [to a smartphone] actually but uhm the reason why I wanted to shift is because (1.5) basically like you said [everyone?] was on social media that kinda thing and it was awesome to have social media, I dunno why, **it's like a bandwagon effect**.

In the next extract, Brandon, Mahmood, and Tasneem recall shifting to WhatsApp. The overlapping speech (marked with square brackets) indicates the extent to which this "bandwagon effect" is co-constructed and a shared sentiment, the strength of this feeling reflected in the evaluative phrases which are marked in bold:

B: you know neh you know neh sometimes neh we don't actually . . . sometimes neh it's not that we choose to use WhatsApp, it's **we get influence to do it**, not that – we don't [[get
M: [[due to uhm
T: [[like **everyone else is using it**
M: due to the **bandwagon effect**

The "bandwagon effect" alludes to the "social" aspect of style and the way in which it functions as an *affiliative* object in the sense of Lucy Suchman. Objects with affiliative powers "are not innocent but fraught with significance for the relations they materialize" (Suchman 2005: 379). Clearly the "bandwagon effect," where social constellations and peer groups cluster and form around specific mobile artifacts, and where perceptions of social value and material capital are tied to these artifacts, is a prime example of the style value of the phone.

The Phone as Extension of Self

The phone, however, is far from a mere fashion accessory. Once we begin to consider the materiality of the phone as a feature of style, we are also made aware of how the phone is also imbued with characteristics of close confidante and friend and inserted into a web of emotions and affect that contributes to how we interact with others.

Turkle introduces the idea of "evocative object" to capture how mobile phones, like other objects once designed as "tools" to assist humans with particular functions, are subsequently experienced by their users "in a much more intimate way, even as extensions of themselves" (*Harvard Business Review* 2003: 3). They serve, she argues, to anchor memories, to provoke new ideas and passions and to sustain relationships – hence "companions to our emotional lives" (Turkle 2007: 5). Her work underscores the growing interdependence of humans and technology and she is well known for her quotation, "we think with the objects we love, we love with the objects we think with" (Turkle 2007: 5).

We find such "emblematic" value in some of the surprisingly vivid and detailed recounts our participants make of their memories of their first mobile phone. They do so in a way that suggests a highly "intimate" relationship with the phone. For example, they recall the make and model of their first phone, its physical appearance ("small, thin, flat, cover flips up"), color ("blue, black, silver"), special features ("dolphin face, mirror screen, color screen, rotating camera, games") and ringtones. They also tell stories of when and from whom they got their first phone (or smartphone) and particularly the *feelings* associated with this acquisition. What is noteworthy about this data is the detail with which they recall the *materiality* of their phones and the *affect* with which these memories are imbued.

T: oh uhm I got my first phone in grade 4 I remember it was a Nokia 3310 and like the **coolest** thing about it was that you could play like that snakey game for the whole day [all laugh] and also like the battery lasted for [[like

N: [[forever and a day

T: jaaa

M: and you could personalize your ringtones also like that [inaudible]

T: exactly

Yet another participant tells of how his first phone had a "dolphin face" because "at that time it was fashion not to have the original face" and another remembers that on her eighteenth birthday, her mother bought her a color screen phone: "It was that black Samsung, you know the one that flips open with the rotating camera." These memories are interspersed with "small stories" (Georgakopoulou 2006) that give detail and context for these first acquisitions, indicating their significance in the lives of the speakers. Threading through all these recounts are statements of *affect* which indicate clearly how the acquisition of these phones evoke strong emotions, further indexing their importance as symbolic resources and "evocative objects" in the constitution of situated selves.

In the extracts below, the evaluative terms (marked in bold) point to the desire and pride that these first phones aroused in their users. *Kwaai* is the local Kaaps word for "cool," *yor* is an expression like "wow," and *awe* is being used here as a marker of affirmation:

N: The camera . . . ja
M: **Yor**, that was **awesome**.
N: It was a **cool** phone.
B: I **wanted** one like that, but I couldn't get one
N: It was **the best**, it was **kwaai**
B: **Awe**, I **actually liked** that phone

Mahmood recalls his first phone which he describes as "a **really cool** phone":

M: It was a Sagem C2 it was just so small [illustrating with his hands] [. . .] and you can like flip it open [. . .] and it had er it had everything, it had camera, it could go on internet [. . .] The only problem there was at first was I couldn't like download Mxit because that was like the in thing but and afterwards I got it right. But it was actually a **cool** phone. **I still miss it** though.

In this extract, Mahmood admits to "still missing" his phone, as though a part of himself was bound up with it. Later he describes himself as "heartsore" when he lost it. For Mahmood, the phone is an *extension of himself*, worn with pride and affection as a statement of his identity. Brandon also remembers with pride the identity his first phone (a Nokia 3310) afforded him. Here *ou* is a colloquial Afrikaans expression signifying "the main guy":

B: If I come with my 3310 people are still gonna think **I'm the ou** because of a 3310

Threading through all these accounts are references to "coolness" (e.g. "yor it was so cool," "I wanted to be like cool and BBM and stuff," "it was a really cool phone"). In our data, then, "coolness" refers to a composite style based on an assemblage of design elements which, we have argued, index a complex range of meanings and values, from ones which affirm local identity and solidarity, to those which signal global mobility and sophistication.

As a final illustration of this, we present one last piece of data, the beginning of a chat between two students, cousins, who are texting each other in a lecture venue at UWC. This chat, like Chat 1, uses Kaaps and the abbreviated spellings reflect local pronunciations. For example, *op siti* (turn 4) and *nti* (turn 8), which are rendered in standard Afrikaans as *op sit nie* ("to put on") and *net nie* ("just not"), reflect local spoken realizations in which the negative particle (*nie*) is assimilated with the previous word. The ritualized *lmk* (turn 9), which stands for *lag my klaar* ("laugh me finished"), is a local variant equivalent to more recognised English initialism, *lol* ("laugh out loud"). (The standard Afrikaans and English translation is given after each turn.)

Female (X) and male (Y), WhatsApp, 2013

1. X: hey
2. Y: hlo
3. X: nou eers *[now only]*
4. Y: ek was op mxit... j wl msi vi jo mxit op siti
   [Ek was op mxit.. .jy wil mos nie vir you mxit op sit nie]
   [I was on mxit... you don't want to put mxit on]
5. X: ha ha not my scene.
6. Y: g3 my n rede
   [gee my 'n rede]
   [give me a reason]
7. X: soema net
   [sommer net]
   [just so]
8. Y: dais mosi n antwrdi
   [daai is mosnie 'n antwoord nie]
   [that's not an answer]
9. X: dit is nti vi my ni en ds uncool lmk
   [dit is net nie vir my nie en dit is uncool lag my klaar]
   [it is just not for me and it is uncool, laugh me finished]

Here, we see how style is explicitly referenced in terms of the notion of "coolness." The young woman (X) does not want to be on Mxit because it is not "cool" (*not my scene, ds uncool*) whereas WhatsApp is. "Coolness" represents a style that has "cachet," a lifestyle choice that inspires "the band-wagon effect," an aspiration saturated with affect and desire. It requires balancing the expression of local connectedness with global aspiration in endlessly diverse and innovative ways. Phones and their associated affordances embody particular social meanings and are thus part of the "assemblage of design choices" available for the styling of desirable interpersonal selves.

Conclusion

In this chapter, we explored the shifting trends in choice of mobile technologies and texting styles of UWC students. We argued that an expanded notion of style should be used to understand our participants' choices. Contextualizing our study within a review of national shifts, we noted throughout how mobile phones, their materiality and their affordances, together with the variable practices of texting, are intimately associated with situated and ideologically informed representations of self and how we relate to others.

With regard to our participants' technological preferences, our data shows clear shifts, while selected elements of their textual style, namely choice of linguistic variety and orthographic forms, remain relatively stable over the same five-year period. We argued that these choices can be interpreted if we adopt a perspective on style as an assemblage of design choices, in which these elements form part of the repertoire on which these participants draw when crafting their own unique styles and identities. Additionally, we argued that what drives these selections is a fluid and complex interplay of factors, including the participants' maturing age, changing identities and ideologies, and a strongly emotive component bound up with personal feeling and aspiration, not simply the outcome of increasingly sophisticated technologies. In other words, technological advances impact on and shape the context, thereby changing the options available to users and allowing new identities and ideologies to develop. But these technological developments are not deterministic; rather, the factors which shape stylistic choice are varied, multidimensional, and composite in nature.

We further argued that our conception of style needs to be expanded to include the phone as part of the repertoire of stylistic elements available to users. We argued that these phones can be seen as extensions or embodiments of the users themselves, and therefore as *de facto* co-constitutive of what it means to be a particular person on a specific occasion in a particular context, thus enacting as well as constituting social identities. They are productive in mediating, co-constructing, and distributing the emotional makeup of the user in relation to the mobile field, as phones carry memories or function as reservoirs of emotion – present or past – and that this is also an important part of how the user relates stylistically to others.

Mobile technologies come and go, and it is in this passage of mobile artifacts, the shift and turn-over of technologies, the historicity of mobile design, the fluidity of affordance and application, and the diversity of texting practices, that style finds its place.

Postscript

Mobile communication and youth styles are rapidly evolving phenomena. Preliminary findings from further data collection in 2016 continue to show an increasing preference for WhatsApp. (Ninety-eight percent of all participants report using WhatsApp in 2016, usually in addition to other applications, notably Facebook and BBM.) The data also show an increased shift towards more standard, monolingual forms, particularly in the chats which use only or primarily English. This suggests that the technological affordances of predictive texting are, in the case of English, driving style shifts towards more monolingual varieties and standard spellings for some users. Yet we also note that this still seems to be matter of choice as participants continue to shift between different registers within one chat, as for Chat 1 in this chapter. However, in those chats which are largely in isiXhosa or Afrikaans, where no inbuilt predictive texting option exists, participants choose texting styles which tend to employ a mix of languages and the abbreviated spellings of textese. This, we suggest, further supports our core argument that texting styles are highly variable and driven by a complex interplay between the evolving technological affordances and the multidimensional and changing presentations of self in different contexts. Thus, we argue, technological advances contribute in highly significant ways to shaping the context, but they are only one of a number of competing factors which drive stylistic choice among our participants.

Acknowledgements

This research was made possible by funding from the National Research Foundation of South Africa. Opinions, findings, conclusions, and recommendations expressed in the article are those of the authors and the NRF does not accept any liability in this regard.

Sincere thanks to Miché Thompson who, together with Nausheena Dalwai, was a research assistant on this project, and to the many students who contributed their data.

4 Nuancing the *Jaxase*

Young and Urban Texting in Senegal

Kristin Vold Lexander

C'est du jaxase, un mélange, quoi. Jaxase – mélange.
On mélange tout, quoi.
L'essentiel c'est que la personne comprend.
["It's *jaxase*, a mix, you know. *Jaxase* – mix.
We mix everything, you know.
What's important is that the person understands."]
Momar 21 years old, high school student

Introduction

Multilingual practices in speech have been developing in urban Senegal for a long time, and not only among young people. McLaughlin (2008a) traces Wolof-French mixing back to the eighteenth century, and the phenomenon has been the subject of several studies (Swigart 1992; 1994; Thiam 1994; Dreyfus and Juillard 2004), which have led to the identification of a proper mixed code dubbed urban Wolof (Swigart 1992) or Dakar Wolof (McLaughlin 2001). Urban Wolof is characterized by alternation of Wolof and French, sometimes mixed with material from the other 25–30 languages used in the country. Young people's way of speaking urban Wolof differs from that of other age groups, with English words being introduced as youth identity markers (Dreyfus and Juillard 2004).

These language practices have been considered mainly as a spoken code, but some studies look at different expressions of urban Wolof in writing, like shop signs (Shiohata 2012), comics (McLaughlin 2001), and newspapers (Kébé 2009). With digital communication, written multilingualism is flourishing in Senegal, for instance in internet discussion forums (McLaughlin 2014), instant messaging and emails (Lexander 2010), and in texting. Momar's statement "We mix everything" characterizes the texting of young Dakarois; when composing SMS messages, Senegalese youth draw on their entire linguistic repertoire.

While many studies of texting focus either on the linguistic aspects (e.g. Anis 2007) or on the social uses of the SMS (e.g. Archambault 2012; Ling and Baron 2013), this chapter embraces both dimensions. Texting is studied as a personal everyday literacy practice (Barton and Hamilton 1998) and the analysis integrates the individual's linguistic attitudes, language, and CMC history (or techno-linguistic biography, Barton and Lee 2013), other literacy and language practices in which the person is engaged, as well as the sociolinguistic context (cf. Sebba 2012). It is hence in accordance with recent developments within the "sociolinguistics of writing" (Sebba 2012; Lillis and McKinney 2013), where important elements are (a) the study of digital communication as *written* communication, (b) the challenging of 'standard' and 'error' as default stance, and (c) the attention to what is meant by writing and where and how it figures in complex communication practices (Lillis and McKinney 2013: 423–430). It is also in line with Deumert's (2014a: 168) remark that studies of mobile communication allow sociolinguists to see things that are fundamental to how language works in social life.

I will start this chapter by briefly reviewing other studies of texting and then recall some of the features of the mobile revolution in Africa. A few characteristics of urban youth language practices on the continent will be presented along with the sociolinguistic situation in Senegal and in Dakar. The second section presents the theoretical and methodological approaches followed in the chapter, while the third part discusses some of the findings. The focus will be on how the label "young" serves as a point of departure for performing other voices or identities in the SMS communication, and how the introduction of Wolof and other Senegalese languages in written communication contributes to nuancing these voices. Three of the most clearly defined voices identified in the collected corpus will be illustrated: (1) the hip-hop style identity, (2) the romantic voice and (3) the articulation of ethnic belonging. Processes like enregisterment and glocalization pattern the heteroglossic practices of the young texters who use their creativity to perform the different voices. Through these processes, African languages are valorized as means for the written expressions of youth identities.

Texting as Youth Practice

The research on texting started in the early 2000s and lexical and stylistic features have been popular topics in linguistic studies of text messages (Thurlow and Poff 2013: 168). A number of studies of the relationship between texting and reading, writing, and spelling abilities (e.g. Plester, Wood, and Joshi 2009) have shown positive relationships between texting and spelling. "Adolescents know the rules but are able to bend them, while retaining the ability to communicate" (Lenhart et al., cited in Ling and Baron 2013: 199). Deumert (2014a: 111) uses the term "small performances" to name such brief and fleeting moments of play in everyday interaction. Through linguistic choices and the combination of forms, these small performances construct particular speaker personae, like "a skillful, creative writer who also has a sense of humor" (Deumert 2014a: 112). Nevertheless, "public and policy-level discourse about texting continues to fixate on its deleterious impact on literacy and standard language use – especially that of young people" (Thurlow and Poff 2013: 171). Such negative attitudes towards texting language are also observed in African countries (e.g. Chiluwa 2008), but the value of the mobile phone as a literacy learning tool is also documented (Dyers 2014).

If youth texting practices have a low status in the news media, they dominate in research on mobile phone use, which has tended to focus more on young people's texting than on adult SMS practices (e.g. Thurlow and Poff 2013). As Ling and Baron point out: After the introduction of the mobile phone, adolescents quickly "became the leading cohort using the technology" (2013: 198). It gives them a communication channel that they can control themselves, thereby making them more independent. What Rainie and Wellman (2012: 11) call the "new networked individualism" marks a shift in people's lives "away from densely knit family, neighborhood, and group relationships toward more far-flung, less tight, more diverse personal networks" (see also Evers, this volume). Mobile technology gives young people more autonomy and privacy vis-a-vis their families, making it easier to enter into other relationships and to maintain these in secret. Since it is a person-based and not a place-based form of communication, the mobile phone allows for more frequent contact with network outside the family, even while physically being at home, with the family. It helps the young to "manage a larger, more diverse set of relationships," where people "function more as connected individuals and less as embedded group members" (Rainie and Wellman 2012: 12–13). For the informants of this study, being young and unmarried means being under a certain degree of control by their family. Texting therefore is a way to create a private sphere, in particular for romantic relationships, allowing a couple to stay in touch even if they cannot meet face-to-face.

However, mobile phones can also be used to have more frequent contact with family members, and in economically underprivileged communities they are shown to be used principally for this (Porter 2012; McIntosh 2010). They make it easier to stay in contact with those who live elsewhere in the country or abroad, for instance through ritualized text messages for religious feasts (Lexander 2011a) and they allow the parents to check if their children are okay, to communicate to them that it is time to come home, etc. One of the high school students in this study said that when her older brother was out late, she was instructed by her mother to text him to ask for his whereabouts and to tell him to come home. Such examples show that it is probably an exaggeration to see the mobile phone as mainly a means for young Senegalese to achieve more individual liberty, but in line with what Brinkman et al. (2009: 74) observe in

Sudan, the mobile phone helps the young operate more freely within the norms of respectable behavior.

The Mobile Phone Revolution in Africa

The growth in the number of mobile phone subscriptions in Africa is impressive: in 2005, the number of subscriptions was equal to 12.4 percent of the population, while nine years later, the number of subscriptions is moving towards a figure of 70 percent (ITU 2015). Africa has leapfrogged technology, moving straight to the mobile phone, which technically is much easier to set up than fixed line telephony is. Senegal is among the countries on the continent with high mobile coverage, reaching a penetration of 111.5[1] percent in June 2014 (Osiris 2014). In 2014, smart phones are common among the urban middle class of Dakar, even if the price of a new handset is the same as in Europe (upwards of 500€), while wages are well below. A simpler mobile phone can be bought new in the street for about 10€ (personal observation, April 2014).

Different aspects of the mobile revolution have been studied; many have focused on economic and social outcomes: how farmers sell their products more easily (Kibora 2009), how news and information circulate faster (Kreutz 2010), and how different software has helped improve health care, political discussions, and banking transactions (Banks 2010), to name but a few. Even people with few economic resources own and use mobile phones; Hahn and Kibora (2008: 104) show how some mobile phone users have a "zero budget strategy," spending as little as possible on use, for instance through the "beeping practice": exchanging messages (like "call me," "I have arrived," etc.) via intentional miss-calls (Donner 2007; McIntosh 2010). Still, within this success story, there are nuances that serve to be noticed, like important differences between the rural and urban population when it comes to access to and use of the mobile technology (Alzouma 2013), and how the shared access to mobile devices may lead to systematic exclusion of particular groups (Burrell 2010). Some linguistic studies of African text messages have also appeared and certain similarities can be identified in texting practices in different African countries, like multilingualism and use of African languages that are otherwise seldom used in writing (Deumert and Masinyana 2008; Deumert and Lexander 2013; Lexander 2011a, 2011b; Deumert 2014a).

[1] The number of subscriptions exceeds the number of inhabitants because many people have more than one SIM-card. The companies differentiate their prices during the day and the night and the different SIM-cards are used to profit from the best prices.

Urban Youth Language Practices in Senegal

There is a trend that modernity and urban status dissociate youth language practices in Africa from ethnic associations (Kiessling and Mous 2004: 316). Likewise, in Dakar, many young people speak urban Wolof and call themselves Dakarois instead of identifying with a particular ethnic group (McLaughlin 2008b: 94). However, urban Wolof is not limited to Senegalese youth language practices; it is the dominant and unmarked choice in spoken communication in urban informal contexts (Swigart 1992: 88).

Urban Wolof is mainly characterized by Wolof-French alternation; that is, the mixing of two languages with quite different roles in Senegalese society. The former colonial language French is the official language and the sole language of instruction in formal schooling and therefore dominant in writing. It is also the language of social mobility, but its prestige has suffered from the high percentage of unemployment among well-educated francophone Senegalese and the success of Wolof-speaking traders (Le Page 1997: 58). The status difference between French and Wolof is also weakening, as French is being used and learnt in the streets while Wolof is entering speech in formal situations where it used to be excluded (Dreyfus and Juillard 2004) (cf. Bock et al., this volume regarding Afrikaans).

In informal spoken communication, standard French is often avoided because the speakers do not want to appear to be too positive towards the former colonial power (Swigart 1994: 179). When mixed with Wolof, however, French comes to index urbanity and modernity. The Wolof spoken in the cities is therefore rarely free from French influence; those who speak "pure" Wolof are considered as *kow-kow* – unsophisticated peasants (McLaughlin 2001: 164). In Wolof classes in University, the students would laugh because they found "real Wolof" (standard Wolof) "so funny!" (personal observation, May 2007) and they did not identify with this variety of the language. Still, some Senegalese intellectuals (Swigart 1994), rappers (Auzanneau 2001), and religious leaders (Lexander 2010) practice and preach a Wolof without French influence, using archaic words and neologisms.

Wolof is also increasingly adopted as the first language of persons from other ethnic groups (wolofization), and it is often referred to as "our national language" in Senegal. Being spoken by as much as 80–90 percent of the population (McLaughlin 2008b: 85), "Wolof speakers provide what could be termed a 'core ethnicity' for the Senegalese state" (O'Brien 1998: 27). While some accept this wolofization, others fear Wolof dominance. Among the speakers of the 25–30 minority languages in Senegal, speakers of the most important of them, Fula, have articulated such skepticism in different ways. In texting, the Fula speakers may use their language as opposed to Wolof to mark their ethnic identity. As we will see below, one of the Fulani informants of this study says that he never uses Wolof when texting, only Fula and French.

French does not only face competition from Wolof: English is also starting to challenge French as the language representing communication with the outside world. This is related to migration to the USA (Dreyfus and Juillard 2004: 63; McLaughlin 2008b: 97) and to music with English lyrics (Auzanneau 2001). Leigh Swigart (1994: 181–182) found in her study of language practices in Dakar that English was associated with "low-life" or street-oriented young men, but it has come to index youth more generally (Bock et al., this volume). The younger generation, both women and men, makes their mixed code unique through the introduction of English words (Dreyfus and Juillard 2004: 246–247).

With the appearance of digital communication, the sociolinguistic dynamics described above have entered the written domain. Urban Wolof practices, usually associated with spoken communication, now appear to a much higher degree in written form in text messages, emails and other digital texts. The role of French as the unique language of writing is challenged as it is mixed with, or replaced by, other languages like Wolof and Fula, other local languages, Arabic, English, and Spanish. Texters both exploit and challenge associations linked to the different languages and linguistic forms when they perform diverse voices in their SMS messages. They thereby value multilingualism and diversity in writing.

Studying Young Texting and Texters: Theoretical and Methodological Considerations

The notion of literacy practice has guided the study on which this chapter is based, and, following Sebba (2012), the ethnographic data play an important role in the analysis of the linguistic play in the individual text messages. Data collection for the present study including texts, observations, and interviews, took place in Dakar in 2005, 2006, and 2007. Informants were recruited through snowball sampling in the university milieu and a total of ten university students, three high school students and two other young Senegalese who had finished their studies made up the pool of informants. The data collection aimed at three aspects: (1) A basis on which profiles of the informants, specifically in relation to use of media and language (similar to techno-linguistic biographies, Barton and Lee 2013) could be built; (2) texts, and data on texts, for qualitative analysis; and (3) texts for quantitative investigation. A combination of methods was thus applied: Photos were taken of all messages saved on the informants' mobile phones at the time of our first meeting (about 500 altogether) and two interviews were conducted with each informant, where the photographed messages as well as texting and language practices in general were discussed. Pascoe (2012: 79) compares text message contact between researcher and informant with the observation: "Both the researcher and respondent can remain in casual frequent contact in the same way they could if the researcher were doing participant observation in the respondent's daily world . . . they can also function much like informal conversations in a physical research site." And, I would argue, collecting text messages is also a form of observation of the informant's daily life – telling the researcher quite a lot of what is going on from day to day, while discussing these texts in interviews gives further insight.

Emails and chatting conversations were collected during observation of the informants' use of the internet in cyber cafés and at home. In addition, their everyday lives at home and at the university, the African language classes at the University of Dakar and other literacy events in the capital were observed to gain data on the local and national linguistic and social context. Finally, the group of informants was extended to include five additional participants and two focus groups that were set up to investigate the age differences identified with certain practices: one for young women in their mid-twenties and one for young men (and one younger girl) in their early twenties. The project started out as a study of electronic literacy practices, but following the unequal importance of different digital media in the informants' everyday lives, texting turned out to be the main object of study.

The analysis focused on the three aspects mentioned earlier: First, the profile of each informant was analyzed based on the data from interviews, observation, and collected texts. Texting literacy practices were compared to other language practices, written and spoken. Second, the corpus underwent a statistical analysis of language use, where the number of words in each language in each message was counted. The objective was to identify the languages – or language combinations – that were the most common, and to measure the quantitative extent to which French is challenged. The messages were also categorized according to content, gender, and interlocutor (age and relationship with the informant), to see if there was a statistical relation between language use and the topic of the message, the sender's and receiver's gender, and the nature of their relationship. Third, the multilingual nature of the texting called for an analysis of the multilingualism of individual messages.

The quantitative analysis showed that messages in a single code made up just over half of the corpus: French only messages made up 47 percent of the corpus, while 5 percent where written in Wolof only and 1 percent in Fula only. The rest of the messages contained linguistic material from multiple languages. This heteroglossia opens up enormous possibilities for linguistic play and it "is essential to creativity" (Deumert 2014a: 121; Hinrichs, this volume; Lee, this volume). According to Bakhtin (1981: 291), all languages are heteroglot: they may be used differently to represent different socio-ideological groups or points of view, different epochs and generations. Heteroglossia can thus be defined as "the coexistence, combination, alternation, and juxtaposition of ways of using the communicative and expressive resources language/s offer us" (Leppänen et al. 2009). And like McLaughlin (2014) observes, the multilingual digital practices of Senegalese integrate these two aspects of heteroglossia: "these diverse and heteroglossic literacy practices allow writers more liberty of expression because they are not subject to the same kinds of normative judgments as French is" (McLaughlin 2014: 31). The very mixing makes different "specific points of view on the world" (Bakhtin ibid.) more acceptable; the texters create images of themselves as conversational participants (Deumert and Lexander 2013: 530) through linguistic play.

Texting can thus be considered as performance, "a mode of communicative display" (Bauman 2003: 9). Deumert (2014a: 110) distinguishes three types of performance: performance-1: things people say and do in their everyday life; performance-2: the way we routinely represent social types; and performance-3: a specially marked, non-routine way of speaking. Here we will consider the two latter and the way they may contrast with each other. The effect of performance-3 often relies on performance-2.

Enregisterment is related to performance-2 and can be defined as "processes through which a linguistic repertoire becomes differentiable within a language as a socially recognized register of forms" (Agha 2003: 231). It is not necessarily differentiable only within a language, but also within a multilingual discourse, as we will see in the following. Digital language can be considered as such a register, and we can also differentiate registers within digital communication.

We will moreover look at language policing: "the production of 'order' – normatively organized and policed conduct – which is infinitely detailed and regulated by a variety of actors" (Blommaert et al. 2009: 203), processes that contribute to socializing young people into texting practices. Finally, the data will be discussed with regard to glocalization (Robertson 1995), used by Koutsogiannis and Mitsikopoulou (2007) in the sense of "a dynamic negotiation between the global and the local, with the local appropriating elements of the global that it finds useful, at the same time employing strategies to *retain* its identity" (Koutsogiannis and Mitsikopoulou 2007: 143, my emphasis). Both French and English appear as glocal languages in Senegal in that they have "international status, but at the same time *express* local identities" (Pakir 2014: 55, my emphasis). As we will see, it can also be about not only retaining and expressing identity, but involves *creating* identity expressions. Through the mixing of global and local linguistic features, through producing local specificities with material from globally shared linguistic forms, glocalized identity expressions are created (see Bock (2013: 83–84) for similar practices in South African digital communication, see Bock et. al., this volume).

Before moving on to the analysis, a presentation of "the young" of this study is needed. All informants in my study shared some of the characteristics that are often associated with youth: they were unmarried, had no children, lived with their parents or other close family (some also had a room at the university campus), and all but two of them were still undertaking studies. However, a study in rural Senegal with the same age group would probably comprise married informants with several children, in a very different situation, different daily activities, different social life – and probably quite different linguistic practices. The informants of the study were also more or less privileged; a study of young workers in the urban informal sector would reflect yet another reality.

Texting Youth Identities

Learning how to text is important for the young texters, because mastering this language game is a way of dominating the mobile phone, of performing, of gaining status (McIntosh 2010; Archambault 2012). The SMS messages and quotes presented here are chosen because they illustrate how young texters perform different identities within the frame labeled "youth." Texting is about creativity and liberty of expression:

Dans les SMS, là, toi, tu crées, toi-même, tu crées.

['In the SMS messages, there you create yourself, you create'] (Christine, focus group)

Tu adoptes du n'importe quoi. Tu utilises du n'importe quoi pour exprimer ce que tu veux.

['You adopt anything, you know. You use anything to express what you want'] (Rama, focus group)

Young urban Senegalese texting implies language alternation from one message to another and language mixing within messages, and it comprises enregistered elements like French neography (Anis 2007) and verlain (reversed syllables) that allow the texters to display themselves as young skillful texters. The texters thus refer themselves glocally, both to a Dakar identity, through the mixed discourse and the use of Wolof, and to a larger group of francophone youth through the same unconventional spelling, the same spelling register, as that used by French speakers elsewhere in the world, and verlain.

The unconventional spelling used for French does not apply to Wolof. Usually the Wolof words are written according to French standard spelling, to facilitate comprehension, since very few actually know the Wolof orthography. The texters even add mute *e*'s and *u*'s, following French spelling rules (which they omit when texting in French), to make sure the text is understood, and only a couple of truncated Wolof words appear in the corpus. However, some use features specific to standard Wolof (like *x* for [x]) to show off through performing a more or less rare knowledge. This illustrates how heteroglossia is emerging both in spite of and because of norms and restrictions (Thurlow 2011: 169): spelling rules are followed, but in creative ways.

Still, texting, like other new media discourse, is not only about form; creative practice is not only expressed through the play with spelling, but also in the pragmatic, relational needs of participants. There is "interactional play," "identity play," and "topical play" (ibid.). For instance, is the use of English words and expressions associated both with being a young Senegalese and with a certain attitude to American culture. There may be references to religious identity as well, mainly Muslim, through the use of Arabic, and to ethnic identity, through the use of minority languages like Fula. One reference does not exclude another. An unusual language choice, a performance-3, like the use of "pure" Wolof in a romantic message, can surprise and impress the receiver.

If creativity through the play with spelling is expected and accepted, excessive use of unconventional spelling is not considered to be positive if the message becomes incomprehensible, and it may lead to a policing response from the receiver. When receiving a message that he could not understand, Mamadou, a sociology student aged 27 at the time, sent the following answer: *Mé sé koi ce message bizarre k tu m'as envoyé* ("But what is this odd message that you've sent me?"). On the other hand, consciously ignoring the liberty from the norms of standard language may also lead to a certain stigmatization. In the following quote, Mamadou draws a line between what he considers as normal and less normal linguistic texting behavior, between youth language and standard French, when he comments on a message in standard French orthography:

MAMADOU: *C'est un copain de la fac, lui, généralement, c'est un peu comme un autre ami, après on va le voir, d'habitude quand il écrit, c'est de façon correcte, claire en français.*
["It's a friend from university, generally, it's a bit like another friend, we will see that afterwards, in general when he writes, it's in a correct way, clear, in French."]

KRISTIN: *Pourquoi* ?
["Why?"]

MAMADOU: *Parce que lui, il fait comme ça, il écrit comme ça. Et pourtant, c'est un jeune comme nous.*
["Because, he, he does it like that, he writes like that. And still, he's young like us."] (individual interview).

Mamadou finds it strange that a young texter, who should be "like us," writes standard French, thereby not marking his youth identity. Youthful texting is thus considered different from adult texting, but the young are still important mediators for their parents and grandparents (see also Jones and Schieffelin 2009; Dyers 2014). The young are asked to text for their elders; they teach them how to text, or they influence their way of texting in indirect ways. When writing messages for her father, Christine is told not to make abbreviations, but she still does: *j'écris comme je le sens après j'efface, donc là, il ne va pas voir ce que j'ai écrit, parce que lui-même, tout ce qu'il sait de son portable, c'est répondre et appeler* (focus group I) ["I write like I want to, afterwards I delete, so that he will not see what I've written, cause himself, all that he knows about his mobile, it's to answer and call."] Also Mamadou sends and receives messages for his mother, often in an abbreviated style. There are even some examples of direct influence from the young to the old:

Par exemple dans les SMS que j'ai eus à noter ici, il y a un qui s'appelle tonton NN voilà, au début, le premier SMS que j'avais à lui envoyer, j'avais pas respecté l'orthographe et autres. Je l'ai écrit comme jeune, quoi, comme je l'avais pensé, et quand je lui ai envoyé le message, tout de suite aprés, il m'a appelé pour me dire : Allô [Mamadou], j'ai lu ton message, ça va, mais sinon dans le message tu as écrit tel mot comme ça. Mais je lui ai dit : Je sais que l'on ne l'écrit pas comme ça, mais dans l'SMS c'est comme ça. Lui, déjà il commençait à découvrir l'SMS, les abréviations et autres, et ça c'était le début. Et maintenant lui, il fait comme nous.

["For instance, in the SMS that I have noted here, there is somebody called uncle NN, well, in the beginning, in the first SMS that I sent him, I did not respect orthography and so on. I wrote it like young, you know, like I had thought it, and when I had sent the message, immediately, he called me to say hello, [Mamadou], I've read your message, it's okay, but you have written this word like that. But I told him: I know that we don't write it like that, but in the SMS messages it is like that. He, already he started to discover the SMS, the abbreviations and other things, and that was the beginning. Now, he is doing it like we do."] (Mamadou, individual interview).

But even if the young influence the adults, they still feel bound by the adult's norms of linguistic behavior and by their indirect language policing. Rama says she doesn't abbreviate when she writes on her father's behalf, and most informants say they use standard French when they send messages to adults:

Mais si en SMS tu veux parler avec une grande personne, pour le respect, le SMS doit être bien écrit, tu dois respecter la grammaire, les accords, les fautes et tout tu dois corriger, ça, ça peut prendre un peu de temps, si tu as assez de crédits, il vaut mieux appeler.

["But, if in SMS messages, you want to talk to an important person in a respectful way, the message should be well written, you should respect grammar, agreement, the errors and you should correct it, that could take some time and if you have enough credits, it is better to call."] (Alioune, focus group).

These "well written" messages to adults should be written in more or less monolingual French, unless the adult addressee has a weak command of the language. There are examples of text messages in Wolof and Fula sent to older relatives when they are more comfortable with these languages. Thus, texters find that they need to adapt to the recipient, or, in some cases, who they text for, respecting that person's language norms and attitudes.

These limitations on "texting young" still leave a great repertoire to choose from in the composition of messages. As noted in Deumert and Lexander (2013: 522) "Being a good texter requires the performance of 'textual linguistic dexterity': the ability to articulate meaning through the skillful use of both global and local forms." The well-trained texters perform, through language choices and linguistic play including African languages, nuanced voices.

The Rapper: A Glocal Identity?

English appears in about 20 percent of the 500 SMS messages collected, but only in the form of single words or expressions. The words used are more or less the same as those found in studies of francophone texting elsewhere (e.g. *big, kiss, now, today*, Cougnon and Ledegen 2010) and hence respond to some kind of global repertoire, while at the same time the words are glocalized into messages or expressions in (urban) Wolof and (Senegalese) French. For instance, the often used greeting in Wolof *namm naa la* ("I miss you") is reformulated to *names u: namm* is Wolof for "miss," the *-es* is added to give it an English sound, and *la* is replaced by the English *you*, written *u*. Such glocal use of English is identified in texting elsewhere in Africa, in Kenya (McIntosh 2010), South Africa (Deumert and Lexander 2013), and Cameroon (Camfranglais) (Feussi 2007). English words may, moreover, be used to perform a more specific hip-hop youth identity. Some of the informants identify with this; others don't.

During the Senegalese presidential elections of 2012 that led to the president's defeat, the local hip-hop movement initiated and organized a considerable political opposition (Fredericks 2014). Hip hop is also associated with particular language practices, and in her study of rap in Dakar and Saint-Louis, Auzanneau (2001) identifies a *langage des rappeurs*, a way of using and mixing language that is proper for rap as well as for the young city-dwellers who listen to rap – practices that are not well-regarded outside of this group. While sharing many of the characteristics of urban Wolof, the hip-hop language practices are singled out through the introduction of both non-standard English words and expressions that refer to American (hip-hop) culture as well as of the use of Standard English that marks an opposition to French colonization. They also make use of other local languages. Auzanneau sees rap as important for identity construction in the African cities, as a space for appropriation and production of models of behavior upon which urban identity processes can be played out (2001: 711). Similar work has been done on hip hop in many parts of the world, showing how it has become a tool for reworking identity around the world (Alim et al. 2009; Cutler 2014), and how code switching serves as an identity marker in this process (Hassa 2010). These functions are also played out in texting.

Two of the participants in the young men's focus group, Amadou and Alioune, aged 21 at the time of the data collection, definitely *are* rappers. Together with two other friends, they have taken the name *Intellectual Weapons* to do rap in English, French, Wolof, and Sereer (Senegalese minority language group), and they exploit the association related to and the vocabulary of the different languages to convey their messages. Hip hop seems to be a typical example of glocalization: Rap in Wolof has strong support in Senegal and the genre is considered as a Senegalese form of expression, while at the same time, American hip hop, widely accepted as the original form of rap music, is very popular in the country, influencing Senegalese music, youth clothing, and dancing. Rap is often associated with rebellion in a global perspective; the rappers identifying with a common set of problems (Cutler 2014).

The Afro-American influence is visible in the use of English in the collected SMS corpus and when commenting on this, the informants often refer to the sender being *young, hip*, or they even refer to Afro-American associations or to spoken language:

Oui, et là, tu vois aussi, il y a des mots anglais, que j'ai mis. Un peu le langage des jeunes, qui parlent, quoi.

["Yes, and there you see it too, there are English words that I've put in. A little bit the language of young who speak, you know."] (Adama, individual interview).

On utilise l'anglais, le français, l'anglais un peu américain, pas l'anglais anglophone, quoi.

["We use English, French, English that is a little bit American, not British English, you know."] (Momar, focus group)

We see that Momar makes the difference between American English with which he identifies and British English with which he does not identify. He thus refers to what Alim (2009a) calls the Hip Hop Nation Language – language practices closely related to African American slang and used not only for rap lyrics, but also for hip-hop conversational discourse (Alim 2009a: 278). Zombie, a geography student aged 31, had received the following message from a friend:

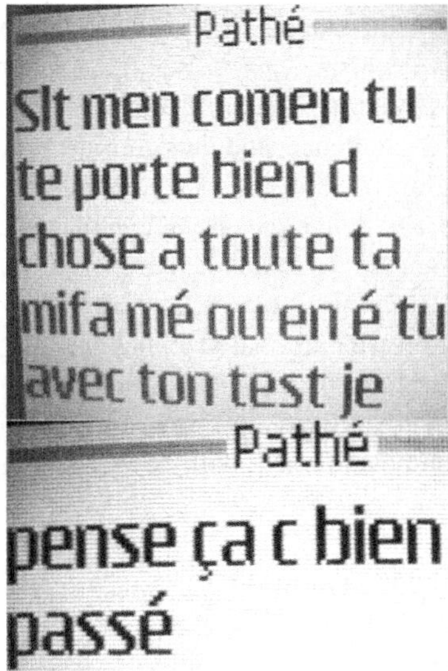

Figure 4.1 SMS 1
Salut ***man****, comment tu te portes? Bien de choses à la famille, mais où en es-tu avec ton test? Je pense que ça c'est bien passé.*

["Hey man, how are you? Best wishes to your family, how is it with your test? I think it went well."]

When commenting on the language use in this text, Zombie qualified the sender as what he calls a "*jump*" or rapper:

C'est un jump, quoi, c'est un rappeur, on le comprend.

["It's a jump, you know, it's a rapper, we understand that."] (Zombie, individual interview)

Only two words seem to qualify the sender as a "rapper": the English word *men* (in the sense of *man*) and the verlain word *mifa* (*famille* with reversed syllables, "family") (cf. Cutler, this volume). This framing, use of only one or two words to define an entire text (cf. Hinrichs 2006), is sufficient to mark his rapper identity. The use of *mé* (*mais*, "but," as an introductory word not signaling opposition), is typical for Senegalese French, and for urban Wolof.

The influence of rap on texting goes the other way as well (see Androutsopoulos 2001), and language practices associated with texting also appear in Senegalese rap. The group Bat'haillons Blin-d uses orthography associated with texting, both in French, English, and Wolof, when writing the

Wolof name *Dëggantaan* of one of their albums *2GunTann* (*2* is pronounced like in French, *Gun* is used like in English, *Tann* is Wolof, Lexander 2007). Both texters and rappers sometimes integrate archaic Wolof words as a way of purifying their language from French influence, and thus contrast it with urban Wolof. There is not, however, an automatic link between youth identity and rap identity; an enregisterment of the *rap language*, is taking place: particular words, mostly from English, become "a socially recognized register of forms" (Agha 2003: 231) that index certain interests, attitudes, and clothing. Some of the features indexed by the register are shared with global hip hop (and the Hip Hop Nation Language, cf. Alim 2009a); others are more specific for urban Senegal, and make up a glocal voice. This hip-hop identity can be shed to perform a romantic voice – or it can be combined with it.

The Enregisterment of the Romantic Voice

Most informants claim that French is the most romantic texting language, and the messages of love were by far the ones where the use of French was the most prominent. The French language offers a greater number of words and poetic formulations for expressing strong feelings of love, and being romantic and texting creatively go hand in hand.

This message, sent by Ousmane to his fiancée Rama, contains several features of French neography found in text messages worldwide: *k* for *que, o* for *au, mwa* for *moi*, and numbers instead of letters (Cutler, this volume). It ends with *jtm*, a closing signature that Rama and Ousmane use in the majority of their messages to each other. Several abbreviations of *je t'aime* ("I love you") are found in the SMS corpus, but *jtm* only is used by Rama and Ousmane:

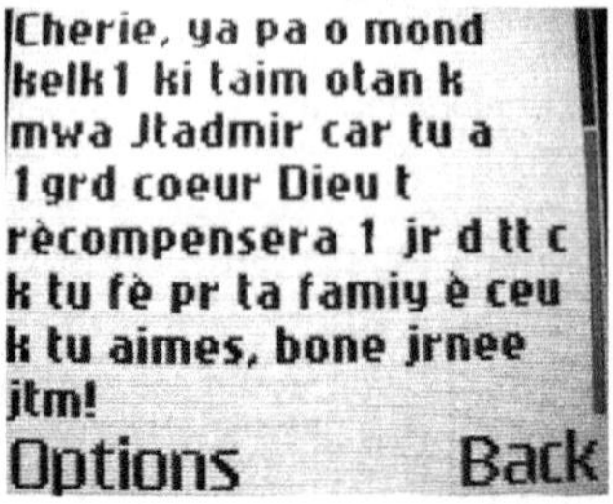

Cherie, ya pa o mond
kelk1 ki taim otan k
mwa Jtadmir car tu a
1grd coeur Dieu t
rècompensera 1 jr d tt c
k tu fè pr ta famiy è ceu
k tu aimes, bone jrnee
jtm!
Options Back

Figure 4.2 SMS 2
["My love, there's no one in the world that loves you as much as me. I admire you because you have a big heart. God will pay you back one day for everything that you do for your family and those that you care about, have a nice day, I love you"]

The global is associated with the personal touch in their creation of their own personal romantic discourse (see also Lexander 2012; 2014), which can be considered as an enregisterment of a personal romantic voice.

Such personal voices are part of the more extended romantic voice. With the SMS message, new possibilities of romantic communication appeared and a new voice could be created. This romantic voice marks a youth perspective on relationships; it refers to Western conceptions of love and contrasts with the traditional view of communication within a couple that according to the Wolof tradition should be distant, even during the first years of marriage (cf. Diop 1985: 100–101). The intimacy that should be reserved for married couples is available on a textual level, thanks to the mobile technology. With the romantic vocabulary available in French language, a separate written romantic voice is enregistered.

This dominant romantic voice does however not exclude Wolof and Fula from the lovers' discourse. On the contrary, texters can make their romantic messages special through the use of languages other than French. Thialguey, one of the Fula-speaking informants, uses almost exclusively Fula in his messages to his fiancée. His language choice is related both to his attachment to the Fula language and to his fiancée's level of French. Playful flirting in texting often takes place in Wolof, which is called the *saay-saay* ('skirt hunter')-language. Still, Wolof free from French influence may be used to perform an even more sincere expression of love, because of its rarity in this communication and because of the difference in vocabulary (Lexander 2012; 2014). We thus see that the texters make contextually specific choices drawing on a range of strategies within their diverse repertoires.

The Articulation of Ethnic Identities

Even if McLaughlin (2001) notes that many Dakarois favor an urban identity over an ethnic identity, and this is followed by the adoption of Wolof as the first language of people from other ethnic groups, ethnic identities or languages are hardly in the process of disappearing in the capital. Migrants from all over the country arrive in the city and bring with them their languages, making sure that multilingualism is constantly nurtured (Dreyfus and Juillard 2004). Some of these migrants are students, like Baba Yaro and Thialguey, who are Fula-speakers coming from areas where Fula is the dominant language. Both Baba Yaro and Thialguey have attended literacy classes in their first language, organized by the movement for revitalization of the Fula language. The two students have however chosen different strategies for their language use in texting.

In Baba Yaro's texting, we find vast linguistic variation; in some messages, it is clear that he is taking on a youth identity in the sense of a young, urban man who knows the latest cool expressions and who can play with language.

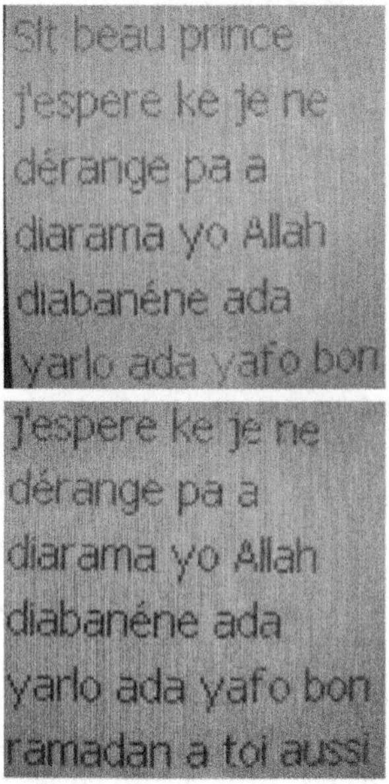

Slt beau prince
j'espere ke je ne
dérange pa a
diarama yo Allah
diabanéne ada
yarlo ada yafo bon

j'espere ke je ne
dérange pa a
diarama yo Allah
diabanéne ada
yarlo ada yafo bon
ramadan a toi aussi

Figure 4.3 SMS 3

Salut beau prince, j'espère que je ne dérange pas. **A jaaraama. Yo Alla jaaban en aɗa yarloo aɗa yaafoo.** *Bon ramadan à toi aussi.*

"Hi beautiful prince, I hope I don't disturb. I thank you. May Allah accept us [our adoration], be lenient on me, forgive me. Happy Ramadan to you too."

At other times, he makes use of the opposition between Fula and Wolof and Fula and French to obtain different effects (see Lexander 2011b). These features also appear in the communication that he receives, like in SMS 3 above, sent by one of his female friends for Ramadan.

Here, the sender combines French neography, indexing their common young age and showing familiarity with texting conventions, with fixed religious expressions used for Ramadan in Fula, indexing their common ethnic identity. Such combinations of formal and informal greetings are quite common in the corpus, and the difference between the two is often marked with an alternation of language.

Demonstrating an urban identity can be particularly important for someone who comes from outside Dakar, like Baba Yaro does, but Thialguey makes different choices in his refusal to use Wolof when texting, instead using French that he sees as more neutral. To his fiancée and his family, and also to Fulani friends, he texts in Fula. Through boycotting Wolof, he states his Fulani identity, opposing the wolofization of Senegalese society and the linguistic dominance of the Wolof majority. McIntosh (2010) makes a similar observation in Kenya concerning texting in Kirigama, the first language of the Giriama of Maldini: "in contexts where ethnic identity is at stake, it can serve as a demonstrative means of indexing 'authentic' Giriamaness and ethnic cohesion" (2010: 340), pointing to "new ways of being Giriama that are simultaneously local and modern" (op. cit.: 337).

However, the use of a minority language does not necessarily involve such a stance; it may also be chosen for purposes of stylization, an imitation of a social type (Bakhtin 1999: 122–123). Many of the young texters seem to find it easier and more precise to be funny or teasing in their first language:

ALIOUNE: *Pour taquiner Amadou par exemple, je peux utiliser des mots sereer.* ["To tease Amadou, for instance, I may use Sereer words."]

AMADOU: *Moi, j'utilise ça, avec des copains quoi . . . c'est pour taquiner, c'est pas pour parler correctement* ["Me, I use that, with friends, you know . . . it's to tease, it is not to speak (write) correctly']. (focus group)

Wolof seems to have a similar position, both for first and second language users. Christine, whose first language is the minority language Joola, but who uses Wolof more, claims that teasing in Wolof is more juicy ("*piquant*"), and less shocking, while the Sereer Amadou says that when the writer uses Wolof, the receiver of the message will imagine the sender's body language:

Tu sais, le wolof, c'est comme l'imagination, tu parles la phrase et la personne imagine les gestes là que tu es en train de faire là-bas, il comprend mieux à l'instant ce que tu es en train de faire.

"You know, Wolof, it's like the imagination, you speak [write] the sentence and the person imagines the gestures that you are making over there, he understands better and immediately what you are doing." (focus group)

Other texters use languages of ethnic groups that they do not identify with to obtain the same humorous effects. In such vari-directional double-voicing (Bakhtin 1984 [1929]), the very choice of language conveys one message while the meaning of the words used convey another. For instance, does Christine use some Sereer words when writing messages to her Sereer fiancé to tease him. The texters thus use the reference to ethnic identities creatively in order to obtain different effects in the text messages.

Conclusion

This chapter has intended to show why and how young Senegalese "mix everything" when texting. On the one hand, the texters make use of a broad linguistic repertoire to express attitudes towards culture and politics, to express a particular conception of love or a particular style, and, on the other, they employ different strategies to express attitudes to the communication in question. Through a series of "small performances," the texters define themselves with nuanced identities; a texter can display him- or herself as both Fula, urban, and romantic in everyday mobile communication and then surprise the receiver with a performance-3, performing a poetic ability. Creative practices like heteroglossia, glocalization, and stylization, while constrained by language policing, are being enregistered in the multilingual texting practices of Sengalese youth. If the texters fail to fulfill the expectations of the receiver, they risk being met with disapproval.

However, these creative practices challenge other expectations in Senegalese society, namely those concerning what languages are proper for writing. Languages like Wolof and Fula, that usually only appear in spoken communication and a very limited and stigmatized written communication, present opportunities in written communication that the dominant French language cannot offer, and we see that these opportunities are not just about "writing speech"; Senegalese texting represents a different way of creatively using and thinking about written language. This is the *jaxase*, the mix, that Momar speaks of in the introductory quote of this chapter. Such mixed practices are giving vitality and value to Senegalese languages, pointing towards a breakthrough for African languages as written languages.

5 Peaze Up! Adaptation, Innovation, and Variation in German Hip Hop Discourse

Matt Garley

Introduction

Glocalization has been characterized as "a process by which globally-circulating cultural resources are recontextualized in local settings" (Androutsopoulos 2009). This definition highlights the interaction between a globalizing culture and the media whereby the cultural resources of that culture are carried around the globe. This includes diverse modes of computer-mediated communication. Hip hop culture is an ideal domain for such questions, as it is a "glocalizing" culture: it has a central node in the United States and is also instantiated in various local hip hop scenes around the globe. In addition, Morgan (2001: 189) aptly notes: "Unlike rock and other musical genres, Hip Hop is based on the co-authorship of artists and urban youth communities." Because of this co-authorship, and in particular the relationship of the artists to youth communities, hip hop reflects, influences, and mediates language use "on the ground" in these communities and beyond, and is thus especially interesting as a domain of sociolinguistic inquiry. The centrality of language to the practice of hip hop, for both artist and fan, makes it particularly well-suited for studies of language behavior and the production of culture.

In this chapter[1], I investigate the use of <z> as an alternative orthographic choice[2] in a roughly 13-million-word corpus (including discussions spanning the period from 2000 to 2011) collected from the German-language internet hip hop discussion forums at MZEE.com. This dataset is supplemented by

[1] Research for this chapter was supported in part by a Deutscher Akademischer Austausch Dienst (DAAD) Graduate Research Grant. In addition, I would like to thank the following individuals: Marina Terkourafi and Julia Hockenmaier for crucial early research guidance, the reviewers for this volume for their helpful contributions and suggestions, multiple friends and associates who participated in the ethnographic research, and finally, editors Cecilia Cutler and Unn Røyneland for their organization of foundational conference panels and their thoughtful and patient work on this volume. Any remaining errors or omissions are my own.

[2] I adopt here the convention of using angle brackets < > for orthographic (written) strings of characters. Whole words from data considered as examples are italicized, and standard IPA forward slashes / / are used to indicate phonemes or strings thereof, and square brackets [] indicate phonetic realizations.

a comparable 19-million-word corpus collected from a US-based, English-language hip hop forum. Examination of the use of <z> in these two contexts illuminates the extent to which language contact, and especially extensive linguistic borrowing from English, has changed the way German youth use language, and this research demonstrates that the linguistic borrowing process and the stylization of English borrowings among German hip hop fans involves the complex application of morphological, phonological, and orthographic knowledge from multiple linguistic systems. This paper also deals with the formulaic use of English *peace*, an expression which functions discursively in global hip hop culture as a greeting, leave-taking, or closing. A number of hybrid orthographic variants are discussed for *peace*, including the orthographic <z>, e.g. *peaze.* I quantitatively analyze the distribution of these variants, comparing usage patterns in a German and a North American hip hop forum. I complement these results by presenting a qualitative analysis of *peace* and its variants, establishing a connection between linguistic features, discursive use, and corpus distribution. By quantitatively establishing large-scale patterns in the dataset, and qualitatively analyzing these patterns, a fuller picture of this heteroglossic linguistic situation can emerge.

Background

German interest in hip hop music and culture dates to the 1980s. In a 2010 ethnographic interview, "Erik,"[3] an established German DJ and 20-year veteran of the scene described to me the initial locus of interest: in communities near US military bases, West German youth would often trade audio and video cassettes with the children of American servicemen. Erik remembered, especially vividly, his prized VHS copy of seminal American hip hop film *Wild Style* (1983). The cultural flow continued throughout the 1990s, mediated by radio play, music-focused television networks like VIVA and MTV, and eventually the internet. German-language rappers achieved initial popularity in the early 1990s, and since then, German hip hop has become a core genre of German popular music, evolving along its own trajectory as it merged with other forms, though certainly not independent of the influence of American hip hop music and culture. As in other parts of the world where hip hop has put down roots, German fans are predominantly teenagers and young adults. Hip hop is popular among both ethnic German and immigrant youth; since the late 1990s especially, ethnic diversity among hip hop artists has become the norm, and many of the most popular German rappers of all time represent ethnic minorities in Germany, like Kool Savas (of Turkish descent), Bushido (of Tunisian descent), and

[3] a pseudonym.

Samy Deluxe (of Sudanese descent). The influence of English language varieties, particularly African American English and Hip Hop Nation Language, is extensive within the subculture, as noted for other hip hop scenes around the globe – see, e.g., chapters in Alim et al. (2009) and Terkourafi (2010). Hip hop, of course, is not the only channel for language contact in this domain. English study to some degree in grade school is common (but not universal) in modern Germany, and the dominance of English as the most prominent working language of the European Union and a de facto lingua franca for international business certainly has an influence on the popularity of English study in Germany. However, for the vast majority of Germans, English is a foreign language – the German sphere is norm-dependent, rather than a locus of a recognized English variety. Complicating matters are the multiple and complex pathways whereby Germans encounter English varieties. While business and government-related uses could constitute what Preisler (1999) terms "English from above," the infiltration of unregulated, less-standardized, and diverse Englishes, primarily through globalizing popular media and the internet, have the effect that Preisler describes as "English from below." Online communications are well-established as data sources for the expression of metalinguistic commentary: Jones and Schieffelin (2009) studied YouTube comments on AT&T commercials featuring "textese," an ideologized form of language involving the spoken rendition of text-message acronym practices. The authors found that commenters engaged with the commercial's language "as a medium for verbal play and as stylistic marker of group membership subject to careful scrutiny" (Jones and Schieffelin 2009: 1075). In the present chapter, my focus on orthography is also informed by Sebba (2007), who establishes the use of orthography, and in particular variant orthography, in youth culture and subcultures, as a marker of sociocultural identity. Overall, then, the linguistic practices of German youth online – engaging in simultaneously global and local subcultural practices, influenced by multiple varieties of foreign-language English (and native-language German), and contending with attendant ideologies of language (described in Garley 2014), are a fertile ground for the investigation of language-contact phenomena.

Data and Methodology

The present study adopts a corpus-sociolinguistic approach to the examination of natural language data, which blends quantitative and qualitative methods. Thus, larger patterns of use are established quantitatively through the analysis of large corpora using automatic methods, implemented here through original tools written in Python. During the quantitative phase of research, lexical items of interest are identified using patterns of frequency and distribution; individual items and sets of items are then analyzed qualitatively in context. This latter portion of the investigation uses the methods of Computer-Mediated Discourse Analysis (Herring 2004; Androutsopoulos and Beißwenger 2008), in that it consists of empirical analyses of texts which take into account the linguistic and social context of their production in order to reach conclusions regarding language as social behavior. The facts of language use in the present corpus underline the ubiquity not only of straightforward English loans in German hip hop culture, but also of word forms which reflect processes of innovation and adaptation. These processes seem at first pass unusual or anomalous, but I argue here that they are reflective of general processes involving the combination of sets of rules from different languages.

The primary dataset here is the multi-million-word MZEE.com internet forum corpus. I collected the corpus from the "Hip Hop Diskussion" subforum in 2011; MZEE.com, a German online retailer for hip hop fashion and accessories, is (as of December 2014) closed for business, but the forums hosted on the site remain open. According to internet use data, the MZEE.com forums were, up until 2009, the most popular German-language hip hop Internet forums in existence[4] (Alexa Internet, Inc. 2012). Participants on these forums are typically German-speaking hip hop fans, expressing their views on topics germane to hip hop culture; as of May 2012, Alexa.com, a site monitoring internet statistics, reported that 84 percent of visits to the site originated in Germany, with roughly 3 percent each originating from Switzerland and Austria, and the remainder originating from other locations worldwide.

After collection, the data from the discussion pages were reformatted and extraneous material was excluded from the corpus. This material included quotes of other users' posts made through the bulletin-board system's affordances and lines repeated from post to post as well as "signatures," and forum-specific emoticons. In order to ensure that like words were being grouped and counted together, punctuation and capitalization were also removed from the version of the corpus intended for quantitative analysis, but a separate XML version with original formatting, punctuation, capitalization, quotes, etc. was used for the qualitative portion of the analysis.

The final MZEE corpus included all posts in the 'Hip Hop Diskussion' subforum from March 2000 to March 2011, allowing for diachronic analysis. The corpus, after processing, contained 12,540,944 words of running text from 381,880 posts. As Iorio (2009: 129) notes, internet communities are often

[4] Historical rankings collected in 2012 from Alexa, a website which provides analytics for multiple sites, ranked MZEE.com over competitors hiphop.de and rap.de. A comparison graph of mzee.com and hiphop.de in terms of historical rankings show that hiphop.de only overtook mzee.com in March 2009.

demographically lean, as little information is available about participants, and even this information is often unverifiable. An investigation of 50 profiles on the MZEE.com forums falls in line with this observation; only 16 users provided their ages, and those who did were 21–31. Twenty-six of the profiles provided gender information and self-identified as "male." These self-reported data points are highly suspect, as there would be good reason for younger or female users to hide these facts: I suggest that there is significant disincentive for users under 21 to provide their age, as doing so would increase the likelihood that their contributions would be dismissed on account of their perceived inexperience in hip hop culture. With regard to gender, Herring (2003: 206) notes that women in many online communities "can present themselves so as to minimize discrimination and harassment" by refusing to self-identify as female. What can, in the end, be inferred about MZEE.com users, is that they are German speakers who share an interest in hip hop, and because of the status of hip hop as a youth-oriented musical genre, are likely to be in the teenager-to-young-adult demographic.

A number of anglicisms, or English borrowings, were identified semi-automatically through the use of a customized German-English classifier, a description of which can be found in Garley and Hockenmaier (2012). The list of anglicisms identified included a number with nonstandard orthographies involving <z>, an observation which motivated the present analysis. The MZEE corpus data provides insights into the use of <z> in the German hip hop sphere. Given the direction of transcultural flows (Pennycook 2007a) from the origins of hip hop in the United States to satellite scenes in Germany and other countries, the present analysis benefits from the addition of comparable English-language corpus. To this end, a 19,385,022-word corpus was collected from the Project Covo forums hosted at SOHH.com (Support Online Hip Hop), a US-based English-language hip hop discussion site. The forum posts were collected from a subforum billed as "The place to be for general discussions on Hip-Hop" and includes posts from 2003 through 2011. As of 2012, Alexa.com reported that 64 percent of traffic on the site originated from the United States, with 10 percent coming from Bermuda, 6 percent from the UK, 3.5 percent from India, and less than 3 percent each from all other countries. Similar cleaning and formatting procedures were used with this corpus, which I will refer to as the "Covo" corpus.

Analysis: Orthographic Stylization in the MZEE Corpus

Orthographic variation is often straightforwardly phonological in nature, which is to say that the representation of English "says" as <sez> or "was" as <wuz>, as Preston (1985: 328) notes of "eye dialect," "reflect[s] no phonological difference from their standard counterparts." Instead, respellings like these, according to Preston, "serve mainly to denigrate the speaker so represented by making him or her appear boorish, uneducated, rustic, gangsterish, and so on." Preston's discussion focused on the use of these alternative spellings to record the real or imagined speech of others, whether interviewees or fictional characters. Such respellings, however, can also constitute a language user's own production, and be used as a form of stylization or language play, and, with the proliferation of written communication online, these alternative orthographies have assumed new meanings and roles for their users. Alongside this social dimension of alternative orthography, there is a practical one: in the two examples above, the use of <z> can easily be interpreted with the phonetic value [z]. However, the relation of orthography to phonotactics, the correspondence between characters and sounds, is not as straightforward in every case – especially when multiple languages are involved.

The substitution of <z> for <s>, primarily seen in plural English word forms, has been considered a hallmark of hip hop orthography, as mentioned by Paolillo (2001: 190) in his study of an Indian diaspora chatroom. While Paolillo identifies the use of <z> as hip hop related, he notes that it "does not necessarily invoke rap in a direct way" and associates the form with a hacker subculture as well, eventually relating the form to a more general vernacular orthography. This more general treatment of <z> fits with Androutsopoulos' (2000) discussion of *grapheme substitution* as a method of stylization in German punk "fanzines," a genre rich with alternative orthography. As noted above, the substitution of <z> for <s> in English could in many cases be considered a quasi-phonetic spelling, as in the hypothetical example of <dogz> for *dogs*, [dɔgz], but not in others, as in <catz> for *cats*, [kæts]. These examples demonstrate the fact that the suffix represented by final <s> has two environment-dependent phonetic realizations in English, a voiced [z] when following a voiced segment, and an unvoiced [s] elsewhere.

In investigating the list of anglicisms produced by the German-English classifier used in the MZEE corpus, it was noted that a number of the most frequently-used anglicisms used alternative orthographies, most commonly involving the substitution of <z> for <s> – in the following examples, the number in parentheses indicates the word form's rank in the final anglicism list. Examples include <beatz> (31st), <bozz> (82nd), <skillz> (87th), <headz> (215th), <kidz> (232nd), <greetz> (240th), and <trackz> (292nd). Most of these examples use <z> as a plural suffix, but <zz> as a replacement for final <ss> is also present. Also found is the form <peaze> (95th), where <z> substitutes for <c>, and alternative forms <peaz> (259th) and <peazen> (261st). While <skillz>, <headz>, and <kidz> would be realized in English with a phonetic [z], the remainder would be realized with a phonetic [s] by most

Table 5.1 *Orthographic-phonemic correspondences in English and German*

English	German
<z> → /z/	<z> → /ts/
<s> → /s/	<s> → /z/ (prevocalically), /s/ (elsewhere)
<c> → /s/ or /k/	<c> → ??? (does not occur in native German forms except in di/trigraphs <ch> and <sch>)
<ts> → /ts/	<ss/ß> → /s/

native speakers. In the English-speaking world, stylized orthographic forms where a <z> would be realized as [s] like <catz> do occur, such as in the children's video game series "Petz" or various American radio stations with "Hitz" in their name, but in German the situation is more complex.

In German, the grapheme <z> corresponds to the phoneme /ts/, so as Androutsopoulos (2000: 527) notes in his examination of German punk zines featuring alternative orthographies, "the /z/ pronunciation which is relevant here is imported from English." To illustrate the situation between languages, I provide in Table 5.1 a chart of common orthographic-phonemic correspondences from English and German relevant to the current study.[5]

Turning back to the situation with <z>, the replacement of <s> with <z> in plural forms borrowed from English is found with regularity in the MZEE corpus, for example with the form *beatz*, which occurs 1,826 times in the corpus. By comparison, the standard plural form *beats* occurs 9,654 times, about five times more often. The high frequency of *beatz* (which is the 31st most common English borrowing in the corpus), however, indicates that it is in fact an established alternative form.

This observation spurred a wider investigation in which a set of all words ending in <z> were pulled from the MZEE corpus, automatically ignoring known German forms like *trotz* "despite" and *schmerz*, "pain." From this set of words, those that had a relative corpus frequency over or near one in one million (those occurring over 13 times in the corpus – and thus less likely to be one-off forms or errors) were hand-coded into several categories. Word forms occurring in names of known artists and albums from earlier compiled lists were automatically excluded.

[5] Note here that <c> does not, by itself, represent a phoneme in native German words, occurring only in the orthographic digraph <ch> → /ç/ or /x/ and the trigraph <sch> → /ʃ/. In certain loanwords, <c> can have the value of /s/, as in *City* or *Service,* but this is among other imported values like /ts/ and /k/ and is in any case not a productive orthography in Standard German.

Table 5.2 *Word stems with a plural produced phonetically as [s], relative frequencies (per million words) and ratios of <z> to <s> in the MZEE and Covo corpora*

	MZEE <z>	MZEE <s>	Covo <z>	Covo <s>	MZEE ratio <z>:<s>	Covo ratio <z>:<s>
beat(z/s)	146.6	769.80	15.32	479.13	0.19 : 1	0.03 : 1
prop(z/s)	12.36	39.31	4.85	288.32	0.31 : 1	0.02 : 1
street(z/s)	2.87	35.72	4.6	182.1	0.1 : 1	0.03 : 1
peep(z/s)	1.28	1.36	1.39	50.81	0.9 : 1	0.03 : 1
hit(z/s)	1.12	44.97	1.29	116.9	0.03 : 1	0.01 : 1
mean ratio z:s					**0.30 : 1**	**0.02 : 1**

Taking those forms identified as English noun plurals (rather than third person verbs, German forms with spurious <z> endings, which I will deal with presently), frequencies relative to corpus size (frequency per million words) were calculated for the form ending in <z> and the form ending in <s> in the MZEE corpus and the Project Covo (US-English) corpus for comparison. Ratios of <z> to <s> for each word form were then calculated, but forms that did not have a frequency greater than one in one million in both <z> and <s> forms in both corpora were excluded. This yielded a list of 30 nominal stems. It was also necessary to make sure that the words under consideration were choice-based or intentional usages. As an example, *eyez* was excluded because a sample of 50 usages of *eyez* in context were references to the 1996 2Pac album and song "All Eyez on Me," and thus did not represent a stylistic choice to use a <z> plural. Samples of all 30 stems were considered in context, and those that were used as part of an artist or song title over ~25 percent of the time, being obligate uses, were discarded, leaving 17 plural forms. The forms were then divided according to whether the plural <s> would be produced phonetically as an [s] or as a [z] in Standard English. The results are presented in Tables 5.2 and 5.3. The values in columns 2–5 are relative frequencies (incidence per million words in each corpus), and are comparable row-wise. The final row contains the mean ratio of <z>:<s> in each case.

In almost every case, the <z> form is used less frequently than the <s>, but still at a rate of over one word per million, suggesting its status as a deliberate alternative orthography. For all of the forms in Tables 5.2 and 5.3, taken together, the mean ratio of <z> to <s> in the MZEE corpus is 0.26:1, whereas it is 0.02:1 for the Covo corpus. A paired t-test comparing the listed forms revealed that the difference in average ratio for the German and English corpora is statistically significant ($p = 0.01$). What these data

Table 5.3 *Word stems with a plural produced phonetically as [z], relative frequencies (per million words) and ratios of* <z> *to* <s> *in the MZEE and Covo corpora*

	MZEE <z>	MZEE <s>	Covo <z>	Covo <s>	MZEE ratio <z>:<s>	Covo ratio <z>:<s>
skill(z/s)	68.26	67.22	20.43	116.12	1.02 : 1	0.18 : 1
head(z/s)	30.14	55.26	4.02	143.72	0.55 : 1	0.03 : 1
kid(z/s)	18.50	144.89	3.15	301.83	0.13 : 1	0.01 : 1
style(z/s)	10.61	85.48	1.70	142.07	0.12 : 1	0.01 : 1
record(z/s)	6.78	243.04	1.14	253.75	0.03 : 1	< 0.01 : 1
gangsta(z/s)	5.66	14.35	2.79	20.53	0.39 : 1	0.14 : 1
hoe(z/s)	4.39	20.17	2.22	81.35	0.22 : 1	0.03 : 1
thug(z/s)	3.51	19.14	3.35	57.31	0.18 : 1	0.06 : 1
jam(z/s)	2.15	81.17	4.08	13.98	0.03 : 1	0.29 : 1
new(z/s)	1.20	79.02	2.43	175.14	0.02 : 1	0.01 : 1
star(z/s)	1.12	28.07	1.55	85.48	0.04 : 1	0.02 : 1
hater(z/s)	1.12	5.1	1.34	77.90	0.22 : 1	0.02 : 1
mean ratio z:s					**0.24 : 1**	**0.07 : 1**

show is that there is a consistently higher usage of the alternative orthography <z> in the German hip hop forums than in the American forums – compared to the <s> forms, <z> forms are used over ten times more frequently by the German hip hop fans. The only word, in fact, where the <z>:<s> ratio is higher in the US corpus than in the German corpus is *jamz*, and upon investigating a sample of uses in context (this was done pre-analysis only for the German corpus) it appears that it is very heavily used in reference to the song "Slow Jamz" by Twista, which perhaps did not enjoy the listener market penetration in the German-language scene that it did in the United States.

This observation connects to research on alternative orthographies in text messaging (in this case understood to include an array of features from abbreviations to respellings and number/letter substitutions) by Deumert and Mesthrie (2012: 557). In seeking a basis for comparison of South African usage of orthographic variables in SMS data, the authors meta-analyze studies on US and UK orthographic variables, noting that "unlike their peers in the Global North, South African texters have extended the norms of usage and employ this new orthography at frequencies that are unlike those reported for 'inner circle countries'." German hip hop fans, then, likewise appear to be engaging in orthographic <z> substitution at significantly higher levels than American fans.

While the use of <z> by native speakers of English in voiced contexts can be motivated phonetically, the use of <z> in unvoiced contexts suggests an aesthetic or stylistic explanation. In a study of American hip hop forum discourse, Beers-Fägersten (2006: 40) finds that “final -z is also used to substitute for the inflectional morpheme /s/, even when the phonological environment would not cause voicing.” In the case of Androutsopoulos’ (2000: 527) German punk zines, he writes that in cases where an orthographic-phonemic correspondence is not present (for example, in considering the use of <x> for <s> in the band name *H-Blockx*):

The crucial motivation for these spelling variants is not phonetic representation, but their indexical or symbolic value as cues of subcultural positioning. In other words, they act as an instruction to interpret the discourse as “subculturally engaged” or “hip.” The relatively more frequent usage of alternative <z> in the MZEE corpus, especially where English phonotactics favors an <s>, does suggest that stylization is a contributing motivation for this type of variation. However, the last rows of Tables 5.2 and 5.3, taken together, tell another interesting story: The average <z>:<s> ratio for the American corpus for words phonetically produced with an [s] plural ending is 0.02 : 1, and with a [z] plural ending, 0.07 : 1, indicating that the “phonetically sensitive” use of <z> is about three and a half times more frequent than the “phonetically insensitive” use of <z>. For the German data, the ratio for words phonetically produced with an [s] plural ending is 0.30 : 1, and with a [z] plural, 0.24 : 1. While the low number of data points prevents inferential statistical analysis, I suggest that there is an element of phonetic consideration when using <z> for English speakers, but that this element is obviated in the German context.

A likely reason for this difference is found in German phonology, and this factor may make the choice of <z> especially attractive in the German context. Word-final devoicing, or fortition, is a productive phonological rule in German whereby voiced stops and fricatives become voiceless word-finally (Fagan 2009: 23). To a German speaker, any word ending in the phoneme /z/ would be realized phonetically as [s]. While the grapheme <z> in German would represent /ts/, <z> in English represents /z/. German hip hop fans could, then, be choosing the English value /z/, applying word-final devoicing from German to make the choice of word-final orthographic <z> or <s> equivalent. In this case, regardless of whether an English borrowing ends in an orthographic <z> or <s>, the pronunciation would in any case be [s]. Phonetic realization, then, plays a role in this spelling variation, with the subcultural positioning afforded by the orthographic choice of <z> as a sort of bonus. This is supported by previous findings in Garley (2014) that (in the same corpus) word-final devoicing contributes to the felicitous extension of the <ed> orthographic suffix to verb forms beyond the third person singular, functioning like <t> for borrowed

English verbs. The interaction of rules from multiple systems, then, make <z> a more attractive option to German hip hop fans.

Moving beyond the notion that phonetic representation is not the only influence on digital (or subcultural, cf. Androutsopoulos 2000) writing, the very idea that writing primarily represents or corresponds to speech has been called into question in some recent sociolinguistic work on digital communication. As an example, Deumert and Lexander (2013: 533) find that in South African SMS practice, the grapheme <d> is substituted for <th>, yielding forms like <dat> for "that," even though the pronunciation of <th> as [d] is "not a salient feature of spoken varieties of English [in South Africa]." While similar practices in Nigeria and Ghana can be tied to features of West African Pidgin, the authors attribute the use of <d> in South Africa to globalized norms which surround digital writing, and which "evoke globally-mediated African American styles of speaking (popularized via hip hop, movies, adverts and television series)." This case holds many similarities to the orthographic alternative <z> considered here – in particular because the grapheme in question is, in both cases, not expected in the context of the relevant spoken language. There is, though, still a very prominent link from speech to writing which is demonstrated by the fact that, in both cases, not just any grapheme can be substituted, and the grapheme chosen represents something phonetic about the word, albeit to a lesser degree of precision. First, <z>, which represents /ts/ in German, would not be as confusing to a German reader expecting an <s> plural as, say, the substitution of <n> or <p> or <q> would be, because /ts/ contains /s/. Consider <*beatn>, <*beatp>, or <*beatq> as graphical representations of the loanword "beats." None is felicitous or especially interpretable, save for the first, which looks like an infinitive verb. In the case of South African texters using <d> rather than <th>, the move is from a digraph representing a coronal fricative to a single character representing a coronal stop – the correspondence of the grapheme to the phonetic form is indeed relaxed, but certainly not missing. An <r> or <w> or <k> would be an extremely unlikely substitute for <d> in <dat>, "that."[6]

Several of the forms excluded from the earlier analysis are worth additional examination. As an example, *greets* "greetings" was found 45 times in the MZEE corpus, while alternative orthography *greetz* was found 345 times. Neither form is in widespread use in the English-speaking hip hop community,

[6] Also relevant here is the case of *pwn*, a term popularized in the early 2000s in internet gaming communities. The origin of the form is debated, but a general consensus has it as a typo for *own* which then took on an ironic intentional usage, and it has the same denotation of dominating/humiliating an opponent (in a videogame). While the graphemic alternation involved, from <o> to <p>, would argue for a complete disregard for phonetic correspondence, the crowdsourced pronunciations at Urban Dictionary [www.urbandictionary.com] as of November 7, 2015 indicate that with few exceptions, speakers pronounce the word as [poʊn].

as *greets* is found ten times in the larger Project Covo corpus (likely to have more German visitors than MZEE has US visitors due to the directionality of transcultural flow) and *greetz* is not found there. One can compare the use of *greets/greetz* in the German hip hop community to the case of Ger. *Handy* "cell phone," whose origins were likely with the early term *handset*. Interestingly, the stylistically playful version with the <z> was found several times more frequently than the version with <s>, and while no additional orthographic play was found with *greets,* the forms *greetzzz, greetzky,* and *greetze* are all found in the MZEE corpus. In addition, the form *greez* subsumes the <t> under the <z>, which is made possible by the <z> → /ts/ correspondence in German, and this is then further re-analyzed as a singular form and given the English <es> plural as *greezes*:

1. Yo, fedde greezes erstmals an alle Hopper da draussen,
   und natürlich an alle Tagger, Sprayer...

   "Yo, phat 'greetses' first to all hip hoppers out there, and
   naturally to all the taggers and sprayers..."

This doesn't go without comment. In a following post quoting the original, another user mocks the first author with an extremely stilted and over-the-top alternative orthography.

2. >"Yo, fedde greezes erstmals an
   >alle Hopper da draussen, und natürlich an alle
   >Tagger, Sprayer..."

   ey yo vedde grietings gähen surügg an [username]. yo.
   "ey yo phat greetings go back to [username]. yo."

This second post includes exaggerated nonce orthographies like *vedde* for *fedde* (for *fette*, "fat"), *grietings* for English *greetings, gähen* for *gehen*, "go," and *surügg* for *zurück,* "back." This, and the analysis of *peace/peaze* later in this chapter, supports the notion that greetings and leave-takings, often not integrated into the syntax of the surrounding discourse, are a particularly popular site for stylization and language play, although not in an uncontested way.

The influence of the stylized English <z> plural is not restricted to English borrowings. German roots contribute to <s>/<z> plural forms, which do not appear in the earlier analysis because they are not found in the US corpus, are *jungs/jungz* "boys," *mädels/mädelz*, "girls," and *leuts/leutz/leuz,* "people."

The forms on the last row of Table 4 are the standard plurals for each of these words; in the case of *Jungen*, the standard form is almost always used only when referring to male children, rather than the extended use of "boys" as male teenagers or adults. The forms *Jungs* and *Mädels* are not due to English

Table 5.4 *Comparative incidence of nouns with <s>/<z> variation in the MZEE corpus*

Word form	Freq.	Word form	Freq.	Word form	Freq.
jungs	4137	*mädels*	611	*leuts*	65
jungz	137	*mädelz*	36	*leutz*	465
				leuz	17
jungen	771	*mädel* (sing. = pl.)	211	*leute*	22765

influence. They, are more commonly used in Central and North Germany (the Southern form would be *Mädeln).* As common colloquial forms they are understood throughout Germany. However, their use in this context (especially with the <z> plural) could be reinforced through English influence. *Leuts/ Leutz/Leuz* is a more obvious case of language play, as the corpus counts show these forms to be relatively low-frequency alternatives. In this case, the forms function as spurious English-influenced plurals for Ger. *Leute* "people," a word with no singular form. Here, the <-s> plural (which is the least frequent plural in German, but is considered the "default") is substituted for the <-e> plural in the original German form. The <s> is then further replaced by <z>, and then (perhaps influenced by the <z> → /ts/ orthographic-phonemic correspondence) the <t> is subsumed under the <z> in *leuz*. Further confirming the association of <z> with language play, *leutzz, leutzzz, leutzn,* and *leutez* are all attested in the corpus, while no alternative forms involving the <s> orthography are found. The next case to be examined will revisit the use of <z>, providing more evidence of the role that word-final devoicing plays in loanword orthography.

Analysis, Part 2: Morphological Adaptations and Hybridization of Stylized Lexemes

While it is likely that the practice has its origins before hip hop culture's genesis, the use of *peace* as a formulaic greeting or leave-taking can carry "specific hip-hop semantics" (Beers-Fägersten 2006: 28). Smitherman (2006: 36) characterizes its use as "Greeting or farewell; originally to indicate uplift, self-love, Black social consciousness." Kearse (2006: 418) includes it in his dictionary of "hip hop and urban slanguage,"as a "term of affection used when greeting, departing, or ending a verbal or written communique with someone. Ex: 'Peace Dawg, how you?' 'Until we see each other again peace.'" In the MZEE forum, *peace* and its variants seem to be narrowed to the leave-taking function, but it is found in a large array of orthographic forms: *peace* (7,855 hits), *peaze* (799 hits), *peaz* (321 hits), as well as *peacen, peece, peeze, peez, peezn, peezee, peesen, peasze, piezen, piis, piiz, piizn,* and a wide range of of idiosyncratic but systematically variant forms where one or more characters in the above choices is repeated, as in, for example, *peeeeeeeeeeeeezzzzzzzzzzzzzzeeeeeeeeeeennnnnn*. In addition, morphologically extended forms like *peazen, peacen, peezn, peesen, piezen, piizn, peacigen, peacesen, peaciano*, and *peacenskofsky* are also attested in the MZEE corpus. This single-word leave-taking, then, is a favored site for stylization or language play by the users of the MZEE forum. In terms of relativized frequency, *peace* is found much more frequently in MZEE (628.4 *peaces* per million words) than in the Covo forum (94.5 *peaces* per million words), indicating that after the form was borrowed from the English-speaking hip hop community, it is used much more heavily in the German community. In a sample of 50 instances of *peace* in context from each forum, only 20 were leave-takings in the Covo forum, with the remainder being use of the word as a noun in sentence contexts (use as a greeting was not seen in this sample) but 49/50 were leave-takings in MZEE, indicating that the word form is borrowed in this community almost exclusively in its discourse function. Users' knowledge of both German and English orthographic-phonemic mapping is also evident – taking the base form as phonologically /pi:s/, the forms with orthographic <ee> display knowledge of a common English representation of /i:/; the forms with orthographic <ii> playfully combine this vowel duplication with the German grapheme for /i/, which is <i>, while avoiding the interpretation of <i> as /ɪ/, which <i> would represent in a monosyllabic word like *mit*, "with."

The orthographic <z> appears in the relatively common alternate form *peaze* and others like *peazen* (apparently including either an infinitive German morpheme *-en* or a plural morpheme *-en,* but see further discussion below) and *peaz*. Through the influence of German orthographic-phonetic norms, the final <e> is dropped in this case.

A common addition to the base form in the above examples warrants further discussion, and provides a further clue to the imagined phonological value of <z>. Forms like *peacen, peazen, piizen, peesn*, and so forth seem to involve the addition of a syllabic (*-e*)*n* to the end of the word. This quasi-suffixation could represent a plural or an infinitive verb ending, as <en> has both roles in German. However, an exchange from the forum sheds light on the morphological status of this suffix:

3a. Wer hilft mir, dass das wort "josen" (bzw. yosen) eingeführt wird?

"Who'll help me introduce the word 'josen' (or yosen)?"

3b. das gibts doch bestimmt schon irgendwo wird ja bei vielen wörtern die endung rangehängt wie bei bis densen, peazen, moinsen usw.

"That's got to be out there somewhere already, this ending is added to many words like bis densen, peazen, moinsen, etc."

In (3a–b), an MZEE.com user wishes to use introduce the word *josen* or *yosen*, which would be the combination of the hip hop *yo* (or the colloquial German *jo*, "yes") with the nonsense suffix *-sen*. The first response is from another user who notes that this *-sen* suffix is already applied to several greetings and leave-takings like *bis dann* "until then" > *bis densen, moin* [regionally] "[good] morning!" or "hello!" > *moinsen*, and, crucially, *peace* > *peazen*. The inclusion of *peazen* in parallel with the other examples in this post suggests that *peazen* is morphophonologically /pi:s/ + /sen/, further supporting the claim that orthographic *peaz(e)* is phonologically interpreted as /pi:s/ rather than /pi:z/ or /pi:ts/ or another alternative. In 2010–2011, I conducted a number of ethnographic interviews with German hip hop fans in Hamburg; these interviews and ongoing research (like these findings on <z>) often led to follow-up questions online with various contacts in the German hip hop scene. "Georg,"[7] a university mathematics student, hip hop radio-show host, and occasional MZEE forumgoer, was a native-speaker consultant in this capacity in October 2011. I asked Georg at that time whether he thought <peazen> was an instance of the *-sen* suffix. His response:

4. Genau wie du es sagst. Das "-sn" ist eine norddeutsche Regiolekt/Dialekt-Endung. Und irgendwie ist der norddeutsche Sprachgebrauch "cool", weil lässig, oder sowas. Bayrisch/Sächsisch wäre da nicht denkbar! Und da hängt man halt mal "-sn" hinten dran und hat was Plattdeutsches, bzw was cooles. Ich denke, das geht in die Richtung eures "whuzzp" ~ "watsn losn?" das liest man manchmal [. . .]

"It's just as you say. The '-sn' is a North German regiolect/dialect suffix. And somehow, North German language use is 'cool' because it's laid back or something. Bavarian/Saxon would be unthinkable there! And there one just hangs '-sn' at the end of something has something *Plattdeutsches*, and something that's cool. I think it's something like your 'whuzzp' ~ 'watsn losn?' One reads that sometimes, even if 'moinsn' is surely the most popular [. . .]"

Georg also wrote this when asked about the pronunciation of <peace> and <peaze>:

[7] a pseudonym.

5. Alles wird gleich ausgesprochen. Ob “c” oder “z” ist nur eine Frage des Geschmacks, oder der Coolheit. “z” ist irgendwie ein digitaler Buchstabe der neuen Generation. Auch in der Raubkopiererei wird oft das “z” verwendet (”warez”), aber auch im Englischen (”whuzzup”). Warum – keine Ahnung. Wahrscheinlich um sich etwas vom Normalsprachlichen zu distanzieren.

   “They’re all pronounced the same. Whether ‘c’ or ‘z’ is just a question of taste, or of coolness. ‘z’ is somehow a digital character of the new generation. ‘z’ is also used often in the realm of software piracy (‘warez’), but also in English (‘whuzzup’). Why – no idea. Possibly to distance oneself somewhat from normal language use.”

These statements from a non-linguist hip hop fan (but an academic, and someone who obviously thinks quite a bit about language) reveal both metalinguistic knowledge and thought about the use of <z> in multiple languages. Georg finds variant uses of <z> to iconize youth culture (“the new generation”) in the sense described by Sebba (2015), drawing on Irvine and Gal (2000) – this orthographic character has become an iconic representation of a particular group. It is interesting that <z> in <peaze> is not directly noted as an English form, as Georg notes that <z> is “also” used in English. To Georg, <z> in this context has acquired a local meaning – one not reliant on, but clearly influenced by, its English origins. German hip hop fans’ extension of <z> to forms like <peaze>, which are not clearly attested in English hip hop usage, is a local instantiation of a global style – simultaneously individual and collective. Fans in this domain are not merely reproducing forms from the English-speaking culture, but stylizing, playing with, and making them their own.

Idiosyncratic capitalizations are another indication of this phenomenon; while the quantitative analyses of the MZEE forum largely ignore capitalization, an in-depth investigation of *peace/peaze* in the MZEE corpus found that certain users favored idiosyncratic capitalizations. *PeacE,* for example, was used 25 times in the MZEE corpus; 23 of these uses were by the same user, as a sort of signature leave-taking:

6. luda is echt fresh, rappt halt voll
   hardcore mäßig!! PeacE!

   “luda[cris] is really fresh, he just raps
   completely hardcore!! PeacE!”

In another case, the orthographic <z> was emphasized through capitalization. The form *peaZe* was found 75 times in the corpus, with the first 23 uses attributed to a single user. This capitalization then seems to have spread to other users.

7. [. . .]ausserdem ist heutzutage fast jeder "grosser" Rapper bei Top of the Pops, The Dome, siehe Azad + Kool Savas, aber natürlich ist das COOL wenn die da auftreten, gel? mein beitrag dazu

   peaZe up!

   [username]

   "[. . .]and what's more, today almost every 'big-time' rapper is on Top of the Pops, the Dome, Look at Azad + Kool Savas, but naturally it's COOL when they appear there, ain't it? that's my input

   peaZe up!

   [username]"

This use of idiosyncratic capitalization as a kind of personal emblem or signature language practice to underline the use of a borrowed leave-taking as a special stylistic resource involves the application of creativity (within certain boundaries) in a playful way.

Discussion and Conclusions

This examination of the language-contact situation among youth in the German hip hop scene online yields several major findings. First, <z> is used as an alternative orthographic choice in both English and German contexts. While it is not unique to hip hop, it does carry, as Androutsopoulos (2000) notes, a subcultural indexicality, and this is used to a much greater extent in the German than the American hip hop scene. In addition, rather than simply copying words from English to German, the borrowing process in the German hip hop community is revealed to involve complex knowledge of orthographic, phonological, and morphological rules from both English and German, as evidenced by the interaction of the English orthographic-phonemic correspondence <z> → /z/ and German word-final devoicing in forms with final <z>. Second, greetings and leave-takings like *greets* and *peace* are particularly fertile sites for stylization and language play, and likely to be favored targets for borrowing. This bears further research; I noted here that elements like *leuts* "people" and *jungs* "boys" are also orthographically manipulated for stylistic purposes, and it is intriguing that these often play a role as vocatives in discourse, i.e. as elements which, like greetings and leave-takings, often do not participate in larger syntactic structures, fulfilling discourse rather than grammatical functions. Finally, the variation found in the formulaic leave-taking *peace* in the German hip hop scene appears to be a stable situation with heavy preference given to the standard English orthographic form *peace.* The form of the variants *peaz, peaze,* and *peazen,* which are relatively frequent when compared against other alternatives, are best explained by the adoption of the English value /z/ for orthographic <z>, but with a twist: the /z/ follows the German phonological rule of word-final devoicing, yielding the form [pi:s] in both cases. Essentially, the application of a combined set of English-German orthographic-phonetic norms and phonological rules allows for a more diverse array of alternate, stylized forms – <peaze> appears nowhere in the Covo corpus.

There is some criticism of the notion that digital writing is beholden to phonological concerns; Deumert and Lexander (2013: 535) suggest that "digital writing ... needs to be studied on its own terms, and not as a reflection of the spoken language." This statement is in many respects true, as the unique and diverse contexts of digital writing, which are "both technical and social", as Herring (2007: 1) notes in her approach to classifying computer-mediated discourse, are key to understanding digital writing. However, digital writing must to some extent be shaped by phonological concerns. There cannot exist a complete lack of systemic correspondence between speech and writing. German hip hoppers, by virtue of a phonological feature of their first language and a variable knowledge of English as a foreign language, are more likely than American fans to do things like produce <peaze> as a stylization and, as I demonstrate in Garley (2014), use the suffix <-ed> anywhere German phonology suggests a <-t> suffix. Stylization in digital writing often involves the extension, combination, and relaxation of required correspondences between phonology and orthography, and the multilingual context of German hip hop fandom affords these language users a broader palette with which to employ language creatively. But, as a general rule, written language cannot, or does not, ignore the spoken form entirely.[8] In the case of <peaze>, the graphemes that can felicitously appear in the terminal pronounced position in the word are constrained to a small set, including <c>, <s>, and <z>. An additional possibility would be <x>, which is a very relaxed grapheme in terms of its phonetic correspondences for various reasons, perhaps because it is, across many cultures, the prototypical mathematical variable. Garley and Slade (2016) discuss the usage of <x>, for example, to represent part of the word "cyberpunk" in the digitally written form <cypx>. Returning to <peaze>, many other options are right out. Anything beyond a small set of graphemes related in their possible phonetic realizations risks too much misinterpretation or confusion. In written language stylization in

[8] This observation would also hold for SignWriting used with a signed language as a writing system.

the digital domain, users are, in theory, only constrained by technology (input devices and software) in their choice of graphemes and symbols for meaning-making; in fact, a large amount of meaning is made non-linguistically, for example by using emoji. But to convey and interpret ideas through language, both writer and audience must have a common basis on which to identify the words being used – and that crucially constrains the realistic possibilities for stylization in most cases to graphemes that could conceivably correspond to the phonetic forms being used. In summary, these results serve to illuminate language practices which are emerging from an asymmetrically multilingual, subcultural domain in which digital engagement is central – illustrating not only extreme instances of language stylization, but also the natural boundaries and limitations on language play.

Part II

Strictly Online

Multilingual Practices in Texting, Blogging, and Commenting

6 Tsotsitaal Online

The Creativity of Tradition

Ana Deumert

> There is nothing like art – in the oppressor's sense of art. There is only movement. Force. Creative power. The walk of the Sophiatown tsotsi or my Harlem brother on Lenox avenue. Field hollers. The Blues. A Trane riff. Marvin Gaye or mbaqanga. Anguished happiness. Creative power, in whatever form is released, moves like the dancer's muscles.
>
> (Keorapetse Kgositsile, 'Bra Willie', *The impulse is personal – a poets credo*; 1966, published in *Negro Digest*, July 1968: 42)

6.1 Introduction

This chapter discusses online mediatizations of a multilingual South African "way of speaking" (Hymes 1974) which is commonly known as Tsotsitaal[1]. The name is a combination of *tsotsi*, referring to a (mostly) petty criminal, and *taal*, Afrikaans for "language." It translates literally as "thug language" or "language of criminals." However, the social semiotics of this way of speaking are considerably more complex than the explicit reference to criminality. They also involve notions of urbanity, a politics of resistance to oppression, youth and masculinity, the art of being streetwise (referred to locally as being "clever"), and performative displays of linguistic virtuosity.

Drawing broadly on Stuart Hall's (1997) work on representation, Asif Agha's (2007) notion of enregisterment and Richard Bauman's (1977; Bauman and Briggs 1990) work on performance, I argue that displays of language – whether online or offline – are complex signifying practices which are imbued with ideology (in the sense of Silverstein 1979). Ideologies constitute a reflexive, meta-pragmatic space where speakers and writers articulate beliefs about the shape and structure of the represented linguistic form, its position and meaning in

[1] The subtitle of this chapter is inspired by Charles Briggs' (1988) book *Competence in Performance: The Creativity of Tradition in Mexicano Verbal Art* (Philadelphia: University of Pennsylvania Press). The work presented here would not have been possible without the support of the National Research Foundation (South Africa), the University of Cape Town, my colleague and partner Nkululeko Mabandla whose memories of Tsotsitaal helped me to understand its history and meanings, and to Anne Storch, who introduced me to the linguistics of secret languages.

the social world, its typical speakers as well as the multimodal ensemble of which it forms part. Representations can, at times, be reductionist, creating an impoverished, even stale and lifeless, version of the linguistic practices they portray (as discussed in Deumert 2014a; Chapter 4). However, they can also give new meanings to vanishing vernaculars, extending their social symbolism across time and space; that is, beyond the realm of body-to-body encounters. I suggest that Tsotsitaal can be understood as constituting part of South African (urban) folklore; that is, it is an artful tradition of speaking, and a mimetic display of this tradition, just as much as it is creative contemporary practice. Online representations of Tsotsitaal draw on a history of media representations – going back to the 1950s – and recontextualize the familiar in new contexts and for new audiences. Rather than seeing folklore as embedded in the "romantic mist" of the past, I follow Dan Ben-Amos (1971: 4), who argued that "the materials of folklore are mobile, manipulative and transcultural," and indeed mediatized and displayed in public contexts (Bauman 1983).

The chapter is structured as follows: 6.2 discusses the history, social meanings and early mediatizations of Tsotsitaal. This is followed by a brief overview of Tsotsitaal and other mixed urban vernaculars in contemporary South Africa (for a broad overview of the sociolinguistic context in South Africa, see Deumert 2014c). Moving into the data analysis, I outline the broad methodological-theoretical framework in 6.4 and discuss Tsotsitaal representations on social media platforms in 6.5 and 6.6. Tsotsitaal is used to achieve particular communicative goals in these online contexts: to index what is colloquially known as *loxion kulca* ("location culture," i.e. the ways of the township[2]); to articulate a voice that evokes the past and that is experienced as aesthetically pleasing; and to show-off, that is, to display linguistic knowledge and skill to an audience.

6.2 Locating Tsotsitaal: Sophiatown and Beyond

In the popular imagination, the origins and history of Tsotsitaal are closely linked to Sophiatown, the multiethnic and multilingual neighborhood of Johannesburg which was destroyed in 1955 when the apartheid government forcefully moved its residents to Meadowlands, Soweto. Sophiatown, also known affectionately as *Kofifi*, was – and is – legendary in South Africa (and beyond, see Hannerz 1996). It was a hub of music, literature, art and politics in the 1940s and early 1950s, and

[2] In South Africa, "township" refers to the ghetto-like urban areas where Black, Coloured (a colonial ethnonym for creole or mixed race) and Indian people were forced to live during apartheid (1948–1994). These areas have persisted post-1994 and South African cities continue to show high levels of segregation. The orthographic conventions used in this chapter follow common vernacular spellings used in South Africa; rendering the terms in IPA is not feasible because of the variety of existing pronunciations.

one of the few places in South Africa were Africans were allowed to own property. However, it was also a slum, overcrowded and impoverished, plagued by high levels of crime. And it was on the streets of Sophiatown – as well as close-by areas such as Marabastad, Alexandra, the Western Native Township and Newclare – that the figure of the *tsotsi* seems to have taken shape.

The term *tsotsi* appears in the sociological literature from the mid-1940s onwards. It is used to refer to young, male criminals, who express an assertive masculinity, and display a strong sense of fashion and style; typically, modeling themselves on the gangsters seen in the popular American movies of the time. The etymology of the word is murky and several proposals have been made. It might be a mispronunciation of *zoot suit*, referring to the fashionable pegged trousers and long overcoats of the time (Glaser 2000). Alternatively, it might originate in the isiXhosa and/or Sesotho verb for 'to sharpen' (*ukutsolisa* and *ho tsotso* respectively), metaphorically referring to the 'sharp' look of the young men as well as their preference for knives. In isiXhosa there is also *itsolo,* an old term meaning "dandy" (Kropf 1899). And, finally, some have suggested that it might be a word play on Tutsi, an ethnic group in Rwanda, which was known for its vicious and fierce warriors (see Molamu 2003, for a discussion of the different etymologies).

The *tsotsi* was not only a figure of fear, but also one of desire and fantasy, of politics, poetry and art. This is illustrated in Kgositile's *Poets Credo* (1968), given as the epigraph to this chapter. The tsotsi was not only dangerous; he[3] was also about music and movement, with a walk as free and distinct as the language that accompanied it. It was an identity which was artful and powerful at the same time, expressing resistance to all forms of oppression. The figure of the *tsotsi* also opened up distant horizons: He linked Sophiatown to Harlem, showed appreciation of American and European fashion, was familiar with jazz and *film noir.* He represented a life which transcended the parochial world of apartheid South Africa: In the midst of brutal colonial oppression *tsotsis* challenged not only authority, but simultaneously played "a game of cosmopolitanism" which held the promise of a different, bigger world (Hannerz 1996: 169; Fenwick 1996; Morris 2010).

Tsotsis were defined by their fashion style, as well as by communicative practice. What kind of a language was/is Tsotsitaal? *Taal*, as noted above, is Afrikaans for "language," and the base, or matrix, language of Sophiatown's Tsotsitaal – both lexically and syntactically – was Afrikaans (Slabbert and Meyers-Scotton 1996).[4] In addition to Afrikaans, the lexicon includes material

[3] Although *tsotsis* could, in principle, be female, the stereotypical persona of the *tsotsi* was (and is) male.

[4] The syntax, however, does not always follow that of standard Afrikaans and Molamu (2003: xxv) speaks about syntactic "violations." There is, for example, variation in word order (see the examples in Bothma 1951), with deletions (copula, pro-drop) being permitted (see the examples in Mesthrie and Hurst 2013; Brookes and Lekgoro 2014).

from various African languages and English (especially in its American guise, picked up from movies), some lexis from other languages (such as French, German, Portuguese, Italian or even Latin) as well as a wide range of creative neologisms. The strong influence from Afrikaans requires explanation – why Afrikaans and not isiZulu, Sesotho or even English (which, also then, was a language of prestige and global aspiration)? Local demographics are unlikely to have played a role. Although Sophiatown and neighboring areas had initially been set aside for Colored occupation, and Afrikaans might have been dominant in the early days, this changed rapidly: Already in the 1920s, Africans made up about half of the local population, this increased to about 85 percent in the 1930s, and to over 90 percent in 1950.[5] A "founder effect" (Mufwene 1996) can explain limited influence, but it does not explain the fairly persistent Afrikaans base, especially in syntax. The use of Afrikaans is better understood as a form of cultural-linguistic appropriation or even parody: taking "the language of the oppressor" and making it one's own, turning it upside down in the process. Afrikaans, the language of Whiteness and purity, thus became the language of Blackness and hybridity (see Deumert 2009, for a discussion of similar processes in Namibia; on linguistic appropriation see also Fanon [1952] 2008).

The use of Tsotsitaal as a voice of resistance against oppression is evident in one of its earliest media representations, Strike Vilakazi's (1956) protest song "Meadowlands." The lyrics of the song articulate different voices. There is the voice of White people, trying to lure Sophiatown residents into leaving their homes and moving to Meadowlands, the government-decreed Black township. This is answered by the voice of the *tsotsis* who speak out, simply, but firmly, against the forced removals. And, finally, there is the coda *sithandwa sam*, a third voice, which links the two stanzas (Sotho, unmarked; Nguni, underlined; Tsotsitaal, italics).

Otla utlwa makgowa are	You'll hear the Whites say
Are yeng ko Meadowlands	Let's move to Meadowlands
Meadowlands, Meadowlands	Meadowlands, Meadowlands
Meadowlands, sithandwa sam	Meadowlands, my love.
Otlwa utlwa botsotsi bare	You'll hear the tsotsis say
Ons dak nie ons phola hier	We won't leave, we are staying here
Phola hier, phola hier	Staying here, Staying here
Phola hier, sithandwa sam.	Staying here, my love.[6]

[5] Letter to Reverend D. Taylor by the Secretary for Native Affairs (February 5, 1946); Summary of Report on Survey of Western Area Townships, City of Johannesburg 1950. Digitized versions are available online: www.historicalpapers.wits.ac.za (collection: AD1715, 5.28). See also the statistics provided in Bothma (1951) for townships in Pretoria.

[6] *Phola* (from isiZulu *ukuphola*) means "to relax, to chill, to sit down and reflect"; *dak* (from English "to duck") means "to leave."

Tsotsitaal also featured prominently in the pages of *Drum*, a South African magazine which was directed at a Black urban audience. Consider, for example, Can Themba's (1956) "picture story" *Baby Come Duze* ("Baby come near"). It is the story of a love triangle, told multimodally in image and text, using the township's "new lingo . . . made of Afrikaans, Zulu, Sotho, English and brand-new words" (with translations provided for the uninitiated; reprinted in Chapman 1989). Or his story *The Urchin* (1963) which features Macala, a ten-year old boy:

Macala suddenly felt in the mood for the jargon of the townships. The near-animal, amorphous, quick-shifting lingo that alarms farm boys and drives cops to all branches of suspicion. But it marks the city slicker who can cope with all its vagaries. (Cited in Manus 2011: 102)

The anthropologist Phillip Meyer (1961: 73–75) suggested that the *tsotsi* – and his language – became part of urban folklore, an almost mythical figure which was not only "terribly dangerous" and outside of "decent" society, but also an icon of urbanity and style. The figure and language of the *tsotsi* allowed writers – and their readers – to imagine, and perform an African modernity that was distinct from that of mission-school educated intellectuals. The *tsotsi* represented a modernity that was streetwise and "sharp" (see above), brash and fast-talking, with a devil-may-care attitude and in opposition to authority. These texts enregistered (Agha 2007) not simply a way of speaking – understood as a collection of socially meaningful linguistic forms which are interpreted as belonging to a specific code or variety – but also a unique way of being in the world, reflecting an aesthetic which valued hybridity and play, and a political orientation which resisted oppression and any denial of freedom.

Tsotsitaal as an aesthetic form and social symbolic representing the experience and voice of Black urban resistance, did not disappear with the end of Sophiatown. It remained part of the semiotic repertoire of South African artists well into the 1980s. An example is Matsemela Manaka's (1981) essay *The Babalaz People* ("those who have a hangover," *ibabalaz*, "hangover," is part of the core Tsotsitaal lexicon)[7]. In this essay, Manaka locates Black (political) theater firmly within the segregated and violent towns that were created by apartheid architecture, with urban vernaculars, such as Tsotsitaal, as its expressive force and aesthetic.

The squatters, slums and ghettos should be its [Black theater's] stage. Mampara ["fake"] bricks, corrugated zinc, the mud and stench in the streets should be its costume. Seqamtho, "tsotsitaal," sepantsola, not sehippie should be its language. (Manaka 1981: 34)

[7] The title evokes Can Themba's (1956) essay *Let the people drink!*, a classic example of Drum writing (reprinted in Chapman 1989).

Manaka's programmatic statement identifies not only Tsotsitaal as the linguistic form appropriate for struggle theater, but also Iscamtho (spelled here Seqamtho) and Sepantsula (spelled here Sepantsola). The latter two refer to multilingual urban vernaculars which draw more strongly on African languages, and thus recontextualize the hybrid aesthetics and political meanings of Tsotsitaal in a different linguistic form (see below). These ways of speaking are distinguished from seHippie, the language and subculture of the Hippies. The latter extended, according to the historian Clive Glaser (1992), beyond the township and "linked up to white hippie culture." Its love-and-peace rhetoric, bellbottom trousers and sandals, stood in contrast to the edgy resistance aesthetic of the township. It is relevant that Manaka puts Tsotsitaal in inverted commas. Tsotsitaal has a unique, or marked, status among the languages listed: It was a language not only of the street, but also – already in 1981 – a language with a history of mediatization.

6.3 What's in a Name? Of Tsotsitaal and Tsotsitaals

The above cited quote by Manaka points to the multitude of (emic) language names that, by the 1980s, were used to refer to mixed urban vernaculars in South Africa. Linguists typically group these into two broad categories (the name most commonly used in the literature and media discourse is highlighted in bold):

(a) mixed vernaculars, that arose in the historical freehold areas of Sophiatown and tend to show strong Afrikaans-influence. These vernacular practices stabilized in the 1940s, have been represented in print since the 1950s, and have been in decline from the 1970s onwards. Language names include: Flaaitaal, **Tsotsitaal**, Kofifitaal, Wietie ("to speak"), lingo; and
(b) mixed vernaculars, that emerged in the apartheid townships and use African languages as their matrix language. These varieties rose to prominence from the 1970s onwards, have been mediated especially through music (in the local genre of *kwaito* as well as in hip hop) and radio, and continue to be widely used (on *kwaito* and hip hop in South Africa see Livermon 2012, Williams and Stroud 2014). Language names include: **Iscamtho**, Sepantsula, Ringas ("speaking slang"), Kasi-Taal ("location language"), lingo.

The idea that we can distinguish two basic types goes back to an early MA thesis, written by Cornelius Vale Bothma in 1951. Bothma distinguishes two forms of what he calls "Tsotsi-taal": *Flaaitaal*, the strongly Afrikaans-based "language of the streetwise," those who are "fly," clever and quick-witted, and *Shalambombo*, a Nguni-based prison argot. Bothma uses Tsotsitaal as a hypernym to refer to both types, a move which, at times, is also made by speakers, linguists, and in the media. In Cape Town, for example, Tsotsitaal can be used to refer to slang lexis embedded in an isiXhosa matrix (Mesthrie and Hurst 2013). Similarly, in Durban isiTsotsi describes an isiZulu-based, non-standard variety that stands in a diglossic relationship to standard isiZulu (Rudwick 2005) (also Slabbert and Meyers-Scotton 1996: 326).

What unites these different types of speech is a partially shared lexicon, which includes many words that go back to the old Afrikaans-based variety of Sophiatown. This was argued most recently by Rajend Mesthrie (2008) (also Schuring 1979; Slabbert and Meyers-Scotton 1996) who proposed "a unified account of tsotsitaal" (with small cap to distinguish it from the Afrikaans-based Tsotsitaal). He describes tsotsitaal in this generalized sense as "a loose set of varieties that flourish in South Africa's townships" (Mesthrie 2008: 95). These varieties display a distinct and recognizable lexis, which can be inserted in an existing matrix language (Afrikaans, English, or an African language), and is typically accompanied by a multimodal ensemble of dress, movement, gesture, and posture (Hurst 2008; Brookes 2014). The historical depth of this lexicon became evident when I was looking at online data from the last few years (2009 to 2015): The majority of the words as well as turns of phrase that were used on Twitter and Facebook were known to older Tsotsitaal speakers in their fifties, and only rarely did a formulation elicit the response "I don't know that one." This suggests that there is a core lexicon which has shown considerable stability across time.

Tsotsitaals, as conceptualized by Mesthrie, are instantiations of what Roland Kiessling and Marten Mous (2004) (also Childs 1997) discuss under the heading of "urban youth languages in Africa." They argue that these vernaculars constitute a typologically unified phenomenon which exists, in various linguistic forms, across the continent (including varieties such as Sheng in Kenya or Nouchi in Côte d'Ivoire), and perhaps even across the world. African urban youth languages are not unlike European multiethnic youth languages such as, for example, *straattaal* in the Netherlands. The linguistic processes (mixing, relexicalization, neologisms, etc.) and the socio-symbolic meanings appear to be fairly similar (youth, masculinity and urbanity, a symbolic sense of Blackness or ethnic identity; e.g. Cornips et al. 2015; see also the other chapters in Nortier and Svendsen 2015).[8]

Mesthrie's argument that tsotsitaalness resides primarily in the lexicon echoes Arnold van Gennep's (1908) early work on special languages which also sees them as lexically and not morphosyntactically defined. Anne Storch

[8] It is important to note that these varieties *index* youth, masculinity, and urbanity *symbolically*, rather than being spoken only by those falling into the demographic categories of "young," "male," and "urban." There is ample evidence that their use might endure across the lifespan (see also Rampton 2011); they function in rural contexts as markers of urban experience; and, although women might avoid these varieties because of their indexicalities of roughness and street culture, they do use them quite deliberately to portray particular social personae.

(2011; 2013) has argued that the linguistic processes which create such a special, and sometimes secret, lexicon are of interest to linguistic theory because they reflect the metalinguistic knowledge of speakers. The lexicon, in other words, is not something that is given; rather, it is dynamic, generative, and creatively constructed, just like morpho-syntax. Borrowing and semantic shifts (including metaphor, metonymy, hyperbole, etc.) feature prominently in the Tsotsitaal lexicon. Examples include *cherry* for "darling" (from French *chérie*; borrowing) and *donkie* to refer to a slow-witted person (from "donkey"; borrowing plus semantic shift). In addition, there are a number of phonological and morphological processes. Khekheti Makhudu (2002) discusses, for example, syllable inversions (Afrikaans *slaan* > *nals*, "to hit"), nasalization (Afrikaans *papier* > *mampier*, "paper"), devoicing (*pasella*, "gift," from isiXhosa *ibhasela*), and reduplication (*naiza-naiza*, "party," from English "nice"). In Louis Molamu's (2003) dictionary we have examples of reanalysis, new ornamental affixes (*amper*, "almost," becomes *amper-kies, mri*, "friend," becomes *mri-tology* or *mri-toza*), word-initial, word-final as well as word-internal truncation, as well as ideophones (such as *gwap-gwap*, "quick passing of time"). Learning how to use these words – and how to create new words – forms "part of people's linguistic education" (Storch 2013: 94), and is integral to the successful performance of this particular way of speaking. That is, speaking Tsotsitaal – or its cousin Iscamtho – skillfully is not solely a question of knowing existing words and enacting them within the expected multimodal matrix (dress, posture, and movement), it is also the ability to expand on what is there, to surprise the audience through a display of linguistic virtuosity and creativity. The remainder of this chapter focuses on the digital representations, enactments, and performances of the old Afrikaans-based Tsotsitaal. Given that fluent speakers of this variety are now mostly in their fifties and older, what representations do we see online?[9]

6.4 Virtual Linguistic Landscapes: Representing Language(s) Online

Stuart Hall's edited volume *Representation* (1997) is a core text in the study of signifying practices; that is, practices through which we create meaning and constitute the world around us. Hall argues that we create social meaning in three different ways: (a) by *interpreting* the world for ourselves and others, (b) by *doing* things, and (c) by *re-presenting* and displaying the world. He writes:

> In part, we give objects, people and events meaning by the frameworks of interpretation which we bring to them. In part, we give things meaning by how we use them, or integrate them in our everyday practices … In part, we give meaning by how we

[9] Iscamtho-like practices are also common online. However, their discussion is outside of the scope of this chapter.

represent them – the words we use about them, the images of them we produce, the emotions we associate with them, the ways we classify and conceptualize them, the values we place on them. (Hall 1997: 3)

As noted in the introduction, Hall's work on representation links to Asif Agha's notion of enregisterment as well as Richard Bauman's work on performance. Representation and performance are kindred theoretical concepts which aim to understand reflexive communicative practices that put language on display in front of an audience, and, in the process of doing so, create – that is, enregister – recognizable ways of speaking that are available for further displays, and that can, over time, become integrated into routine daily practices. Thus, the repeated use of Tsotsitaal in the pages of *Drum* created, already in the 1950s, an image of how to speak and write, of how to represent the language of the street corner. This then became the source for further media displays, first in the context of struggle theater and writing, later in movies such as *Mapantsula* (1988) and soap operas such as *Isidingo* (which premiered in 1998). These displays created a model of language and associated speaker personae, that was available for further recontexualizations (Bauman and Briggs 1990) and resemiotizations (Iedema 2003) in interaction, off-line and online.

The idea that the internet constitutes a vast semiotic landscape was argued by Jane Hill (2005). Jane Hill made use of Google's search engine to trace the intertextual meanings of *mañana* ("morning, tomorrow") in what she calls Mock Spanish, that is, the use of Spanish lexical items by monolingual English speakers to project a "positive colloquial persona." These practices are offensive to native speakers of Spanish as they inadvertently reproduce racist stereotypes. Mock Spanish occurs in everyday interactions, but is particularly prominent in media representations, ranging from movies (such as the *Terminator*) to slogans on T-shirts and coffee cups. In her 2005 article, Hill advocates the use of Google searches as a tool for tracing the intertextual linkages and meanings of such heavily mediated forms. She argues that:

This [online, Google-enabled] research technique allowed me to reproduce in a very short span of time the experience that an ordinary English speaker might have over several months or even years, being exposed to multiple contexts of /man'yanə/. (Hill 2005: 117)

Google searches – of text, images, and videos – provide quick access to a vast range of language-on-display, constituting what we might call a "virtual linguistic landscape" (Ivkovic and Lotherington 2009; Androutsopoulos 2013a). An image search for Tsotsitaal, for example, provides an interesting and thought-provoking collection (public search, December 22, 2014; browser: Firefox, location: South Africa). Most noticeable is the preponderance of academic representations of this linguistic practice. Two out of the top five images reproduce the first page of an academic paper (Slabbert and Myers-Scotton 1996; Makhudu 2002). Another image – depicting greeting routines in cartoon-like fashion – accompanies a newspaper article written by another linguist (Hurst 2013). The remaining two images reference popular culture: one shows the cover of a recently produced album (by the American indie rapper Ten and Tracer), the other an image from a blog, depicting a young Black man dressed in twenty-first century township fashion (jeans, T-shirt, sneakers and soft hat). Scrolling down further we see more iconic representations of Black male township youth (and style), an advert of the mobile phone company *8ta/heita* (whose name is inspired by an old and well-known Tsotsitaal greeting), books about Tsotsitaal, more blogs, as well as images from the Oscar-winning South African movie *Tsotsi* (2005), which introduced the figure of the Tsotsi to global audiences. In these digital representations Tsotsitaal becomes visible as an object of academic study and point of reference for local, as well as global, popular culture: Its deep local embedding notwithstanding it works as a meaningful term for an American rapper with no identifiable connections to South Africa.

Google searches are particularly helpful when investigating what we might call hegemonically-sanctioned representations. Thus, just like editors, search engine algorithms create regimes of visibility by sorting, ranking, and filtering content that is available online (Bucher 2012; Introna and Nissenbaum 2000). With the exception of product reviews (such as Tripadvisor) and Wikipedia entries, user-generated content on social media platforms generally receives low rankings on Google, and much remains entirely invisible in broader web-searches (this includes tweets, Facebook, and YouTube comments).

The following analysis focuses on two social media platforms: Facebook and Twitter. YouTube is not included because of the general paucity of user-generated material: Although a search for "Tsotsitaal" returned 61 results, only 23 were about linguistic practice (date of search: December 22, 2014; four years later, in June 2018, this had grown to over 300 videos tagged "Tsotsitaal"). The majority of these (n=18) were professionally or semi-professionally produced music videos, TV programs and documentaries, or trailers/interviews for movies such as *iNumberNumber* (2014) or *Hijack Stories* (2000), which make use of Tsotsitaal/Iscamtho in the dialogue. Given the academic interest in Tsotsitaal and related practices, it is perhaps not surprising that two further videos were recordings of academic presentations about Tsotsitaal. Only three videos could be classified as user-generated content. These were unedited amateur recordings of staged multilingual performances. Two were recordings of the same spoken word poet; the third, an impromptu rap performance. Linguistically, although tagged as "Tsotsitaal," neither of them uses the Afrikaans-based variety which is the focus of this chapter, and all three represent Iscamtho-like practices.

The question of access is relevant here. Online engagement in South Africa is historically mobile-centric, and, as such, has favored text- and image-based practices (see Deumert 2014a, Chapter 3). Thus, while YouTube provides only limited data, online representations of the Afrikaans-based Tsotsitaal are fairly common on Facebook and Twitter, two social media platforms which allow easy access via phones. Writing Tsotsitaal online is not habitual practice. It is experienced self-consciously as marked, as exploring a different and unfamiliar voice.

1. Texting my bf in tsotsi taal, so funny [May 2013; female; Twitter].
2. The way I text in tsotsi taal when chatting with Sanny. Nno maan. Makes me feel like I'm standing @ a urinal : D [September 2013; male; Twitter][10]

The examples discussed below were taken from the public timeline of Twitter and from public sites on Facebook (data collection took place in 2014, when the chapter was written). Demographic information (race, gender) is based on visual inspection of the avatar: Although avatars do not necessarily reflect the actual gender/race of a user, they can be taken to reflect the projected or desired race/gender.

6.5 The Pleasure of the Past: Afrikaans *aka* Tsotsitaal

Using Twitter's search function and looking over a large number of tweets (going back to 2009) which either talk about Tsotsitaal or offer performances of Tsotsitaal, two observations can be made: (a) There are almost no posts by White South Africans on the topic which thus seems to belong to the contested space of what has been referred to as Black Twitter (Brock 2012; Florini 2014); and (b) many writers express great appreciation for the "old school" Afrikaans-based Tsotsitaal, even though, or perhaps precisely because, it is rarely heard in everyday spoken interactions, except among older people.[11]

3. These o'ladies be speaking tsotsi taal lol. . .I love it when old people speak tsotsi taal mixed with Afrikaans [October 2014; female; Twitter]
4. My stepdad and I speak in that old school tsotsi taal. . .he's 64 this year. Awesome. [February 2014; male; Twitter]
5. I'm really fascinated by old man with their tsotsi taal and kasi swag! They were the pioneers of cool [January 2014; male; Twitter]

[10] A note on spelling: While linguists spell Tsotsitaal quite consistently as a composite noun (indicating perhaps its "language-like" character), digital writers tend to spell it as two words.

[11] Such positive evaluations were clearly the majority view. However, there are also some who dislike the old Tsotsitaal, consider it to be "too Ghetto" and as inappropriate for grown-up men and women.

6. How kool is these old Tyma Tsotsi taal??? "Ons gat jou Pazamiesa hieso" ["we will chase you away"]#YizoYizo [August 2012; male; Twitter]

The models for this type of speech – which is characterized as "smooth," "cool," "dope," "turn on," "deep," "fascinating," "boss" – are not one's peers, but one's elders and, in addition, media representations. Popular characters in South African TV series which are regularly mentioned as models are Bra Gibb (in *Yizo Yizo*, played by Dominic Tyawa), Bra Tiger (Patrick Shai) from *Zone14* and Papa G (Georgie Zamdela) from *Isidingo*.

At the same time as writers express appreciation and admiration, they also articulate a sense of inadequacy, and a wish to learn and improve their skills:

7. Working on my tsotsi taal [November 2014; female; Twitter]

8. :""D I want to learn how to speak tsotsi taal like the old timers [December 8, 2013; male]

9. I wanna learn how to tweet in tsotsi-taal... That's gonna be so dope for when I have my kasi ["township"] moments! [June 2012; male]

On Facebook, a number of virtual classrooms have playfully inverted the idea of school or university as the place where one learns to speak "proper." Instead, they propose to "teach" the language of the streets.

10. Ikasi Ringas ["township talk"] – School of Tsotsitaal [started 2012]
TsotsiTaalLanguageSchool (TTLS) [started 2014]
UniVersity of TsotSi-taal LinGo [started 2013]
School of iRingas aka Tsotsi Taal [started 2012][12]

The most popular of these is *Ikasi Ringas* (with over 14,000 likes in 2014; it went up to over 17,000 in 2018)) which emphasizes diversity, authenticity, celebration, sharing, and learning in the *about* feature:

Ikasi Ringas is a community that aims to celebrate and spread authentic South African township lingo. Expand your township vocabulary and share language unique to various South African townships

The design of the site creates a classroom that is quite unlike the classrooms readers will have experienced at school. The image on the site is of Bonginkosi Dlamini aka Zola, a well-known Kwaito musician who provided the soundtrack to the movie *Tsotsi*. And instead of a stern teacher, there is a team of administrators which provide status updates with "cool" and "crazy" words, advice on how to engage in appropriate streetwise interactions ("Next time umntu aku buza ['a person asks you'] 'Ku hambani?' meaning what's

[12] In January 2015, I counted about a dozen of such pages which were all created between 2011 and 2014.

popping . . . tell them 'ku hamba iinyawo umzimba ubaya iskelem' ['the feet are walking, the body has been tricked into following']", February 2013); challenges readers to the occasional quiz ("A simple quizz for friday what does the abbreviation 'MVV' in tsotsi taal mean?", August 2013),[13] and provides ample scope for user contributions ("WHAT DO YOU CALL A 'BACK YARD ROOM'[14] IN YOUR HOOD?", May 2014).

Although English and Iscamtho-like practices dominate on these pages, Afrikaans influence is persistent, and old Tsotsitaal lexis keeps re-appearing. Thus, among the responses to the above question of how to refer to a "backyard room," we find *pozi* (already attested in Bothma's, 1951, wordlist; possibly from *posisie*, "position"), as well as a range of other Afrikaans-based terms: *hoki* (from *hoek*, "corner"), *kisti, kist, ekhistini* (from *kis,* "box," but with the final *–t* as in Dutch; also used in South African English to refer to a large wooden chest), *palamente* (vernacular spelling of *parlement*, "parliament"), *huis* ("house") and *spookhuis* ("ghost house"). Old Tsotsitaal lexis also features in the responses to the question: "how do you say I love you in Tsotsi taal? (June 2014). Particularly favored is the intensifier *blind* (meaning "very") and the verb *frostana* (from Afrikaans *verstaan*, "to understand"), giving rise to several versions of the phrase: *ngiyakufrostana blind blind*! (literally, "I understand you totally"). While this example, just as the one provided in the original question, uses isiZulu as the syntactic matrix, other respondents offer a range of phrases which draw on Afrikaans lexicon as well as syntax:

11. ek is lief voor jou ["I love you"]
ill be a lover jou vir wena skat ["I'll be your lover, for you, dear"]
ek es mal van jou ["I am crazy about you"]

Remembering and acknowledging Afrikaans words in Tsotsitaal is common practice and can even be turned into a competition:

12. Tsotsitaal words that are taken from afrikaans – (my spelling sucks) Kak, bell, Vat se, geen, traap, scooner, verstaan, gister, sister, ekse, fede, bow(build), groont, groet, mooi, plaat, spaan, vaar, bestier, stier, vaslaap, skomel, draai, blom, skierlek, water siek, and many many more. What other words can you think of? (May 2013)

I suggested above (in 6.2) that Tsotsitaal allowed speakers to appropriate Afrikaans, a language which – its complex and multi-racial speaker base notwithstanding – was historically and symbolically associated with Whiteness and oppression. And indeed one of the reasons which has been given for the rise of Iscamtho-like practices, and the decline of the Afrikaans-based Tsotsitaal, are the Soweto protests of 1976, when high school students

[13] The answer is *mooi van ver*, meaning "beautiful from afar."
[14] A back-yard room refers to an informal dwelling which is built at the back of a house.

protested against the introduction of Afrikaans as a compulsory subject, and carried posters with slogans such as "to hell with Afrikaans." Karen Calteaux (1994) comments on the situation of the early 1990s as follows: "the youngsters of today no longer know Afrikaans and dislike it . . . the youngsters of today tend to prefer Iscamtho . . . Iscamtho is thriving but Tsotsitaal will die out without a trace." Similarly, Andrew Molefe (2011) lamented in his "Thinking Aloud" column in *The New Age* that "tsotsi taal is now a threatened species. There are few people left in the township who can still praat ['speak'] the language with the flair of its original hip form" (see also Molamu 1995; Childs 1997; Brookes and Lekgoro 2014).[15]

Yet, online, on Twitter and Facebook, the tradition of the old-style Tsotsitaal, the language of Sophiatown, continues, symbolically creating "a connection between aspects of the present and an interpretation of the past" (Bauman 1992: 32). This link between old and new, past and present, is established also in other media discourses. In 2002, Tokollo Tshabalala aka Magesh released the kwaito hit *No.1 Tsotsi*, which earned him the affectionate nickname *tsotsi van toeka af* ("old-style Tsotsi"; on musical representations of Sophiatown in kwaito, see also Livermon 2012). The expression *tsotsi van toeka af* was then picked up by those writing in digital spaces to express a sense of continuity, a way in which the township experiences under apartheid still resonate today. This is illustrated in (13), where the writer links the *tsotsis* of Sophiatown to kwaito/hip hop and contemporary *loxion kulca*:

> 13. Tsotsi van tuka,tsotsi van kofifi,kwaito all the way [June 2013; male; Twitter]

The style and language of the old-school tsotsi is not only valued and desired, it is also performed. And although knowledge is mostly of a fragmented nature, limited to just a few words and phrases, writers use these fragments to create performances for their online audiences (on linguistic fragments in performance, see Williams and Stroud 2014). In these written performances the emphasis is not on the invention of novel forms, creative word play and linguistic manipulation – practices which index the fluent and proficient speaker – but rather on articulating a recognizable historical voice.

6.6 The Pleasure of the Knowledge: Performing Tsotsitaal

The affordances of, especially, Twitter are well-suited for cultural-linguistic performances in the absence of full proficiency. The service's message format is

[15] www.thenewage.co.za/printstroy.aspx?news_id=325&mid=186.

minimalist (with a maximum of 140 characters), and there is no expectation that a tweet would be anything but a "small performance." The concept of "small performances" draws on Alexandra Georgakopoulou's (2007) discussion of "small stories." Like "small stories," "small performances" are embedded into everyday social practice. They are momentary, fleeting, and non-routine displays of linguistic skill for an audience. Perhaps the most pervasive small performance genre in digital spaces are greeting routines (Androutsopoulos 2013b). Greetings and salutation rituals allow participants to frame their social relationships in particular ways, evoke shared tradition and history, and make it possible for people with minimal linguistic skills to engage successfully in an interaction by relying on fragments of knowledge. The tweet in (14) shows an exchange of greetings between two male writers, including iconic and old-style forms such as *fede* ("how are you"), *ekse* ("hello"), and *authi* ("young man"), as well as the creative spelling /xap/ for "what's up." The exchange took place on Twitter around lunchtime in July 2013.

14. @K_M: Morning tweeps
@C_M_D: Woi woi bosso wat se authi? ["hey boss, what are you saying?"]
@K_M: Xap broer fede? ["what's up brother, how are things?"]
@C_M_D: Grand bos! ["cool boss!"]
@K_M: Hola ["hey"]

Tsotsitaal performances on Twitter are often framed by explicit announcements, in which the writers state their intention that they will now write Tsotsitaal. This establishes a clear performance frame, and invites the audience to enjoy and evaluate the display they are about to see and read.

15. Ok let me try tweeting in tsotsi taal. [August 2013; male; Twitter]

16. I will start tweeting in tsotsi taal . . . [May 2013; male; Twitter]

These comments draw attention to "the act of expression" itself (Bauman 1977), an interactional move which is central to definitions of performance as artful language. And the responses show that audiences appreciate such displays. In response to, for example, (14), readers reacted with a clear sense of anticipation.

17. *graps a chair* :) [August 2013; female; Twitter]

18. *camps on your TL* ♥♥,) /\ [August 2013; female; Twitter; TL= timeline]

It is not only Tsotsitaal that is displayed in a performative frame online, but any language can become a focus of performance in the digital space of Twitter.

Consider the exchange between @LNW (female) and @P_P (male) in (19), which draws on a wide range of linguistic resources – urban isiZulu, Tsotsitaal, English – in a self-conscious and reflexive performance of the genre "expressing affection." In each post the writer first performs a particular way of speaking, and then provides an explanation of how the linguistic performance should be read, i.e. as isiZulu, Tsotsitaal, or old school.

19. @P_P mara siyathanda nina neh! ["but we love you, hey"] ♥♥ lmfao how do u like my Zulu?

    @ LNW BLIND BLIND vele siyathandana !! ["totally of course we love"] Lol ♥♥ lmao how do u like my tsotsi taal ?

    @ P_P lmao ahhh sweetheart! Wena ["you"] ul always be my baby!!! Lmfao. . .how do u like my old school? [January 2013; Twitter]

In addition to linguistic fragments, reflecting a broad appreciation of, and admiration for, words and expressions belonging to the Afrikaans-based Tsotsitaal, we also see more sustained performances on Twitter. In early 2012, @JM (male) tweeted – early in the morning – four short Tsotsitaal performances. The total number of tweets posted by @JM on that day was 52. Thus, these performances were just a small portion of his digital engagement on the day. He self-consciously flagged the tweets as representing not just Tsotsitaal, but Kofifitaal, the original language of Sophiatown.

20. Sy is jou vrou. Let her have some fun. Tlogela go nna iscefe se ndoda. Los daai Delilah ["She is your wife/girlfriend . . . Stop being a weak man. Leave that unfaithful woman"; February 12, 2012, posted at 6:52am]
21. Ons phola hier ['We stay here'; posted at 7:01am; retweeted once)
22. Ek nyisa daai moegoe ka my twa en hy di gatas bel. Dom kop. (Kofifi Taal on Twitter) ["I threatened the idiot with my gun, and he called the cops. Stupid person"; posted at 7:07am]
23. Want ek is dik so. Ek vat nie tshandis. Jy gaan tshwerr! ["Because I am fed up like that. I don't take nonsense. You will go!"; posted at 7:08am]

None of the four tweets given in (20) to (23) is directed at anyone in particular (as indicated by the absence of the @ feature), nor do they comment on events that have happened on @JM's timeline (such as perhaps a friend having trouble with his girlfriend, or a disagreement with someone). Rather, they are standalone performances which not only put linguistic forms on display, but also the social voice of the most prototypical resident of Sophiatown: the tsotsi, with his rough and tough masculinity. In addition to written, verbal performances, images tagged as *tsotsi van Kofifi* are posted regularly on Twitter: They are mostly, but not exclusively, photographs of well-dressed young men who stand in a culturally recognizable posture that is at once cocky and confident. All these performances – written as well as visual – keep the tradition alive, creatively representing it in a new digital form. They are an example of what Alistair Pennycook (2007b: 286) called "creativity as recontextualization"; that is, creativity as mimesis, as the "performance of sameness."

The small stories paradigm mentioned above considers the role of brief narrative moments in interaction. Similarly, work on performance has emphasized the interactional aspects of language-on-display (Bauman 1977). In the case of @RM's Tsotsitaal tweet there was Twitter-style audience interaction which further recontextualized the postings: (21) was retweeted; and (23) was retweeted and tagged #GeorgieZamdelaTweet by a reader, thus comparing the linguistic display on Twitter to the virtuoso and much-admired Tsotsitaal performances of George Zamadela, Papa G in the TV series *Isidingo*.

The Facebook and Twitter data discussed here form part of the virtual linguistic landscape. Although not easily accessible via Google search engines, these performances are part of the digital experience of individuals as they read their timelines or check into Facebook. These performances display and represent language in a visual mode, and contribute to new forms of enregisterment in person-to-person interaction as well as popular culture.

6.7 Conclusion: Don't be *Tjatjarag*

Old Afrikaans Tsotsitaal words and expressions, the linguistic world of the 1950s to 1970s, remain in circulation today; they are desired and appreciated, enacted and performed, seen and read. Media discourses have long been part of the history of Tsotsitaal, starting with *Drum* in the 1950s, struggle theater and writing of the 1960s and 1970s, movies and TV since the 1980s, and, in the twenty-first-century digital media. Today, knowledge of this way of speaking tends to be fragmented. It is often limited to individual words, and the focus is on small, fleeting performances. Yet, it remains popular.

The way in which old words linger and can, through mediatization, be infused with new life can be illustrated with the example of *tjatjarag*, another Tsotsitaal word meaning "over-eager" or "nosy." The journalist Lesiba Langa describes how, in his youth, the word was used by school teachers and his grandmother when angry or reprimanding someone. It was a word that belonged to the speech of older people. But then, in 2010, Julius Malema, the youth leader of the ANC used it in an outburst against the BBC journalist Jonah

Fisher: "Let me tell you, before you are *tjatjarag* [audience laughs], this is a building of a revolutionary party and you know nothing about the revolution. So here you behave or else you jump." Malema's outburst received considerable local and international media coverage, and suddenly *tjatjarag* was all over South Africa "being mentioned in hang-out spots" and "on social network sites the word has been thrown around excessively."[16] It features on T-shirts, has inspired its own "keep calm and don't be tjatjarag!!!" series, and gone global with entries in the *Urban Dictionary.*

Thus, as suggested by Louis Molamu (1995: 154), we might not yet be seeing the end of Tsotsitaal. Even though it is *spoken fluently* mostly by "grey-haired" men, it nevertheless continues to "supply a considerable stock of words and phrases" to everyday language. *Tjatjarag* is one of those Tsotsitaal words that has crossed into general South African slang. In the process it lost some of its tsotsitaalness, its link to the social, political and cultural world of Sophiatown, and the edgy resistance aesthetic that went with it. Other words and expressions, however, retain their link to the world of the past more strongly, and writers and readers take delight in using them. Showing off one's linguistic virtuosity in online texts does not mean that new words are created and invented, rather it is about displaying one's knowledge of a historical voice. Being able to perform the old Afrikaans-based Tsotsitaal for an audience is not something everyone can do. It requires work and effort, skill and knowledge.

[16] www.supersport.com/football/blogs/lesiba-langa/Dont_be_tjatjarag. The interaction between Malema and Fisher is available at: www.youtube.com/watch?v=EpIcwctC7nQ.

7 "Pink Chess Gring Gous"

Discursive and Orthographic Resistance among Mexican-American Rap Fans on YouTube

Cecelia Cutler

Introduction[1]

At a press conference a few months before the U.S. presidential election of 2016, award-winning Mexican-American journalist Jorge Ramos of the U.S. Spanish language television network Univision repeatedly attempted to ask candidate Donald Trump a question about immigration. Trump derisively told him to sit down and refused to address him, saying that Ramos spoke out of turn. As Ramos, a Mexican-born U.S. citizen, was being physically removed by Trump's security detail, Trump told him to "Go back to Univision" and a Trump supporter shouted, "Get out of my country." Ramos was eventually allowed back into the press conference, but only after having endured the indignity of exclusion as a representative of the largest U.S. Spanish language news service. Yet, it seemed to be his Spanish language accent that initially led him to be identified as "other" and denied the right to speak.[2] In other words, phenotype is not the only way in which bodies are singled out for exclusion and policing (Ramos is blue-eyed and of European descent); language, in this case, rather than appearance (phenotype, dress, religion) was the trigger for racialization and exclusion. The incessant challenges that many Spanish-accented individuals face in the U.S.A. are also a theme in various online spaces where Mexican-American and other Latino youth gather to express their feelings and frustrations. The present chapter examines some of the writing practices of young bilingual Mexican-Americans on YouTube, focusing on the discursive and orthographic means through which they contest monolingual and standard language ideologies and engage in counter-hegemonic narratives about Mexicans, Mexican-American history, and identity. The data include a YouTube video by the artist "Jae-P," who was born in Los Angeles to

[1] I am extremely grateful for the input and suggestions of a number of readers, particularly Matt Garley, Karl Swinehart, and Unn Røyneland. The shortcomings are entirely my own.

[2] Upon winning the presidency, Trump immediately had all Spanish language content from the White House website removed (Bierman 2017).

Mexican immigrant parents, and the comments (N=453) posted by viewers. The analysis looks at how YouTube commenters signal stances through code choice, as well as through discursive, and orthographic means. In addition, it explores how YouTubers draw on their bilingual and multistylistic repertoires to express discursive alignments/distance within and across ethnolinguistic boundaries.

This chapter approaches YouTube as a "potential site of cosmopolitan cultural citizenship – a space in which individuals can represent their identities and perspectives, engage with the self-representations of others, and encounter cultural difference" (Burgess and Green 2009: 77). YouTube offers both content creators and audiences the chance to participate in the "mundane but engaging activities that create spaces for engagement and community-formation" (Uricchio, 2004: 148, cited in Burgess and Green, 2009: 75). Through audience practices such as quoting, favoriting, commenting, and sharing, viewers can evaluate, discuss, and curate the content in ways that are personally meaningful to them (Burgess and Green, 2009: 76). Moreover, digital spaces such as YouTube offer Diasporic populations such as Mexicans and Mexican-Americans a way to engage politically with the nation of origin (Sharma 2014; Swinehart, this volume). The current chapter examines the practice of commenting on YouTube video content in order to examine how audience members construct narratives about who they are and their relationship to the society in which they live.

Background

The oldest evidence of humankind in the geographical U.S. dating back to 35,000 BC was found in the U.S. state of Texas (Chávez 2001: 17). These early inhabitants and their descendants lived in the region continuously until the mid-twelfth century CE when they began migrating south and settled in what is now Mexico and Central America, giving rise to the Aztec culture (Anzaldúa 1999). *Aztlán*, the Nahuatl word for the home of the Aztec people was the historical name for this region which encompasses what is now the American southwest (Chávez 1984; Gonzalez 2001; Muñoz 1989). Sixteenth-century Spanish colonization brought renewed settlement to the region, this time by Spaniards, Indians (Indigenous people), and Mexicanos (people of mixed Spanish and Indian heritage). In 1821, Mexico achieved independence from Spain whereupon these territories became part of the newly formed *Imperio de Mexico*. Two centuries later, following the Mexican–American War of 1846–1848, large numbers of Mexican nationals became de facto inhabitants of the U.S.A. when 2.1 million square km of territory (encompassing most modern-day states of Arizona, California, Colorado, New Mexico, Nevada, Texas, and Utah) was transferred from Mexican to U.S. sovereignty upon the signing of the Treaty of

Guadalupe-Hidalgo (Moll and Ruiz 2008: 364). The Mexicano and Indian landowners living on the U.S. side of the new border were massacred, harassed, and lynched by jealous neighbors, causing many to abandon their ranches and flee to Mexico (Chávez 1984). Thus, the ancestors of many Mexican-Americans have ties to the American southwest dating back at least as far back as the Spanish Colonial Period (1519–1821). The border between the U.S.A. and Mexico has been a continually contentious space and tensions have been exacerbated in the twentieth century as Mexico has become increasingly impoverished relative to the U.S.A., leading to mass migrations to *El Norte* (the North). As of the 2014 U.S. Census, people of Mexican origin constitute the largest single group of Latin Americans with 35 million currently living within U.S. borders. Latinos make up 17 percent of the U.S. population, of whom 64 percent are of Mexican origin.

The growing numbers of Mexican migrants in the U.S.A. have triggered what Chavez (2008) refers to as the Latino Threat Narrative as – "a set of culturally entrenched discourses that construct U.S. Latinos as linguistically and culturally dangerous" (cited in Carter 2014: 210; cf. Mendoza-Denton 1999; Rodriguez 1983). This narrative frames Spanish-speaking immigrants as unable or unwilling to learn English, reluctant to integrate into larger society, and more insidiously, as conspiring to re-conquer the southwestern U.S.[3] A similarly prejudiced frame positions Spanish speakers and the Spanish language as disrupting the security of monolingual white public space (Hill 2009). Attacks on Spanish through political movements like English First and numerous "official" English campaigns, objections to the public use of Spanish, and the rejection of Spanish as a language that merits proper idiomatic translation in official signage are ubiquitous facts of life in the U.S.A. (Hill 2009: 122–123). The psychological effects of internalizing impoverished conceptions about one's language have been dubbed "linguistic terrorism" (Anzaldúa 1999: 58), causing Spanish speakers to fear using their language in public places and abandonment of Spanish among some immigrants. Adopting some of the same rhetoric and slang as the Chicano Rights Movement of the 1960s (see footnote 6), Mexican-American rap artists' choice to rap in Spanish can be framed as a counter-narrative, proclaiming the rights of Mexican-Americans to exist and practice their language and culture within the geographical and cultural boundaries of white hegemonic "American" culture.[4]

[3] The most recent U.S. Census data show that 74 percent of Spanish speakers in the U.S.A. report being able to speak English "well" or "very well" (Ryan 2013) (www.census.gov/prod/2013pubs/acs-22.pdf).

[4] Ownership of the term "American" is hotly disputed by the inhabitants of countries in the Americas outside of the U.S.A. Citizens of the U.S.A. tend to use this term exclusively to refer to themselves, whereas citizens of Mexico, Colombia, Argentina, Brazil, etc. also claim this identity and resent the fact that U.S. residents do not recognize them as fellow "Americans" as well (Martinez-Carter 2013).

Mexican-American rap emerged in the 1990s with groups such as Cypress Hill and Kid Frost in what Androutsopoulos and Scholz (2003) refer to as the transculturation process or the spread of hip hop from African American youth to other groups within national borders and beyond. At the time, most well-known Mexican-American rappers performed in English and tried to conform to the linguistic patterns of African American youth and Hip Hop Nation Language or HHNL (Alim 2004). However, in the early 2000s, in response to their growing popularity, a number of bilingual Mexican-American rappers were signed to the Spanish language music division of the Univision television network. Artists like Kinto Sol, Akwid, and Jae-P rapped in Spanish over beats infused with the sounds of older popular Mexican music styles such as *banda, cumbia*, and *norteño*. In 2008, the rapper Jae-P was a finalist in the Latin Music Awards in the Latin rap/hip-hop album category. He has a large following on Facebook and YouTube and has continued to rap and produce video content on social media in the intervening years.[5] One striking aspect of his work is that he chooses to rap almost exclusively in Spanish despite his own bilingual proficiency and that of many, if not most, of his fans in the U.S.A. His Facebook page and the comments of people responding to his video are in Spanish, as are a majority of the YouTube comments analyzed here.

Jae-P's song, "Ni de aquí ni de allá" (not from here [the USA], nor from there [Mexico]) references a common experience among Mexican migrants and Mexican-Americans who feel rejected in their parents' country of origin and in the country where they were born or were brought to as young children (Anzaldúa 1999; Franquiz and Salazar-Jeréz 2013; Carris 2011). The title of the song expresses the ambivalence that many such young people have both towards the homeland and the adoptive country, the feeling that they are not entirely at home in either culture, and the struggle they face to define their identities as a result. Writing about Mexican-American youth, Zentella (2009: 332) notes, "In effect, they are neither real Americans nor real members of their ancestral culture."

Performed entirely in Spanish, the video is set against a backdrop of visual references to Mexican-American life in California – small, one-story dwellings, low-rider cars, backyard parties, and musical references from *banda* melodies accompanied by traditional instruments like the trumpet and the

[5] At the time the video and comments were downloaded in 2012 at the following link, https://youtu.be/Sfu5MVKffR0, there were 453 comments and the video had been viewed just under 1.9 million times. According to *Billboard* magazine, Jae-P's debut album, *Ni de Aqui Ni de Allá* (Neither from Here Nor There) from 2003 sold more than 140,000 units (www.billboard.com/artist/304030/jae-p/biography). Currently, as of February 2017, his Facebook page has just over 26K likes and the video of his new song which is posted on his Facebook page, Broken Wingz, garnered 1.3 million views.

accordion.[6] The content of the song hinges on a few common themes: (1) a yearning to belong, (2) Mexican-Americans/Latinos as an up-and-coming social force, and (3) pride in Mexican/Indigenous/Latino identities ("raza" and "brown pride"). The lyrics highlight the struggles of Jae-P and people like him to gain acceptance in the U.S.A., lamenting the fact that despite learning English and working hard, to the gringos, he'll always be a "wetback" and a "fucking joke" (*para el gringo soy un wetback, un pinche chiste*). Neither his face nor his skin are acceptable forms of identity in the U.S.A. (*ni cara ni mi piel fue la forma aceptada MADE IN THE USA*). The rallying cry "brown pride" which appears in numerous comments in the corpus, signifies feelings of otherness and being "out of place" or "ni de allá" (Anzaldúa 1999; Fránquiz and Salazar-Jeréz 2013; Carris 2011; Muñoz 1989). Referencing the instrumental motivations of his parents who brought him to the U.S.A. as a child, Jae-P raps that this is where the money is (*aqui esta la lana ...*) and as his grandmother used to say, first you just have to "suck it up" (*primero hay que tragar*). Despite his allegiance to Mexico and desire to return there (*Mexico yo te quiero y me quiero regresar*), he doesn't feel accepted there either (*Pero tu gente no me entiende y jamás me acceptará*). Ultimately, there is hope as Jae-P raps that despite his two accents, he will prevail (*Con dos acentos en la lengua llegaré a triunfar*), proclaiming that the next generation will reap the benefits of his hard work when he says that one day, his child will be the president of the U.S.A. (*Mi hijo será presidente de este pinche país*).

Language is specifically thematized in the song as Jae-P recounts how he learned English (*apprendí hablar inglés*), but despite his two accents (*dos accentos en la lengua*) gets dismissed as linguistically incompetent in Spanish by a dismissive female voice, "this guys doesn't know how to talk" (*este güey no sabe hablar*) (cf. Zentella 2007 on *pochos*). He exhorts his listeners to learn English because this land will be "ours" again someday (Porque esta tierra será *nuestra* otra vez).[7] The song, its metalinguistic observations about language and its uptake by viewers on YouTube showcase current political debates surrounding the status of Spanish and Latinas/os in the USA. Emergent in the dialog between the song and the comments is a collective assertion of the rights of Spanish speakers to use their language in "white public space" (Hill 2009) and the contestation of received histories and discourses about what types of bodies are licensed to be in the U.S.A.

[6] As rap and pop music gained popularity in the early 2000s, *banda* music styles were fused with rhymes and rap beats among young Mexican-American rappers like Jae-P.

[7] Gloria Anzaldúa (1999: 32) writes that in every Chicano and Mexican lives the myth of the prized lost territory and the desire to reclaim it through a "silent invasion."

Data

The data for this chapter consist of 453 comments collected on YouTube in 2012 following the "explicit" version of the rap song posted in 2007 by BIGBEARURDADDY. All of the comments were manually copied and pasted in a word document and then the comments, usernames, and date were extracted and entered into an excel spreadsheet and coded for different types of orthographic patterns (e.g. letter repetition, non-standard punctuation, hybrid/non-standard orthography), type of comment (reply to another post, response to video), and theme (ethnic pride, nationalism, etc.).

About two-thirds of the comments appear to be in Spanish, although it was often difficult to assign a language at the sentence or word level. What is the "matrix" language when an English lexeme sits adjacent to a Spanish lexeme, marked as a plural with an orthographic form from hip-hop culture (<z>)? (e.g. <FUK ALL SEROTEz> "fuck all Salvadorians"). In other instances, the interpretation of a Spanish lexeme may rely on the English pronunciation of a grapheme (e.g. syllabic use of the grapheme <s> as in <sto> for *esto*). Thus, trying to definitively determine the language or code of a given sentence or word forces us to question the boundedness of English and Spanish as distinct languages and adopt a more fluid conception of linguistic repertoires as sets of resources that may come from disparate sources (Agha 2008; García 2009). Agha (2008) challenges the grammar-centric idea that each code can be identified as having discrete boundaries. Moving away from such a perspective to an interpersonal one, he argues, allows us to observe how the social-indexical values of speech-forms are reevaluated through the reflexive activities of speakers under conditions of linguistic and cultural contact. Specifically, we can see how changes in the "social types" stereotypically indexed by speech are experienced and negotiated by speakers as aspects of their identities (Agha 2008: 254–255).

In addition to a repertoire that blends Spanish and English linguistic resources, the comments also contain elements of Mexican Spanish and Chicano "Caló" slang, other varieties of Spanish (e.g. Salvadorian, Guatemalan, Castilian, and Argentine), Chicano English (Fought 2003; Galindo 1995; Santa Ana 1993), Hip Hop Nation Language (HHNL) (Alim 2004), and American English (cf. Anzaldúa 1999). Mexican-American hip-hop culture is represented at the lexical level with range of slang expressions such as *vato* and *pura neta* which seem to have been recycled from Caló or slang of the Pachuco or Mexican migrant culture (Ramirez 2006, Castro 2000).[8] Adopting Agha's perspective allows us

[8] Selected Mexican-American slang in the YouTube comments corpus
büey (other variants include güey, guey we, wei, and wey) – dude (cf. Bucholtz 2009)
carnal – (noun) friend, "homie," "brother"

to see how language users draw on complex repertoires that contain bits and chunks from more than one language variety and writing system. The choice to use one variant over another can be interpreted as indexing social types, which can tell us about how young people align or disaslign with various possible identities, discourses, and stances (e.g. Mexican, American, Latina/o, indigenous, brown, white/güero, etc.).

The gender identities of participants are difficult to determine conclusively in what Iorio (2009) calls "demographically lean" online sites such as YouTube. However, judging from ubiquity of male-gendered Spanish usernames (e.g. <JAVIER. . .>) and from morphological and other forms of male gender marking within the comments (e.g. <ESE LOKITO> "crazy gang banger"), the sample appears to be dominated by male users, which aligns more broadly with male-dominated participation in hip hop (Cutler 2014). The age of the contributors is also difficult to verify, since users do not always post personal information on their own pages; however, based on the tiny photos posted by some users and the kinds of activities they reference in the comments (listening to rap music, orienting to "norteño" or "sureño" gangs, playing video games), most appear to be young people in their teenage years or early twenties.

Theoretical Overview

The linguistic and orthographic hybridity of the data point us to analytical tools such as Bakhtinian heteroglossia, polyphony, and more recent concepts such as polylanguaging (Jørgensen et al. 2011). Heteroglossia entails the coexistence of and often tension between different types of speech within an utterance, whereas the polyphony relates to the assignment of multiple values (meanings) to a written sign or the multiplicity of sounds associated with a symbol or character belonging to the writing system of a spoken language (Coe 1999). As Deumert (2014a: 109) writes, adopting a Bakhtinian perspective allows us to get beyond seeing language not only as a "social fact characterized by conventions and norms," but also as a "source of creativity and art and which produces utterances that are unpredictable and multi-voiced." In contrast to analyzing the data as simply a form of code switching which relies on an

cholo/a – (noun) Chicano gang member
gringo – (noun) White (European-American) (pejorative)
güero – (adj.) light-skinned, fair; (noun) (alternatively guero or wuero)
pendejo – (adj. or noun) "stupid," "dumbass"
pinche – (adj.) fucking
pocho – (noun) derogatory term for Americanized Mexicans who don't speak Spanish.
raza – (noun) lit. "race"; term referring to one's own people
rola – (noun) "track"/"song"
ruca – (noun) "homegirl"; "girlfriend" (alternatively ruka, rruka)

a priori view of languages as discrete, identifiable entities, frameworks like polylanguaging (Jørgensen et al. 2011) and translanguaging (García 2009) assume no such fixed boundaries. Rather, "[l]anguage users employ whatever linguistic features are at their disposal to achieve their communicative aims as best they can, regardless of how well they know the involved languages" (Jørgensen et al. 2011: 34). Some of the data illustrate this kind of unconscious deployment of linguistic resources; yet in other instances users appear to be making deliberate choices in their written utterances that reveal an understanding of how to capitalize on the interplay between two or more systems and associated registers as a way to index "social types" which they use to negotiate aspects of their identities (Agha 2008: 254). Examples of this type also have the potential to be heteroglossic or polyphonous (Bakhtin 1981; 1984). Thus, multilingual YouTubers, empowered by the creative freedom afforded to them by the looser strictures of online writing (Garley 2014), deploy their repertoires in ways that tell us something about their understanding of how languages are socioculturally associated with values, meanings, and speakers (Jørgensen et al. 2011).

Methodology

Following Androutsopoulos and Tereick (2016), this chapter examines YouTube comments as a resource for discourse participation and examines the attitudes users express towards the reference video and/or their contribution to the ongoing discourse. It adopts a mixed method research design combining orthographic analysis (Darics 2013; Iorio 2009; Sebba 2007; Shaw 2008; Soffer 2010) and Computer-Mediated Discourse Analysis (CMDA) (Androutsopoulos and Beißwenger 2008) in order to analyze the writing practices and discursive means through which Mexican-American youth resist hegemonic English and white culture and the ways in which they themselves are constructed discursively in the U.S. popular imagination.

For the analysis of orthography, the chapter employs tools from studies of orthographic practices, both in CMC and in other forms of less-regulated writing. Sebba (2007: 24) describes orthography as a set of socially and ideologically organized practices that are determined by the kinds of literacy practice for which they are designed. Using and controlling standard language is a marker of power and orthographic choices are associated symbolically and metaphorically with "social, cultural and linguistic identities and hierarchies" (Coupland 1985:155 cited in Jaffe and Walton 2000: 562). Specifically, standard orthography is ideologically associated with middle-class status and educational attainment, whereas non-standard orthography often marks a speaker as having low linguistic and social capital; moreover, written speech is seen as deviant, non-conformist, and an affront against "everything regular and established in society" (Hinrichs and White-Sustaíta 2011: 48).

CMC writing, according to Sebba (2007) exists somewhere between the highly regulated space of academic writing and the completely unregulated spheres like graffiti (Sebba 2007: 44). However, in CMC, non-standard orthography often serves very specific pragmatic functions, including the expression of creativity, personality, affect, emotional involvement, and informality (Danet et al. 1997; Darics 2013; Peuronen 2011). Others point to its role in rendering spoken words (Soffer 2010; Herring 2012; Cho 2010) and in stereotyping and positioning the language it represents vis-à-vis the standard (Jaffe and Walton 2000; Hinrichs and White-Sustaíta 2011). Furthermore, because of its associations with non-conformity, non-standard orthography may also mark an utterance or stance as deviant or rebellious. Lastly, it may play a central role in identity construction and creation such as demarcating group boundaries and showing an oppositional stance with respect to the mainstream (Sebba 2007: 56).

Analysis of YouTube Comments: Resisting Hegemonic Language and Culture

The data are divided into two sections. The first consists of examples illustrating how language choice and stance are strategically deployed to convey resistance to hegemonic English and white American culture within the USA. The second section analyzes how writers express this resistance through creative use of orthography, which they also deploy to challenge the way they are portrayed and to assert pride in their identities.

Language Choice and Counter-Hegemonic Stances

Speaker stance is defined as speakers' positioning with regard to both the content and the form of their utterances (Jaffe 2007). One powerful way to convey a stance of resistance is through language choice, manifesting not only in the preference for one language – in this case, Spanish – but also in discursive resistance towards English and hegemonic American culture.[9] This linguistic resistance is echoed in the empowering discursive stances that YouTubers take in their comments regarding the status of Mexican-Americans in the USA.

[9] Fought (2003: 200–203) notes the symbolic importance of language competence (even if it's partial competence) among Mexican-American youth as a marker of identity. While some feel that being proud of who you are is paramount, others privilege knowledge of Spanish and disparage those who lack the ability to use it.

Responding to the *Ni de aquí ni de allá* YouTube video, the favored status of Spanish within this space emerges in the conversational turn shown in 1 and 2 below when DellM's request for an English translation of the song triggers kika's rebuke that he learn some Spanish instead of expecting bilinguals to bear the entire communicative burden (all names are pseudonyms). The repetition and vari-directional scare quotes around the lexeme <"translate"> marks this kind of labor as something English monolinguals ought to be doing themselves. In effect, yokicamaja's comment demonstrates a role reversal of the two languages wherein Spanish is the dominant, unmarked language and English is the interloper. By insisting that English monolinguals make the effort to learn the lingua franca, she casts the hegemony of English into doubt. This counter-hegemonic challenge is heightened through non-standard forms such as the clipped form <bout> (about), an emphatic expression of national/ethnic pride, <mexicana para toda la vida>, self-proclaimed gang affiliation, <sur 13>, and the HHNL form <da> (the).[10] The polyphony of her utterance indexes multiple personal alignments as well as heteroglossic tensions between Spanish and English.

1. DellM Can someone please translate the song for me please.or tell me a website where i can translate the song
2. kika how bout u learn some spanish and then you can "translate" it yourself mexicana para toda la vida sur 13 all da way!

Expressions of ethnic pride as in 2 align with a preference for Spanish and the use of creative orthography in the corpus. Indeed, comments containing expressions of regional, national or ethnic pride were slightly more likely to be written mostly in Spanish compared with the average across the remainder of the corpus; they were also more likely to contain creative orthography compared with the remainder of the corpus, pointing to the symbolic, counter-hegemonic role that language choice and orthography can play in augmenting the illocutionary force of an utterance (Sebba 2007). Comments expressing ethnic pride also show how many young Mexican-Americans feel about themselves, their relationship to the United States and white Americans. Many comments convey a strong sense of self-worth and pride about their origins in Mexico in exclamations such as <pura raza> (pure race), <100% Mexicano>,

[10] Chicano gang culture in California is organized along semantic North–South oppositions: the "norteños" or northerners vs. the "sureños" or southerners. Mendoza-Denton (2014: 97; c.f. Fought 2003) describes the former as Chicanos who, broadly speaking, align with U.S. Mexican-American culture and English and the latter, as recent immigrants who align more with Mexico, Indigenous identities, and the Spanish language. Sureños use the color blue and employ eponyms containing the number 13 and/or some combination of S, South, Sur or South Side (e.g. SUR 13, South Side 13, X3, 100 Sureño, Sur X3, SS 13). Norteños are known for wearing red and using eponyms with the number 14 (e.g. Norte 14, X4, NS 14, Nor Cal, Puro Norte).

and <brown pride>, an analog to the "black pride" movement, dating back to the Civil Rights era of the 1960 and 1970s which challenged negative images associated with people of color in the U.S.A.

A frequent theme among these comments is the call to reclaim territories formerly belonging to Mexico that are now part of the U.S.A. The Nahuatl term *Aztlán* refers to the ancestral home of the Aztec people (Anzaldúa 1999: 33). It came into widespread use during the 1960s among members of the Chicano student movement (Muñoz 1989: 77) and has since become a rallying cry for people of Mexican descent to reclaim lands seized by the U.S.A. from Mexico in 1848. Currently, invoking the term is part of a practice among young Latinos in the U.S.A. of assigning alternative toponyms to an area as a way to assert personal ownership of an area (cf. Quist 2018).

Assertions of linguistic and cultural pride in the YouTube comments are often pitted against hegemonic (white) American culture which is framed in oppositional ways. Sinaloa picks up on a line from the song about having more kids to take back what is <nuestro> (ours) which he explicitly states does not include gringos, Germans, and the other blonde people (<otros wueros>). By implication, the speaker indexes his disaffiliation with these groups while asserting his non-European, indigenous heritage. The pragmatic force of his utterance is marked by several orthographic variations such as phonemic <k> in <kitarle> and morphemic <k> in <lo k es nuestro> (what is ours), the non-standard spelling of the curse word <chingen> (from *chinguen* "fuck"), and by a sureño gang identifier <puro sur 13> (pure south 13).

3. sinaloa semon tengan mas morriyos para kitarle lo k es nuestro chingen a su madre los gringos y alemanes y oros wueros puro sur 13
   hell yeah, have more kids in order to take back what's our fuck the mothers of the gringos and the Germans and other white people pure south 13.

Calling out to an imagined young male audience with the vocative <wey> in 4, DJ makes pragmatic use of quotations to critique the appropriation of the term, <"americanos">, proclaiming gringos to be the real <wetbacks> (illegal immigrants) because they had to cross an entire ocean to arrive in the U.S.A. The comment is written in a relatively standard register apart from absent diacritics, capitalization, and punctuation and <ke> for *que*. Gringos are recast as hypocrites, racists and fools whereas Mexicans are framed as the real Americans with a territorial claim based on seniority or right of return. Lexical forms like <wey>, <mamones>, <pinches>, <gringos>, <pendejos>, and <chingar> index the writer's Mexican identity and locate his complaint within a geohistorical context.

4. DJ mira wey, se les critica por mamones y racistas wey. estos pinches gringos se creen "americanos" cuando ellos son los wetbacks, cruzaron

todo el pinche atlantico wey, son bien mamones y pendejos. y si hay ke chingarnos a los gringos y menos critica
look dude, one can criticize them for being dumbasses and racists, dude. these fucking gringos think they're "americans" when they are the wet-backs, they crossed the whole fucking atlantic, dude, they're really dumbasses and fools. and yes we have to fuck up the gringos instead of complaining.

These sentiments are echoed in 5 below in vihuela's hybrid Spanish-Nahuatl expression <HONOR AZTLAN>). Anzaldúa (1999) calls Aztlán the "other" imagined Mexico, which connects ancient Indigenous people on both sides of the recently established U.S.A.–Mexico border. This is followed by the subjunctive exhortation <VIVA MEXICO> (long live Mexico). Building on these nationalist sentiments, vihuela further constructs a Mexican origin audience with collective first person plural pronouns such as <nuestra> (our) and verb forms such as <recuperamos> (we'll recover). With plentiful swagger, vihuela represents Mexicans and Mexican-Americans as agentive actors in a historically justified movement to reestablish *Aztlán*, and to even extend its boundaries beyond the 48th parallel up to the 49th in Canada.

5. vihuela AZTLAN HONOR VIVA MEXICO CABRONES EN TODO CANADA Y E. U. recuparamos nustra tierra que nos quitaron esos putos les hicimos una invasion masiva y no[s] nadamas esos estados todo estados unidos y llegamos hasta canada puro aztlan honor.......................
HONOR TO AZTLAN LONG LIVE MEXICO MOTHERFUCKERS IN ALL OF CANADA AND U.S. we'll recover the land that these fuckers took from us we made a massive invasion and swim across these states the entire united states and make it all the way to canada. pure aztlan honor.

In sum, the examples in this section illustrate how language choice and discursive assertions of resistance towards hegemonic English, received representations of Mexican-Americans, and interpretations of historical events collude to create an empowered stance (cf. Mendoza-Denton 1999). These comments construct a collective sense of solidarity and common purpose with other Mexican-origin youth in the U.S.A. The next section turns to a discussion of orthographic creativity – in particular, the ways in which users deploy their multilingual repertoires in their online writing to add layers of meaning to their utterances. The ubiquity of CMC forms points up the important symbolic role that creative and non-standard forms of writing take on in online spaces like YouTube and their role in adding affect and subtlety to a written utterance.

Orthographic Creativity

Virtually all the comments in the corpus depart from standard written norms in their tendency towards lack of punctuation and capitalization, in line with other electronic forms of so-called "fingered speech" (McWhorter 2013). Moving beyond these ingrained CMC forms, around half of the comments also contain CMC conventions such as serial vowels, consonants and punctuation as well as mixed use of capitalization, bilingual forms, and rebus spellings. A number of the conventions found in the corpus are used by Spanish speakers across the Spanish-speaking world. These include <k> for the morpheme *que* (that/which/what) or the phoneme /k/, using the grapheme <d> in place of the homophonous prepositional morpheme *de* (of) or <t> for the clitic pronoun *te* (you, direct object). The Spanish conjunction *porque* (because) and the interrogative *por qué* (why) are often written <x q>, where <x> stands for *por* and <q> stands for *que* (<x k> is another variant). Other, more complex shorthand forms rely on bilingual English-Spanish competence in order to be interpretable, although arguably some may have already become conventions in their own right. One such pattern relies on the English pronunciation of the grapheme <s> (pronounced /ɛs/) substituting it for the syllable *es* in Spanish words. (The Spanish pronunciation of the grapheme <s> is bisyllabic, i.e. /ese/). In 6, the author is telling off other commentators who say they don't like Jae-P or the song in an utterance that contains Spanish and English words rendered in a hybrid resistance orthography. Her use of the grapheme <s> in place of the syllable /ɛs/ lends the utterance a clipped, menacing tone, perhaps analogous to stopped fricatives in English (*dese* and *dose* for *these* and *those*) (cf. Deumert's discussion of <da>, 2014a: 108). The author augments this toughness through a collection of non-standard spellings including initial geminate <r> in <rruka> (perhaps a case of prosodic writing for emphasis), morphemic <k> and <c>, phonemic <k>, <b> for /v/, <i> for the conjunction *y* (and), and colorful curse words (*guanga, garrapstrosa*). This example also contains a dialectal form in which the grapheme <c> is used for the Spanish clitic pronoun *se* in the first line (<c skucha>) which works because of the homophony between them in seseo varieties such as Mexican Spanish.

6. Chica1 se ke soy rruka y k c 🅂kucha mal… pero como me kaga el puto palo jente mamona ojetes de mierda ke dicen k no les gusta esta musica y k they hate cholos y cuanta mamada. … pero aki tienen ke 🅂tar los hijos de su puta guanga garrapastrosa madre 🅂kuchando 🅂to! kien putas los manda?? xq no ban i chingan su madre asta k se le ponche una llanta al tren y a su puta madre!!!
   I know that I am a gang girl and that it's hard to hear. … but I can't stand these dumbass pieces of shit who say that they don't like this music and that they hate cholos and what bullshit. . .but they have to come over here,

> *sons of their slutty dirty mother, and listen to this! who the fuck asked them?? Why don't they go and fuck their mothers until they puncture a tire on the train and fuck off!!!*

A similar pattern is found in morphemic uses of <k>. Besides the phonemic use of <k> (e.g. <aki> instead of *aqui*), the grapheme <k> can also stand in place of the complementizer or prepositional morpheme *que* (that, which). Unlike the grapheme <k> which is pronounced /ka/ in Spanish, the English pronunciation of <k> is nearly homophonous with the Spanish pronunciation of *que* (/ke/), thus presupposing a bilingual reader. Perhaps one reason for using <k> in place of *que* is to save time by shaving down the number of letters from three to one, yet the grapheme <k> has functions beyond simply reducing the number of keystrokes needed to type out a word.

Schieffelin and Doucet (1994) and Sebba (2003) note the cultural symbolism of using <k> in Romance languages such as French and Spanish where it is lacking. Debates in the 1980s about whether to employ <k> in written Haitian Creole centered on its "Anglo Saxon" feel and the rejection of its French linguistic and cultural origins that its adoption would entail. Sebba (2003) notes that in Spain, <k> has become a marker of anti-establishment groups or of those who sympathize with such activities (cf. the *okupas* squatter movement in Spain, Michael Newman, personal communication). Thus, in Spanish and other Romance languages, <k> has become enregistered as a marker of sub-cultural non-conformity through the visible rejection of standard orthography. This is very likely its function in the YouTube commentaries discussed here, even in places where it appears to serve a short-hand function. For example, in 7, <k> co-occurs in an expressed stance of defiance about staying in the U.S.A., lending pragmatic power to the utterance as a rejection of standard orthography and dominant social discourses about the residency rights of immigrants.

> 7. DD aqui donde me gusta y aqui me voy a kedar!!!!!!!!!!!
> *Here where I like (it) and here I'm going to stay!!!!!!!!!!!*

Like, <k> and <s>, the grapheme <z> is also a vessel for social meaning. Androutsopoulos (2000) has noted its subcultural associations for German punk fans, and Garley (this volume) observes its symbolic value for German hip-hop forum participants for signaling a hip-hop affiliation. In 8, the grapheme <z> is a plural marker in the HHNL expression *haterz* (people who criticize and denigrate others), positioning the author, RP, as an insider who is knowledgeable of HHNL lexis as well as the written norms of HHNL. Other aspects of the author's identity are signaled in his multilingual polyvocal repertoire (English, Spanish, Caló, HHNL) and self-locating geographical identifiers that point to his first-generation immigrant status with roots in Mexico and California. The renaming of places (e.g. California as <califas>) is a common strategy among young people for signaling and contesting ownership to a place (Paunonen et al. 2009, cited in Quist 2018). According to Castro (2000), *califas* is an affectionate and proprietary in-group term for California that has been in use since at least 1940 among Mexican-American youth.

8. RP born in guanajuato raised in califas fuck yeah cabrones fuck haterz

Serial vowels and consonants function pragmatically and iconically to convey enthusiasm. In 9, the Mexican Spanish expression <chida> (cool) contains 54 <i>'s which mimics a drawn-out exclamation of delight and personal identification the author feels with the content of the song. The author further cements his connection to the lyrics and to other Mexican-Americans by opting to use Chicano slang terms such as *chida* (cool), *la rola* (song), and *compas* (friends).

9. Jason G esta chiiiiiiiiiiiiiiiiiiiiiiiiiiiiiiiiiiiiiiiiiiiiiiiiiiiiiida la rolla compas)
this is a cooooooooooooooooooooooool song dudes

The non-standard use of capitalization also has subcultural significance. For instance, in 10, the mixture of upper and lower case letters seems to index a countercultural subjectivity and a stance of resistance towards normative patterns of writing, and perhaps by extension, conventional received forms of knowledge about the world.

10. B Martinnnes esTA ChIdO la rOLa)
this is a cool song

If orthographic practices were to be ordered on a scale of consciousness, conventional CMC forms like <u> for "you" or the number <4> in place of the preposition "for" would be at the lower end since they eventually become part of unreflexive, unconscious practice. Social meaning is more likely to be located in the conscious, deliberate, and pragmatically complex choices that writers make in their CMC utterances. In 11, PedroG uses Anglicized spelling to phonetically render a Mexican Spanish curse on white Americans, <pinches gringos> (fucking gringos). According to UrbanDictionary.com, the term *pinche gringo* is used "when arrogant white people piss off a Mexican or Mexican-American person."
(www.urbandictionary.com/define.php?term=Pinche%20Gringo)

11. PedroG pink chess gring gous
fucking gringos

The polyphonous graphemic representation in the example reflects the author's knowledge of English spelling, while simultaneously voicing a generalized sentiment about white Americans among many people of Mexican heritage. It illustrates how Spanish speakers monitor white ways of speaking and mock white pronunciation of Spanish as a way to reclaim power and disrupt the dominant sociolinguistic order (Carris 2011: 476). Combining the English morphemes <pink> and <chess> for *pinches* (fucking) signals how we "hear" the vowels by inscribing auditory information into a written utterance, providing an "interpretative framework signaling how the verbal message should be understood by the reader" (Darics 2013: 144). The author renders the tense high vowels /i/ and /e/ of Spanish as the lower, lax English vowels, /I/ and /ɛ/ by choosing English lexical items to represent the Spanish syllables. Similarly, the diphthongal <ou> in <gring gous> mimics the diphthongal vowel pattern found in American English, contrasting with the monophthongal /o/ of Spanish.[11]

This example illustrates how the surface level interpretation of an utterance (a curse on gringos) acquires additional layers of meaning through the polyphony of the written utterance which is at once both Spanish and English and a heteroglossic rendition of a Mexican voicing a gringo speaking Spanish (Bakhtin 1981; 1984). As Deumert (2014a: 109) writes, rather than arbitrary mixtures of linguistic forms, such "highly crafted utterances. . .combine forms for maximum effect" allowing writers to "articulate different voices" and create "artful tensions and semantic conflicts" which draw from the writer's entire repertoire.

The examples in this section illustrate how YouTube commenters draw on their multilingual and multistylistic repertoires and orthographic competencies to express resistance towards standard written norms, standard language ideologies, and hegemonic American culture. The final section turns to a discussion of the implications of this data in terms of prior and future work on creative orthography and counter-hegemonic discourse in YouTube comments and other CMC spaces.

Discussion/Conclusion

This chapter has focused on some of the hybrid, multi-voiced discursive and orthographic practices that bilingual Mexican-American youth use to signal their alignments, stances, and identities on YouTube. Through language choice and discursive references to Mexico's pre-1848 borders, young Mexican-Americans stake out stances of resistance towards hegemonic English and express nationalist and anti-colonial sentiments. Posting comments in Spanish is an act of

[11] Getting Americans to utter the expression "pinches gringos" is the subject of a YouTube video in which unwitting tourists in Mexico are asked to name the color and object in a series of hand-drawn pictures, the first of which is "pink cheese" and the second, "green ghost" (www.youtube .com/watch?v=PVU6o9tGUIw).

counter-hegemonic resistance and a challenge to the dominance and hegemonic status of English as the language of power, education, and the internet. Commenting in Spanish (or rapping in Spanish) can also be interpreted as a way to "keep it real" in the hip-hop sense by opting to express oneself in a socially marked and stigmatized minority language (in the U.S.A.), but one that for young Latinos also indexes something essential and elemental about their identities (Androutsopoulos and Scholz 2003; Cutler 2014; Rickford & Rickford 2000). The comments shown here illustrate how Latino youth contest their marginalized status not only by choosing to express themselves in Spanish, but also through the emphatic assertion of ethnic and local and translocal identities (e.g. Michoacano, Guanajuato, Califas, Azteca, and/or citizens of *Aztlán*). Moreover, embracing the subaltern status of Spanish connects YouTubers to the larger Mexican diaspora and to other Spanish-speaking communities. Despite the dominance of Spanish in the corpus, many YouTubers also signal their multilingual competence by deftly blending elements of English orthography, HHNL lexis, and Chicano slang in their posts.

At the level of discourse, we have seen how Mexican-American youth discursively align with other Latinos and Spanish-speaking immigrant communities and distance themselves from *gringos*. Constructing who is defined as part of the in-group helps to forge a discursive bond between young people of Mexican origin and the broader Spanish-speaking diaspora living in the U.S.A. and abroad. These alignments lend rhetorical clarity to alternative versions of history such as the framing of white Americans as the real "wetbacks" and Mexicans as the real "Americans."

As a number of previous studies have observed (Deumert 2014a; Sebba 2007), writing in CMC draws on both oral and written expression, at times attempting to "create the experience of spoken words" (Soffer 2010: 313, cited in Darics 2013: 134), and in other moments, reflecting displays of creativity. Commenters on YouTube make quite elaborate use of the available system of symbols in order to add the flavor and tone to their utterances that is found in oral expression. Aspects of body-to-body communication (Deumert 2014a) such as facial gestures, intonation, pitch, volume, playfulness, and irony get conveyed through writing practices such as serial punctuation, hybrid orthography, mixed upper case and lower case writing, rebus spellings, and affective markers. These practices are somewhat comparable to stylization in spoken language, allowing authors to embellish their utterances with semiotic clues as to the identity or stance of the author, and/or the illocutionary force of an utterance.

YouTube has for some time provided a space where written norms can be played with and contested, calling into question the relative status of dominant and marginalized languages (Jones and Schieffelin 2009; Peuronen 2011; Shaw 2008). The data show how bilingual Latino youth contest standard written norms in their use of non-standard orthography and language mixing, thereby challenging the hegemony of standard English as well as Spanish, the boundaries between the languages, and the power of those who enforce them.

In a more overarching sense, the data exemplify how YouTube audience practices like commenting constitute a form of local activism in the context of political struggles among Latinos to embrace Spanish and raise critical consciousness about "structural and political impediments to unity and equality" (Zentella 2007: 36). For multilingual, immigrant youth in particular, YouTube is a place where native language rights and other kinds of privileges are asserted, such as the right to stay in the U.S.A., to live in territories that were once part of Mexico, and to express alternative histories of the U.S.A. Using one's full linguistic repertoires and drawing on contrasting graphemic norms may be done for efficiency's sake, but it also works to convey multiple stances, alignments, and identities (Canagarajah 2004; Jaffe 2007). Choosing to rap or post comments in Spanish while challenging the hegemony of English, flouting standard written norms, and transgressing language boundaries is a defiant act of identity for young bilingual Latino youth that signals a re-fashioning of their identities and language practices as hybrid and transnational (Zentella 2007: 36).

8 Virtually Norwegian

Negotiating Language and Identity on YouTube

Unn Røyneland

Introduction

Early January 2017 the city of Oslo suffered heavily from pollution due to a combination of extensive traffic and cold weather. To resolve this problem, the city commissioner for environment and transport, Lan Marie Nguyen Berg, issued a ban on driving diesel cars certain days. The same day a right-wing politician, who was very upset by the ban, posted a message on her Facebook wall where she attacked Nguyen Berg in extremely offensive language. She called Nguyen Berg a Vietnamese bitch, and told her to go back to Vietnam or North Korea where communists like her belong (Dagsavisen January 17, 2017). The message was quickly picked up by the media, where it provoked resentment and launched a massive debate. The right-wing politician defended herself by saying that this was a private message posted on her Facebook wall, and that this kind of language use is quite common in her dialect. Both excuses were heavily criticized and dismissed in the following debate. As a politician, you are a public figure and hence cannot expect that a post on your Facebook wall will not be spread and taken up by the media. The idea that this kind of language use has anything to do with dialect was also rejected; it is simply degrading and racist language. Still, it is interesting that the politician – in an attempt to defend herself – used both arguments. It illustrates how people tend to think about Facebook as a private site – although they have hundreds of "friends" – and also that the use of dialect is quite common in private writing in Norway. In a comment on the attack from the right-wing politician, Nguyen Berg said that what she found most offensive and difficult to deal with was the attack on her national identity. Her father came from Vietnam as a refugee to Norway back in the 1960s, but she herself is born and raised in Norway and has no other nationality.

Sadly, this kind of trolling and bullying of people with immigrant backgrounds, and also challenging of their identity as Norwegian, are not at all a rarity; in fact, it is often found in the YouTube commentaries posted in response to the rap videos of several of the Hip Hop artists of mixed backgrounds that I have been following over the last decade. In this chapter, I will discuss identity negotiation, metalinguistic commentary, and language policing online, looking at a rap video and YouTube commentary where language, place, and belonging are thematized. Drawing on Bucholtz and Hall's (2004; 2005) work on identity negotiation and Michael Bakhtin's (1981) concept of heteroglossia, I argue that hybrid identities are particularly difficult to negotiate, and are often rejected and policed along with the mixed linguistic practices with which they tend to be associated. Essentialist ideas of identity and belonging as well as purist language ideologies seem to be quite widespread among young people online. Mixed language use gets policed, and language correctness is often used as an argument for who is or is not considered to be Norwegian.

Background

Over the last decades, Norwegian society, like many others in Europe, has changed substantially as a result of increased globalization, mobility, and labor- and refugee-driven immigration. Today, approximately 17 percent of the national population of 5.2 million has either migrated to Norway or is born in Norway to foreign-born parents (Statistics Norway 2017). Until the 1960s Norway was a relatively homogeneous society with little immigration. Migration patterns were characterized by emigration rather than immigration, but this changed in the mid 1960s partly as a consequence of the country's economic upturn (Vassenden 2012: 7). Today, as many as one-third of the population in the capital, Oslo, have an immigrant background. The largest immigrant groups come from other European countries, particularly Poland, Lithuania, and Sweden, but immigration to Norway has its origin from a large number of countries. The first group who came as labor immigrants in the 1960s originates from Pakistan and hence the largest group of Norwegian-born with foreign born parents has a Pakistani background. The largest refugee groups originate from the Balkans, Somalia, Iraq, Syria, Vietnam, and Eritrea.

Linguistic diversity in Norway

Although immigration to Norway is relatively recent, Norway has always been linguistically diverse, as there are several national minority languages, two written standards of Norwegian (*Bokmål* and *Nynorsk*)[1] and substantial dialect diversity. In 1993, Norway ratified the European Charter for Regional or

[1] Bokmål is historically a Norwegianized variety of Danish, whereas Nynorsk was created on the basis of Norwegian dialects during the mid-nineteenth century (Haugen 1966; Jahr 2014; Røyneland 2016). Since a parliamentary resolution in 1885, the two standards have coexisted as legally equal written representations of Norwegian. Nynorsk has had a minority status since

Minority Languages for four languages: *Sami* and *Kven* as "regional or minority languages" and *Norwegian Romani* and *Romanes* as "non-territorial languages" (Lane 2011; Wiedner 2016). In addition, Norwegian sign language is acknowledged as a fully-fledged language with fundamental values. Dialects in Norway differ considerably (at all linguistic levels) between regions; unlike most other European countries, dialects are used within all social domains, formal as well as informal, and diglossia is rare (Nesse 2015; Røyneland 2009; Sandøy 2011). Norwegians are, on the contrary, expected to keep their dialect – even after many years living away from their place of origin. With increasing inter- and intra-regional migration, this means that communication between Norwegians very often is "polylectal" (Røyneland 2017).[2] In addition, it has become increasingly normal to use dialect in writing on social media, particularly on Facebook and YouTube, and in text messaging (e.g. Rotevatn 2014).

Until a few decades ago, over 95 percent of Norway's population spoke Norwegian as their first language (Engen and Kulbrandstad 2004). With increasing globalization and migration, however, this has changed dramatically. The linguistic situation in Norway is marked by increasing complexity with a large number of immigrant languages adding to the already existing diversity, and English becoming a second language to most young Norwegians (Rindal 2015). There is no public registration of exactly how many different languages are spoken in Norway, but numbers from *The Norwegian Directorate for Education and Training* (UDIR) suggest that between 150 and 200 languages are spoken among pupils in Norwegian schools (Wilhelmsen et al. 2013).

In recent years, new linguistic practices or styles have emerged in multilingual and multiethnic urban environments across Europe, also in Norway, particularly in the capital, Oslo, where a high proportion of the inhabitants have immigrant background (e.g. Opsahl 2009; Svendsen and Røyneland 2008). These heteroglossic linguistic practices are characterized by the inclusion of linguistic features from many different varieties, used by people with several ethnic backgrounds, either to express their minority status or as a reaction to that status, aiming to upgrade it, or both (e.g. Clyne 2000; Eckert 2008b; Quist 2008; Svendsen and Røyneland 2008). The gradual enregisterment (Agha 2005) of this speech style is still an ongoing process, in which the media, artists, the primary users, and we as researchers, all participate. In the media, it is commonly referred to as "Kebab-Norwegian" and often framed in negative

the very beginning in terms of number of users (approx. 13 percent), power and prestige (Røyneland 2016).

[2] In 1878, the Norwegian Parliament decided that no particular spoken standard should be taught in elementary and secondary schools. This principle is still valid today and has no doubt been essential for the continued use of local dialects in Norway and for the contentious position of the oral standards (e.g. Jahr and Mæhlum 2009).

terms; as a threat to the Norwegian language, a hindrance to entering the job market, or an obstacle for social advancement more generally (Ims 2014; Svendsen and Marzo 2015). On the other hand, several artists, particularly rappers, strongly oppose the idea that this linguistic practice is something negative or problematic, and use it in their artistic work. In fact, recent work on language and identity among urban youth suggests that hip hop plays a decisive role not only in the formation and propagation of the new linguistic practices, but also in the ideological struggle for acceptance and legitimization of the style (e.g. Brunstad, Røyneland and Opsahl 2010; Cutler and Røyneland 2015; Opsahl and Røyneland 2016). In several of the most recent secondary school textbooks – published between 2013 and 2016 – linguistic and functional descriptions of the speech style is covered in their chapters on language variation and dialects, and lyrics from these performers have been included (Opsahl and Røyneland 2016: 48). These pedagogical works discuss the linguistic practices of current rap music in an engaging, non-dismissive manner, and juxtapose the emerging speech style with dialects and sociolects. Including discussions of these practices in their textbooks and handling them as part of the Norwegian dialect landscape, serve to normalize and legitimize them, and hence contributes significantly to the ongoing process of enregisterment.

Linguistic Characteristics of Multiethnolectal Norwegian

The multiethnolectal speech style is characterized by a wide range of co-occurring linguistic features, including an association of these features with certain social practices. Most of these features may be conceived of as contact phenomena; some of them are typical second language features, others may be the result of language or dialect contact, while yet others may be the part of more general changes in progress. A typical feature of the speech style is an extensive, and also extended, use of loanwords from immigrant languages. Many are swearwords or expressions that index cultural taboos or proscriptions, while others come to play the role of discourse markers with specific discourse functions (e.g. “wallah” = *I swear by Allah* (Arabic)) (Opsahl 2009). Other common features of the speech style are violations of the syntactic verb second constraint, rendering an XSV word order, where “X” is a topicalized element, “S” the subject and “V” the finite verb (e.g. *“Egentlig vi er norske” XSV *Really we are Norwegian* instead of standard V2 “Egentlig er vi norske” XVS *Really are we Norwegian*), as well as some morphological developments (e.g. grammatical gender simplification like the use of masculine gender with neuter nouns) (Opsahl and Røyneland 2016: 46). A prevalent prosodic feature, which probably is the most salient feature of the speech style, is a specific ‘staccato’ sounding intonation that is most likely due to vowel-length equalization combined with syllable-timed pronunciation (in contrast to the traditional Norwegian stress-timed pronunciation) (Svendsen and Røyneland 2008). Several of these features are found in urban multiethnolectal speech styles across Scandinavia and in other parts of Europe (see articles in Nortier and Svendsen 2015; Quist and Svendsen 2010).

Data and Methodology

In this chapter, the main focus is on online data – more specifically a rap video by the Norwegian-Chilean-Peruvian rapper *Pumba*, where issues of belonging and identities are thematized, and the comments following this video. The video has been uploaded three times on YouTube (September 2009, December 2009, and August 2012). The first upload, which is the one that will be used here, has by far the most views and comments: 438,410 views and 661 comments (by January 2017). The other uploads only have a few thousand views and a handful of comments. Most of the comments are from the first years after the video was uploaded, but comments continue to be added – either as direct response to the video or as response to previous comments.[3] In the analysis, both comments directed to the video and comments to previous comments will be discussed. In order to download and process the comments in a systematic way, I used the scraping tool *YouTube Scrape.*[4] The results include the commentaries, usernames, dates and other information that was downloaded to an Excel file for further processing and analysis (the last download was done in January 2017). Although there is no way to determine the exact age, gender, ethnicity, or background (social, national, regional) of the people engaging in the thread, it may be possible to get some information from a close reading of their usernames, writing styles, use of dialectal and/or multiethnolectal features, mixing of languages, and through an analysis of the content of their comments (provided that these data are not produced by someone putting on a "fake" identity).

My interest in CMC data, and more specifically in rap videos by rappers of immigrant background, has its origin in long-standing research on the linguistic practices of adolescents in multilingual environments in Oslo through the UPUS/Oslo-project.[5] This research began with ethnographic fieldwork and sociolinguistic interviews and conversations which provide in-depth, personal

[3] 2009–2010: 42 comments; 2011: 138 comments; 2012: 185 comments; 2013: 130 comments; 2014: 40 comments; 2015: 42 comments; 2016–2017: 56 comments.

[4] http://ytcomments.klostermann.ca

[5] The Upus/Oslo-project was a Norwegian Research Foundation funded project that ran from 2005 to 2009. The aim of the project was to study linguistic practices among adolescents in multilingual parts of Oslo. Five researchers were part of the project; Toril Opsahl, Bente Ailin Svendsen, Finn Aarsæther, Invild Nistov, and Unn Røyneland.

narratives and accounts of participants' identity formation and also their involvement in hip-hop culture (e.g. Cutler and Røyneland 2015; Svendsen and Røyneland 2008). These ethnographic data provided the basis for identification and analysis of these communities of practice and their associated language styles and ideologies. Thus, I turned to CMC as a way of supplementing the foundational sociolinguistic data and gaining an understanding of the changing ways in which today's youth connect with one another and negotiate their multiple identities and belongings online.

YouTube

As pointed out by Androutsopoulos and Tereick (2016), YouTube has received less scholarly attention than other media platforms such as Facebook or Twitter. However, YouTube is becoming one of the most important social media platforms globally – including in Norway. Since its foundation and launch in the USA in 2005, YouTube has become the leading video-sharing website worldwide, and it is currently the third most popular website globally (cf. Androutsopoulos and Tereick 2016). YouTube is now available in 76 languages and exists in localized versions in 90 countries – primarily in the global North.[6] The Norwegian version of YouTube was launched in February 2013. According to Statistics Norway, YouTube is by far the most popular media platform for viewing videos.[7] Since 2008, the majority of online videos are viewed on YouTube (60 percent) as compared with other online streaming video services, and the most active viewers are children and adolescents (Statistics Norway 2015: 106). On the whole, the relative proportion of people who watch film, TV, or video online has increased steadily and significantly in the same period (from 13 percent in 2007 to 43 percent in 2015).

A recent study of media trends in Norway shows that 44 percent of young people under the age of 30 watch YouTube videos every day (Strømmen 2017). The second most popular genre after humour snippets is music videos. Facebook is by far the most used social network and, interestingly, also the most important media channel for those under 30. As many as 89 percent use Facebook every day and 43 percent report Facebook to be their most important news source. Facebook and YouTube are the two most important media channels in young Norwegians' everyday life (92 percent and 85 percent respectively), and hence outperform The Norwegian public broadcaster NRK, commercial TV channels and radio stations, and online newspapers. This stands in sharp contrast to the media habits of those aged over 50, for whom traditional print or broadcast media still are the most important media

[6] https://en.wikipedia.org/wiki/YouTube#Localization
[7] www.ssb.no/forside/_attachment/269027?_ts=15533e71088

channels and news sources. Only 5 percent of people over the age of 60, and 21 percent of those between 45 and 60, use YouTube on a daily basis. Against this background, there are good reasons to believe that most of the people who engage in the comments thread in my study are relatively young. As we have seen, it is mostly young people who watch videos on YouTube, and it is also mainly young people who are interested in the musical genre in question.

Ethical Considerations

The online nicknames used by the participants in the thread following Pumba's video are quite interesting as they reveal a good deal about their background and stances regarding issues pertaining to immigration. However, in order to protect the user's privacy, I have chosen to replace their nicknames with similar pseudonyms. This does not entail, of course, that their anonymity is secured. YouTube is a "public" space and anyone can enter the videos and find the comments in question. Furthermore, the user's online identity may in many cases be reconstructed simply by entering a string of the comment in a search engine. Still, obscuring the nicknames, or monikers, makes access less immediate and provides a first barrier. YouTube videos and comments are publicly available and may be conceived of as similar to an online newspaper thread. The video and the comments analyzed here do not contain highly sensitive personal data.

On a more general note, one of the challenges in working with CMC data is that we often lack information about users' ages. This raises ethical considerations, particularly regarding the use of data from potentially underage users who may not be aware of the consequences of posting comments online. Their awareness of which pages are "public," and hence open for anyone to access, and which are "private" may not be well developed. As well, public pages may at times contain discussions of topics of a rather private nature. As pointed out by Bolander and Locher (2014: 17), the division between the public and the private is becoming increasingly blurred and should be conceived of as gradable rather than absolute. This poses considerable challenges to online data collection – and to our conceptualizations of what is private and public, and for whom.

Theoretical Orientation

Identity, Belonging, and Category Memberships

> Membership of a category is ascribed (and rejected), avowed (and disavowed), displayed (and ignored) in local places and at certain times, and it does these things as part of the interactional work that constitutes people's lives. [. . . It is] not that people passively or latently have this or that identity

> which then causes feelings and actions, but that they work up and work to this or that identity, for themselves and others, there and then, either as an end in itself or towards some other end. (Antaki and Widdicombe 1998: 2).

The view of identity as something that is continuously co-constructed and contextually bound, put forward by Antaki and Widdicombe (1998), is shared by many scholars within contemporary sociolinguistics and it is also one I adhere to. Bucholtz and Hall (2005) discuss five principles of identity construction: the *emergence* principle, the *positionality* principle, the *indexicality* principle, the *relationality* principle, and the *partialness* principle. The first two principles are concerned with the ontological status of identity: that identity is an emergent rather than a pre-existing product, and that identities encompass both macro- and mico-level categories, and more temporary and interactionally specific stances and participant roles. The third principle is concerned with the mechanism whereby identity is constituted and negotiated, whereas the fourth principle emphasizes identity as a relational phenomenon. The fifth, and last, principle focuses on the partialness of any given identity. Identities are always co-constructed, and always relational and contextually bound. Identities may in part be an outcome of others' perceptions and representations, and in part an effect of larger social and material structures and ideological processes. In the following discussion and analysis of my data, principles 3 and 4 will be of particular interest:

> (3) *The indexicality principle*: Identity relations emerge in interaction through several related indexical processes, including: (a) overt mention of identity categories and labels; (b) implicatures and presuppositions regarding one's own or others' identity position; (c) displayed evaluative and epistemic orientations to ongoing talk, as well as interactional footings and participant roles; and (d) the use of linguistic structures and systems that are ideologically associated with specific personas and groups (Bucholtz and Hall 2005: 594).

> (4) *The relationality principle*: Identities are intersubjectively constructed through several, often overlapping, complementary relations, including similarity/difference, genuineness/artifice, and authority/delegitimacy (Bucholtz and Hall 2005: 598).

Following Bucholtz and Hall (2005) and also the works of Sacks (1992), Schegloff (2007), and Stokoe (2012) on membership categorization analysis (MCA), I will look at how identities are negotiated online through evoking common categories, activities, and attributes. This includes, for instance, explicit mentioning of membership categories or labels like "Norwegian," "Pakistani," "foreigner," and mentioning of attributes and practices associated with certain categories like, for instance, that Norwegians eat potatoes and drink alcohol, Norwegians speak Norwegian, and not "broken" Norwegian or other languages, and that Norwegians are white. Different practices or attributes may also invoke a category without it being explicitly mentioned: for instance, including someone skiing in a rap video without explicitly stating that this a Norwegian practice may still invoke a stereotypical Norwegian.

The identity negotiations in Pumba's video and in the thread of comments revolve around questions of similarity and difference, (in)authenticity, (il) legitimacy, genuineness and artificiality. Who has the right to claim certain identities, how mixed or hybrid identities are perceived, and on what grounds different identities are accepted or rejected, are questions that are raised in the video and negotiated in the various threads.

Heteroglossic Language Use and Metalinguistic and Metapragmatic Commentary

The multiple varieties in which these online discussions are performed point to analytical tools such as Bakhtinian heteroglossia and voicing. Some of the comments are performed in standard written language, but many use a combination of features from different styles, registers, and varieties. According to Bakhtin (1981: 291), all languages are heteroglot in the sense that they may be used differently to represent different socio-ideological groups or points of view, different epochs and generations. Heteroglossia can thus be defined as "the coexistence, combination, alternation, and juxtaposition of ways of using the communicative and expressive resources language/s offer us" (Leppänen et al. 2009: 1082). However, as pointed out by Vigouroux (2015: 244), heteroglossia does not simply refer to "the simultaneous use of different chunks of 'named languages' or registers," but, more significantly, it often entails tensions and conflicts between different types of varieties or features, based on the historical associations they carry with them. In this way, heteroglossia inscribes both speakers and addressees "within a history of language use, of social stratification and ideological relationship" (Vigouroux ibid.).

Language use itself is often the topic of discussion, and may involve overt or covert evaluative language use such as metalinguistic or metapragmatic commentary, crossing, and stylization (Coupland 2007; Rampton 2011; Silverstein 1993). Metalinguistic and metapragmatic commentary is often related to evaluations of correctness, legitimacy, and authenticity. In the analysis, I am particularly interested in explicit and implicit metalinguistic and metapragmatic comments; that is, language about language, where evaluations of correctness and purity, language policing, legitimacy and authenticity, and expressions of connections between language use and identity, are explicitly or implicitly made. Language policing is here understood as: "the production of 'order' – normatively organised and policed conduct – which is infinitely detailed and regulated by a variety of actors" (Blommaert et al. 2009: 203). In the CMC data, we see both instances of hegemonic and anti-hegemonic language policing. In some discussions it is connected to correctness, and who, by implication, has demonstrated the competence required to be acknowledged as an authentic Norwegian. In other instances, the use of certain features may be policed, since they are seen as connected to nationalism and racism.

Analysis: Negotiations of Language and Identity

Negotiations of National Identity and Belonging

In his rap *Hvor jeg kommer ifra* ("Where I come from"), the Norwegian-Chilean-Peruvian rapper, Pumba, problematizes his mixed background and multiple belonging. Pumba displays his multifaceted memberships and affiliations – a common fact of life for many young people with immigrant background – as he opposes the very idea of belonging as something simple or singular. Yet, a claim to a multiple identity and several affiliations is, in his experience, not easily accepted. In the lyrics from the song shown in extract (1), Pumba shows how he and other youth of mixed backgrounds both feel at home and alienated no matter where they go. Both in Norway and in the countries of his parents' origin he feels charged with lack of authenticity as people he meets want to know where he "really" comes from, hence what his "real" identity is. This urge to place people in unambiguously defined national, ethnic or social categories expresses quite an essentialist view of what identity is – or ideally should be.

Excerpt (1)

"Hvor jeg kommer ifra"	**"Where I come from"**
Stanza 1	*Stanza 1*
Hva skjer 'a? Jeg må bare forklare asså	What's up? I just have to explain
Når vi drar til hjemlandet, vi er nordmenn, skikkelig å	When we go to our home country we are Norwegians, real ones
Og når jeg er her så er jeg chilener, peruaner, svarting du veit	And when I'm here, I'm Chilean, Peruvian, blacky, you know
Hvor faen er jeg fra?	Where the fuck am I from?
[. . .]	[. . .]
Tenker på det ene språket, snakker med det andre	Thinking in one language, speaking with the other
Chorus	*Chorus*
Folk som jeg møter spør meg ofte hvor jeg kommer fra	People that I meet often ask me where I come from
Jeg veit da faen, men alt jeg veit er at jeg er her i dag	I don't know, damn, but all I know is that I'm here today
Mine foreldre jobba hardt for å få meg inn hit	My parents worked hard to get me here
Bodd her nesten hele mitt liv, er noen ganger i tvil	Lived here almost all my life, sometimes I doubt

As we can see in this excerpt, Pumba, both highlights his mixed background and questions simple category ascriptions. His delivery, like that of many other rappers of immigrant background, is characterized by a clear non-traditional staccato intonational pattern that is typical of the urban multiethnolectal speech style. He also has instances of so-called lack of inversion, or violations of the syntactic verb second constraint ("X, *vi er nordmenn" "*X, we are Norwegians*" XSV instead of standard verb second "X, er vi nordmenn" XVS "*X, are we Norwegians*"), a feature which also has been described as characteristic of multiethnolectal Norwegian. In addition to these features, he also has typical eastern-Oslo, working-class phonological features such as diphthongs instead of monophthongs ("veit" instead of "vet" "*know*"), and eastern-Oslo morphological features like the past tense inflectional form *-a* instead of the upper middle-class, western-Oslo variant *-et* ("jobba" instead of "jobbet" "*worked*").

Pumba is frustrated by not being accepted by his new homeland, and also by being "othered" in his parents' homeland. There he is seen as a real, authentic Norwegian, whereas in Norway, he is seen as a "*blacky*" – a skin color traditionally not associated with Norwegians, and hence an attribute that works in an exclusionary way. The racial label "svarting," which can be translated to "blacky" or "nigger," is generally understood as derogatory, but may take on different valences depending on context and interlocutors. Here it is clearly pointing to the fact that the color of his skin prevents him from being accepted as an authentic Norwegian, and to his position as someone "in-between." The first stanza ends with a question directed as a challenge to himself and to the audience: *So, if I'm not from there and not from here, where the f* am I from?*

As pointed out by Bucholz and Hall (2005: 602), mixed or "hybrid" identities seem to be particularly susceptible to denaturalization and illegitimization. Whenever an identity violates ideological expectations, like an unexpected combination of language, skin color, and claims of identity, it may be rejected and accused of being false and inauthentic. This process, which Bauman has labelled *traditionalization*, may be compared to the "act of authentication akin to the art or antique dealer's authentication of an object by tracing its provenance" (Bauman 1992: 137, here after Bucholz and Hall 2005: 602). This feeling of being seen as inauthentic or impure is shared by many of Pumba's followers. Throughout the video, however, this is exactly the kind of exclusionary and essentialist discourse Pumba advocates against.

In the video, a multicultural, mixed Norway is put on display, including a number of unexpected combinations of attributes and activities. In the beginning of the video, we see Pumba positioned as the classic thug, dressed in baggy pants and a hoodie and seated in a golden chair (see www.youtube.com/watch?v=bt_ds7S3LO0). Although playing on the stereotype of the tough, criminal immigrant, both verbally and visually, it is obviously ironic and throughout the video he takes a clear stance against the assigned identity as the dangerous immigrant: “Media labels everyone / I don’t understand why / calls us criminals / but we have built up Oslo.”[8]

A bit later we see Pumba with a group of boys, one with the text “Zoo York” on his hoodie, pointing to the increasingly mixed population of Oslo like New York, and a black boy waving the Norwegian flag. Throughout the video, we see flags from many nations: Philippines, Morocco, Albania, and Norway and people wearing clothes in the colors of different national flags (for instance “Vince,” a guest rapper with Ghanaian background, wearing the colors of the Ghanaian flag). We see people of different skin colors dressed in traditional costumes from different countries around the world, but also combinations of stereotypically Norwegian attributes and activities, and foreign attributes. So, for instance, we are presented with a woman wearing a Norwegian police uniform and a hijab, a dark-skinned ski-instructor called “Abdoul,” a black man wearing “bunad” (a traditional Norwegian national costume) and eating “kvikk lunsj,” which is an iconically Norwegian chocolate that “all” Norwegians would bring with them and enjoy on their ski-outings.

Here we see a mixing of category-bound attributes and activities that is clearly humorous, but also carries a very serious intent. Pumba’s basic message here is that wherever you originally came from, you still belong in this country. He makes the point that immigrants are not criminals, but have contributed to building the country and are part of its basic fabric; there are immigrants in all layers of society and in many different occupations. They have a legitimate right to be here:

“hvis du er afrikaner eller du er en same/så er konklusjonen at vi alle er en del av landet”

If you are African or Sami / the conclusion is that we are all a part of this country

Contesting and Endorsing Comments

In the thread of comments following Pumba’s video there are broadly speaking two major groups: one that aligns with him and another that totally disaligns and rejects his claim to Norwegianness. Some comments are aimed directly at the video whereas others form part of longer sub-threads between commentators where issues of immigration, integration, and racism are debated. A few comments directed to the content of the video may serve as illustrative examples of quite commonly expressed protectionist/nationalist or plain racist attitudes:

[8] “media stempler alle / jeg skjønner ikke hvorfor /kaller oss kriminelle /men vi har bygd opp Oslo”

1. *RushQ* GTFO, du er ikke norsk (2011)
   GTFO, you're not Norwegian
2. *Wolf* Norge er du ihvertfall ikke fra! (2016)
   You're not from Norway, anyway!
3. *KaiTN* Jævla tulling du er Pakis for faen (2017)
   Fucking moron you're a god damn Paki
4. *SB4* Nordmann? Du er neger, hvordan kan du være en nordmann :S? (2013)
   Norwegian? You're a negro, how can you be Norwegian :S?
5. *Honest* Jeg blir provosert av det her. Man blir ikke norsk selvom et stykke papir sier det, så ryk og reis hjem til Afrika!! (2015)
   I'm provoked by this. You don't become Norwegian even if a piece of paper says so, so just get yourself back to Africa!!
6. *MrNo* Jævla svartsvidde jævla, hut dåkker te hælsika, fette kræftfræmkallanes musikk :) (2016)
   Fucking black-burned fuckers, get yourselves the hell out of here, cunt cancer causing music :)

The first two comments simply reject Pumba's claim to be "part of this country." The first comment from *RushQ*, opens with GTFO (an acronym for "get the fuck out"), an English loan commonly used also by young Norwegians, whereas the next comment is written solely in Norwegian (standard Bokmål). The next three comments also deny Pumba's Norwegian identity and make overt mention of identity categories, labels, and attributes. Pumba is ascribed an identity as "Paki" (derogatory for Pakistani), he is called a "negro" and told to go back to "Africa." Since the Pakistanis were the first immigrants to come to Norway in the 1960s, they are often seen at the prototypical immigrant and "Paki" is often used as a common label for anyone with an immigrant background. Also, as will be discussed in detail below, "black" and "negro" are attributes often ascribed to all immigrants, regardless of their actual skin color. The last comment (from *MrNo*) is a plain racist utterance where Pumba, and presumably all the dark-skinned people ("black-burned") that appear in the video and immigrants in general, are told to leave the country, and the music is described in an extremely derogatory manner. The comment contains several distinctive northern Norwegian dialect features (underlined in the Norwegian original), such as the use of the second person plural pronoun "dåkker" (*you*) ("dere" in standard Bokmål), the use of non-standard phonology *-e-* instead of *-i-* ("fette" *cunt*) and *-æ-* instead of *-e-* ("hælsika" (*the hell*) "kræftfræmkallanes" (*cancer causing*))[9], and the

[9] This phenomenon, often referred to as, *lowering* is quite common in many Norwegian dialects, but is particularly widespread in Northern Norwegian dialects, where it may also function as a shibboleth (Mæhlum and Røyneland 2012).

dialectal inflectional form *-anes* instead of standard *-ende*. The use of dialect here may index pure and real Norwegian. Due to our colonial history, rural dialects became a particularly powerful symbol of Norwegianness (Mæhlum and Røyneland 2012; Røyneland 2017), and are by many still seen as more authentic and national than urban dialects, which were mixed with Danish, or the written standard Bokmål, which is based on Danish. However, participants who align with Pumba also use dialect in their comment. Hence, the use of dialect, although indexing Norwegianness, is not connected to one specific socio-ideological group. It may be used to voice quite distinct, even opposing, attitudes and convictions. The social meaning of dialect is contextually bound and may also be negotiated in discourse. Both *Edward* and *AnnieG* take explicit anti-racist stances, while mixing English, dialect, and Bokmål:

7. *Edward* -fra en ekte nordmann, I love all my foreign friends! å æ hate alle rasistiske nordmenn, vi har oss sjøl å takk for dem kriminelle vi har, norsk eller ikke. Så ha testikla/eggstokka å face up to that shit! Pumba *e* kos <3 (2013)
   -from a real Norwegian, I love all my foreign friends! And I hate all racist Norwegians, we have ourselves to thank for the criminals we have, Norwegians or not. So have testicles/ovaries to face up to that shit! Pumba is nice <3
8. *AnnieG* jævla rasistår! eg e største kviding du finne! har mer svarte vennår en andre <3 eg e albanår bitch! uten oss utlendinger har dokk ingenting bitch ass !!! (2013)
   fucking racists! I'm the biggest whitey you can find! have more black friends than others <3 I'm Albanian bitch! without us foreigners you have nothing bitch !!!

Edward positions himself as a "real Norwegian" who embraces multiculturalism and hates racism. Like *RushQ* above, he also uses several distinct dialect features in his comment, such as the first person pronoun "æ" (*I*) ("jeg" standard Bokmål), loss of the unstressed vowel *-e* (apocope) "å takk" (*to thank*) ("å takke" in standard Bokmål), and the indefinite plural form *-a* instead of *-er* "testikla"/"eggstokka" (*testicles/ovaries*), all features typical of Mid- and some Northern Norwegian dialects. While *Edward* distances himself from racist utterances, and aligns with Pumba, he still positions himself as a "real Norwegian," hence indicating that some Norwegians are more "real" than others. At the same time, *Edward*'s self-labelling is clearly a challenge to the idea that "real" Norwegian entails insularity and nationalism. This is underscored by the mixing of different codes; standard Norwegian, local dialect, and English – notably, he switches to English when orienting toward his "foreign friends."

AnnieG also takes a clear stance against racism when she calls herself the "biggest whitey" and states that she is Albanian. She uses southern Norwegian dialect features in combination with features from Bokmål, Nynorsk, and English: *bitch* has become a quite common English loanword, the first person singular pronoun "eg" (*I*) is both a feature of Nynorsk and western/southern Norwegian dialects, the second person plural pronoun "dokk" (*you*) is used in southern and northern dialects, whereas the indefinite plural form *–år* is a very characteristic feature of southern Norwegian dialects: "vennår" (*friends*) "albanår," but she also uses the Bokmål form *-er* "utlendinger," *(foreigners)* a combination of Bokmål and dialect inflection. This mixed and heteroglossic language use may be read as a linguistic signal of her embracing variation and diversity. The use of dialect features, may, as in the case of *RushQ* also be understood as an affirmation of their Norwegianness. They are "real" Norwegians, but not racists. Hence the use of dialect does not have to be understood as a nationalist and exclusionary move, but rather as an index of authenticity.

Many of the participants in the thread support and align with Pumba in wanting to claim a legitimate place for themselves, and tell similar stories about being alienated and "othered" both in the country of origin and in Norway. They voice the same frustration and confusion as in Pumba's lyric – "where do I 'really' belong?" This indicates a conception of belonging and identity as something singular, something you ought to have only one of, whereas what they experience is a sense of multiple belonging and mixed identities. They also voice their frustration at being told to go home to their own country, when Norway *is* their home. A rather long comment by *MariaM* may serve as an example:

9. *MariaM* Denne sangen oppsummerte alt det jeg alltid har følt. Selv er jeg halvt marokkaner, så jeg vetta f*n hvor jeg kommer fra, men det jeg vet er at jeg føler en tilhørighet til Norge. Jeg er født her, og har vokst opp her, og snakker Norsk, men siden jeg er "svart" blir jeg behandlet som det, og innvandrere har mer lyst til å bli kjent med meg enn nordmenn xD Er sikker på at de fleste andre "svartingene" som er født og oppvokst her føler akkurat det samme, og er dritlei å bli fortalt at jeg skal "dra tilbake til hjemmelandet dit!", for DETTE er hjemmet mitt;) (2016)

> *This song summed up all that I have always felt. I'm half Moroccan, so I donno where the f* I come from, but what I know is that I feel a belonging to Norway. I'm born here, and have grown up here, and speak Norwegian, but since I'm "black" I get treated like that, and immigrants are more eager to get to know me than Norwegians xD I'm sure that most other "blacks" who are born and raised here feel exactly the same, and are sick of being told that I should "go back to your home country!", because THIS is my home;)*

Her comment has received 33 likes and six comments, mostly in support of her view but also comments like: "Ut ur norge, svartingahelvete." "*Get out of norway, black hell.*" Interestingly this comment has Swedish features (for instance the use of the Swedish preposition "ur" which would be "av" in Norwegian). *MariaM*'s comment is basically written in standard Bokmål with the occasional slang word. Referring to herself as "black," using quotation marks, *MariaM* is invoking the voice of the majority, white Norwegian. She says that she gets treated as "black," meaning that she gets "othered." She is clearly rejecting the label, highlighting its socially constructed meaning in the context of Norway. Neither Pumba nor *MariaM*, who says she is half Moroccan, are particularly dark skinned. As pointed out by Bucholz and Hall (2005: 599), in order for groups or individuals to be positioned as alike, they need not have exactly the same attributes, but must merely be understood as sufficiently similar for current interactional purposes. In the Norwegian context, it is quite common among adolescents to refer to anyone who looks darker than an ethnic northern European, as black. Even kids with an eastern European or middle-Eastern background may be referred to – and refer to themselves – as black. Hence, black does not necessarily index African descent, but merely non-white and by implication non-Norwegian. As we may see, *Blue4* and *AdeleZ*, both with an eastern European background, express similar experience and frustration, although people from this area normally would be considered "whiteys":

10. *Blue4* det er sant asz når jeg er i kosovo er jeg potet når jeg er i norge er jeg Albaner (2011)
It's true like when I'm in Kosovo I'm potato when I'm in norway I'm Albanian
11. *AdeleZ* Hvor jeg kommer ifra? Født i norge Men Fra Albania/kosovo!!! kaller ikke meg selv norsk az, riktig riktig i hjemlandet blir man kalt norsk, er du her du blir kalt utenlandsk! :S confusing (2010)
Where do I come from? Born in norway But From Albania/kosovo!!! don't call myself Norwegian like, correct correct in the home country one is called Norwegian, are you here you are called foreigner! :S confusing

Blue 4 says that he is seen as a "potato" in Kosovo, but as Albanian in Norway. "Potato" is a slang word for Norwegian – the label index whiteness and Norwegianness, as eating loads of potatoes, is a stereotypical activity associated with Norwegians. *AdeleZ* says she doesn't call herself Norwegian, although she was born in Norway, since she is seen as a foreigner. There seems to be a general feeling among many of the commentators engaging in the thread that their identities are dismissed, censored, or simply ignored.

This feeling of not being accepted is shared by many adolescents of immigrant background in Norway. A longitudinal study of more than 4,000 adolescents from Oslo conducted over a four-year period (2006–2010) shows that more than half of the adolescents with immigrant backgrounds (N=575–581) do not feel Norwegian, largely because they don't feel that they are allowed to "be Norwegian" due to the color of their skin (Frøyland and Gjerustad 2012: 48). Approximately 80 percent of Norwegian-born kids with immigrant backgrounds and adolescents who immigrated before the age of 7 report that they identify as both Norwegian and foreign, whereas 93 percent of the adolescents who came after the age of 7 identify as foreign. The numbers are particularly high among adolescents with a non-Western background and one of the reasons they cite is color. They don't look Norwegian and hence will never be accepted as Norwegian since "whiteness" is seen as an essential part of what it means to be Norwegian.

Issues of identity and belonging are also frequently discussed by the adolescents in the UPUS corpus, and skin color is referred to by some as an important gatekeeper; it is what prevents them from identifying as Norwegian and excludes them from being accepted as Norwegian. Responding to the question, "what would you have answered if somebody asked where you are from?" most of the adolescents with immigrant backgrounds answer the country of their parents' origin. Many report that they don't feel that they are entitled to say Norwegian, that they will never be accepted as Norwegian because they don't look Norwegian. Like Pumba, many oppose simple category ascription and refuse to self-identify as either the one or the other; they feel they are both or mixed. Lukas, a young boy born and raised in Norway with Nigerian parental background, may serve as an example:

12. Lukas ja (.) på hudfargen føler jeg meg som nigerianer men på språket (.)
føler jeg meg som norsk
yes (.) with skin color I feel Nigerian but with language (.) I feel like Norwegian

His skin color places him in Nigeria and his language in Norway, although he reports speaking and mixing features from a number of languages on a daily basis, including Yoruba, English, and multiethnolectal Norwegian.

Metalinguistic and Metapragmatic Commentary

In this rap, Pumba connects his confusion and sense of multiple identities and belonging to his experiences of being multilingual (see excerpt 1): "*Thinking in one language, speaking with the other.*" This theme is picked up and starts different threads between several participants in the comments: *TimTale* shares Pumba's bilingual experience, whereas others, like *KimN* and *eme333*, either adhere to a one-ethnicity-one-language ideology or criticize Pumba's Norwegian, connecting it to second-language immigrant talk or multiethnolectal speech.

13. *TimTale* tenker med det ene språket og snaker med det andre, haha skjenner meg igjen (2015)
    thinking with one language and speaking with the other, haha I recognize this
14. *KimN* Han er fra Latin Amerika og Morsmålet hans er Spansk... Just sayin' (2016)
    He is from Latin America and his Mother tongue is Spanish... Just sayin'
15. *eme333* Fra Chile, bodd 19år i norge, men snakker som en paki? WTF??? (2014)
    From Chile, lived 19 years in norway, but speaks like a Paki? WTF???

To speak "like a Paki" is clearly not what you would be expected to do if you have lived in Norway since childhood, according to *eme333*. Pumba's speech style, which contains a number of multiethnolectal features, seems to be connected only to being foreign. It is not perceived to be a new way of speaking Norwegian that adds to the Norwegian dialect landscape, as is now common in most recent high school textbook discussions of multiethnolectal Norwegian.

In the following exchange, we shall see that using correct orthography becomes a stand-in for authenticity and Norwegianness. Even minute errors in spelling and grammar may lead to challenges to one's claim to be Norwegian. In a lengthy discussion between *Wolf* and *OceanA* about who is and who is not Norwegian, *Wolf* finally rejects *OceanA*'s claim to be 100 percent Norwegian, and having both Norwegian mother and father, by attacking his language. As we can see, both language and the type of discourse associated with a certain group are used to delegitimize and de-authenticate *OceanA:*

16. *Wolf* "+*OceanA*": har du ikke, snakker som en jævla pakkis og høres ut som en!" (2017)
    You don't have, talk like a fucking Paki and sounds like one.

However, *Kiss*, another participant, supports *OceanA*, and challenges *Wolf* as being ignorant. The counter-claim here is not simply that people of immigrant background should count as Norwegians. Rather, it is likely that *Kiss* is invoking the fact that ethnic Norwegians also speak multiethnolectal Norwegian (cf. Opsahl 2009).

17. *Kiss* Wolf har ikke du hørt om norske som snakker kebab norsk? (2017)
Wolf haven't you heard about Norwegians who speak Kebab Norwegian?

In a rather lengthy discussion between *AppS5* and several other participants, but particularly *Roger9* and *Martin4*, a quite interesting shift of language style occurs in conjunction with a shift towards a metalinguistic discussion where the question of who is the most legitimate speaker is at stake. After several racist comments by *AppS5*, written in a combination of standard Bokmål orthography, abbreviations typical of CMC writing, English loanwords, and with many northern Norwegian dialect features (underlined), *Martin4* responds in a similar style of writing:

18. *Martin4* Du og rasisten i dæ kan sug kuken min :) det kan forsåvidt landet ditt også :) Internet thug fitte. . .du e norlending? avtale møte bitch? (2014)
You and the racist inside you can suck my dick :) the same goes for your country :) Internet thug cunt. . .you're a northerner? schedule a meeting bitch?

Martin4 challenges *AppS5*'s racist views while, like *AppS5*, using several northern Norwegian dialects features such as the second person singular pronoun "dæ" (standard "deg" *you*), and the apocopated form "sug" (standard "suge" *suck*). *AppS5* answers in a very aggressive way using a large number of northern Norwegian dialect features (underlined in the Norwegian original).

19. *AppS5* Æ e internet thug ja, det ekke æ som sett å true med juling over internett. Ha litt selvinnsikt, eller blir det for komplisert for ei apa? Og nei, æ hold mæ unna utlendinga, eneste dokker duge til e å lage junkfood og voldta 14 åringa. Æ e dessverre verken sulten eller 14. (2014)
I'm an internet thug, yes, it's not me who threatens beatings over the internet. Have some self knowledge, or is that too complicated for an ape? And no, I keep away from foreigners, the only thing you're good at is to make junk food and rape 14 year olds. Unfortunately I'm neither hungry nor 14.

At this point *Roger9* enters the stage and takes a very clear stance against *AppS5*'s utterances. He does so in standard Bokmål, which, however, contains a few misspellings (underlined) and abbreviations.

20. *Roger9* hhahahahha d er kansje noe av det mest tilbakestående jeg har lest i hele mitt liv, du hadde kansje blitt tatt litt mere serriøst om du faktisk ga menig i det du sa, kjenner en pakkis som har bod i norge i 4 år som gir mer mening en hva du akkurat skrev. jævla norske fjell ape. (2014)
hhahahahha this is maybe some of the most retarded stuff I have read in my whole life, you would maybe have been taken a bit more seriously if you actually gave meaning to what you're saying, know a Paki who has lived in norway 4 years who makes more sense than what you just wrote. bloody Norwegian mountain ape.

The topic "who knows Norwegian the best" is introduced here, and is at the very heart of the rest of a rather long discussion. *AppS5*'s Norwegian skills and ability to make sense are compared to the skills of an immigrant who has been in the country only a few years. Finally, he is labeled a Norwegian mountain ape – that is, an ignorant person living on the periphery – a characterization that invokes the use of dialect features placing *AppS5* in the northern periphery. *AppS5* hits back, accusing *Roger5* of lacking the ability to express himself in a comprehensible way. Instead of entering into a discussion about the matter at hand, it becomes a metalinguistic and metapragmatic discussion. The aim is clearly to dismiss the other person's arguments on the grounds of lacking linguistic competence. Interestingly, *AppS5* abruptly changes to a writing style quite uncommon for informal CMC interactions. He stops using dialect features completely and sticks to standard Bokmål, with standard punctuation, no abbreviations or emoticons. Hence, he refrains from using what *Roger9* has labelled a marginal voice from the periphery (i.e. "*bloody Norwegian mountain ape*"), and assumes a geographically unmarked, authoritative voice using an authoritative supra-regional, standard language. *Roger9*, on the other hand, though writing in a slightly more "polished" language, continues to produce typos or misspellings (underlined), and persists in using slangwords, non-standard abbreviations, emoticons, and phrases in English:

21. *Roger9* om du virkelig ikke skjønnte hva jeg skrev så er d 2 alternativer 1: du kan ikke norsk 2: du er helt retardert – whatever makes u happy :).en normann som klager over utlendinger men kan ikke skrive sitt eget språk engang var hele "meningen" i kommentaren, jeeze folk må ha allt med t-skje. (2014)

> *If you really didn't understand what I wrote then there are 2 alternatives 1: you don't know Norwegian 2: you're totally retarded – whatever makes u happy :) a Norwegian who complains about foreigners but who cannot even write his own language was the entire "message" of the comment, jeeze people must have everything with a t-spoon.*

AppS5's reaction to this is first to correct *Roger9*'s misspellings and question his Norwegian identity. Hence, lack of linguistic competence is used as a justification to discredit *Roger9*'s arguments as well as to cast doubt on his authenticity and legitimate right to present an opinion.

22. *AppS5* Skjønte* retarded* nordmann* alt* teskei* Hvilken nordmann er det som ikke kan skrive sitt eget språk her? Den eneste med språkvansker her er deg. [...] Jeg kan norsk, men det kan tydeligvis ikke du. (2014)
Understood retarded* Norwegian* everything* teaspoon* What kind of Norwegian doesn't know how to write his own language? The only one with language difficulties is you. [...] I know Norwegian, but you obviously don't.*

It is interesting to note that two of the corrections are slightly off track, since one is correcting a Norwegianized form of the English loan "retardert" to the correct English spelling "retarded," and the correction of "t-skje" to "teskei" is only partly warranted since both "skje" and "skei" are correct spellings – the only deviation is the use of "t-" instead of "te," which is a pretty normal abbreviation, not least in informal writing. *Roger9*'s response is to insist on his Norwegianness and even refer to his grades at school:

23. *Roger9* jeg kan norsk jeg, tar jeg ikke helt feil gikk jeg ut fra skolen med en 5'er også .. [...] (2014)
I know Norwegian I, if I'm not mistaken I graduated with an A minus too.

After yet another provocation from *AppS5*, where he indicates that his message is too complicated to understand for an unskilled person like *Roger9*, *Roger9* responds by insisting on his language competence and ends his comment with crying out (upper case) a swear phrase in Croatian:

24. *Roger9* hør her din mammaknuller, <jeg kan ikke norsk ? wow du er virkelig stokk dum...hvordan i helvete kan jeg ikke norsk når jeg er født i norge og har bod her i 23 år snakker norsk hjemme og blandt vennner så ikke snakk piss jævla fjell ape. [...] IDI U PICKU MATRINU ! (2014)

Listen up you motherfucker, <I don't know Norwegian? Wow you're really thick as a brick... how the hell do I not know Norwegian when I was born in Norway and have lived here for 23 years speak Norwegian at home and among friends so don't talk shit fucking mountain ape GO FUCK YOURSELF !

AppS5's reaction to this is simply to continue policing *Roger9*'s language, while insisting on language correctness – with what can be interpreted as a condescending smile:

25. *AppS5* Beklager, norsk RETTSKRIVNING da. Ser ikke ut som det er en av dine sterke sider :) (2014)
Sorry, Norwegian ORTHOGRAPHY. Does not seem to be one of your strong sides :)

Here we see an example of how linguistic purity and prescriptive correctness is used as a proxy for national belonging in an anti-immigration discourse. However, the strategy of linguistic policing is challenged by anti-racists, who undercut its rhetorical force by inverting the argument. This is what happens when *TheMan* responds to *OldNorse*'s comment "styg utlending sang" (with only one *g* in *stygg*) "*Ugly foreigner song*" as follows:

26. *TheMan* Jeg må nesten le av deg, du burde kanskje lære deg å skrive Norsk. Det skrives stygg din idiot, burde få flere innvandrere hit, så kan vi sende ut rasister som deg ut av landet (2016)
I almost have to laugh, you should probably learn how to write Norwegian. It is written ugly you idiot, we should get more immigrants here so that we can send racists like you out of the country.

Conclusion

As we have seen in the different examples from commentaries posted in response to Pumba's video, and also in the video itself, features from different languages and dialects, including multiethnolectal features, and typical CMC features like emoticons, abbreviations, and non-standard spelling are used by young people engaging on YouTube. This illustrates how CMC offers people the ability to interact using features from dialects, styles, and registers that have no written standard, opening up new possible meanings and domains of use for hitherto marginalized codes and features. We have seen that the use of non-standard features gets policed in cases where correct orthography is used as a measure of how legitimate your claim to national identity and belonging is. At the same time, dialect features may be invoked in order to marginalize voices, as they are taken to index insularity and lack of authority. Hence, the use of different chunks of "named languages" or "registers," enters into a heteroglossic struggle. The tensions and conflicts between different varieties, styles or features are to a large extent based on the historical associations they carry with them – like the use of dialectal and multiethnolectal features versus standard features. However, their meaning is also interactionally negotiated and constructed. From an historical perspective, dialectal features may be seen as indexing national authenticity, but, used while uttering racist opinions, they may be understood as a signal of excessive nationalism. The social meanings of dialectal features are actively contested and used for different, often opposing, purposes. This is also the case when it comes to multiethnolectal features and more generally to multilingual practices. Mixing languages or using multiethnolectal features may be taken to show a lack of linguistic competence, as in one of the comments to Pumba's performance: *"19 years in Norway and speaking like a Paki, WTF?"* (example 13), or as an expression of young people with minority backgrounds' mixed identity and multiple affiliations: *"thinking with one language and speaking with the other, haha I recognize this"* (example 15). "Pure," non-mixed Norwegian is sometimes taken as an absolute requirement for "Norwegians." The point for Pumba and many other young people with mixed backgrounds, however, is precisely not to claim *one pure identity*, but to assert the validity of identities that are multiple and mixed.

9 Footing and Role Alignment Online: Mediatized Indigeneity and Andean Hip Hop

Karl Swinehart

The Mediatized Interaction Order

> While we often speak of society as though it were a static structure defined by tradition, it is, in the more intimate sense, nothing of the kind, but a highly intricate network of partial or complete understandings between the members of organizational units of every degree of size and complexity, ranging from a pair of lovers or a family to a league of nations or that ever increasing portion of humanity which can be reached by the press through all its transnational ramifications. – Edward Sapir, *Communication* (1951 [1931])

One wonders how much Edward Sapir would have to edit this line from his short essay, "Communication" to update it for the twenty-first century. Perhaps not terribly much. Published first in 1931, these words approach the prophetic for how they identify the profound "transnational ramifications" of global communications' spread and for describing the complex networked interconnections resulting from them. Precisely such transnational ramifications have animated a broad range of social science inquiry under the banner of "globalization" in recent decades, including the contributions to this volume. Sapir underscores that societies exist at many scales, are dynamic in nature, and he pushes us to consider the very concept of society itself as an abstraction resulting from communicative processes. In his view, it is only from moments of communicative action that bonds of groupness become forged. These moments of connectivity may or may not be organized through highly institutionalized means, such as national educational systems, elections, social services, and the like. The fact that a sense of belonging to a society may be anchored to state institutions like these, whether positive or negative, contentious or banal, can too easily convince those engaging in them that "society" and the nation-state are one and the same. This need not be the case, is often not, and Sapir reminds us that societies exist at many scales, both smaller than, and increasingly beyond the limits of nation-states (cf. Bock et al., this volume; Evers, this volume; Garley, this volume).

Some consequences of Sapir's placing communicative processes at the center of his definition of society include recognizing society as a dynamic, rather than a static object, and also recognizing the unevenness in how a society's members understand their own and others' participation in it. This raises an interesting question for research on language and communication. If any "society" is dynamic and operative within "a highly intricate network of partial or complete understandings (Sapir 1951: 104)," how do its members stake out positions vis-à-vis one another and the unevenly shared understandings of the social groups to which they, and others, belong? How does this happen in the even more profoundly networked circumstances of contemporary life?

The first of these two questions motivated much of the work of the sociologist Erving Goffman (1922–1982), while the second question attracted his attention radically less so (more on this below). Goffman, like Sapir a generation before him, also recognized large-scale sociological phenomena as experienced through communicative encounters. For Goffman, however, these would be primarily everyday face-to-face encounters, a domain of human activity that he termed the *interaction order* (Goffman 1983: 2). In arguing for the interaction order as a privileged site of social scientific inquiry, Goffman emphasized that, "It is a fact of our human condition that, for most of us, our daily life is spent in the immediate presence of others: in other words, that whatever they are, our doings are likely to be, in the narrow sense, *socially situated*." Sociolinguist and scholar of Computer Mediated Communication (CMC), Ana Deumert, points out that Goffman's privileging of face-to-face encounters situates his approach within what the post-structuralist French philosopher Jacques Derrida termed a metaphysics of presence (Deumert 2014a: 9; Derrida 1976). Derrida identified a long trajectory within Western thought, reaching back to Socrates, through Rousseau, and into the twentieth century that privileged physical co-presence and orality as primary and authentic in contrast to writing and text, which became dismissed as variously degenerate or inauthentic (Derrida 1976). If it was a prejudice of his own metaphysics of presence that limited Goffman's view to face-to-face encounters, scholars researching language and communication in the twenty-first century cannot afford to ignore that the "fact of our human condition," to reanimate Goffman's words, also includes a thorough penetration of mobile new media in our communicative everyday. Acknowledging this, Deumert expands Goffman's notion to what she calls a *mediated interaction order* (Deumert 2014a). But beyond simply updating the notion of interaction order to include interactions mediated through text and other media, how else might we make use of Goffman's insights within CMC contexts, i.e. within a mediated interaction order?

A central contribution from Goffman's analysis of the interaction order was to move beyond an overly idealized notion of "speaker" and "addressee." For Goffman, face-to-face encounters operate within participation frameworks that combine both a production format for participants' utterances (more on this in the next section) and participants' status vis-à-vis one another, particularly as ratified or unratified participants. This status may change in the course of interaction in part through what Goffman calls footing, or, "the alignment we take up to ourselves and the others present as expressed in the way we manage the production or reception of an utterance" (Goffman 1981: 128). This chapter brings Goffman's notions of footing, role alignment, and participation frameworks more broadly to a CMC context to illuminate the mediation of social relations that fit into Sapir's definition of "society" above, and within speech communities that, while physically dispersed, are discursively engaged and digitally connected.

Indigenous Andeans Online

The CMC context in this chapter is an indigenous one originating in the central Andes, in the Bolivian city of El Alto, and reaching far beyond it, to enclaves of Andean migrants in Europe, the United States, and large South American cities like Buenos Aires. The central Andes is home to one of the largest concentrations of speakers of Amerindian languages in the Americas, with speakers of Quechua and Aymara comprising the two largest indigenous ethnolinguistic groups of the region. Quechua languages are found from Ecuador through Peru and Bolivia and into northwest Argentina in a territory that is coextensive with the pre-colonial reach of the Inca Empire, and they are spoken by as many as ten million people (Adelaar 2004). The contemporary distribution of Aymara speakers includes a number approaching three million people who reside in Bolivia, Peru, and Chile in the Andean high plain, or *altiplano*, surrounding Lake Titicaca. The largest single concentration of Aymara speakers by far is found in the city of El Alto, a city of nearly one million inhabitants that makes up nearly half of the metropolitan region of Bolivia's capital of La Paz. Quechua and Aymara have official status in Bolivia and Peru, and Kichwa, as it is called in Ecuador, has legal recognition but not official status. Despite advances in the use of indigenous languages in education and media, a general trend of language shift towards Spanish dominance persists.

Like others throughout the region, indigenous Andeans have migrated in recent decades beyond their traditional communities not only to local urban centers, but also to Europe, North America, and other South American cities like São Paulo and Buenos Aires. While indigeneity suggests a foundational, perduring relationship to territory, Aymara and Quechua migrants do not necessary leave their indigenous languages behind upon arrival to cities in

Europe or elsewhere in Latin America. This chapter illuminates how one multilingual CMC context becomes a site where dispersed, yet digitally connected, persons maintain, contest, and sometimes reject practices, particularly linguistic ones, associated with Andean indigeneity and other forms of group membership, including membership in a global hip-hop music scene. In what follows, we encounter indigenous Andeans, Aymaras from the city of El Alto, communicating with their counterparts abroad, with other hip-hop artists and fans through the musical genre of hip hop. We also encounter the talk from these very hip-hop fans and artists in response to their hip hop, and the communication that unfolds is profoundly multilingual. In this regard, the linguistic practices we encounter in this chapter can be considered to fall within the realm of what Janis Androutsopoulos calls "networked multilingualism," or multilingualism shaped by being digitally connected and embedded within the global digital mediascape of the web (Androutsopoulos 2015: 188).

This chapter emerges from a larger project on Aymara language media that included a focus on Aymara language hip hop in El Alto (Hornberger and Swinehart 2012; Swinehart 2012a; Swinehart 2012c; Swinehart 2012d). As we will see below, these artists place importance on building and engaging a fan base through the internet, particularly through uploading videos to YouTube. The data comes from videos they have posted there and the comments these generated online. We will begin with the artists themselves and a video in which they address their audience through the posting of a YouTube video and, from there, move on to examine comments posted to one of their most widely viewed videos, for the song "Chamakat Sartasiry," to consider the means through which their audiences perform acts of footing to establish diverse forms of alignment and disalignment to one another and others (imagined and real) within this transnational network.

Saludos/Greetings and Participation Frameworks

A group of five rappers in the highland Andean city of El Alto, Bolivia gather around the video camera of a computer in their makeshift recording studio in the home of one of the group's members. Wearing a now internationally recognizable hip-hop fashion of bomber jackets, sweatshirts, and baseball caps turned backwards, they look in to the camera and address the audience in Spanish (Table 9.1).

Calls of "check check" and "yeah yeah" open Grober and Rolo's greetings to their fans. These phatic microphone checks, like their clothing, form part of a now internationally recognizable communicative repertoire that linguist H. Samy Alim and others have called Hip Hop Nation Language (HHNL) (Alim et al. 2009). The fourth to speak, Eber, dedicates his greeting to everyone who loves hip hop in Latin America. They title the video "Saludos" or

Table 9.1 *Wayna Rap – Saludos*

Grober: Yeah, Yeah ¿Qué tal mis hermanos? desde El Alto, Bolivia representando. Ésto es Wayna Rap junto aquí a Grober, mi persona.	Grober: Yeah, Yeah. What's up my brothers? From El Alto, Bolivia representing. This is Wayna Rap, together here with me, Grober, myself.
Rolo: Y aquí Rolo representando a El Alto, Bolivia, Wayna Rap Clan.	Rolo: And here Rolo representing El Alto, Bolivia, Wayna Rap Clan.
Inzano: Check check acá me dicen Inzano acá representando. No se olviden triple v punto myspace punto com barra wayna rap	Inzano: Check check here they call me Inzano (Eng: Insane) here representing. Don't forget www.myspace/wayna rap
Eber: Hola yo soy Eber Coromata. Un saludo pa todos los locos de Latinoamérica que aman la cultura hip-hop	Eber: Hello I'm Eber Coromata. Greetings to all the crazy ones of Latin America who love hip-hop culture.
Grober: yeah yeah muy pronto estaremos trayéndoles buenas sorpresas junto a Wayna Rap.	Grober: yeah yeah very soon we'll be bringing you good surprises together with Wayna Rap.
No se olviden estamos aquí por las calles de El Alto y La Paz	Don't forget we're here on the streets of El Alto and La Paz.
Wayna Rap – Saludos (uploaded May 31, 2008) www.youtube.com/watch?v=z5AJaLdMotc&feature=related	

"Greetings," situating it within the genre of the *shout-out*, or a greeting from hip-hop artists to their fans and fellow artists viewing them online. We might also note that the title, like their greeting, is in Spanish, not Aymara, and presupposes their online audience as a Spanish speaking one. Their greeting includes a promise of more music videos to come – there will be "good surprises." When those videos come they are not in Spanish, but in Aymara, some times include Quechua, and often have Spanish subtitles. The final, edited version opens with the group's name moving across the screen and is set to a soundtrack of the group's song "Chamakat Sartasiry (Coming out of the Darkness)."

These artists form the collective Wayna Rap. They are multilingual rappers who perform in Aymara, Spanish, and Quechua. Many of them are the children of rural Aymara migrants to the city of El Alto. Part of their motivation to compose and perform their rhymes in the Aymara language stems from their observing the language being abandoned by urban Aymara youth and fears of the language dying out in their, or future, generations (Hornberger and Swinehart 2012; Swinehart 2012d). In a country marked by sharp racial and class divides, performing in Aymara also matters to them as a gesture of anti-racist Indian pride. As indigenous cultural brokers, they understand themselves as protagonists in what many Bolivians refer to as "el proceso de cambio" (the process of change), more boldly described as decolonization by Aymaras and non-Aymaras alike.

The group's name includes the Quechua and Aymara word for "youth" or "young" – "wayna." In this clip they refer to themselves as "Wayna Rap Clan," a name that resonates with parallelism alluding to a more widely known 1990s US hip-hop collective and inspiration for their own work – Wu Tang Clan. Wayna Rap first came together as a collective in 2003 (the video is from 2008). At the time of recording, these were the core members of the now, largely disbanded collective. Eber and Inzano, for example, have moved on to other projects like *Nación Rap*, *Diztinto*, and *Raza Insana*. An important feature of YouTube is its capacity not just as a media-sharing platform but also an interactive social network that connects media producers and their audiences. Digitally mediated communicative events like this video clip have afforded these artists tremendous mobility – their web presence has been crucial for developing an audience in Bolivia and abroad, and has resulted in their being invited to perform in Venezuela, Argentina, and Europe.

From the title of this clip, "Saludos" (greetings), to their embodied stance of gazing into the camera, this video invokes a model of communication that, while being multi-party, implies a dyadic framework of speaker and addressee, the speaking artist, and their viewer on the other side of the screen. The idea of face-to-face communication as a straight forward, dyadic exchange between speaker and addressee is the very model that was helpfully deconstructed by Goffman who recognized that within any given interaction, in fact, there exist more precise characterizations of the speakers' relationship to the utterance – what he called "participation status." Beyond simply a speaker, he elaborated a range of possibilities noting that, "an utterance does not carve up the world beyond the speaker into precisely two parts, recipients and non-recipients, but rather opens up an array of structurally differentiated possibilities, establishing the participation framework in which the speaker will be guiding his delivery" (Goffman 1981: 137). Beyond there being simply a "speaker," the one physically producing the sound of the message is certainly the *animator* of the utterance, but may or may not be its *author* and may or may not represent the moral, institution, or evidential anchor to a given utterance – the *principal*, in Goffman's terms. Goffman expanded the notion of the speaker into author, animator, principal, and elaborated a finer grain set of possible roles for the "addressee," which he broke down into unaddressed recipients, ratified participants, and bystanders with an awareness that, "a ratified participant may not be listening, and someone listening may not be a ratified participant" (Goffman 1981: 132).

The "Saludos" clip seems to invoke a relatively straightforward framework of speakers and an audience, but we can see even here how Goffmanian notions of principal, author, and animator give us a more complex picture. We can consider, for example, the calls of "check, check" and "yeah, yeah" as not only words of Wayna Rap's own authoring, but instead, as words belonging to all rappers, or even musicians more broadly, famously used to check a microphone before initiating a performance, that here are merely *animated* by Grober and Rolo. Similarly, their declarations of representing El Alto, Bolivia, sound almost formulaic for their resonance with other rappers' claim to representing their hood, city or region. These forms of citation through the animation of linguistic practices that form part of HHNL may do as much to situate them characterologically as rappers for their audience as do their clothing and the accompanying music. What of the notion of principal? While these artists are speaking for themselves individually, introducing themselves one by one to their current or potential fans, they simultaneously ground their address to institutional frameworks and systems of value and morality larger than their individual selves – in the Goffmanian sense, other principals are invoked. For one, they speak not only as individuals, but as a group, Wayna Rap, and beyond representing the hip-hop collective itself, as mentioned above, they are representing their home city of El Alto, Bolivia.

Many viewers take up the call to communication, leaving their own *saludos* in response to Wayna Rap's videos in the YouTube comment space. These greetings come from other Bolivians, but also from migrant Bolivians in other parts of South America, the United States and Europe, and include many responses addressed directly to the artists, encouraging them to continue in their work – "*Adelante,*" "*Viva Bolivia!*" keep up the good work etc. In the following sections, we will consider comments left by diasporic Andeans to the video for their song "Chamakat Sartasiry" (for more on this track, see Swinehart 2012d).

CrazyQueen: Deixis and Footing

This comment (Table 9.2) was left by someone using the name CrazyQueen1916. She opens her comment by noting that she is "Bolivian from her heart" (*Boliviana*

Table 9.2 *CrazyQueen's Comment*

soy Boliviana de corazon y_ estoy en Valencia España y es la primera vez que veo este rap boliviano en aymara y me parece genial ojala pudieramos grabar muchas cosas mas similares para no olvidar y llevar siempre adelante nuestros idiomas y culturas MUCHAS FELICITACIONES de una amiga mas . . . para vosotros.
CrazyQueen1916
I am Bolivian in my heart and_ I'm in Valencia Spain and it's the first time that I see this Bolivian rap in Aymara and it seems great to me I hope we could record many more similar things to not forget and to carry forever forward our languages and cultures MANY CONGRATULATIONS from one more friend . . . for you.
CrazyQueen1916

de corazón). We do not know if this means she is figuratively Bolivian or literally a Bolivian who resides in Spain. Either way she makes this affiliation explicitly. We will see below, however, that the language she uses in her comment gives a number of indications that she speaks peninsular Spanish. For example, her use of the pronoun *vosotros* (second-person plural) and the adjective *genial* are both widely recognized as belonging to the register of Spanish spoken in Spain, not in the Andes. Despite being text and not recorded speech like the video above, the appearance of items belonging to a distinct register of the language, in this case peninsular Spanish, have the effect of locating her socially in the world much like the appearance of tokens of HHNL like "check, check" and "respresentando El Alto" do in the "Saludos" video. These kinds of voicing effects (Bakhtin 1981) are powerful mechanisms of non-referential indexicality that point to kinds of social personae that have become associated with these registers through processes of enregisterment (Agha 2005; Swinehart 2008). In what follows, however, we will see that the referential indexicality within in this comment also matters for how she positions herself socially. In other words, the referential indexicality of her comment is every bit as much a form of social indexicality as is the non-referential indexicality of her peninsular Spanish. Tracing the shifts in CrazyQueen's use of referential indexicality, particularly the role of pronominal and verbal deixis, illuminates a varied set of footings that this member of Wayna Rap's audience takes up towards them as artists, towards their music and also others on the internet.

Roman Jakobson (1957) and later Michael Silverstein (1976) illuminated the central role of indexicality in language through their analysis of shifters – locative deictics like *this*, *that*, *here*, temporal deictics like *now*, first- and second-person pronouns, and verbal tense. These signs become meaningful through co-textual arrangement with and in relation to other signs. This is why Jakobson also called these duplex signs, for how they collapse the levels of code and message, of grammatical system and speech event, into one (Jakobson 1957). Verbal tense, like other shifters, operates through "*deixis*, which indicates the spatio-temporal relations of some presupposed referent in the speech event to speaker, hearer, or other referent" (Silverstein 1976: 25). Deictic reference functions to anchor language to the moment of interaction and represented moments of interaction, or *narrated events* in Jakobson's idiom, in order to diagram participant roles within them. Interlocutors use deixis to typify the contexts of their own and others' talk and activity. Thus, deixis provides an important means to establish one's footing. In CrazyQueen's comment, we find her shifting through a number of footings that position her differently with regard to whom she addresses and also concerning the Goffmanian category of principal, discussed above, all within a very short stretch of discourse. While the author and animator remain CrazyQueen throughout, the principal invoked shifts through her comment.

Tracing the deixis of verbal inflection and pronominal reference across this small comment allows us to diagram the shifting principals CrazyQueen voices in this short stretch of text (Table 9.3).

She opens with a series of verbs (*soy* "I am," *estoy* "I am," *veo* "I see") and a dative pronoun (*me* "to me") anchored to first-person subjectivities of identity (*soy* Boliviana de corazón "I am Bolivian in my heart"), location (*estoy* en Valencia "I am in Valencia"), and cognition (*veo* "I see," *me* parece "it seems to me"). Here there is a neat alignment between author, animator, and the principal – she is speaking for herself and herself alone.

From the opening line addressing Wayna Rap, she then shifts to admonishing online bystanders about "not forgetting and always advancing our languages and cultures." This almost formulaic language belongs not to the intimate personal register of the opening line, but to a pious voicing of multicultural, or even traditionalist, platitudes. There is also a shift from the first-person singular to a first-person plural (*pudiéramos* "(that) we could"; *nuestro* "our"). This "we" could either be a "we" of a universal humanity or perhaps she is speaking specifically of a "we" that affiliates with or lays claim to indigenous Andean languages and cultures (cf. Cutler, this volume). Considering the large number of descendants of Andean migrants residing in Spain, this could also be a reasonable interpretation. Either way, we can consider the first-person plural an exclusive *we*, one that addresses other online viewers of the video rather than the artists, who, after all, are already doing precisely what she says ought to be done. Who is the principal invoked with these admonitions? The shift to a first-person plural makes the principal invoked now more than simply CrazyQueen1916 herself, whether simply the other viewers of the video, other indigenous Andeans, the children of Andeans in Europe, or all people interested in human patrimony more broadly.

The closing line brings yet another shift, this time marked through another shift in deixis but also through the visual poetics of the message form itself. In addition to a shift from the (exclusive) first-person plural to third-person reference, there is a change in font size through a shift to all caps: MUCHAS FELICITACIONES de una amiga más … para vosotros "MANY CONGRATULATIONS from one more friend … for you." The change in font brings us to a feature specific to CMC that Ana Deumert, drawing on Jakobson (1957), has likened, in its most creative and excessive cases to the Futurist poets of the early twentieth century (Deumert 2014a: 123–145) for foregrounding the materiality and textual form of the message itself. For as much of an oxymoron as "textual prosody" might seem, we could also consider the change of font the introduction of a prosodic element into the message. While metadiscursive norms online are in flux and still very much emergent, writing in ALL CAPS is often described and perceived as the textual equivalent of a raised voice or shouting. Taking this into account, CrazyQueen1916's

Table 9.3 *Shifts in Footing through CrazyQueen's Comment*

Verbal and Pronominal Deixis	*Comment*	*Addressee*	*Principal*
1.			
1st sing. "I am" (identity)	**soy** Boliviana de corazon	Wayna Rap	Crazy Queen1916
I am (place)	Y **estoy** en Valencia España		
"I see"	y es la primera vez que veo este rap boliviano en aymara		
1st person dative "seems to me"	y **me** parece genial		
2.			
1st plural exclusive/– addressee	ojala **pudieramos** grabar muchas cosas mas similares	other viewers	Andeans, Indigenous,
1st pl. possessive	para no olvidar y llevar siempre adelante **nuestros**		Linguistic Minorities,
	idiomas y culturas		"human patrimony"
3.			
3a.	MUCHAS FELICITACIONES	Wayna Rap	Wayna Rap Fans
1st sing. visual: text. prosody			
3b.			
3rd sing	de una amiga mas . . .		
3c.			
2nd pl. / peninsular Spanish	para **vosotros**.		

stylistic shift is at once deictic, visual, and prosodic. In this message she digitally shouts with enthusiasm and praise, as "another friend," another fan in the adoring crowd online. This is followed by another visual break made by three dots followed by "for you," or even better yet, "for *y'all*," as the second person plural used here is a regionally marked one – *vosotros* – used stereotypically by speakers of peninsular Spanish. The visual and textual organization of her comment could be understood as moving readers' attention across distinct subject positions, from a first-person voice, to a broad fan base. The deictic shifts follow a trajectory of expansion, moving from an intimate conversation with the artists, to a call to other participants to "value our languages," finishing with a stance of public praise.

The BolivianOG: From Byplay to the Online Dis

CrazyQueen shifted her footing rapidly within a short stretch of discourse, addressing the artists, but not them alone. She also crafted her message to address other anticipated viewers online. Others also make use of the comments section in a similar fashion, to engage with other viewers of the videos, sometimes in ways that make it seem as if others online, rather than the initial posters of the video themselves, are the intended addressees of the message. In the following example, we find another Bolivian artist, but this time one based in the United States. He differs from CrazyQueen in terms of his country of residence but also the language in which he writes (and raps) – he posts in English not Spanish, much less Aymara. His name is BolivianOG, a name that positions him as an "original gangster" or "OG." He also comes to Wayna Rap's video from a different place in another sense, whether or not he too is a *boliviano de corazón*. He is an artist himself and not simply another fan. He comes to Wayna Rap's video as another contender in the field of global hip hop, and one whose very name betrays his aspirations of authenticity. In the following comment, we find BolivianOG hailing viewers of Wayna Rap's message in order to direct their attention elsewhere, to listen instead to his music:

> ***search BIG WICKED THE BOLIVIAN OG MIX_***
> ALLEYBOYSATCX3

The addressivity of this comment is simpler than CrazyQueen1916's message in terms of grammatical structure and functionally distinct from hers both in terms of the participation status invoked and the participation framework it projects. The imperative English verb "search" anchors the comment within a participation framework that bypasses Wayna Rap to address directly other viewers online. This comment provides an illustration of the commentator's awareness of the "array of structurally differentiated possibilities" afforded online viewers. Just as Goffman identified in face-to-face interaction, in the

CMC context these possibilities also include being addressed recipients or unaddressed recipient(s), ratified participants or bystanders. Goffman points out that, "a ratified participant may not be listening, and someone listening may not be a ratified participant" (Goffman 1981: 132). These varied statuses establish hierarchies of participation in which there exists "subordinate communication" that is "manned, timed and pitched to constitute a perceivably limited interface to what might be called the 'dominating communication' in its vicinity" (Goffman 1981: 133). Big Wicked BolivianOG's comment provides an instance of online *byplay*, or a participation framework in which ratified participants sidestep, directly engaging the primary initiators of the communicative event, in this case Wayna Rap, to reach out to other participants. It is a kind of parasitic communication facilitated by the very networked, open infrastructure of the internet itself. Unlike the "Saludos" that we saw earlier, or CrazyQueen's "para vosotros," the imperative command *search* is directed at other viewers of Wayna Rap's video to invite them to another communicative encounter, to check out *his* Bolivian hip hop, one that while being 113 percent Bolivian, is in English.

As an intervention in this multilingual CMC context, BolivianOG's positioning of the English language as the medium for authentic (even Bolivian) hip hop runs in direct opposition to the intervention Wayna Rap make with their Aymara lyricism. This implicit contestation of Aymara language use is made more explicitly elsewhere through racist attacks on Wayna Rap and denigrations of the Aymara language. A commentator by the name José Zavala, for example, uses the term *colla* (highlander) in a pejorative sense, evokes the stereotype of Aymaras chewing coca leaves, and belittles the Aymara language calling it *porquería* ("a mess") and less than a language, a mere dialect:

vallan a comer coca collas e mierda. la porqueria q hablan no se considera idioma, si no un dialecto

go eat coca shitty *collas*. the mess you speak isn't considered language, but a dialect

The message combines a common orthographic error ("vallan" for "vayan," Eng. "go"), an abbreviation ("q" for "que," Eng. "that"), alongside an orthography evocative of lowland Bolivian phonology (the attenuation of "de" to "e," Eng. "of") in order to hurl an anti-Indian insult into the mix of comments below Wayna Rap's video (cf. Cutler, this volume). He evokes a stereotypical figure of a coca-leaf-chewing highland Andean and uses an insult – "colla e mierda" ("shitty colla") – salient among the repertoire of anti-Indian epithets associated with racialized east–west regional conflicts in Bolivia (see Swinehart 2012b for a fuller discussion). The author of this comment stakes out a footing of an eastern Bolivian, or "camba," who treats highland Indians like shit ("colla de mierda") and their speech (much less verbal art) as less than fully qualifying as language ("un dialecto"). The insult is directed at Wayna Rap, but also other *collas* who would watch the video and scroll through the comments below it. This kind of anti-Indian racism is precisely what Wayna Rap aims to combat with their Aymara language hip hop. However implicit, the assertion by BolivianOG, that Bolivian hip hop is to be found elsewhere and, once found, will be in English, amounts to an affront (a *dis* even) that shares a symmetry with José Zavala's openly racist insult insofar as it too undermines Aymara's status as a legitimate language. In a mode of byplay, in a footing attached to a US-centric hip-hop identity, BolivianOG implores viewers to look elsewhere for Bolivian hip hop, and *search* for it in English.

Role Alignments

So far, we have considered participation frameworks in terms of deixis, addressivity, and shifts in footing that invoke varied Goffmanian principals, but what of participants' intersubjective orientation to social roles within these encounters? In this section, we examine the visible mediation of national (Bolivian), indigenous, and hip-hop group membership through *referential alignment* (an orientation to the denotational meaning of a message), *characterological alignment* (identification with the figures animated through discourse), and *register-mediated alignment* (identification with *ways* of speaking) (Agha 2007: 177–179; Swinehart 2008).

With BolivianOG, for example, we learn something of the nature of his alignment with social roles by following his instructions and conducting of the search he has told the viewer to conduct. What we find on his page is that what matters most for him is not indigeneity at all, but the fact that he is "113 percent Bolivian" and, clearly, that he is a rapper making hip-hop music. In this sense, there is a direct characterological alignment that unites BolivianOG with Wayna Rap and, potentially at least, with their online audience. The overlap here is with a model of conduct for being a kind of person in the world, an alignment to a hip-hop register, that is a broader semiotic register that includes embodied, physical demeanor, gestural repertoire, vestiment, although not with a more narrowly linguistic register, or even Hip Hop Nation Language.

For CrazyQueen1916, in contrast, it is not clear that the genre of hip hop itself is of any particular importance to her. This may or may not be the case, but what matters to her, at least what we can recover from her comment, is that the music is sung in Aymara, in an indigenous language. The fact that Wayna Rap perform their music in an indigenous language is what is foregrounded as mattering above and beyond the genre or even the referential content of what the lyrics "mean" in their denotational, referential capacity. In this sense, her comment is mediated by her alignment to the linguistic register in which they perform.

This kind of register-mediated alignment may result in what applied linguist Netta Avineri has termed metalinguistic community (Avineri 2014), or a community that orients towards a linguistic code independently of their own proficiency in it through metalinguistic commentary. While there are obvious differences between the Yiddish case examined by Avineri and the sociolinguistic situation facing Quechua and Aymara speakers, the close link in both cases between language shift and experiences of cultural eradication, assimilation, and even genocide create conditions in which metalinguistic communities flourish and conversations about *nuestros idiomas y culturas* ("our languages and cultures") take on the sense of urgency we find in CrazyQueen's comment. And, indeed, there are many examples of comments left in response to Wayna Rap's videos that display this kind of register-mediated alignment celebrating Wayna Rap's use of Aymara and Quechua.

In YouTube's capacity as a social network it permits tracing the author of a comment back to an individual's profile (if they have one), as we saw above with Big Wicked Bolivian OG. In what follows, we will examine two more comments in response to the video "Chamakat Sartasiry" and consider them in light of the self-presentation of those who wrote them through their respective YouTube profile pages. Both display a register-mediated alignment with Wayna Rap's performing in Aymara and Quechua, albeit from radically perspectives.

First we can consider the following comment left by M. Lukaña (Table 9.4): The Quechua that opens the comment, *kawsachunku*, is grammatically equivalent to the Spanish that opens the following line, *qué vivan*, i.e. both can be glossed with the English exhortation "Long live." This parallelism evokes the repetition of a translator at a public meeting, who toggles clearly between one language and another. Lukaña also uses the name of Quechua, the name for the Inca Empire, *Tawantin Suyu*, and also *Abya Yala*, a phrase from the Kuna language that many indigenous and Indianist activists have adopted as an alternative name for the American continents. In this way, he also aligns with the political perspective put forward by these artists singing about indigenous uprising, making this also a case of referential alignment.

Upon visiting M. Lukaña's YouTube site, we find him to be a multilingual, Dutch-, English-, Spanish-, and Quechua-speaking citizen of the Netherlands

Table 9.4 *Long live Quechua and Aymara!*

Kawsachunku Qhichwa Aymarawan! Que vivan todos los pueblos de **Tawantin Suyu** y **tukuy llaqtankuna sumaq**_Abya yala.	**Long live Quechua and Aymara!** Long live all the peoples of **Tawantin Suyu** and **all its cities good**_Abya yala

Bold = Quechua

of Peruvian origin and also a student of linguistics. His affiliation to the world of hip hop is clear through the self-presentation in his profile, where a photo reveals him with a baseball hat turned to one side and sporting a gold chain. Not only is his alignment with hip hop, though, his words of encouragement to Wayna Rap come written in a mixed code of Quechua and Spanish and convey a pro-indigenous message. Taking this fuller picture into account, we can appreciate that Lukaña's comment also provides an example of networked multilingualism (Androutsopoulos 2015) – we find a diasporic Andean using the internet as a space to encounter contemporary indigenous Andean cultural production like Wayna Rap and to engage with other speakers of indigenous Andean languages (cf. Hinrichs, this volume).

While Lukaña aligns neatly with all of the role fractions made available through Wayna Rap's video, in terms of referential, characterological, and register-mediated alignments, we can also find radically more narrow and fractionally aligned orientations to Wayna Rap's music video. The following comment from "Ainamarka" is a case in point. Ainamarka was one of the few to leave extensive comments exclusively in Aymara (Table 9.5).

The author of the first line, in the Goffmanian sense, is not Ainamarka, but Wayna Rap, as this comes from the refrain to the song "Chamakat Sartasiry" to which he is leaving a comment: "(The) Aymara, Quechua is coming, with force, with force, he's coming." Here, Ainamarka is the animator, beginning his own comment with Wayna Rap's lyrics. After this first line, however, the rest of the comment is his own. He writes in Aymara, albeit with an idiosyncratic orthography, and also marks a departure in terms of propositional stance. "Chamakat Sartasiry" is one place of many, including the "Saludos" video above, where Wayna Rap make calls for pan-Latin American solidarity. Ainamarka, however makes a call for unity to an end that does not feature in Wayna Rap's lyrics anywhere – a call to worship Satan. Even his name, *ainamarka*, in Aymara could be glossed in English as "underworld" ("*ayna*-" below, under; "*marka*" land, country). Following the link to this user's profile,

Table 9.5 *Ainamarka's Comment*

Aymara_ Quechua juthaskiwa chamampy chamampy juthaskiwa	Aymara_Quechua is coming, with force with force he's coming
Tacke marka latinoamerica jiwantañani uckja Bastardo jesucristoj!!	All the countries of Latin American let's kill that Bastard Jesuschrist!!
Adorañani Sajra supay 666 ukjaru!!	Let's worship Satan 666 then!!

we find out that he is one of the thousands of Bolivian migrants to the city of Buenos Aires, his profile stating that he is a descendant of "Aymara Warriors." His profile, however, does not make him out to be particularly invested in hip hop. The main video clip he has posted is Bach and his profile photo is a shirtless "selfie" with flexed muscles that one might find on an online dating site. This is not to say there is only a register-mediated alignment, and nothing characterological in Ainamarka's alignment with the figures presented in the "Chamakat Sartasiry" video. Whether it's his comment about being an "Aymara Warrior" or a stated interest in meeting up with extremists from Afghanistan, there may be a characterological alignment with a "tough guy" persona that resonates for him from the demeanor and embodied performance visible to him in Wayna Rap's video, a kind of masculinity that constitutes yet another semiotic fraction extractable from the composite hip-hop register.

Conclusion

The talk we encounter in and surrounding Wayna Rap's video "Chamakat Sartasiry" unfolds in many languages – Spanish, English, Aymara, and Quechua – and in consequentially different registers of these languages, like peninsular Spanish and lowland Bolivian. Many things are done with these languages – songs sung, fans greeted, artists praised, Indians insulted, audiences solicited, comrades sought out, identities affirmed. But what does this diversity do? For one thing, this multilingualism functions as one of the mechanisms for staking out varied sorts of footings with regard to one another and to Wayna Rap's music. While not the only mechanism through which footing is achieved, it is an important one. Whether Jesús Zavala's contemptuous "colla e mierda," hurled with a textual voice that "sounds" like a lowland Bolivian *camba*, or the *vosotros* included in CrazyQueen's gushing approval, linguistic features indexing regional provenance contribute to the overall configuration and meaning of these messages. CrazyQueen and Jesús Zavala's comments stake out radically opposing metalinguistic evaluations concerning the status and use of the Aymara language. One is an instance of the very prejudice and denigration that Aymara speakers face, while the other provides a call for more indigenous language cultural production.

In this sense, we can also see how the multilingualism within these CMC encounters is generative of a metalinguistic community (Avineri 2014), and in ways that facilitate the use of indigenous languages. Like CrazyQueen, Markos Lukaña's bilingual exhortation celebrates indigenous cultural practices and provides one example of how to do this – through using the language in public. Whatever one makes of Ainamarka's call to worship Satan, he does this in Aymara; this forum becomes for him a space in which he listens to the Aymara language and expresses himself in it. For languages like Aymara that, despite its many speakers, continue to undergo processes of language shift among new generations, the creation of CMC fora for language use like the one examined here is promising (cf. Lexander, this volume).

In examining the language of these videos and the comments left in response to them, this chapter has extended Goffman's insights on face-to-face communication to a multilingual CMC context and to "talk" of a different temporal frame and material durability than what Goffman had in mind with "the interaction order." Still, as in face-to-face encounters, tracing the shifts in footing and role alignments achieved in multilingual CMC encounters across multiple scales, from the smallest comment posted in response to a video, to more elaborate representations of selves (and ideal selves) on profile pages, proves analytically productive. We see, for example, CrazyQueen shift between an intimate conversation with artists she admires, to more public (seemingly rehearsed even) admonitions to her fellow viewers to "advance our languages and cultures." Big Wicked Bolivian OG tries to poach off Wayna Rap's site to increase his own online visibility. We have personal profiles of a bookish hip-hop fan in Amsterdam and a bodybuilding Bolivian metal head in Argentina, who, for one moment online, share Aymara hip hop as a mutual point of attention and cultural commentary. The tracing of footing and role alignment in these cases illuminates how these digitally dispersed individuals orient not just to one another but also to larger social aggregates of group belonging.

Here, we can reflect again on Sapir's words that open this chapter concerning the communicative nature of society. In addition to being ahead of his time in characterizing society as a network, we could also acknowledge the extent to which he flipped the script concerning the traditional subject of expertise of his era's anthropology – "the primitive tribe." In that same 1931 essay "Communication," he counters the view that so-called primitive languages were less complex or capable of eloquence, artistry, and sophistication than Western ones (Sapir 1951: 105). Jesús Zavala's remarks insulting Aymaras and their language provide an unfortunate reminder that such views have survived into the twenty-first century. Sapir closes the essay by going on to say that, in fact, "we" are just like "them," noting that "The multiplication of far-reaching techniques of communication . . . increases the sheer radius of communication so that for certain purposes the whole civilized world is made the psychological equivalent of a primitive tribe" (Sapir 1951: 108). Would he have anticipated that, within a only few generations, members of "tribes," as the Aymara were certainly considered in his day, would be engaged in transnational conversations about music, politics, and culture? Sapir also alluded to his own fear that the spread of telecommunications could have a flattening effect on culture in ways that anticipate some contemporary critics of globalization. The brief examination of diasporic Andeans' discourse online here, however, provides a cast of characters that are anything but homogeneous.

A Satan worshipping, muscle building, sometimes Bach listening, sometimes hip-hop enthusiast, politically Indianist Bolivian migrant may seem a marginal figure within the many intersecting communities to which he belongs. Despite the many ways he may indeed experience marginality as a Bolivian migrant in Argentina, within this CMC context he is not marginal but at the center of his own network of interaction. As an individual node within a networked context there is one sense in which no one can be marginal if there is no center. If we are to return to the initial questions of how it is that senses of groupness are negotiated within networked contexts, it seems inadequate to simply acknowledge, or celebrate even, the kaleidoscopic, fractal array of possible identities that coalesce within them. The challenge, instead, is to understand how these sometimes overlapping, sometimes diverging, alignments towards diverse semiotic fractions become linked to social actors, institutional frameworks, and value projects. Whether these projects have names like hip hop, indigeneity, or the Aymara language, they are all framed by sociohistoric formulations to which these alignments are anchored, and reflexively extend. What can we learn from tracing online discourse? We learn something of the affordances of CMC for varied participation frameworks, but also, hopefully, some outlines of ongoing social history.

10 The Language of Diasporic Blogs

A Framework for the Study of Rhetoricity in Written Online Code Switching

Lars Hinrichs

Introduction

This chapter investigates rhetoricity in written online code switching (WOCS). The notion of *rhetorical* code switching (CS), as introduced in Hinrichs (2006), refers to a quality of language-contrasting behavior in computer-mediated writing which, as I argue, distinguishes it from CS in speech.[1]

In general, rhetorical language has since antiquity been understood as figurative language, i.e. language which uses imagery (metaphors, figures, tropes, and schemes); as such it is the conceptual opposite of literal language. In literal language, linguistic forms serve to convey only their unaltered referential meaning.[2] Figurative language, by contrast, is characterized by meaning which arises not from direct reference to objects, but from semiotic tropes such as metaphor, symbolism, iconicity, simile, metonymy, etc.

Conditions of textual production play a part in whether and how rhetoricity occurs: to the extent that rhetorical language is more elaborate, unpredictable, creative, and artful than literal language, and that it requires, in addition to the cognitive work of giving shape to intended message content, reflection on and application of aesthetic principles, it takes more effort to produce. And therefore, the modality of writing – especially in asynchronous modes – is more conducive to rhetoricity than spontaneous speech because it exerts fewer time constraints on linguistic production. Deumert (2014a) makes a very similar

[1] I thank Susan Herring for her comments on this paper, made when it was presented in her workshop at NWAV 2012; Axel Bohmann for multiple rounds of commentary; the editors of this volume for their careful reviews of the manuscript at multiple stages; and Erica Brozovsky for help with the formatting of the manuscript. I am especially indebted to Christian Mair, who in a conversation in 2002 casually mentioned the discrepancy between the use of language features traditionally coded as spontaneous/informal and the overall "rhetorical" nature of some types of online language use. The usual disclaimers apply.

[2] The main exception to this observation is catachresis, i.e. conventionalized metaphors such as *leg of a chair* which historically have entered the realm of literal language "under the pressure of necessity", i.e. due to the lack of another, literal referent for a certain thing or concept (Freinkel 2012: 210).

point for mobile technologies: she finds that due to material constraints on written language production, mobile and digital language is often more carefully constructed than speech.

Much like semiotic tropes, the interactional meanings of CS vary: there are some types in which CS creates interactional meaning in a simpler, quasi-literal logic, and other types in which the meanings of CS are constructed from complex juxtapositions of intertextually embedded voices and stances. Since CS is able to contribute so vastly to the process of invoking the voices of others in one's own discourse, I argue that this, the construction of complex and hybrid voices, is the most strongly rhetorical discourse function of CS in general. My proposal that CS participates in a continuum of meaning creation types, from least to most rhetorical is linked to the following well-known passage from Bakhtin's work:

> Our speech, that is, all our utterances (including our creative works), is filled with others' words, varying degrees of otherness or varying degrees of "our-own-ness." . . . These words of others carry with them their own expression, their own evaluative tone, which we assimilate, rework, and re-accentuate. (Bakhtin 1986:89)

In Gumperz's framework (1982), switches among codes create meaning either in a "situational" or a "metaphorical" way. (The best-known iterations of Gumperz's framework contain the situational-metaphorical contrast; see further discussion below.) In situational CS, speakers in bilingual/bidialectal communities select codes based on features of the interactional setting (addressee, topic, or location) and by following communally held expectations for the co-occurrence of prestigious situations with prestigious codes. In metaphorical CS, speakers draw on these co-occurrence expectations when they switch codes *as if* a feature of the external situation had just changed, when really the variables of addressee, topic and location have remained constant. As I show, situational switching is barely relevant in the study of WOCS (see also Hinrichs 2006: Chapter 3). In other words, practically all CS in digital writing is "metaphorical," as defined by Gumperz. But within the class of metaphorical switches, there are important typological distinctions whose differences are rooted in their different respective degrees of figurativeness and, hence, we find degrees of rhetoricity. This paper offers a descriptive and classificatory approach to the phenomenon of variable rhetoricity in WOCS.

As I have mentioned, written online communication is conducive to greater rhetoricity, relative to speech, owing primarily to constraints on production: writing allows for more time to think (especially in asynchronous modes). However, it is also fostered by two additional aspects of the context of the discourse that I will consider as data in this study.

1. Increasing global mobility and diversity in urban settings (Vertovec 2007; Bock et al., this volume), and the resulting increase in the frequency of communication among people of different backgrounds in general (Blommaert and Rampton 2011), result in a destabilization of traditionally homologous language ideologies. That is to say, while traditional ideologies associated one language to one territory (the English speak English, Italians speak Italian ...), the factual inaccuracy of such simple correlations becomes increasingly salient as non-native speakers of locally dominant languages increase in number and the quantity of languages in diversifying locales grows (Blommaert 2013).
2. Rhetoricity, specifically as an aspect of the way in which multiple, contrasting linguistic resources are combined in discourse, is also more likely to be found in the discourse of young people – i.e. of adolescent and emerging adults – than of adults (cf. Bock et al., this volume; Lexander, this volume). In this paper, I will not pursue in detail the issue of life stages and the ways in which they relate to the rhetoricity of WOCS (but see Hinrichs 2016).

Data and Method

Data for this study were collected through a form of sociolinguistic online ethnography[3] (Jonsson and Muhonen 2014; Kytölä 2012). I followed multiple blogs written by Jamaican authors from 2007 until 2011. A subset of the data that informs the present study was analyzed and discussed in previous publications (Hinrichs 2012; Hinrichs and White-Sustaíta 2011). Observation and data collection for the present study continued past the time when the earlier studies were conducted, so that the present paper also draws on some more recent additions to the corpus. While none of the blog authors are personally known to me, I interacted with some of them in informal email interviews, which complement my observation of publicly visible interactions in online fora.

The blogs I observed were of the "personal journal" type (Herring et al. 2006), with a few exceptions where writers also followed a partly professional genre (see, e.g., example [10] below, taken from a personal journal blog with occasional fashion reviews).

In total, 48 different writers were followed, 21 of them male and 27 female. All writers can be described as being at a stage in life that immediately precedes full adulthood: they are all 18 years or older (the oldest writer is in his early thirties), but they have not yet fully settled for a career and fixed life partner.[4]

[3] Critics of online ethnography have questioned the extent to which it truly shows the socially and physically immersive aspects of traditional ethnography (e.g. Kelly-Holmes 2015).

[4] In gathering demographic information about writers, I primarily used what writers made available on their public profiles, or what could be inferred from their writing about themselves. Therefore, specifics such as writers' *exact* age could not be obtained for each individual.

Most are university students; many are single. Arnett refers to this life stage as "emerging adulthood" (Arnett 2003; Bigham 2012; Hinrichs 2016). While the sample emerged nearly balanced for gender purely by chance, I intentionally selected writers to reflect "homeland" and "diaspora" residence in an even distribution. As a result, 23 of the writers reside in Jamaica, and 25 are diasporic individuals, residing in Great Britain, Canada, the United States, or (in one case) another island nation in the Western Caribbean.

Overall, the modestly sized corpus contains 190 blog post and comment samples, amounting to a volume of 47,274 words. The samples were catalogued with running numbers, which are cited in this chapter to identify data excerpts. Blog posts are labeled with a number, whereas comments are labeled with both the number of the master post under which they occur and an additional ordering number prefixed with <–c>.

Most individuals who are linguistically socialized in Jamaica grow up with some degree of access to both Jamaican Creole (JC) and Jamaican English (JE). The vast majority of Jamaicans speak JC as their first language at home, acquiring English during their years in the educational system. JE is the dominant language of literacy, since no official standards exist for the written use of JC; in fact, language activists are still pushing for the official recognition of JC as a language by the national government (Brown-Blake 2008). Therefore, when JC is used in online writing, writers rely on impromptu and conventionalizing practices of transliteration, which in turn draw on the plentiful etymological links between JC and English words, but which also, in some cases, systematically depart from English orthographic models (Hinrichs and White-Sustaíta 2011).[5]

Jamaicans in the diaspora, including members of the first and of subsequent generations, typically have access to some form of JC, but tend to use or converge toward a different, local form of Standard English. For example, many members of the Jamaican community in Canada speak Canadian English and JC (Hinrichs 2014).

In referring to JC, it should be noted that the term *Creole* is used mostly by linguists, whereas native speakers most commonly use the term *Patois* (with stress on the first syllable). Since the present chapter is interested in the contextual meanings of different linguistic resources' written uses, but not in typological, creolist, or linguistic-descriptive questions, I use the terms *Creole*, or the abbreviation *JC*, and *Patois* interchangeably.

However, information about gender, occupation, country of residence, *approximate* age and, of course, the fact that writers were of Jamaican background could be verified for each individual writer.

5 Outside of digital contexts, written uses of JC are limited to experimental approaches by literary artists, or signage (Devonish 1996).

Code switches between English and Creole were marked manually. In distinguishing Creole from English, the criteria described in, e.g. Hinrichs and White-Sustaíta (2011: 51–52) (see also Hinrichs 2006: Chapter 2) were applied: the label "Creole" was assigned (i) at the clause level and (ii) only when overt morphosyntactic or lexical markers were present. Meanwhile, orthography was generally ignored in this metric because nonstandard spellings occur even in clearly English passages.[6] Reductive markers of Creole substrate interference in English such as copula deletion were *not* considered sufficient to mark a clause as Creole if no other features were present.[7]

The methods used in analyzing the data fall broadly into the group of methods described by Herring (2004) as "computer-mediated discourse analysis." At its center lies the qualitative, interpretive analysis of the sociocultural meanings indexed by the construction of language contrast through CS.

Toward a Rhetoricity-Based Framework of Written Online Code Switching

Preliminaries

As mentioned in the introduction, the construction of sociocultural meaning through CS can function metaphorically, in the same sense as referential meaning, which can be constructed through both literal and metaphorical language use. In the case of CS, the literal dimension corresponds to Gumperz's category of situational CS.

As I have argued, situational CS is extremely rare in digital writing (Hinrichs 2006: Chapter 3). It involves, in Gumperz's definition, "a simple, almost one-to-one relationship between language usage and social context" (Gumperz 1982: 61). De-emphasizing the aspect of volitional switching, Gumperz models situational switches as *reactions* on the part of speakers to changes in *setting*, *topic*, or *addressee*. Over the years, much critique has been leveled at this, the situational part of Gumperz's framework (e.g. Auer 1984: 90, who criticizes the rather static notion of "situation" underlying it).[8] It is rare for the setting or the

[6] There are exceptions to this tactic. In a small number of cases, insertions were marked as Creole by orthography, but not morphosyntactically. These cases were also included if it was clear that nonstandard orthographic choices were indexical of exclusively Creole phonology. For an example, cf. example (1) below.

[7] My classification provides a practical solution to the issue of identifying codes in mixed discourse. As I lay out elsewhere (Hinrichs 2006: Chapter 2), it does not intend to contribute to theoretical debates about the appropriateness of labels such as *creole, pidgin*, etc. (Mufwene 1997), or the nature of the creole continuum (see, e.g. chapters in Hinrichs and Farquharson 2011).

[8] Gumperz himself abandoned the distinction between situational and metaphorical CS in later work. This move was resonant with critiques that his model had received over the years.

addressee of electronically mediated discourse to change turn-internally. Topics do change turn-internally in CMD, of course, but only very few topics seem to produce robust correlations with code switches in predictable directions (Hinrichs 2006).

Due to the problematic absence of volition from the definition of situational switching, and because instances of "a simple, one-to-one relationship" between changes in setting/topic/addressee and language use are so very rare in digital data, I propose that this framework for the discourse functions of WOCS dispense with the category entirely, and that it focus instead on a plausible grouping of CS discourse functions, arranged in a continuum from less to more rhetorical types.

Gumperz's notion of metaphorical CS posits the dynamics of situational CS as its reference point at the literal level. The model was initially developed on a case study of language in Hemnesberget, a coastal village in northern Norway. In the community, a locally restricted dialect, Ranamål (R), coexists with one of the national standard varieties of Norwegian, Bokmål (B). Residents prefer using R in informal interactional contexts, e.g. in talk among personal friends and family members, while B serves as the language of education, business interactions, public discourse, most outgroup interactions, and so on.

According to Blom and Gumperz's account (1972), the sociolinguistic situation in Hemnesberget closely resembles diglossia as originally described by Ferguson (1959), featuring a set of two varieties of the same language that are in fairly strict complementary distribution across social domains and contexts of use. Ferguson introduced the binary of "H" versus "L" codes: H is the high-prestige code (here, B) and L is the low-prestige code (here, R). In Fishman's (1967) elaboration, the dynamics of diglossia are shown to operate in ways similar to those described by Ferguson in fully bilingual (as opposed to merely bidialectal) settings. By and large, diglossia is thought to be an apt descriptor of Jamaica as a sociolinguistic setting, where JC functions as L and JE as H. While creolists and Caribbeanists have argued about whether the notion of a "*strict* separation of codes" (emphasis added) applies in the Jamaican situation, Devonish (2003) has pointed out the ways in which the distribution of codes among social domains in Jamaica, however strict or loose it may be, is representative of the linguistic consequences of colonialism (cf. Swinehart, this volume).

As a description of the socio linguistic situation in a small-town Norwegian locale, Blom and Gumperz's (1972) study has received criticism from Norwegian linguists: the possibility of B and R existing as distinct codes in the repertoires of speakers in Hemnesberget has been questioned (Mæhlum 1996). As Røyneland (2009: 11) notes, diglossia may have been historically present in Norway, during the "language struggle" of the nineteenth century pursuant to Norway's political independence from Denmark: while Denmark and what is now Norway had been seen as a mostly coherent linguistic space prior to 1814, newly independent Norway was now in need of a defined standard of its own. Proposals varied in their degree of adherence to the Copenhagen model of Danish, but they all involved a move toward endogenization of Norwegian linguistic norms. In this scenario, the emergence of Bokmål (in the nineteenth century) much resembles a type B situation with spoken diglossia, but we hardly find type B areas, "with code switching between discrete varieties, in *present-day* Norway" (Røyneland 2009: 19; emphasis added).

With these caveats upon the epistemology of Blom and Gumperz's study in mind, we can nonetheless identify those aspects of their model of CS in society from which the present paper departs. Situational switching, in Gumperz's framework, is best illustrated in a diglossic community, where there is a linguistic repertoire, shared at the community level, which comprises one and only one H, and only one L. This is a precondition for changes in interactional context to prompt predictable code selections. Metaphorical CS, on the other hand, involves switches which, in contrast to situational CS, are *not* prompted by changes in the interactional context, but which are made proactively by speakers in order to contextualize the referential content of their discourse. In a frequently cited list, Gumperz names six contexts in which metaphorical CS typically occurs:

1. quotations (direct quotations or reported speech)
2. addressee specification (to direct a message to one of several addressees)
3. interjections (or sentence filters)
4. reiteration (either literally or modified)
5. message qualification (e.g. sentence and verb complements)
6. personalization vs. objectivization (e.g. degree of speaker involvement).

(Gumperz 1982: 75)

This list of CS contexts is problematic, not only because it is non-exhaustive (as Gumperz concedes), but also because it mixes CS *functions* with CS *sites*. For example, "personalization" is a function of CS, but "reiteration" is simply a location for a stretch of discourse which repeats content; as such it does not state what exactly the switch adds to the message. All the label suggests is that the switch draws attention to the reiteration itself. But the list coheres in one central sense: in all six cases, metaphorical CS acts primarily as a highlighting device. Switches from one code to the other are explained as primarily intended to draw attention to discourse, and if they are soon followed by a switch back into the original code, then they serve to expose one stretch of discourse as in some way different from the surrounding discourse. It is undeniable that the identity of the codes also matters in bringing additional meaning to each individual case of language alternation – sometimes more so, sometimes less.[9] In the case of Gumperz's study, the meaning added by the identity of the code can typically be inferred from its role as either H or L in the local diglossia, which opens up a kind of indexical field (Eckert 2008a) of broadly overt-prestige-oriented functions for H and covert-prestige-oriented functions for L. However, the contrasting potential of CS is both primary and essential to all types in Gumperz's list, along with a strongly local orientation of the analytical perspective: switches are analyzed individually and case by case, but not at the level of the text or interaction.

Situational switching is rare in modalities other than speech, e.g. in written online discourse or in multilectal, super-diverse communities in which participants' repertoires vary at the individual level, and which do not show the simple and homogeneous sociolinguistic order of an established diglossia. Meanwhile, metaphorical switching is anything but rare in such domains – in fact, it is quite frequent in written online discourse (Hinrichs 2006: Chapter 4) – and this is due precisely to the fact that metaphorical switching is primarily a focusing device and works through contrast. Additional meanings, ones that might be metaphorically inferred from the underlying diglossic logic of situational switching, are non-essential to its functioning. Therefore, the notion of situational switching is absent from the framework presented here.

In the three groups of CS functions discussed below, which represent increasing degrees of rhetoricity, those functions that construct meaning primarily from contrast form the first group. The other two groups are those that are noticeably more rhetorical because the indexical values of the codes involved, as well as their relation to topic and the writer's stance, contribute to the interactional meaning in crucial ways, unlike in the first group. The notions of voice, intertextuality, and heteroglossia, which are familiar from sociolinguistic reworkings of Bakhtin's writings (1981; 1984; 1986) in recent years, are helpful in organizing these types.

Rhetoricity in Three Types of WOCS Discourse Functions

Type I: Switching for Contrast Gumperz coined the term "contextualization cue" as an inclusive descriptor for the function of CS in conversation (1982). CS adds meaning to discourse, not by explicitly altering its referential meaning, but by contextualizing it: the fact that speakers switch to another code for certain stretches of speech informs listeners that those segments need to be understood – or contextualized – somehow differently than the preceding discourse. In a diglossic community, all speakers command, by and large, identical linguistic repertoires, at least with respect to the dual nature

9 See Auer (1992) on the continuum from "contrastive" to "inherent" CS functions. In particular, Sebba and Wootton (1998) address the issue of code sequence in the analysis of CS meanings.

of their composition: they comprise an H and an L code, and those show regular structural and social differences from one another. Switches from one of those codes to the other therefore are not jumps to linguistic resources that are in any way external: both codes are integral parts of each individual speaker's voice. This does not imply, however, that community members are unable to construct voices of other people: CS is only one of a range of strategies that speakers can use to construct others' voices; it is complemented by structural variation at all levels of linguistic analysis.

In this type, where switching primarily functions to construct the semiotic device of contrast, speaker stance toward the current topic of discussion, in other words: toward the stance object (Du Bois 2007), does not necessarily change either. In (1), the switch into Creole in the first sentence is a modification of the content of the main message, adding non-essential information to the primary strand of discourse.[10]

1.
[. . .] Nikki, while sitting and reading about new super

bug (**some staph sumting or de odder**) in the newspaper:
some staph something or the other

"Lawd!!! Who is it that really comes up with all these

names for bacteria? [. . .]" <b03>

In this example, Gumperz's Type 5, "message qualification," best describes the location of the switch in discourse (without addressing its function). The linguistic-structural contrast created by the switch acts as a highlighter to the fact that this insertion does not advance the discourse in the same way that the surrounding material does, and that, instead, additional information is provided. As such, the code switch reduplicates the contextualization delivered typographically by the parentheses that enclose the switched passage.[11]

In (2), the author is reflecting on the advantages and disadvantages of professional childcare. The first sentence of the excerpt (in English) makes

[10] In presenting data extracts, the following conventions were followed: regular font – English text; **boldface** – Jamaican Creole text; underlining – text in codes other than English or JC; *italics* – interlinear glosses of Creole text. Elision marks in square brackets ([. . .]) were applied wherever material from an original post was omitted. Reference indices from my corpus were included in angular brackets for each data sample.

[11] Throughout my presentation of data, I cite as CS functions those that I regard as primary, but I hasten to concede that many instances of CS operate through multiple methods at once. For example, it would not be wrong to provide a reading of double-voicing in (1) – perhaps, the voice of an uneducated, naïve persona is invoked here in order to construct a stance of puzzlement in the face of the scientific facts being discussed in the newspaper – but I would argue that this interpretation is secondary to the one of providing defining information on the noun phrase immediately preceding the switch.

a general statement, while the following passage in JC presents the core message (Sebba and Wootton 1998), i.e. the true and personal motivation for the writer to make the preceding argument.

2.
[. . .] I believe that sometimes it is more important to

suffer the financial hardship than to leave our chil-

dren to the whims and fancy of others. **Bottom line is**
The bottom line is

that is dat is not fi dem pickney and dem nah look
((error)) those are not their children and they do not

afta dem like yuh. I am not saying that there
look after them like you do

are not circumstances [. . .] <b12>

The code switch in (2) signals to the reader that the argument in the JC insertion is to be read differently from the surrounding discourse. The reader infers, e.g. from the fact that the topic has not changed, that the material in the insertion is to be read not as coordinate to the environment, but as a restatement of previous message content – in this case, with greater specificity.

Example (3) contains a similar case of increasing specificity from prior discourse to code-switched material. But primarily, the switch highlights a change from more informational to more involved narration: from the telling of a story about a mango-stealing dog to a statement of the narrator's own, very personal evaluation of the dog. This type of stylistic juxtaposition, highlighted by CS, is captured in Gumperz's category 6, "personalization vs. objectivization." An additional, parallel juxtaposition in this excerpt is in the contrast between a speech act of story-telling and the explicitly performative speech act (Austin 1975), borrowing the Rastafarian verbal convention of *faiya-bon* (> "fire-burn," Farquharson 2005) to curse one of the actors in the story.

3.
[. . .] Here I was saying how worthless she was letting

strangers into the yard when in fact the protector is

the criminal. Well if she is going to be stealing my

mangoes then she and I cannot co-exist, . . . **fyah bun fi**
curses on

mango tief!!! Anyways enough crap from me today. [. . .]
the mango thief <b11>

Out of Gumperz's six types of metaphorical switches, there is one that does not easily fit my definition of "CS functions derived primarily from structural contrast, but no alternation of voice or stance" (i.e. Type I): it is the "switching for quotations" kind, because it necessarily involves the inclusion of others' voices. By contrast, in all the other contexts the functions of CS do not derive from other-voicing. Therefore, I consider code switches that co-occur with direct or indirect quotations as the simplest and most straightforward case of the integration of another's voice.

Type II: Polyvocal CS Type II captures cases of CS use in contexts of intertextuality. Following a common understanding among readers of Bakhtin (e.g. Linell 2009: 120), I consider intertextuality and polyvocality to be two sides of the same coin, or more precisely: the latter is a result of the former.

Intertextuality and polyvocality are observed at the level of the discourse, whereas the related phenomenon of heteroglossia exists at the social level.[12] Whenever CS contributes to the construction or invocation of others' voices, it adds to the referential value of a discourse in a more complex way than is the case in Type I switching. Type II, which I label "polyvocal switching," encompasses switches through which either textual material from, or the voice of, an *identifiable, concrete personal or textual source* is integrated.

Example (4) demonstrates Gumperz's class "switching for quotations," a direct speech quote is delivered in another code than the surrounding narrative. Gumperz discusses that in the context of reported speech, CS can be motivated by either or both of two potentially competing goals: to use structural contrast as a way to highlight the material in the switch as somehow distinct from surrounding discourse (as all other classes that I include in Type I), and/or to reproduce the speech of others in as true to the original a way as possible, which implies mimetic code choice based on how the original quote was said (Gumperz 1982: 82–83). Since in reported speech, the constraint of authenticity acts upon code choice in addition to the incentive of its highlighting function, this function is not included in Type I, but represents instead the simplest type of switching in the context of intertextuality. In (4), a writer reports her own words, which occurred in a conversation she had with a man, a would-be suitor, after church one recent Sunday.

[12] In Bakhtin's original formulation, heteroglossia described the coexistence and contrasting use of social voices in competition (Bakhtin 1981). Heteroglossia was thought of as the linguistic-symbolic site of class struggle. In more recent uses of the term (e.g. Bailey 2007; 2012), authors have focused more on the notion of the alternating use of social codes, and its difference from multidialectalism, but have not dwelled on the Marxist dimensions of the term.

4.
[. . .] Perhaps I smiled a bit too sweetly on occasions,

or spoke too engagingly, which has led him to make

this ludicrous request now.

"Yu waan mi fi do wha?" My voice is shrill and laced
you want me to do what?

with incredulity. [. . .] <b40>

The writer here reports her own words from a concrete and identifiable context. Since the writer is bilingual and biliterate in English and JC, we are unable to judge whether she represents her words in the code they were spoken in: either one is a plausible choice, given her repertoire. What she provides is a stylization of her own response, drawing on linguistic contrast with the surrounding narrative.

Examples of clearly traceable intertextuality vary in terms of the amount of flagging that is provided. A code switch can itself act as a flag to an intertextual insertion, but since this study is only interested in CS to begin with, our focus is on *additional* flag types. In (4), an explicit quotative is missing, but at the typological level quotation marks signal the passage in JC as an insertion, and the reference to the writer's speaking voice is easily read as a statement of who made the utterance.

In (5), the JC insertions are just as readily decoded as embeddings of the voices of others based on the typographical cue of double quotes that enclose both. This time, however, speaker identity is more diffuse: a group of "some guys" is mentioned, but the quote is never explicitly attributed to them except by implication. It is unclear whether all of the "guys" spoke the words, or only a subset.

5.
[. . .] I passed some guys **"browning, you look good enuh"**
browning,[13] *you look good you know*

and I responded "thanks" with a smile. Not all of our

men are haggardly [*sic*] and disrespectful. **"Waah mi**
want me to

walk wid you baby" "No thanks :)" [. . .] <b88>
walk with you baby

When reported speech is part of a narrative, as it is in (4) and (5), and code switching is reserved for the speech of some of the characters, but not all, CS

[13] *Browning* – (n.) 'light-brown-skinned girl' (Cassidy and Le Page 1980).

becomes a tool for the organization of narrative that serves, in effect, textual economy: despite the potential complexity in the array of a narrative's personae, quotatives and declarations of speaker identity for each given piece of reported speech are minimized as the contextualizing function of CS assumes their function (Hinrichs 2006: 127–132).

In the following example, the process of re-entextualization of external textual material is even more minimally signposted: a Jamaican proverb is cited, then discussed. The source of the quote is de-personal, as is usually the case with proverbs. Almost by necessity, then, there is no quotative; we also don't find any other form of material flagging aside from the code change.

6.
Oh Lord . . . I am late with this one.

A fas' mek anansi deh a 'ouse-tap
because of his curiosity, Anansi [a spider and mythical creature] has to be at the top of the house [in the attic][14]

Interpretation

-continue writing

-do the Dr. Doolittle approach on dogs and reptiles.

[. . .] <b51–c03>

While in (6), a proverb is embedded that has no identifiable author but a fixed phrasing, and which thus constitutes formulaic CS (Bullock and Toribio 2009; Namba 2010), example (7) evokes a stereotypical concept which can occur in many different formulations and types of embedding. The idea is: "Jamaican women are strong." In my study of Jamaican email, I noted that there is a certain voice that writers frequently adopt, often by switching into JC (Hinrichs 2006: 119–126). Here, the writer does not speak in the voice of a Jamaican woman's character; instead she makes a general statement about Jamaican women.

7.
[. . .] I NEVER saw my daddy lay his hand on my mother,
and he never beat my sister or me. Plus, if he had
tried that with my mother, she would've dealt with his
case. **Yu nuh mess wid a Jamaican ooman**, lol. [. . .] <b95–c01>
you don't mess with a Jamaican woman

Yu nuh mess wid a Jamaican ooman is not a formulaic statement (attempts to read it as intertextually connected to the phrase *Don't mess with Texas!*

14 See Watson (1991: 32) on the proverb cited here.

should prove unsatisfying), but the sentiment is widely acknowledged among Jamaicans and has been represented and discussed often in vernacular stories and poems, cf. Louise Bennett's poem "Jamaica Oman" (reprinted in Donnell and Welsh 1996: 145–146; for a critical reading see Cooper 1988). With its lack of explicit cues as to its own intertextuality, this Creole insertion demonstrates an important dimension of rhetoricity in WOCS: the switch into a different code, one that is itself indexically linked to the sociocultural construct that is invoked – serves as the sole evidence of polyvocality.

In summary, examples (4)–(7) have presented a cline of increasing rhetoricity in the discourse functions of WOCS. With greater rhetoricity, the semiotic-indexical load of individual switches increases, while the contribution of their contrastive, highlighting function (Type I) to the overall function of switches within texts becomes relatively less important.

Type III: Heteroglossic CS In contrast to Type II, Type III covers those switches in which other-voicing indexes an *opaque source*. Most typically, the indexed sociocultural unit is a *social code* as opposed to a concrete person or text. A social code is a distinct way of speaking that is recognized within a given cultural space. In the Jamaican context, a very well-known and easily recognized social code is Rastafarian speech, which has been described in the linguistic literature as a variety of JC (Pollard 1980; 1986; Slade 2014; Hinrichs 2015). This variety, Dread Talk (DT), is spoken consistently by practicing members of the Rastafarian religion in Jamaica. It differs from JC mostly at the lexical level. (There are also a handful of morphological, but no phonological or syntactic differences.) When words from the DT lexicon are used within JC passages, they act as critical "code markers": forms with sufficient indexical load to define the code of a certain stretch of discourse (Saville-Troike 2003). In example (8), a JC clause is inserted into an otherwise English blog comment, and within the JC insertion, a DT lexical feature (bold-underlined) serves to mark the insertion as DT.[15] The sample is a comment on a blog post that included a photo of a female fashion model with very short hair.

8.
Although **mi bun fire fi the ball head thing**, she does
I despise the baldhead thing

[15] The DT lexeme is a verbalized version of *faiya-bon*, discussed in the context of (3) above. Incidentally, the spelling <bon> reflects a use of the phonemic Cassidy-orthography for creole languages (Cassidy 1982), which is typically used by linguists. The spelling <bun>, on the other hand, is a nonce transliteration that the blog writer employed.

look captivating! <b05–c01>

The (male) writer voices disdain for the woman's short haircut; in doing so, he indexes a Rastafarian voice. While my attempts to interview the writer personally by email were unsuccessful, his online profile suggests that he is not a Rastafarian himself and that he splits his time between living in New York and in the Greater Kingston area of Jamaica. The use of DT forms thus appears as a form of unidirectional double-voicing: by assuming the social code of DT, he invokes the identity of a Rastaman, speaking on his behalf. The Rasta voice supports the direction of his own discourse, since it is among the beliefs of Rastafarianism that hair should be allowed to grow freely (Chevannes 1994). This fact is general knowledge among persons from the West Indies. Playful assumption of a Rastafarian voice by non-Rastafarians is common among Jamaicans and around the world.[16] The code switch in (8) thus illustrates how a Type I highlighter function can coincide with CS used in a heteroglossic language practice. Unlike Type I switches, this kind can work productively as a strategy of meaning creation among speakers who do not share a particular social code as part of their "own"[17] repertoire: the writer in (8) uses DT without being Rastafarian, and his readers understand and appreciate this act of playful double-voicing without "owning" DT themselves (this does not rule out the possibility that members of the readership may actually be practitioners of Rastafarianism).

In a similar way, (9) draws attention to the speaker's identity and repertoire. It is another example of double-voiced invocation of the Rastafarian voice by a non-Rastafarian.

9.
[. . .] Stood 2 hours in line at the Tax Office to get the car licenced [*sic*]. Paid out $2000.00 of hard earned money **just so that Babylon don't hold down black man**. Imperialism at its best. [. . .] <b26>

In this instance, we can speak of varidirectional double-voicing: the writer reports paying $2,000 (about $15–20 in US currency) "just so that Babylon don't hold down black man." The idea that Babylon, i.e. the pervasive system of Western oppression, imposes rules, collects fees and levies fines in order to continue the subjugation of blacks that began with slavery is a deeply held belief in Rastafarianism. In this sense, Rasta discourse aligns with the speaker's experience of anger at the charge. However, the notion that by paying the relatively small fee of $2,000, a person might keep Babylon at bay is humorous

16 See Hinrichs (2006) for numerous examples, also Hinrichs (2015).

17 The notion of "ownership" of linguistic codes is used here in the sense of Rampton (1995; 1998). It is central to a definition of linguistic crossing: when speakers use linguistic codes that do not "belong" to them, they engage in crossing.

in the way it trivializes the Rasta meta-narrative. The Rastafarian voice is assumed in this example with concurrent signs of non-seriousness, which signal an asymmetry in the writer's alignment with DT as a social code. Overall, a sense of playfulness characterizes this heteroglossic play with voices, much as in (8).

To end this section, I discuss a sample from a female writer who at the time of data collection maintained a blog in a hybrid genre: it is part personal journal and part fashion review blog. The writer imagines her audience as being composed of both personal friends, who are likely to appreciate her journal-type entries more, and strangers who are interested in her fashion writing. In an email interview, she wrote that based on her blog's visitor tracking statistics,

> 45% of my visitors are from Jamaica, 34% from US, quite a bit from the Caribbean and the rest splattered around the world. I'm guessing that a big heft of that US figure has Jamaican heritage but who knows. . .

While she uses JC frequently in her writing, the length of insertions seems limited. When I asked her if she had any sort of personal principles regarding the amount of JC she uses on her blog, she answered:

> Good point! I do try to limit the amount of patois so that if someone doesn't get exactly what I'm saying, they would have gotten the gist anyhow from the surrounding sentences.

She is based in Kingston, Jamaica, and her social networks do not include Americans:

> I sure am living in Kingston, Jamaica, born, raised and nevah lef yah! LOL
>
> I travel fairly often but I've never lived outside of Jamaica, my longest time away from home was 4 months in the US. [. . .]
>
> Most of the persons I come in contact with from the states (this goes for Britain too) are Jamaicans. I can't think of anyone outside of Jamaica that I have a close relationship with that I speak with often and the few who I can think of I message them more often than speaking on the phone so not much slangs are shared.

Nonetheless, her blog is a good example of heteroglossia. As with previous examples in this section, she draws not only on codes that can be considered her own by virtue of her biography, such as Jamaican English and Creole. She also regularly draws on forms that structurally and in terms of linguistic practice can be considered borrowings from African-American Vernacular English (AAVE). Example (10) is excerpted from a lighthearted narrative about her disappointing experience of first procuring and then using tamarind twigs as a healing substance against a rash, a traditional Jamaican recipe.

10.
[. . .] I walked for almost an hour past mango tree,
breadfruit, ackee, cherry, sweet sop, sour sop, **all**
even
orange to rhatid. No damn tamarind. . . just
some frickin' orange trees
when I was heading back home bound to scratch myself
into ugliness. . . I saw it. . . a huge ass tamarind tree at
the back of what must be a crack house, you know the
kind. . . I saw a dude[18] leaning up against a rotting car
and motioned to him. He cut me down a couple twigs and
of course offered to come rub me down. Yeah fat chance
negro. . .
Back at home with the miracle stuff. . . yeah **the damn**
the damn
thing nay worth shit!!! I guess I was supposed to
thing in't/wasn't worth shit
boil enough to fill ma bathtub and go soak in it but I
couldn't be bothered with all that so I did it the rag
down way. Never work for shit. [. . .] <b100>

In this passage, unmarked Standard English alternates with JC insertions (in bold), AAVE insertions (underlined), and hybrid mixes between JC and AAVE (bold-underlined). The story has a three-part structure: In the first part, the writer recounts the unsuccessful beginning of her search for a tamarind tree. In the second part she finds a large tamarind and interacts with a "dude" who helps her by cutting down some twigs. The last part reports that the treatment turned out to be ineffective and gives a brief evaluation of the experience.

When we consider the identity of the inserted codes, there emerges a trajectory from lower-mesolectal JC in the first insertion (l. 2–3) across two shorter AAVE insertions and one hybrid form to a fully AAVE insertion in the final position, in which the conclusive evaluation of the story is delivered. Without overburdening this observation, we may say that there is a meta-discursive story told by the writer's language choices throughout the excerpt: as she undergoes an ultimately frustrating experience with her attempt to procure and apply a local-traditional remedy, she gradually shifts from using JC to AAVE, which is indexically linked to the metropolitan-modern identity of African-American culture (cf. Lexander, this volume). Her linguistic choices provide a commentary on the narrated experience: by shifting from JC to AAVE for her inserts, she executes, at the symbolic level of linguistic choice,

[18] *Dude* is a borrowing from mainstream informal American English, as opposed to AAVE.

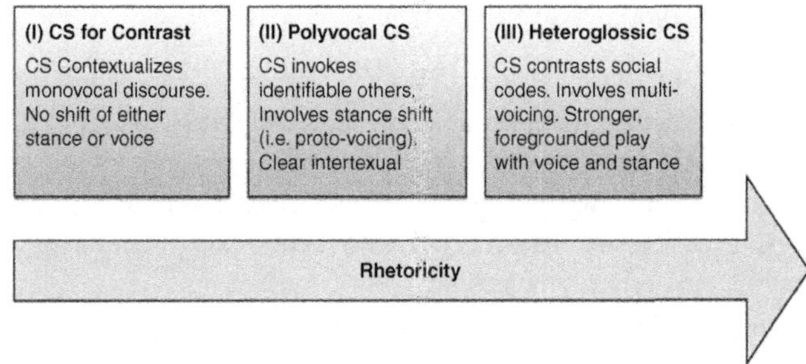

Figure 10.1 Discourse functions of written online code switching in three types, from least to most rhetorical.

the departure of a young person from her community's rural traditions and concurrent orientation towards the transnational figure of the Black Atlantic.

The heteroglossic use of CS complicates any existing notions of the link between speaker/writer identity and foregrounds the very fact that code users have access to a range of codes that is as disparate as the globalizing nature of their communicative environment would suggest. For example, the fact that the writer of example (10) switches variably from English into JC and AAVE would be misread as an ultimately unified claim of identification with the Black Atlantic. It also, as we know, does not index any personal ties to African-American cultures. Rather, the speaker shows herself to be alternating with ease between the symbolic inventories of her local culture on the one hand, and the metropolitan culture of black Americans on the other. The medium of multicodal expression is the message here, one might say. The playful mix of different social codes outside of any expectable indexicalities based on speakers'/writers' biographies creates a certain levity of interactional style which ultimately serves as a mode of confronting the relational complexity of life in a rapidly globalizing, diversifying world.

Thus, it becomes apparent that Type III switching, the most rhetorical type, is also the most figurative. Rather than merely employing codes that are shared at the community level, speakers/writers can switch codes *as if* they were members of certain communities, *as if* their own biographies had actually provided them native-speaker-like access to these codes, and *as if* these codes were all indexical of essential aspects of their core identity. Compared to this type, then, Types I and II appear relatively more "literal," and less rhetorical (see Figure 10.1): indexical links between codes and sociocultural meanings are clearer, individual linguistic repertoires are more a matter of common knowledge and less a matter of identity play.

Conclusion

The framework for the analysis of WOCS discourse functions according to their degrees of rhetoricity that I have presented captures most or all instances of WOCS and their discourse functions. It is important to recognize that more than one function type may be assigned to any given example of a switch. Most commonly, Type I functions co-occur with Type II or III functions, but other combinations are certainly possible.

I have suggested that the effects of globalization favor greater rhetoricity in WOCS behavior. My data show that the transnational position of diasporic writers leads to more rhetoricity in diasporic writing. At the same time, I have shown that the electronic medium itself, as a site and agent of globalization, fosters rhetoricity. Future research might treat this observation as a testable hypothesis and ask whether WOCS data written in highly diverse, metropolitan contexts for highly mixed audiences shows more highly rhetorical switch types than data produced in more traditional, peripheral settings that show fewer effects of globalization.

As my examples have suggested, rhetoricity is also especially at home in *young* people's language practices. For writers whose identities are not yet fixed in ways that mark adulthood – with firm commitments to careers, life partners, and so on – rhetoricity is a mode of playful, temporary alignment with a range of identities. In Bakhtin's original writings on the pervasiveness of multiple social voices and languages in discourse, he saw these as ways in which speakers could implicitly and symbolically negotiate social struggle under politically oppressive circumstances. Young people in most societies are typically in non-hegemonial, materially powerless positions. Thus, rhetoricity in language use becomes an important mode of connecting the self to the world at the levels of ideation and self-expression.

11 The Korean Wave, K-Pop Fandom, and Multilingual Microblogging

Jamie Shinhee Lee

Introduction

Korean pop culture products have recently become increasingly popular outside Korea, particularly in Asia. The widespread and growing popularity of Korean contemporary cultural products such as TV shows, movies, and K-pop beyond the Korean domestic market has been noticed in the media. According to Huat and Iwabuch (2008: 2), "the flood of Korean pop culture – film, pop music and especially TV dramas – into the rest of East Asia came to be known very quickly as the 'Korean Wave' by the PRC audience in 1997." The Korean Wave also known as "Hallyu" (韓流) signifies Korea's emergence as "a new epicenter of mass media and popular culture in East Asia" over the past ten years (Nam 2013: 209). Hallyu is positively viewed since it is "an authentic local response to the homogenizing force of cultural globalization" (Nam 2013: 227). Hallyu is also considered "cultural hybridization between Western universalism and Asian exoticism (or particularism) that is pivotal in attracting transnational audiences" (Oh and Park 2012: 368).

Hallyu involves a range of Korean pop culture commodities, but melodramas have been particularly successful (Yin and Liew 2005 cited in Park 2010: 159). Along with Korean dramas, K-pop has become a vital force in the Korean Wave, enabling several Korean "girl groups" and "boy bands" to be popular and successful beyond Korea. These "Hallyu stars" have their websites created and maintained by well-established management companies, and fans all over the world can obtain information about these stars' latest albums, upcoming performances, and scheduled public appearances through these websites. These websites often have a message board where fans can post messages to their favorite groups and members. As Korean popular culture products are distributed in the global market, consumers are no longer limited to Koreans anymore; transnational fans often exchange their opinions and comments online.

This paper examines microblogging called "fan board" on one of the most successful South Korean entertainment management companies. The fan board is mainly for fans to post relatively short messages for the artists they admire. In theory, fan board participants can respond to one another's posts; however, in reality, fan board messages tend to contain predominantly one-sided praise for their stars. Although it is not explicitly stated whether censorship is practiced for so-called *akphwul* ("vicious reply"), it is not far-fetched to assume that some type of "language management" occurs since the website is maintained by the stars' management companies. This particular company, SM Town (Company S hereafter), has an official YouTube channel streaming its star artists' recent music videos. Among the artists Company S manages, Super Junior and Girls' Generation are possibly the two most successful K-pop groups that have a robust global fan base.

This chapter examines their fan board micro posts, focusing mainly on multilingual practices, messages, and features of computer-mediated communication (CMC). Earlier research on CMC is generally based on monolingual data and deals mostly with English. No extensive academic attention has been given to multilingual CMC with the exception of a few recent studies (see, e.g. Androutsopoulos 2015; Danet and Herring 2007b; Deumert 2014a). Furthermore, the interplay between globalization and language fellowship in online pop music fandom has not been the main focus of sociolinguistic research. This study aims to address questions regarding the linguistic resources fans recruit to mark their different yet intertwined identities as individuals, highlighting their L1 backgrounds, accentuating their group identity, and demonstrating their knowledge and skillful usage of linguistic devices in CMC. It will be further investigated how a sense of audience, or knowing who may read their posts (K-pop stars for example) contributes to their linguistic choices.

Linguistic Impact of *Hallyu*

Hallyu has facilitated spreading Korean popular culture as well as the Korean language. Increasing popularity of Korean dramas and K-pop has led to growing interest in learning the Korean language. In her study of student motivations for learning Korean, Sotirova (2014: 7) mentions Hallyu as a main factor and notes that Korean Studies program students are mostly Hallyu fans. The Korean language students in Sotirova's study rely not only on traditional instructional materials such as textbooks and lectures, but also on K-pop and Korean dramas and movies, especially for learning colloquialisms.

The Office of Ethnic Communities of the New Zealand Government published an article in 2013 entitled "Korean Wave motivates Kiwis to learn Korean," which discusses the impact of the pop star Psy's success with his song "Gangnam Style." The New Zealand Government report mentioned earlier notes that "as the song gained global popularity, an increasing number of people with no knowledge of the Korean language started singing along to 'Oppan Gangnam Style' which translates roughly to 'Big Brother in Gangnam Style'." According to a CNN report, Psy's music video "has surpassed 2,147,483,647 views on YouTube, maxing out the site's original view counter" (Griggs 2014). It is further noted in the New Zealand Government report that "The Korean Education Centre, supported by the Korean Ministry of Education, has embraced this trend and is actively promoting Korean language education in intermediate schools across the Auckland region." According to a senior advisor at the Korean Education Centre, approximately 1,700 students take Korean as a second language in 15 schools.

Despite the importance of transnational fans in Hallyu, linguistic studies on K-pop fandom are still limited in number and scope. The involvement of K-pop fans is generally discussed in terms of "fan activism" (Jenkins 2012) and "spontaneous mobilization of the fans by themselves" (Lee 2015: 109). In discussing K-pop fan communities in Palestine and Israel, Otmazgin and Lyan (2013: 70) argue that fans act as "cultural mediators" and "harbingers of globalized culture." Otmazgin and Lyan specifically comment on language usage in K-pop fandom, noting that "an integral part of K-pop fandom includes participating in Internet forums dedicated to Hallyu, in Hebrew (for Israeli Jews) and Arabic (for Palestinians), and sometimes in English and Korean as well" (Otmazgin and Lyan 2013: 75).

Mixed elements in K-pop are identified as forms of "textual impurity of hallyu" (see e.g. Jenkins et al. 2013; Jin and Yoon 2014). Jin and Yoon (2014: 1286) argue that "Korean pop cultural texts tended to be identified by their hybrid and impure attributes." Jenkins et al. (2013: 263) define "impurity" as "unexpected mixing and mingling of cultural materials." However, this "textual impurity" is argued to improve K-pop's transnational accessibility and enhance its global appeal. For example, Jin and Yoon (2014: 1286) report that most respondents in their research appreciate and prefer "the mixture of Korean and English" in K-pop because it makes the content "more familiar and interesting." Jin and Yoon (2014: 1288) conclude that "the technological affordances of social media and fans' sociality interplay with each other and rapidly spread hallyu as a set of impure cultural forms."

Then how does digital communication fit into the discussion of Hallyu? Jung's (2011) research on K-pop fandom in Indonesia shows that social media affects K-pop fans' communicative practices and plays a critical role in disseminating K-pop song texts online. Jin and Yoon (2014) observe that "while the mainstream media were unable to provide North American fans with the prompt cultural and linguistic translation of Korean content, the fans kept translating and circulating hallyu materials, especially via participatory online social networking or video-streaming portal sites" (Jin and Yoon 2014: 1285).

Linguistic Choices and Digital Communication

Digital communication has become an integral part of routine interactions with others. As far as language issues in online communication are concerned, research generally reports two tendencies: "the dominance of English as a lingua franca of transnational communication and the representation of linguistic diversity online" (Androutsopoulos 2006: 428). Dąbrowska (2013: 66) notes that "English is frequently chosen as a language of Facebook posts, even when used between non-native users of it." Considering the power of English in many domains of modern society and its widely recognized practical function as a lingua franca, it is no surprise that English is favored in interactions among electronic communicators who do not share the same native language. This study, however, argues that English is used neither exclusively nor dominantly in CMC among fans from different L1 backgrounds. English is definitely present, but it often co-occurs with other languages including fans' first languages although the intelligibility of messages written in languages other than English is not always guaranteed. Furthermore, many fans also utilize Korean as a foreign language which they possess little to no knowledge of in order to index membership in K-pop fandom.

The language choices speakers make are influenced by several social factors including interlocutors, context, and subject, to name just a few. Social distance, relative status or role, degrees of formality, and functions or goals of interaction also affect language choices (Holmes 2013). Solidarity, group identity, and a sense of belonging often motivate speakers to choose one code over the other as argued in Gumperz's (1982) *we code* and *they code*. Similar to code switching in face-to-face interactions, switches in CMC achieve several pragmatic functions (see Hinrichs, this volume). For example, Dąbrowska (2013: 76–77) notes that Hindi-English switches are used to emphasize and reinforce messages, express emotions, show respect and wishes, and indicate emotional distancing.

Electronic media normally feature informal or semi-formal language (Dąbrowska 2013). Non-standard spelling or "orthography that deliberately rejects the norm" known as "rebellion spelling," to borrow Sebba's term (2003), is quite common. Shaw (2008: 42) notes that non-standard spelling is generally used "for comic purposes" and concludes that the existence of variable spellings is a reflection of postmodernism and an indicator of "the tensions of global and local, the borrowed and mixed identities, and the freedom to choose one's belongingness" (Shaw 2008: 49). He also asserts that features representing colloquial styles such as *gonna*, *-in*, *ya* occur without specific affiliation with particular ethnic or local identities (Shaw 2008: 48). It is noted that many of the CMC features are regularly used regardless of their nationalities. African American Vernacular English (AAVE)-influenced or hip-hop related spellings such as <da> for "the" and <dat> for "that" are also found in all three groups that Shaw (2008: 48) investigated (i.e. the USA, England, and Ireland). Shaw suggests that "an American voice of this kind has covert prestige everywhere (ibid.)."

Punctuation and spelling are often discussed as noteworthy features in CMC (e.g. Baron and Ling 2011; Lewin and Donner 2002; Shaw 2008). Baron and Ling (2011: 61) comment specifically on a structured nature of punctuation in textspeak and propose two principles: "A principle of parsimony" and "A principle of information load." The principle of parsimony refers to "omit punctuation, especially periods, at ends of messages" and the principle of information load is mainly concerned with the idea that "question marks carry more discourse information than periods and exclamation points because they signal a request for a response from interlocutors" (Baron and Ling 2011: 59). Shaw (2008: 48) summarizes major spelling-related CMC features such as number/letter rebus, clipping, abbreviation, initialisms, expressive oral and visual respelling, representation of spoken forms, and regularization of irregular spelling.

Although previous research provides useful findings on various aspects of CMC, most of the earlier studies focus on cyber texts constructed by single-language groups. If several groups are examined, their linguistic behaviors are compared and often contrasted separately without considering the interaction among these groups. Also, most studies deal with English CMC data. A transnational nature of e-communication is implicitly acknowledged but not discussed explicitly as a topic.

Data

Among the several popular Hallyu K-pop groups, the present study focuses on Super Junior and Girls' Generation. These two groups are selected mainly because they are arguably the most successful Korean pop groups that became famous relatively early in the Korean Wave yet continue to demonstrate high staying power even today. Super Junior is one of the earliest and most successful groups created and managed by Company S. It has two sub-groups: Super Junior T and Super Junior M. Super Junior T consists of six members (Lee Teuk, Hee Chul, Kangin, Shindong, Sungmin, and Eunhyuk) and debuted with the album Lokkukhe on February 25, 2007. Super Junior M is composed of eight members (Sung Min, Eunhyuk, Donghae, Shiwon, Lyuwook, Kyuhyun, Zhou Mi, and Henry), according to the information available on the Super Junior Fan board.[1] Girls' Generation, mostly known as *Sonyeoshidae* (소녀시대) in Korea and

[1] It was retrieved from http://superjunior-t.smtown.com/pages/superjunior-t/version01/Index.asp (March 6, 2014).

affectionately dubbed Soshi or SNSD, is a nine-member Korean female group that has been active since 2007. Its members are Taeyeon, Yuna, Yuri, Jessica, Sunny, Tiffany, Sooyoung, Hoyyeon, and Seohyun. Three members with English names (i.e., Jessica, Sunny, and Tiffany) were born in California and educated partly outside Korea.

I visited Company S's website on a monthly basis and randomly collected the first ten fan board messages for the two hallyu groups mentioned above. A total of 100 messages were collected from April through August in 2014. Approximately 33 percent were exclusively in Korean. English only messages comprise 35 percent of the data and 32 percent of the posts involve language mixing. This chapter takes a qualitative approach to the data, examining mainly discourse features, and is not concerned with frequency or number of occurrences of a particular feature. The fan board shows messages from fans with different first language backgrounds around the globe including Australia, Brazil, Indonesia, Iran, Thailand and so forth. Fan board messages are written in English, Korean (in Hangul or in the Roman script), Chinese, Japanese, Thai, and Spanish. Korean words are notably incorporated even into English posts written presumably by non-Koreans. A multilingual nature of the fan board was noticeable and, in a sense, expected considering these two groups' global fans worldwide.

What is particularly noteworthy is non-Korean speaking fans' use of Korean expressions – mainly kinship terms, address terms, and encouraging or congratulatory remarks (cf. Garley, this volume). A few predominant patterns and themes emerged from a linguistic analysis of these messages. The following analysis focuses on five noticeable discourse features: Korean address terms and greetings, Korean colloquialisms, Konglish,[2] language mixing and CMC features.

Analysis

Korean Address Terms and Greetings

According to Speech Accommodation Theory, "converging towards the speech of another person is a polite strategy. It implies that the addressee's speech is acceptable and worthy imitating" (Holmes 2013: 245). The Hallyu fans in the present study perform speech accommodations mainly through adopting Korean expressions. The most frequently appearing Korean words happen to be address terms directed towards the artists.

[2] It refers to a Koreanized variety of English, which is not generally intelligible to speakers other than Koreans. It is often evaluated negatively by language purists (Lee, in press). Ahn calls it "Phony English" and views it "neither Korean nor English" (cited in Choe 2000). For structural features of Konglish, see Kosofsky (1990) and Kent (1999).

A brief discussion of Korean address terms should be in order here. Both gender and age become a determining factor influencing the choice of an address term in Korea. If both the speaker and the hearer are female and the speaker is younger than the addressee, the term *unni* is appropriate. However, when both the speaker and the hearer are male and the speaker is younger than the addressee, the word *hyung* is proper. If the speaker is male and the hearer is female and the speaker is younger than the addressee, the term *nuna* should be used. On the other hand, when the speaker is female and the hearer is male and the speaker is younger than the addressee, the term *oppa* is suitable. Super Junior fans in this study predominantly use the term *oppa* ("an older brother"), whereas Girls' Generation fans mostly use the term *unni* ("an older sister"). Based on gender identity markers available on fan boards including names and pictures, one can sometimes figure out the gender of an individual without much effort. However, there is no guarantee that e-communicators on the fan board always reveal their identity truthfully, including gender. Age is another sociolinguistic variable which is hard to know because e-communicators do not normally mention how old they are. However, K-pop fans are generally believed to be fairly young, between the ages of 14 and 22, and mostly females (Otmazgin and Lyan 2013).

What is noteworthy though, is the fact that only *unni* and *oppa* appear. The term *hyung* does not occur in the data and *nuna* appears only once. This implies, according to the rules of Korean address terms explained above, that all fans who used the terms *unni* and *oppa* should be younger than the members of Super Junior or Girls' Generation (most likely tweens, teens, and twenty-somethings). However, it cannot be verified that all fans using *unni* and *oppa* are in fact younger than the members of Girls' Generation and Super Junior. Also, fans using *oppa* and *unni* should be all female since these are gender-exclusive address terms in the Korean language. Again, information such as this cannot be clearly confirmed or denied in online communication, but it will be hard to argue that there are absolutely no male fans among those who used *oppa* and *unni* in this study.

Another noteworthy pragmatic feature in the microblog messages in this study is that not only Korean fans but also non-Korean fans use Korean address terms even when their messages are written exclusively in English. It is quite possible that global fans may not necessarily fully understand this rather complicated address term system in Korean but simply focus on the gender of the group and use *unni* to Girls' Generation and *oppa* to Super Junior. In other words, global fans may not consider their own gender and use these Korean address terms indistinguishably. Excerpt (1) is posted by an Indonesian fan who uses the Korean address term *oppa* to write a message directed towards a member of Super Junior named Yesung.

1. YESUNG **OPPA SARANGHAE** WE WILL WAITING FOR YOU !!!
   "Older Brother Yesung, I love you! We will be waiting for you!!!!"

The message above could be from a female fan because the term *oppa* can be used only by female speakers when addressing an older male, but no distinctive gender identity marker can be inferred from the fan's login ID. It is also noteworthy that the Korean expression *saranghae* ("I love you") instead of its polite counterpart *saranghaeyo* is used here even though the use of *oppa* indicates that the confessor is younger than the confessed, i.e. Yesung. If the confessor is younger than the confessed, the polite verb ending suffix *-yo* is used, but it is clearly absent in the excerpt. It is paradoxical that the Indonesian fan uses an expression lacking the polite ending *-yo*, which gives the impression that she is older than Yesung, but calls him *oppa* ("an older brother"). Yesung is currently inactive, and this particular fan's wish for Yesung to rejoin the group is conveyed in the expression "WE WILL WAITING FOR YOU !!!," which contains a syntactic deviation i.e., auxiliary deletion. Similarly, excerpt (2), a fan message from Turkey, features another instance of the Korean address term *oppa*, but this time the English plural marker is attached to *oppa,* i.e., *oppas*.

2. **oppas** thanks for coming to turkey !!!! it was an amazing show please come back again soon =)
   "Older brothers, thanks for coming to Turkey!!!! It was an amazing show. Please come back again soon =)"

In expressing her gratitude for Super Junior's successful show in Turkey, this Turkish fan addresses the members of Super Junior as *oppas*. What is noteworthy is that the hybrid plural form, i.e. the English plural marker bound morpheme -s attached to the Korean free morpheme *oppa*, is used in place of the Korean plural form *oppa-tul* ("older brothers"). Also, it should be noted that a few oft-cited CMC features including the use of lower case (e.g. turkey) (Frehner 2008), multiple exclamation points (e.g.!!!!), and emoticons indicating a smiley face (e.g., =)) (Baron and Ling 2011) are used here. Korean address terms are also used by Girls' Generation fans. Considering that their addressee is a "girl group," *unni*, not *oppa,* is expected to occur. Excerpt (3) below has an example of that.

3. Annyeong SooYoung **Unnie**! I am your No.1 fan in my school and I am just like you, both of us love eating <3 I love you ! **Saranghae** Sooyoung
   "Hi, Older Sister SooYoung! I am your number one fan in my school and I am just like you. Both of us love eating. I love you! I love you, Sooyoung."

Excerpt (3) above is directly addressed to a member of Girls' Generation, Soo Young. This particular fan highlights their shared passion for food and expresses her love for Soo Young. Her message contains the address term *unni* but with a slightly modified spelling (i.e. *unnie*), which is listed as one of the "101 Korean pop culture words you absolutely MUST know" (Acton 2013). The elongated final vowel can carry an enhanced tone of intimacy. In addition, Baron and Ling's (2011) "principle of parsimony" is at play since several punctuation marks are omitted including periods and commas, which is reported to be fairly common in CMC. Furthermore, we see the heart symbol emoticon "<3" indicating love, which is followed by the English expression "I love you!" and subsequently reinforced by its Korean verbatim translation "*Saranghae*." Similar to the inappropriate use of the plain style in excerpt (1), this fan seems to indicate that she is younger than Soo Young by using the address term "*unnie*," but her greeting at the beginning (i.e. "*Annyeong*") replaces the usually expected polite counterpart *Annyeonghaseyo*. Her inappropriately informal speech is also repeated in her Korean expression "Saranghae" ("I love you"), lacking the polite sentence ending suffix *-yo*. Violating co-occurrence constraints in Korean in her post makes the message appear discourteous and ill-mannered by Korean standards. However, her identity as a global fan may help her avoid criticism because her attempt to use some basic Korean words to connect with the group she admires is likely to be appreciated as a sign of a dedicated fan.

Complicated Korean address terms and honorific endings can be challenging to non-Korean speakers, but some global fans in the present study demonstrate a rather sophisticated understanding of Korean kinship terms. In excerpt (4), a Brazilian fan of Super Junior deliberately uses an improper address term, creating a humor effect.

4. Good night **Ajeossis**! **kekekeke**
   How are you? I'm from Brazil
   I just want thank for the Super Show 5 Brazil, was perfect, I felt like a beautiful dream, I hope can live this all again someday!
   We're ~brazilian fans~ waiting to SS6!!!!

The word "*Ajeossi*" literally means "an uncle," but it is not an exclusively blood-related kinship term. Korean speakers use it to address an older married male who is not a close acquaintance. *Ajeossi* is often contrasted with *oppa*, which refers to a young male. *Oppa* is generally used to indicate some level of familiarity or intimacy between the speaker and the addressee. The term *oppa* is preferred even by older males since it indexes youthfulness. All members of Super Junior are single and most members are in their twenties, so the term *oppa* is appropriate. However, by addressing Super Junior as *ajeossis*, the Brazilian fan intentionally flouts the linguistic etiquette. The use of *kekekeke* mimicking a chuckle shows that her use of the improper address term was intended for comic purposes. Acton (2013) lists *kekeke* as another one of "the 101 Korean pop culture words you absolutely MUST know" and explains its discourse functions as follows: "When using 'hehehe' just doesn't sound cute enough to express your laughter. Some people actually 'kekeke' out loud, which is not recommended. Keep the kekeke-ing to texting. Over use of the kekeke can go from cute to annoying real quick. Use sparingly. Kekeke." In place of *kekekeke,* Koreans would use ㅋㅋㅋㅋ in textspeak to represent a laugh. For non-Koreans who would not necessarily know how to type in Korean, *kekekeke* is a reasonable alternative to its Korean CMC equivalent. Notably, similar to excerpt (1), the hybridized plural form of *ajeossi* (i.e. *ajeossis*) is created through affixation combining the Korean free morpheme *ajeossi* and the English-bound plural morpheme *-s*. Moreover, common CMC features such as use of lower case ("we're brazilian fans") and omission of punctuation ("I'm from Brazil") are present as well. Also, it is worth mentioning that an initialism that can be understood only by fans familiar with Super Junior's international tour dubbed "The Super Show" is used along with the number 6 indicating that the next show will be their sixth worldwide concert tour.

Another Korean address term-related example is found in excerpt (5) below, but it is seems to be unique as it features the only occurrence of the Korean address term "nuna" in the data. The term 누나 (*nuna* "an older sister") suggests that the poster of this message is a male who is younger than the two Girls' Generation members mentioned in the message (i.e. Yuna and Yuri). Also, it features a phonetically-oriented spelling of the expression 어디이쪼요 (*etiic-coyo*) in place of the standard expression 어디있어요 (*etiisseyo*), which is immediately followed by an apology for his "broken Korean."

5. . . .윤아 누나, 유리 누나??. . .어 디이쪼요? . . . sorry, broken korean..
   . . .Yuna nuna, Yuri nuna??. . .etiiccoyo? . . .sorry, broken Korean..
   "Older Sister Yuna, Older Sister Yuri?? Where are you? Sorry for my broken Korean."

Linguistic "errors" made by global fans are not commented on by others. Their linguistic insecurity manifests itself in the form of self-deprecation, which is likely triggered by self-awareness of their "non-native" Korean speaker status. Unlike crossing (Rampton 1995), global fans' provisional use of Korean may not be sanctioned as "wanna be" behavior mainly because they have already earned their group membership as fans first. Using some linguistic resources (i.e. Korean expressions) may strengthen their status as a "kolswu" ("die hard" or "fanatic") fan.

Excerpt (6) showcases another message written in Korean. The messages from global fans discussed earlier in the chapter (i.e. excerpts (1)–(4)), are written mostly in English with some Korean address terms. In earlier excerpts, even Korean greetings and colloquial expressions are represented in English transliterations through the Roman script. In contrast, excerpt (6) below features a lengthy message mostly in *Hangeul* (the Korean alphabet).

6. 안녕하세요 슈퍼 주니어~!! 나는 미셸 요 그리고 난 내가 모든 음악을 사랑한다 말하고 싶어 ~:D. . .
   Annyenghaseyyo Super Junior~!! Nanun Michelle-yo. Kuliko nan nayka eumakul saranghantako malhako siphe ~ :D. . .
   "Hi Super Junior~!! I am Michelle. And I want to say I love all of your music ~:D"
   . . .또한 내가 좋은 일을 계속 고맙다는 말을하고 싶었다! . . .And sorry, for my bad Hangul!;o;..
   . . .ttohan nayka cohunilul kyeysok komaptanun malul hako siphessta! . . . . . .And sorry, for my bad Hangul!;o;..
   "I also wanted to say thank you for continuing to do a good job!. . .And sorry, for my bad Hangul!"

The message above is written in awkward Korean containing several syntactic deviations. A simple greeting such as안녕하세요 (*annyenghaseyyo* "How are you?") at the beginning of the message is the only partially grammatically correct and socially appropriate part of the message. This particular fan apologizes for her limited Korean language skills at the end. Her concern for "bad *Hangeul*" is additionally reinforced by the text-based emoticon ";o;" indicating a feeling of nervousness or embarrassment.

Some languages have rather rigid co-occurrence restrictions regarding various styles. Korean is one of them. Depending on the relationship between the speaker and the hearer, one of the six verb suffixes, namely intimate (*-na*), familiar (*-e*), plain (*-ta*), polite (*-e yo*), deferential (*-supnita*), and authoritative (*-so*), will be used in Korean (Trudgill 2000: 93). In excerpt (6), this particular fan's Korean does not sound "natural" because it does not follow co-occurrence restrictions in Korean. In fact, she mixes three different styles in one discourse. When she states that she loves all Super Junior's music, she switches to the familiar ending *-e* (어) instead of the polite ending *-eyo* (어요) and then changes again to the plain suffix *-ta* (다) in the subsequent sentence.

Although Korean CMC allows informal expressions and abbreviations more liberally than face-to-face communication, co-occurrence style constraints are not generally violated. Failure to adhere to co-occurrence style constraints can still be considered impolite in Korean CMC. If a speaker "upshifts" from familiar to polite, it would not be offensive to the hearer. On the other hand, "downshifting" from polite to familiar is viewed as improper and could be perceived as a serious social blunder since it shows a lack of respect for the addressee. However, similar to excerpt (3), her attempt to use Korean expressions may be appreciated by native speakers as an indicator of her enthusiasm as a global fan even though her message clearly shows that she lacks communicative competence in Korean. No specific comments on global fans' use of Korean are found in the data, but foreigners' attempts to speak Korean are generally recognized positively in the form of compliments and/or pleasant surprises. It is not uncommon for Koreans to offer a compliment like "hankwukmal calhasineyyo!" ("Your Korean is good!") even when foreigners make grammatical and pragmatic errors.

In addition to inappropriate shifts between different styles, her message also contains multiple instances of the redundant first-person pronoun, which is pragmatically inferable and therefore normally omitted in a pro-drop language like Korean. She uses three different forms yet essentially the same nominative case of the pronoun "I" in Korean (i.e. "*nanun*," "*nan*," "*nayka*"). Lexical redundancy is also evident in her use of superfluous conjunctions such as 그리고 (*kuliko* "and") and 또한 (*ttohan* "also"). Moreover, we see unusual lexical choices as well. For instance, 좋은 일 (*cohunil*) means "a good thing or good news," not "good work" which is presumably intended here as in "keep up the good work." Furthermore, morphologically, her utterance shows that she has not mastered the ways in which verbs are conjugated in Korean. After her name, Michelle, only the polite verb suffix *-yo* appears without the verb "be" itself. Korean speakers would insert the verb root *-i* before adding the suffix.

Multiple morpho-syntactic deviations in excerpt (6) clearly indicate that this fan does not have native fluency in Korean. However, the fact that she chose to communicate in the band's native language, not her own, signifies something sociolinguistically powerful. Holmes (2013: 242) argues that speech convergence is a polite strategy indicating that "you are on the same wavelength". Excerpt (6) is a revealing example of speech accommodation attempting to strengthen the bond between the group and an individual fan through use of a shared language.

Korean Colloquialisms

Bell's (1984) *audience design*, the idea that speakers formulate and adjust their speech with a particular addressee in mind, is useful for analysis of the use of Korean colloquialisms in otherwise predominantly English fan board messages in this study. Bell (2009: 268) notes that the concept of audience design can be applied to mass communication as well as face-to-face interaction. As he argues, "the basic tenet of audience design is that style is oriented to people rather than to mechanisms such as attention. Style is essentially a social thing. It marks interpersonal and intergroup relations."

Contemporary Korean slang expressions are commonly incorporated into fan messages in this study. The transnational K-pop fans in the present study seem to have a clear sense of audience and design their language accordingly.

They demonstrate a rather skillful incorporation of up-to-date and informal expressions that are popular among young Korean speakers and possibly among Hallyu fans. Two of the most frequently used colloquialisms turn out to be대박 (*taypak*) and 짱 (*jjang*), which indicate excitement, delight, and enthusiasm. In excerpt (7) below, a Girls' Generation fan excitedly comments on their successful new album. It contains the slang expression대박 (*taypak*), which means "a big success" or "a great hit."

7. i already hear all song in the album..,its 대박!!! (taypak)
   "I've heard all the songs on the album. It is a huge success!!!"

Excerpt (8), a message from a Malaysian fan of Super Junior, contains another tremendously popular Korean slang expression, *jjang* ("awesome").

8. super junior **jjang**!!!!!!!!!!!
   annyangbuseyo,,, hai super junior!! iam your fan from malaysia!!! eventho iam not a fanatic one because iam not really know your group members, but i love your song!!! iam really love to saw donghae, eunhyuk, kangin, khuhyun, siwon, and ryeowok!!!!! these are my fav members.. but,, other members also best,, i love u all,, oh,, and of course the most adorable sungmin. . .. hehehe. . .

In addition, excerpt (8) has several syntactic deviations the most notable being overextension of the verb "am" (e.g. Iam not really know. . ., iam really love. . .) and inappropriate tense-marking (e.g., "love to saw. . . "). Furthermore, we observe a few features typical of CMC: a lack of capitalization and 11 exclamation points in the first line when she praises Super Junior. This excessive use of exclamation points coupled with the Korean colloquial expression "*jjang*" unequivocally magnifies her praise of the band she so admires. In contrast to her explicitly expressed admiration for the entire group, her personal attachment to one member, Sungmin, is revealed somewhat timidly as indexed by her giggle or muffled laughter, i.e. hehehe.

Use of "Konglish"

Some fan board messages include so-called "Konglish" expressions which are generally understood by Koreans and used for intranational communication among Koreans. These expressions are not necessarily intelligible to non-Koreans. It is linguistically significant to note that some Hallyu fans in the present study use Konglish, although it is not for "intranational" communication among Koreans. This type of conditional use of Konglish can be viewed as a form of *crossing* (Rampton 1995); crossing refers to provisional use of linguistic features that are not generally affiliated with speakers themselves.

As a result, crossing may be subject to an unfavorable characterization of inauthentic, unauthorized language use by second-language learners. However, transnational discourse space such as K-pop fandom may not mark it as "inauthentic"; rather it can be arguably viewed as a sign of linguistic loyalty and dedication. Excerpt (9) shows a message written by a supposedly Chinese fan of Donghae, a member of Super Junior M.

9. fighting!!!

The expression "fighting" is commonly used as a catchphrase to cheer at sports events in Korea, but it is also generally used to encourage someone to do a good job. An entry on the K-pop dictionary blog by MTV K reads, "pronunciation: hwaiting. noun. a term used as a word of encouragement it can also be used as a cheer." A follow-up comment on the same blog states, "one of the most commonly used phrases in Korea is absolutely everywhere in K-Pop. While most of you may know what it means. . .for those of you who don't – now, you don't have to wonder why all your favorite idols keep telling you to 'fighting!'" This particular fan, whose ethnic background is presumed to be Chinese based on the login name, encourages Donghae to keep up the good work by offering a Koreanized English expression. In a situation to encourage someone in action, Chinese speakers would generally use the expression *jiayou* (加油), which literally means "add gas or refuel." However, this Chinese fan uses Konglish as a linguistic convergence strategy to encourage a Korean speaking member of Super Junior. Girls' Generation fans also use the expression "fighting" as shown in excerpt (10) below. However, unlike excerpt (10), it is orthographically represented in Korean, i.e., 파이팅 ("fighting").

10. 파이팅!!. . .i just want to ask..did you girls ever chat with your fan using some other application?..?..

Multilingual Practices

Along with English, Korean, and Konglish, other languages are also found in the data including Chinese, Japanese, Thai, and Spanish.

Excerpt (11), a message written by the Brazilian fan discussed earlier in excerpt (4), shows Chinese expressions in pinyin (phonetic transcribing system for Mandarin Chinese) addressed to Henry and Zhou Mi, ethnically Chinese members of Super Junior. The expressions *xie xie* ("thank you") and *wo ai ni* ("I love you") are offered specifically to two members who speak Chinese. Henry Lau, of Chinese ancestry, was born and raised in Toronto, Canada. English is his first language but he speaks several languages including Chinese and Korean. Zhou Mi is originally from Wuhan, China.

11. Henry and Zhoumi in next time I want hug you <3
    Thanks for coming!!!!
    Xie xie and wo ai ni 8D

Also, notice that EMC features such as the heart shape "<3" indicating "love," multiple exclamation points "!!!!", and "8D", a manic face indexing insanity or hypomania, are used to express intense affection towards these Chinese-speaking members of Super Junior M. Although they are not extensively used, Spanish expressions occasionally appear. A message from a Miami fan in excerpt (12) below is a case in point.

12. Hola amigos. My name is Stephanie, and I just wanted to say what a great video you have on Netflix. It was the first time hearing about your group so I wanted to let you know it was excellent. I'm glad to see there is plenty of talent around the world.

She starts with a Spanish greeting, which indexes her regional affiliation. Considering that she is from a city highly populated with Latin-Americans, Spanish is a reasonable linguistic choice to mark her local identity. Although the Spanish greeting she uses is very basic, the members of Super Junior (whom she identifies as her main addressee as indicated in the pronoun "you") would not necessarily understand Spanish. Therefore, it is challenging to view the use of Spanish here as a form of audience design, unlike the use of Korean in other examples. Excerpt (13) is a message from a Japanese fan mostly written in Japanese with a few English expressions.

13. 今君は You're here スーパージュニア
    Ima Kimi-wa You're here Super Junior
    Now you-nom You're here Super Junior
    'Now you are here, Super Junior.'
    初めて その時のように 記憶するよ Dear You
    Hajimete sono tokinoyouni kiokkusuruyo Dear You
    First time that time like remember-verb suffix Dear You
    "I'll remember just like the first time we met Dear You."

When linguistic resources are not fully at their disposal, some fans are apologetic and attempt to provide some alternatives. Consider the following message sent from Spain.

14. Well, i really like this website, althouth i don't understand it well, anyway, I wanted to say that I'm already supporting you, guys. I like your music and I think All of you are funny and tender uniquely. I've been crazy looking for a way to contact you, it is not the same to speak Spanish to Korean, I hope this serves as something. Regrets from spain and let me tell you, that you have a NEW BIG FAN.

The author reveals how little he (inferenced by the login name provided) can understand when he visits Super Junior's website. Their website is not exclusively in Korean as it contains some English as well. This Spanish-speaking fan understands some but not all of the information on the website. Nonetheless, he wants to express his support for the group. Writing a fan message exclusively in Spanish would not be communicatively appropriate since the members of Super Junior do not have proficiency in Spanish. However, writing a fan message in Korean is not feasible for him because he lacks Korean language skills. Thus, he opts for a third language, English, to convey his message.

Eastern/Asian CMC Features

Although I mentioned a few CMC features earlier in the chapter whenever relevant, I will point out additional CMC features that are rather unique to Korean or Asian contexts. According to Park et al. (2013), different emoticons are used by online communicators in Eastern and Western countries. They note that the horizontal style is favored in Western countries using the colon (:) for eyes and different mouth shapes expressing feelings, whereas the vertical style is preferred in Eastern countries using the underscore (_) for the mouth and various shapes and characteristics representing emotions for eyes (Park et al. 2013: 467–468). For example, to express happiness, :) is commonly used in Western countries, while ^^ is frequently used in Eastern countries. The present study shows that Hallyu fans utilize mostly vertical style emoticons. Below are a few examples.

> 15. i know you girls have FB page but the page did not reply my message... i am sad... ㅠ.ㅠ ... i will always support you girls.

In the message above posted by a fan in Malaysia, the emoticon indicating a sad or crying face, ㅠ.ㅠ, is used to express disappointment about not receiving any replies to his or her Facebook message. ㅠ.ㅠ, generally pronounced yu yu, phonologically approximates crying and visually represents tears streaming down one's face. This text-based emoticon is commonly known to most Korean internet users, but its meaning is unlikely to be immediately clear to non-Koreans. Although we do not know whether or not this particular fan in Malaysia is an ethnic Korean, it is noteworthy that he or she incorporates a Korean text-based emotion into a predominantly English text.

Excerpt (16), a message from a Super Junior fan in the Philippines, contains emoticons indexing a kiss " :**" and a happy face " ^^". This particular fan uses only Korean and the emoticon in the post. The Korean expression 사랑해 (saranghae) means "I love you" in the familiar style similar to Excerpt (1), but unlike Excerpt (1), the address term *oppa* is not used here. This is possibly because the message is directed towards the entire group (i.e. Super Junior) not just one member as in Excerpt (1).

16. 사랑해 슈퍼주니어 :** ^^
    Saranghae Super Junior :** ^^
    'I love you Super Junior :** ^^

Lewin and Donner's (2002) research on bulletin board messages lists the inappropriate use of lower and upper case letters as one of the most prevalent CMC features. Messages written exclusively in lower case are fairly common in the data. Excerpt (17), a message from a German fan named "steffi" writing to a member of Super Junior about his birthday, is an illustrative example of this.

17. hello eunhyuk oppa my name is steffi and i'm from germany also i'm a big fan of super junior. i have noticed that today is your birthday so I wanted to gratulate you. please have a nice day with your friends and have a nice party.^-

She addresses Eunhyuk as "eunhyuk oppa," which is a combination of his name and the address term *oppa*. Capitalization is noticeably absent in the text. Also, similar to other messages, an emoticon is used to indicate a wink, "^.-", which is used suggestively as a form of flirtation. What is unusual about this text is the use of an archaic verb such as "gratulate" in Netspeak (Crystal 2001). Arguably, the selection of the verb "gratulate" is motivated by a principle of parsimony (Baron and Ling 2011).

Conclusion

The Korean Wave (Hallyu) has produced a group of highly successful and globally popular K-pop stars. Data dealing with fan board messages for two powerful K-pop groups in the present study show multilingual practices in cyberspace. Along with English and Korean, Chinese, Japanese, Konglish, Spanish, Thai, and other languages are used. Messages in English and Korean tend to be lengthier than the other languages. Language mixing is also common. Language mixing in this study seems to have two main functions. Global fans use Korean to demonstrate their active interest in K-pop stars' linguistic heritage and use their native language to highlight their own national identity. Despite the fact that many of these global fans do not speak Korean, they tend to demonstrate linguistic convergence strategies utilizing certain Korean expressions. These Korean expressions range from simple greetings and address terms to contemporary slang expressions to highly Koreanized English expressions. Because they do not possess native fluency in Korean, their use of Korean address terms and colloquial expressions is not always socially appropriate, often showing limited communicative competence particularly in Korean honorific systems and co-occurrence constraints. However, I argue that the bond between stars and their fans is not based on linguistic accuracy but on linguistic fellowship, which relies on perceived shared interest and mutual support. In that regard, the sometime incorrect use of kinship terms such as *oppa* ("an older brother") and *unni* ("an older sister") is particularly noteworthy as it contributes to the enhanced, albeit imagined, closeness between the fan and the artist. Global fans also incorporate contemporary Korean colloquial expressions into their messages. When the text contains Korean sentences beyond the usual, well-known phrases, fans often apologize for their "poor Korean."

Most sociolinguistic studies on linguistic insecurity focus on English. "Non-native" speakers of English often suffer from English language anxiety (Lee 2014). The desire to learn English or speak "better" English is often instrumentally motivated and strengthened by the status and power the English language enjoys around the world as a global language. So-called small languages such as Korean have not experienced such success so far. However, what we observe in this study, albeit on a much smaller scale, is the increasing power of the Korean language as a result of the Korean Wave. As the status of Korea as a successful exporter of pop culture products improves, more fans are exposed to the Korean language, which is leading to an increased interest in learning and using Korean expressions (similar to Asian teenagers reciting English lyrics and rap due to their vested interest in American pop music and MTV). Song Hyang-geun, president of the International Korean Language Foundation notes that "a recent study revealed that most students are taking the class for their personal interests so that they can understand more about Korean dramas or send fan letters to Korean stars" (cited in Lee 2012).

Lee (2012) reports that "the Ministry of Culture, Sports and Tourism, in partnership with Korea Broadcasting Advertising Corporation, announced their plan to introduce an easy and entertaining way of learning the Korean language. The lessons make use of content from K-pop music programs and hit Korean dramas that played a central role in leading the Hallyu craze."

In addition, websites advertising Korean language programs outside Korea mention the ability to understand Korean dramas as a learning outcome. Ngee Ann Polytech, a Singaporean university, advertises its Korean language program with the catchphrase "Stay on top of the K-pop wave by learning to speak Korean!" (Ngee Ann Polytech, School of Interdisciplinary Studies).

Technology-enabled social networks and platforms such as YouTube, Twitter, Facebook, and devices like smartphones allow Hallyu artists to easily and conveniently communicate with their fans regardless of their place of residence. Their fans can be better connected with other fans around the globe as well. Language resources can be easily shared and distributed using technology. Although they all speak different languages, fans can still communicate and identify with one another using the language only they can recognize without abandoning their L1 identity. As shown in this study, fans construct a fan group identity via strategic use of Korean address terms indicating familiarity with and closeness to the artists. In other words, using Korean expressions, particularly kinship terms, creates a sense of belonging and strengthens solidarity and group identity. Korean serves as a connector, a relationship-building device, and a social bonding tool.

Another significant sociolinguistic feature in the data is global fans' reference to their own regional identity. They generally reveal their local affiliation at the beginning of their messages, explicitly mentioning city or country names. Their national identity is often highlighted through brief L1 greetings such as Spanish *hola* and Chinese *xie xie*. However, global fans, particularly those who do not speak English as their mother tongue, do not write their fan messages exclusively in their native languages. Fans from Brazil, for example, do not write in Portuguese. Spanish-speaking fans do not use Spanish exclusively. Rather, they tend to opt for English. This seems to be done out of consideration for the main audience, i.e. K-pop stars who speak Korean and understand English but not necessarily other languages.

In addition, most global fans in the study are fairly well versed in CMC. Their messages contain oft-cited CMC features including clipping, initialisms, expressive respelling, unconventional spelling, representation of spoken forms, multiple exclamation points, and emoticons. Notably, several initialisms and text-based emoticons used by global fans in the data show that linguistic in-group membership is presumed to a certain degree; these expressions are not easily decipherable without some familiarity with contemporary Korean text-speak and acronyms.

The transnational fandom and its multilingual practices in online communication discussed in this study indicate that global fans make linguistic accommodations to Hallyu K-pop stars. Languages that are unknown to the artists are not generally used or minimally used. As a linguistic convergence strategy, global fans frequently utilize Korean kinship terms and popular Korean informal expressions. Arguably, this type of linguistic convergence (quantitatively significant or not) may facilitate forming and solidifying fellowship, which is so greatly desired in a fandom.

References

Acton, Dan 2013. *101 Korean pop culture words you absolutely MUST know*. www.dramafever.com/news/101-korean-pop-culture-words-you-absolutely-must-know/

Adelaar, Willem 2004. *The Languages of the Andes*. Cambridge: Cambridge University Press.

Afsaruddin, Asma 2010. Where earth and heaven meet: Remembering Muḥammad as head of state. In J. Brockopp (ed.), *The Cambridge companion to Muḥammad*. Cambridge/New York: Cambridge University Press. 180–198.

Agha, Asif 2003. The social life of cultural value. *Language & Communication* 23: 231–273.

Agha, Asif 2005. Voice, footing, enregisterment. *Journal of Linguistic Anthropology* 15 (1): 38–59.

Agha, Asif 2007. *Language and Social Relations*. Cambridge: Cambridge University Press.

Agha, Asif 2008. What bilinguals do. In Angela Reyes and Adrian Lo (eds.), *Beyond yellow English: toward a linguistic anthropology of Asian Pacific America*. Oxford: Oxford University Press. 253–259.

Agha, Asif 2011. Large and small scale forms of personhood. *Language & Communication* 31(3): 171–180.

Alexa Internet, Inc. 2012 *Mzee.com site overview*. www.alexa.com/siteinfo/mzee.com

Alim, Samy 2004. Hip hop nation language. In Edward Finegan and John R. Rickford (eds.), *Language in the U.S.A*. Cambridge: Cambridge University Press. 387–409.

Alim, H. Samy 2009a. Hip hop nation language. In Alessandro Duranti (ed.), *Linguistic Anthropology: A Reader*. Oxford: Blackwell. 272–289.

Alim, H. Samy 2009b. Translocal style community: Hip-hop youth as cultural theorists of style, language, and globalization. *Pragmatics* 19(1): 103–127.

Alim, H. Samy, Awad Ibrahim, and Alastair Pennycook (eds.) 2009. *Global Linguistic Flows: Hip Hop Cultures, Youth Identities, and the Politics of Language*. New York/London: Routledge.

Alzouma, Gado 2013. Dimensions of the mobile divide in Niger. In Massimo Ragnedda and Glenn W. Muschert (eds.), *Digital Divide. The Internet and Social Inequality in International Perspective*. London: Routledge. 297–308.

Androutsopoulos, Jannis 2000. Non-standard spellings in media texts: The case of German fanzines. *Journal of Sociolinguistics* 4(4): 514–533.

Androutsopoulos, Jannis 2001. From the streets to the screens and back again: On the mediated diffusion of ethnolectal patterns in contemporary Germany. *LAUD Linguistic Agency* Series A, Nr. 522.

Androutsopoulos, Jannis 2006. Introduction: Sociolinguistics and computer-mediated communication. *Journal of sociolinguistics* 10(4): 419–438.

Androutsopoulos, Jannis 2007. Bilingualism in the mass media and on the Internet. In Monica Heller (ed.), *Bilingualism: A social approach*. Basingstoke: Palgrave Macmillan UK. 207–230.

Androutsopoulos, Jannis 2008. Potentials and limitations of discourse-centred online ethnography. *Language@Internet* 5(8). www.languageatinternet.org/articles/2008/1610

Androutsopoulos, Jannis 2009. Language and the three spheres of hip hop. In H. Samy Alim, Awad Ibrahim, and Alastair Pennycook (eds.), *Global Linguistic Flows: Hip Hop Cultures, Youth Identities, and the Politics of Language*. New York/London: Routledge. 43–62.

Androutsopoulos, Jannis 2011. From variation to heteroglossia in the study of computer-mediated discourse. In Crispin Thurlow and Kristine Mroczek (eds.), *Digital Discourse: Language in the New Media*. Oxford: Oxford University Press. 277–298.

Androutsopoulos, Jannis 2013a. Online Data Collection. In C. Mallinson, B. Childs, and G. Van Herk (eds.), *Data Collection in Sociolinguistics: Methods and Applications*. New York: Routledge. 236–249.

Androutsopoulos, Jannis 2013b. Participatory culture and metalinguistic discourse: Performing and negotiating German dialects on YouTube. *Discourse* 2: 47–71.

Androutsopoulos, Jannis 2013c. Code-switching in computer-mediated communication. In Tuija Virtanen, Dieter Stein, and Susan C. Herring (eds.), *Pragmatics of Computer-Mediated Communication*. Berlin: De Gruyter Mouton. 667–694.

Androutsopoulos, Jannis 2014. Languaging when contexts collapse: Audience design in social networking. *Discourse, Context & Media* 4: 62–73.

Androutsopoulos, Jannis 2015. Networked multilingualism: Some language practices on Facebook and their implications. *International Journal of Bilingualism* 19(2): 185–205.

Androutsopoulos, Jannis and Michael Beißwenger 2008. Introduction: Data and methods in computer-mediated discourse analysis. *Language@Internet* 5(2): 1–7. www.languageatinternet.org/articles/2008/1609

Androutsopoulos, Jannis and Arno Scholz 2003. Spaghetti funk: Appropriations of hip-hop culture and rap music in Europe. *Popular Music and Society* 26(4): 463–479.

Androutsopoulos, Jannis and Jana Tereick 2016. YouTube: language and discourse practices in participatory culture. In Teresa Spilioti and Alexandra Georgakopoulou (eds.), *The Routledge Handbook of Language and Digital Communication*. Abingdon/New York: Routledge. 354–370.

Anis, Jacques 2007. Neography: Unconventional spelling in French SMS text messages. In Brenda Danet and Susan C. Herring (eds.), *The Multilingual Internet: Language, Culture and Communication Online*. Oxford: Oxford University Press. 87–115.

Antaki, Charles and Sue Widdicombe 1998. Identity as an achievement and as a tool. In C. Antaki and S. Widdicombe (eds.), *Identities in Talk*. London: SAGE publications. 1–14.

Anthonissen, Christine 2013. "With English the world is more open to you": Language shift as marker of social transformation. *English Today* 29(1): 28–35.

Anzaldúa, Gloria 1999. *Borderlands: La Frontera: The New Mestiza*. San Francisco: Aunt Lute.

Archambault, Julie S. 2012. "Travelling while sitting down": Mobile phones, mobility and the communication landscape in Inhambane, Mozambique Africa. *The Journal of the International African Institute* 82(3): 393–412.

Arnett, Jeffrey J. 2003. *Adolescence and Emerging Adulthood: A Cultural Approach*. Upper Saddle River, NJ: Prentice Hall.

Asad, Talal 1986. *The idea of an anthropology of Islam. Occasional papers Series*. Centre for Contemporary Arab Studies. Washington D.C.: Georgetown University Press. 1–23.

Auden, Wystan Hugh 1967. *Collected Shorter Poems, 1927–1957*. New York: Random House.

Auer, Peter 1984. *Bilingual Conversation*. Amsterdam: John Benjamins.

Auer, Peter 1992. Introduction: John Gumperz' approach to contextualization. In Peter Auer and A. di Luzio (eds.), *The Contextualization of Language*. Amsterdam: John Benjamins. 1–37.

Austin, John L. 1975. *How To Do Things with Words*. Oxford: Oxford University Press.

Auzanneau, Michelle 2001. Identités africaines: Le rap comme lieu d'expression. *Cahiers d'études africaines* 163–164: 711–734.

Avineri, Netta 2014. Yiddish endangerment as phenomological reality and discursive strategy: Crossing into the past and crossing out the present. *Language & Communication* 38: 18–39.

Back, Michele and Miguel Zepeda 2013. Performing and positioning orthography in Peruvian CMC. *Journal of Computer-Mediated Communication* 18(2): 119–135.

Bailey, Benjamin. 2007. Heteroglossia and boundaries. In Monica Heller (ed.), *Biligualism: A Social Approach*. New York: Palgrave. 257–274.

Bailey, Benjamin. 2012. Heteroglossia. In Marilyn Martin-Jones, Adrian Blackledge, and Angela Creese (eds.), *The Routledge Handbook of Multilingualism* (Routledge Handbooks in Applied Linguistics). London: Routledge. 499–507.

Bakhtin, Mikhail M. 1981. *The Dialogic Imagination: Four Essays by M.M. Bakhtin*. (Edited by Michael Holquist. Translated by Caryl Emerson and Michael Holquist.) Austin, TX: University of Texas Press.

Bakhtin, Mikhaïl M. 1984 [1929] Problems of Dostoevsky's poetics. (Edited and translated by Caryl Emerson.) *Theory and History of Literature* 8. Minneapolis: University of Minnesota Press.

Bakhtin, Mikhail M. 1986. *Speech Genres and Other Late Essays*. (Edited by C. Emerson and M. Holquist.) Austin, TX: University of Texas Press.

Bakhtine, Mikhaïl M. 1999. *Estéthique et théorie du roman*. (Translated by Daria Oliver, original in Russian 1975.) Paris: Gallimard.

Banks, Ken 2010. Social mobile: Empowering the many or the few? In Sokari Ekine (ed.), *Sms Uprising: Mobile Phone Activism in Africa*. Cape Town: Pambazuka Press. 32–39.

Baron, Naomi 2008. *Always On: Language in an Online and Mobile World*. Oxford: Oxford University Press.

Baron, Naomi 2013. Instant messaging. In Susan Herring, Dieter Stein, and Tuija Virtanen (eds.), *Pragmatics of Computer-Mediated Communication*. Berlin: De Gruyter Mouton. 135–161.

Baron, Naomi S. and Rich Ling 2011. Necessary smileys and useless periods. *Visual Language* 45(1–2): 45–67.

Barrett, Rusty 1999. Indexing polyphonous identity in the speech of African American drag queens. In M. Bucholtz, A.C. Liang, and L. Sutton (eds.), *Reinventing Identities: The Gendered Self in Discourse*. New York: Oxford University Press. 313–331.

Barton, David 2015. Tagging on Flickr as a social practice. In Rodney H. Jones, Alice Chik, and Christoph A. Hafner (eds.), *Discourse and Digital Practices: Doing Discourse Analysis in the Digital Age*. Abingdon/New York: Routledge. 48–65.

Barton, David and Mary Hamilton 1998. *Local literacies. Reading and Writing in One Community*. London: Routledge.

Barton, David and Carmen Lee 2013. *Language Online: Investigating Digital Texts and Practices*. Abingdon/New York: Routledge.

Bauman, Richard 1977. *Verbal Art as Performance*. Prospect Heights, IL: Waveland.

Bauman, Richard 1983. Folklore and the forces of modernity. *Folklore Forum* 16: 153–158.

Bauman, Richard 1992. Folklore. In R. Bauman (ed.), *Folklore, Cultural Performances and Popular Entertainments*. Oxford: Oxford University Press. 29–40.

Bauman, Richard 2003. *A World of Others' Words. Cross-Cultural Perspectives on Intertextuality*. Oxford: Blackwell.

Bauman, Richard and Charles Briggs 1990. Poetics and performance as critical perspectives on language and social life. *Annual Review of Anthropology* 19(1): 59–88.

Beers-Fägersten, Kristy 2006. The discursive construction of identity in an Internet hip hop community. *Revista Alicantina de Estudios Ingleses* 19: 23–44.

Beger, Gerrit, Priscillia Kounkou Hoveyda, and Akshay Sinha 2011. From "What's your ASLR" to "Do you wanna go private?" *UNICEF Digital Citizenship Safety Report*. www.unicef.org/southafrica/SAF_resources_mxitstudy.pdf

Beheshti, Jamshid and Andrew Large 2013. *The Information Behavior of a New Generation: Children and Teens in the 21st Century*. Lanham, MD: Scarecrow Press.

Bell, Allan 1984. Language style as audience design. *Language in Society* 13(2): 145–204.

Bell, Allan 2009. Language style as audience design. In Nikolas Coupland and Adam Jaworski (eds.), *The New Sociolinguistics Reader*. New York: Palgrave Macmillan. 265–275.

Belling, Luc and de Julia Bres 2014. Digital superdiversity in Luxembourg: The role of Luxembourgish in a multilingual Facebook group. *Discourse, Context & Media* 4–5: 74–86.

Ben-Amos, Dan 1971. Towards a definition of folklore in context. *The Journal of American Folklore* 84(331): 3–15.

Berezkina, Maimu 2016. "Language is a costly and complicating factor": A diachronic study of language policy in the virtual public sector. *Language Policy*. DOI:10.1007/s10993-016-9422-2.

Bierman, Noah 2017. No habla Espanol? The White House website no longer speaks Spanish. *Los Angeles Times*. www.latimes.com/la-bio-noah-bierman-staff.html

Bieswanger, Markus 2013. Micro-linguistic structural features of computer-mediated communication. In Susan Herring, Dieter Stein and Tuija Virtanen (eds.), *Pragmatics of Computer-Mediated Communication*. Berlin: De Gruyter Mouton. 463–485.

Bigham, Douglas S. 2012. Emerging adulthood in sociolinguistics. *Language and Linguistics Compass* 6(8): 533–544.

Blom, Jan-Petter and John Gumperz 1972. Social meaning in linguistic structure: code-switching in Norway. In John Gumperz and Dell Hymes (eds.), *Directions in Sociolinguistics*. New York: Academic Press. 407–434.

Blommaert, Jan 2013. *Ethnography, superdiversity and linguistic landscapes: Chronicles of complexity*. Bristol/Buffalo: Multilingual Matters.

Blommaert, Jan and Ben Rampton 2011. Language and superdiversity. *Diversities* 13 (2): 1–22.

Blommaert, Jan and Ben Rampton 2012. Language and superdiversity. MMG Working Paper, (12-09).

Blommaert, Jan, Helen Kelly-Holmes, Pia Lane, Sirpa Leppänen, Mairead Moriarty, Sari Pietikäinen and Arja Piiraijnen 2009. Media, multilingualism and language policing: An introduction. *Language Policy* 8(3): 203–207.

Bloomfield, Leonard 1933. *Language*. New York: Holt.

Bock, Zannie 2013. Cyber socialising: Emerging genres and registers of intimacy among young South African students. *Language Matters: Studies in the Languages of Africa* 44(2): 68–91.

Bock, Zannie, Nausheena Dalwai, and Christopher Stroud, this volume. Cool mobilities: youth style and mobile telephony in contemporary South Africa. In Cecelia Cutler and Unn Røyneland (eds.), *Multilingual Youth Language in Computer-Mediated Communication*. Cambridge: Cambridge University Press.

Bolander, Brook and Miriam A. Locher 2014. Doing sociolinguistic research on computer-mediated data: A review of four methodological issues. *Discourse, Context & Media* 3: 14–26.

Bothma, C. V. 1951. 'n Volkekundige ondersoek na die aard en ontstaansoorsake van Tsotsi-groepe en hulle actiwiteite soos gevind in die stedelike gebied van Pretoria. MA dissertation. University of Pretoria.

Boyd, Danah 2011. Social network sites as networked publics. Affordances, dynamics, and implications. In Z. Papacharissi (ed.), *A Networked Self. Identity, Community, and Culture on Social Network Sites*. New York/London: Routledge. 39–58.

Briggs, Charles 1988. *Competence in Performance: The Creativity of Tradition in Mexicano Verbal Art*. Pennsylvania, PA: University of Pennsylvania Press.

Brinkman, Inge, Mirjam de Bruijn, and Hisham Bilal 2009. The mobile phone, "modernity" and change in Khartoum, Sudan. In Mirjam de Bruijn, Francis Nyamnjoh, and Inge Brinkman (eds.), *Mobile Phones: The New Talking Drums of Everyday Africa*. Bamenda (Cameroun)/Leiden: LANGAA/Africa Studies Centre. 69–91.

Brock, André 2012. From the blackhand side: Twitter as a cultural conversation. *Journal of Broadcasting & Electronic Media* 56(4): 529–549.

Brookes, Heather 2014. Gesture in the communicative ecology of a South African township. In M. Seyfeddinipur and M. Gullberg (eds.), *From Gesture in Conversation to Visible Action as Utterance: Essays in Honor of Adam Kendon*. Amsterdam: John Benjamins. 59–73.

Brookes, Heather and Tebogo Lekgoro 2014. A social history of urban male youth varieties in Stirtonville and Vosloorus, South Africa. *Southern African Linguistics and Applied Language Studies* 32: 149–159.

Brown-Blake, Celia 2008. The right to linguistic non-discrimination and creole language situations: The case of Jamaica. *Journal of Pidgin and Creole Languages* 23 (1): 32–74.

Brunstad, Endre, Unn Røyneland, and Toril Opsahl 2010. Hip-hop, ethnicity and linguistic practice in rural and urban Norway. In Marina Terkourafi (ed.), *The Languages of Global Hip-Hop*. London: Continuum. 223–256.

Bucher, Taina 2012. Want to be on the top? Algorithmic power and the threat of invisibility on Facebook. *New Media & Society* 14(7): 1164–1180.

Bucholtz, Mary 2009. From stance to style: gender, interaction, and indexicality in Mexican immigrant youth slang. In Alexandra Jaffe (ed.), *Stance: Sociolinguistic Perspectives*. New York: Oxford University Press. 146–170. http://escholarship.org/uc/item/6kg5m8kb

Bucholtz, Mary and Kira Hall 2004. Language and Identity. In Alessandro Duranti (ed.), *A Companion to Linguistic Anthropology*. Malden, MA: Blackwell. 369–394.

Bucholtz, Mary and Kira Hall 2005. Identity and interaction: A sociocultural linguistic approach. *Discourse Studies* 7(4–5): 585–614.

Buckingham, David and Rebekah Willett 2013. *Digital Generations: Children, Young People, and the New Media*. New York: Routledge.

Bullock, Barbara E. and Almeida Jacqueline Toribio 2009. Themes in the study of code-switching. In B.E. Bullock and A.J. Toribio (eds.), *The Cambridge Handbook of Linguistic Code-Switching*. Cambridge: Cambridge University Press. 1–17.

Burgess, Jean and Joshua Green 2009. *YouTube: Online Video and Participatory Culture*. New York: John Wiley.

Burrel, Jenna 2010. Evaluating shared access: Social equality and the circulation of mobile phones in rural Uganda. *Journal of Computer-Mediated Communication* 15 (2): 230–250.

Calteaux, Karen V. 1994. A sociolinguistic analysis of a multilingual community. PhD dissertation. University of Johannesburg (formerly Rand Afrikaans University).

Canagarajah, Suresh 2004. Subversive identities, pedagogical safe houses, and critical learning. In Bonnie Norton and Kelleen Toohey (eds.), *Critical Pedagogies and Language Learning*. Ernst Klett Sprachen. 116–137.

Canard, Marius 1999. Da'wa. In *The Encyclopedia of Islam*. CD-ROM, version 1.0. Leiden: Brill.

Carrington, Victoria 2015. 'It's changed my life': iPhone as technological artifact. In Rodney Jones, Alice Chik, and Christopher Hafner (eds.), *Discourse and Digital Practices: Doing Discourse Analysis in the Digital Age*. Oxford: Routledge. 158–174.

Carris, Lauren Mason 2011. La voz gringa: Latino stylization of linguistic (in) authenticity as social critique. *Discourse and Society* 22(4): 474–490.

Carter, Phillip M. 2014. National narratives, institutional ideologies, and local talk: The discursive production of Spanish in a "new" US Latino community. *Language in Society* 43(2): 209–240.

Cassidy, Frederic G. 1982. *Jamaica Talk: Three hundred Years of the English Language in Jamaica*. Second edition. London: Macmillan Caribbean.

Cassidy, Frederic G. and Robert B. Le Page 1980. Dictionary of Jamaican English. Second edition. Cambridge University Press.

Castro, Rafaela 2000. *Chicano Folklore: A Guide to the Folktales, Traditions, Rituals and Religious Practices of Mexican Americans*. Oxford: Oxford University Press.

Chapman, Michael (ed.) 1989. *The Drum Decade. Stories from the 1950s*. Pietermaritzburg: University of Natal Press.

Chávez, John R. 1984. *The Lost Land: The Chicano Image of the Southwest*. Albuquerque, NM: University of New Mexico Press.

Chávez, John 2001. The Chicano homeland. In Gabriel Melendez, Jane Young, Patricia Moore, and Patrick Pynes (eds.), *The Multicultural Southwest: A Reader*. Tucson, AZ: University of Arizona Press. 11–21.

Chavez, Leo 2008. *The Latino Threat: Constructing Immigrants, Citizens, and the Nation*. Palo Alto, CA: Stanford University Press.

Chevannes, Barry 1994. *Rastafari: Roots and Ideology*. Syracuse, NY: Syracuse University Press.

Chigona, Agnes and Wallace Chigona 2008. MXit it up in the media: Media discourse analysis on a mobile instant messaging system. *The Southern African Journal of Information and Communication* 9: 42–57.

Childs, G. Tucker 1997. The Status of Isicamtho, an Nguni-based urban variety of Soweto. In Arthur K. Spears and D. Winford (eds.), *The Structure and Status of Pidgins and Creoles*. Amsterdam: John Benjamins. 341–372.

Chiluwa, Innocent 2008. Assessing the Nigerianness of SMS text-messages in English. *English Today* 24(1): 51–56.

Cho, Thomas 2010. Linguistic features of electronic mail in the workplace: A comparison with memoranda. *Language@Internet* 7(3). www.languageatinternet.org/articles/2010/2728

Choe, Sang-Hun 2000. Bad English plagues South Korea's pride. *Times Union* A7.

Clyne, Michael 2000. Lingua franca and ethnolects in Europe and beyond. *Sociolinguistica* 14: 83–89.

Coe, Michael D. 1999. *Breaking the Maya Code*. New York: Thames and Hudson.

Cooper, Carolyn 1988. That cunny Jamma oman: Female sensibility in the poetry of Louise Bennett. *Race & Class* 29(4): 45–60.

Cornips, Leonie, Jürgen Jaspers, and Vincent de Rooij 2015. The politics of labelling youth vernaculars in the Netherlands and Belgium. In J. Nortier and B.A. Svendsen (eds.), *Language, Youth and Identity in the 21st Century. Linguistic Practices across Urban Spaces*. Cambridge: Cambridge University Press. 45–70.

Cougnon, Anne and Gudrun Ledegen 2010. *c'est écrire comme je parle*. Une étude comparatiste des variétés du français dans l'écrit-sms Réunion-Belgique. In Michaël Abécassis and Gudrun Ledegen (eds.), *Les voix des Français, vol. II, Modern French Identities* 94. Bern: Peter Lang. 39–57.

Coupland, Nicholas 1985. "Hark, hark, the lark": Social motivations for phonological style-shifting. *Language and Communication* 5(3): 153–171.

Coupland, Nikolas 2007. *Style: Language Variation and Identity*. Cambridge: Cambridge University Press.

Crystal, David 2001. *Language and the Internet*. Cambridge: Cambridge University Press.

Crystal, David 2006. *Language and the Internet* (Second edition). Cambridge: Cambridge University Press.

Cutler, Cecelia 1999. Yorkville crossing: White teens, hip hop, and African American English. *Journal of Sociolinguistics* 3(4): 428–442.

Cutler, Cecelia 2014. *White Hip Hoppers, Language and Identity in Post-Modern America*. New York: Routledge.

Cutler, Cecelia and Unn Røyneland 2015. "Where the fuck am I from?": Hip-Hop youth and the (re)negotiation of language and identity in Norway and the US. In Jacomine Nortier and Bente Ailin Svendsen (eds.), *Language, Youth and Identity in the 21st Century. Linguistic Practices across Urban Spaces*. Cambridge: Cambridge University Press. 139–165.

Cutler, Cecelia, this volume. "Pink chess gring gous": discursive and orthographic resistance among Mexican-American rap fans on YouTube. In Cecelia Cutler and Unn Røyneland (eds.), *Multilingual Youth Language in Computer Mediated Communication*. Cambridge: Cambridge University Press.

Dąbrowska, Marta 2013. Functions of code-switching in Polish and Hindi Facebook users' posts. *Studia Linguistica Universitatis Iagellonicae Cracoviensis* 130: 63–84.

Dagsavisen 2017. Aina Stenersen (FrP) tar sterk avstand fra partifellens "trønderske banneord". www.dagsavisen.no/oslo/aina-stenersen-frp-tar-sterk-avstand-fra-partifellens-tronderske-banneord-1.913834

Dalwai, Nausheena 2010. The use of intimate language by UWC students in social networking media. Unpublished Honours paper, Linguistics Department, University of the Western Cape.

Dalwai, Nausheena 2015. Social networking among UWC students: Instant messaging genres and registers. MA dissertation. Linguistics Department, University of the Western Cape.

Danesi, Marcel 2003. *My Son is an Alien: A Cultural Portrait of Today's Youth*. Lanham, MD: Rowman & Littlefield.

Danesi, Marcel 2015. *Language, Society, and New Media: Sociolinguistics Today*. New York: Routledge.

Danet, Brenda 2001. *Cyberpl@y: Communicating online*. Oxford: Berg Publishers. Companion.

Danet, Brenda and Susan C. Herring 2003. Introduction: The multilingual internet. *Journal of Computer-Mediated Communication* 9(1).

Danet, Brenda and Susan C. Herring 2007a. Multilingualism on the internet. In Marlis Hellinger and Anne Pauwels (eds.), *Handbook of Language and Communication: Diversity and Change*. Berlin: Mouton de Gruyter. 553–594.

Danet, Brenda and Susan C. Herring (eds.) 2007b. *The Multilingual Internet: Language, Culture, and Communication Online*. Oxford: Oxford University Press.

Danet, Brenda, Lucia Ruedenberg, and Yehudit Rosenbaum-Tamari 1997. "HMMM...WHERE'S THAT SMOKE COMING FROM?" Writing, play and performance on internet relay chat. *Journal of Computer-Mediated Communication* 2(4). http://onlinelibrary.wiley.com/enhanced/doi/10.1111/j.1083-6101.1997.tb00195.x/

Darics, Erika 2013. Non-verbal signaling in digital discourse: The case of letter repetition. *Discourse, Context & Media* 2(3): 141–148.

Dawood, Nessim Joseph 2000. *The Koran: With a Parallel Arabic Text*. London: Penguin Books.

De Decker, Paul and Jenn Nycz 2011. For the record: Which digital media can be used for sociophonetic analysis? *University of Pennsylvania Working Papers in Linguistics* 17(2): 51–59.

Derrida, Jacques 1976. *Of Grammatology*. Baltimore: John Hopkins University Press.

Deumert, Ana 2009. Namibian Kiche Duits: The making (and decline) of a Neo-African language. *Journal of Germanic Linguistics* 21(4): 349–417.

Deumert, Ana 2014a. *Sociolinguistics and Mobile Communication*. Edinburgh: Edinburgh University Press.

Deumert, Ana 2014b. Sites of struggle and possibility in cyberspace. Wikipedia and Facebook in Africa. In J. Androutsopoulos (ed.), *Mediatization and Sociolinguistic Change*. Berlin: Mouton de Gruyter. 487–514.

Deumert, Ana 2014c. South Africa's language ecology – hierarchies, hegemonies and resistances. In E.-H. Jahr, P. Trudgill, and W. Vandenbussche (eds.), *Language Ecology of the 21st Century: Social Conflicts in their Linguistic Environment*. Oslo: Novus. 123–151.

Deumert, Ana 2016. Linguistics and social media. In Keith Allan (ed.), *Routledge Handbook of Linguistics*. London: Routledge. 561–573.

Deumert, Ana, this volume. Tsotsitaal online – the creativity of tradition. In Cecelia Cutler and Unn Røyneland (eds.), *Multilingual Youth Language in Computer Mediated Communication*. Cambridge: Cambridge University Press.

Deumert, Ana and Sibabalwe Oscar Masinyana 2008. Mobile language choices – the use of English and isiXhosa in text messages (SMS): Evidence from a bilingual South African sample. *English World-Wide* 29(2): 114–147.

Deumert, Ana and Rajend Mesthrie 2012. Contact in the African area: a Southern African perspective. In Terttu Nevalainen and Elizabeth Closs Traugott (eds.), *The Oxford Handbook of the History of English*. Oxford/New York: Oxford University Press. 549–559.

Deumert, Ana and Kristin V. Lexander 2013. Texting Africa: Writing as performance. *Journal of Sociolinguistics* 17(4): 522–546.

Devonish, Hubert 1996. Vernacular languages and writing technology transfer: the Jamaican case. In P. Christie (ed.), *Caribbean Language Issues, Old and New: Papers in Honour of Professor Mervyn Alleyne on the Occasion of his Sixtieth Birthday*. Kingston, Jamaica: University of the West Indies Press. 101–111.

Devonish, Hubert 2003. Language advocacy and "conquest" diglossia in the "Anglophone" Caribbean. In C. Mair (ed.), *The Politics of English as a World Language: New Horizons in Postcolonial Cultural Studies*. Amsterdam: Rodopi. 157–177.

Diego, Alvaro R. and Anais H. Lage 2013. La oralización de textos digitales: Usos no normativos en conversaciones instantáneas por escrito. *Caracteres* 2(2): 92–108.

Diop, Abdoulaye-Bara 1985. *La famille wolof*. Paris: Karthala.

Donnell, Alison and Sarah Lawson Welsh (eds.) 1996. *The Routledge Reader in Caribbean Literature*. London: Psychology Press.

Donner, Jonathan 2007. The rules of beeping: Exchanging messages via intentional "missed calls" on mobile phones. *Journal of Computer-Mediated Communication* 13 (1): 1–22.

Dreyfus, Martine and Caroline Juillard 2004. *Le plurilinguisme au Sénégal. Langues et identités en devenir*. Paris: Karthala.

Du Bois, John 2007. The stance triangle. In R. Engelbretson (ed.), *Stancetaking in Discourse: Subjectivity, Evaluation, Interaction*. (Pragmatics and Beyond New Series 164.) Amsterdam: John Benjamins. 139–182.

Durham, Mercedes 2003. Language choice on a Swiss mailing list. *Journal of Computer-Mediated Communication* 9(1).

Dyers, Charlyn 2009. From ibharu to amajoin: Translocation and language in a new South African township. *Language and Intercultural Communication* 9(4): 256–270.

Dyers, Charlyn 2014. Texting literacies as social practices among older women. *Per Linguam* 30(1): 1–17.

Eckert, Penelope 2008a. Variation and the indexical field. *Journal of Sociolinguistics* 12 (4): 453–476.

Eckert, Penelope 2008b. Where do ethnolects stop? *International Journal of Bilingualism* 12(1–2): 25–42.

Eckert, Penelope 2012. Three waves of variation study: The emergence of meaning in the study of sociolinguistic variation. *Annual review of Anthropology* 41: 87–100.

Engen, Tor Ola and Lars Anders Kulbrandstad 2004. *Tospråklighet, minoritetsspråk og minoritets-undervisning*. Oslo: Gyldendal Akademisk.

Ess, Charles and the AoIR Ethics Working Committee 2002. Ethical decision-making and Internet research. Recommendations from the AoIR ethics working committee. www.aoir.org/reports/ethics.pdf

Eurostat Survey 2016. Digital economy and society statistics – households and individuals. http://ec.europa.eu/eurostat/statistics-explained/index.php/Digital_economy_and_society_statistics_-_households_and_individuals

Evers, Cécile, this volume. Alienated at home: the role of online media as young orthodox Muslim women beat a retreat from Marseille. In Cecelia Cutler and Unn Røyneland (eds.), *Multilingual Youth Language in Computer Mediated Communication*. Cambridge: Cambridge University Press.

Evers, Cécile 2016. "Diasporic Belonging: The Life-Worlds and Language Practices of Muslim Youth from Marseille." Dissertation, University of Pennsylvania.

Fagan, Sarah M. B. 2009. *German: A Linguistic Introduction*. Cambridge: Cambridge University Press.

Fanon, Frantz [1952] 2008. *Black Skin and White Masks*. (Translated by C.M. Markmann and with forewords by Z. Sadar and H.K. Bhabha.) London: Pluto Press.

Farquharson, Joseph T. 2005. Faiya-bon: the socio-pragmatics of homophobia in Jamaican (Dancehall) culture. In S. Mühleisen and B. Migge (eds.), *Politeness and Face in Caribbean Creoles*. Amsterdam: John Benjamins. 101–120.

Fenwick, Mac 1996. "Tough guy, eh?": The gangster-figure in drum. *Journal of Southern African Studies* 22(4): 617–632.

Ferguson, Charles A. 1959. Diglossia. *Word – Journal of the International Linguistic Association* 15(2): 325–340.

Feussi, Valentin 2007. A travers textos, courriels et tchats: Des pratiques de français au Cameroun. *Glottopol* 10: 70–85.

Fishman, Joshua A. 1967. Bilingualism with and without diglossia; diglossia with and without bilingualism. *Journal of Social Issues* 23(2): 29–38.

Florini, Sarah 2014. Tweets, tweeps and signifyin': Communication and cultural performance on 'Black Twitter'. *Television & New Media* 15(3): 223–237.

Fought, Carmen 2003. *Chicano English in Context*. London: Palgrave.

Fránquiz, Maria E. and Maria del Carmen Salazar-Jerez 2013. Ni de aquí, ni de allá: Latin@1 Youth Crossing Linguistic And Cultural Borders. *Journal of Border Educational Research* 6(2): 101–117.

Fredericks, Rosalind 2014. "The old man is dead": Hip-hop and the art of citizenship of Senegalese youth. *Antipode* 46(1): 130–148.

Frehner, Carmen 2008. *Email – SMS – MMS: The Linguistic Creativity of Asynchronous Discourse in the New Media Age*. Bern: Peter Lang.

Freinkel, Lisa 2012. Catachresis. In R. Greene and S. Cushman (eds.), *The Princeton Encyclopedia of Poetry and Poetics*. Fourth edition. Princeton, NJ: Princeton University Press. 209–211.

Frøyland, Lars Roar and Cay Gjerustad 2012. Vennskap, utdanning og framtidsplaner. Forskjeller og likheter blant ungdom med og uten innvandrerbakgrunn i Oslo. [Friendship, education and plans for the future. Differences and similarities among youth with and without an immigrant background in Oslo.] NOVA Rapport 5/12. www.hioa.no/Om-HiOA/Senter-for-velferds-og-arbeidslivsforskning/NOVA/Publikasjonar/Rapporter/2012/Vennskap-utdanning-og-framtidsplaner

Galindo, D. Letticia 1995. Bilingualism and language variation among Chicanos in the southwest. In Wayne Glowka and Donald Lance (eds.), *Language Variation in North American English*. New York: Modern Language Association. 199–214.

García, Ofelia 2009. *Bilingual Education in the 21st Century. A Global Perspective*. London: Wiley Blackwell.

Garley, Matt 2014. Seen and not heard: The relationship of orthography, morphology, and phonology in loanword adaptation in the German hip hop community. *Discourse, Context and Media* 3: 27–36.

Garley, Matt, this volume. Peaze up! adaptation, innovation, and variation in German hip hop discourse. In Cecelia Cutler and Unn Røyneland (eds.), *Multilingual Youth Language in Computer Mediated Communication*. Cambridge: Cambridge University Press.

Garley, Matt and Julia Hockenmaier 2012. Beefmoves: dissemination, diversity, and dynamics of English borrowings in a German hip hop forum. *Proceedings of the 50th Annual Meeting of the Association for Computational Linguistics:* 135–139.

Garley, Matt and Benjamin Slade 2016. Virtual meatspace: word formation and deformation in cyberpunk discussions. In Lauren Squires (ed.), *English in Computer-Mediated Communication: Variation, Representation, and Change*. Berlin: Mouton de Gruyter. 123–148.

Gee, James P. 2015. *Social Linguistics and Literacies: Ideology in Discourses*. New York: Routledge.

Gennep, Arnold van 1908. Linguistique et sociologie. II, Essai d'une théorie des langues spéciales. *Revue des Études Ethnographiques et Sociologiques*. 327–338.

Georgakopoulou, Alexandra 2006. Thinking big with small stories in narrative and identity analysis. *Narrative Inquiry* 16(1): 122–130.

Georgakopoulou, Alexandra 2007. *Small Stories, Interaction and Identities*. Amsterdam: John Benjamins.

Glaser, Clive 1992. *School, Street and Identity: Soweto Youth Culture 1960–1976*. Paper Presented to the University of the Witwatersrand, Graduate Seminar.

Glaser, Clive 2000. *Botsotsi: The Youth Gangs of Soweto, 1935–1976*. Oxford: James Currey.

Gleave, Robert 2010. Personal piety. In J. Brockopp (ed.), *The Cambridge Companion to Muḥammad*. Cambridge/New York: Cambridge University Press. 103–122.

Goffman, Erving 1981. Footing. In Erving Goffman, *Forms of Talk*. Philadelphia: University of Pennsylvania Press. 124–161.

Goffman, Erving 1983. The interaction order: American Sociological Association, 1982 presidential address. *American Sociological Review* 48(1): 1–17.

Gonzalez, Juan 2001. *Harvest of Empire: A History of Latinos in America*. London: Penguin.

Google Public Data World Bank 2017. World Development Indicators. www.google .com/publicdata/explore?ds=d5bncppjof8f9_

Graham, Luke 2015. How smartphones are helping refugees in Europe. CNBC special report. www.cnbc.com/2015/09/11/how-smartphones-are-helping-refugees-in-europe.html

Gramsci, Antonio 1994. *Letters from Prison*. Vol. 2 (Edited by Frank Rosengarten. Translated by Raymond Rosenthal.) New York: Columbia University Press.

Griggs, Brandon 2014. "Gangnam style" breaks YouTube. *CNN*. www.cnn.com/2014/ 12/03/showbiz/gangnam-style-youtube/index.html

Grosjean, François 1997. The bilingual individual. *Interpreting* 2(1–2): 163−187.

Grosjean, François 2008. *Studying Bilinguals*. Oxford: Oxford University Press.

Grosjean, François 2010. *Bilingual: Life and Reality*. Cambridge, MA: Harvard University Press.

Gumperz, John 1982. *Discourse Strategies*. Cambridge: Cambridge University Press.

Hage, Ghassan 2005. A not so multi-sited ethnography of a not so imagined community. *Anthropological Theory* 5(4): 463–475.

Hahn, Hans P. and Ludovic Kibora 2008. The domestication of the mobile phone: Oral society and new ICT in Burkina Faso. *Journal of Modern African Studies* 46(1): 87–109.

Hall, Stuart (ed.) 1997. *Representation*. London: Sage.

Hannerz, Ulf 1996. *Transnational Connections. Cultures, People, Places*. London: Routledge.

Harvard Business Review Staff 2003. Technology and human vulnerability. An interview with Sherry Turkle. In *Harvard Business Review*. hbr.org/2003/09/tec hnology-and-human-vulnerability#

Hassa, Samira 2010. Kiff my zikmu: symbolic dimensions of Arabic, English and Verlan in French rap texts. In Marina Terkourafi (ed.), *The Languages of Global Hip Hop*. London: Routledge. 44–66.

Haugen, Einar 1956. *Bilingualism in the Americas: A Bibliography and Research Guide*. Tuscaloosa: University of Alabama Press.

Herring, Susan C. (Ed.) 1996. *Computer-Mediated Communication: Linguistic, Social, and Cross-Cultural Perspectives* (Vol. 39). Amsterdam: John Benjamins.

Herring, Susan C. 2003. Gender and power in online communication. In Janet Holmes and Miriam Meyerhoff (eds.), *The Handbook of Language and Gender*. Oxford: Blackwell. 202–228.

Herring, Susan C. 2004. Computer-mediated discourse analysis: an approach to researching online behavior. In Sasha A. Barab, Rob Kling, and James H. Gray (eds.), *Designing for virtual communities in the Service of Learning*. New York: Cambridge University Press. 338–376.

Herring, Susan C. 2007. A faceted classification scheme for computer-mediated discourse. *Language@Internet* 4. www.languageatinternet.org/articles/2007/761

Herring, Susan C. 2012. Grammar and electronic communication. In Carol A. Chapelle (ed.), *Encyclopedia of Applied Linguistics*. Hoboken, NJ: Wiley-Blackwell. http://onlinelibrary.wiley.com/doi/10.1002/9781405198431.wbeal0466/full

Herring, Susan C., Lois Ann Scheidt, Inna Kouper, and Elijah Wright 2006. A longitudinal content analysis of weblogs: 2003–2004. In M. Tremayne (ed.), *Blogging, Citizenship and the Future of Media*. New York: Routledge. 3–20.

Herring, Susan, Dieter Stein, and Tuija Virtanen (eds.) 2013. *Pragmatics of Computer-Mediated Communication*. Berlin: Mouton de Gruyter.

Heyd, Teresa 2014. Folk-linguistic landscapes: The visual semiotics of digital enregisterment. *Language in Society* 43(5): 489–514.

Heyd, Teresa and Mirka Honkanen 2015. From Naija to Chitown: The new African diaspora and digital representations of place. *Discourse, Context & Media* 9: 14–23.

Hill, Jane 1999. Styling locally, styling globally: What does it mean? *Journal of Sociolinguistics* 3(4): 542–556.

Hill, Jane H. 2005. Intertextuality as source and evidence for indirect indexical meanings. *Journal of Linguistic Anthropology* 15(1): 113–124.

Hill, Jane H. 2009. *The Everyday Language of White Racism*. New York: John Wiley.

Hinrichs, Lars 2006. *Codeswitching on the Web: English and Jamaican Creole in Email Communication*. (Pragmatics and Beyond New Series 147.) Amsterdam: John Benjamins.

Hinrichs, Lars 2012. How to spell the vernacular: a multivariate study of Jamaican emails and blogs. In A. Jaffe, J. Androutsopoulos, M. Sebba, and S. Johnson (eds.), *Orthography as Social Action: Scripts, Spelling, Identity, and Power*. (Language and Social Processes 3.) Berlin: Mouton de Gruyter. 325–358.

Hinrichs, Lars 2014. Diasporic mixing of world Englishes: the case of Jamaican Creole in Toronto. In E. Green and C. Meyer (eds.), *The Variability of Current World Englishes*. (Topics in English Linguistics 87.1.) Berlin: Mouton de Gruyter. 169–194.

Hinrichs, Lars 2015. Tropes of exile in everyday Caribbean-diasporic speech: the reindexicalization of Dread Talk in the Jamaican diaspora. In H. Zapf and J. Hartmann (eds.), *Censorship and Exile*. (Internationale Schriftenreihe des Jakob-Fugger-Zentrums 1.) Göttingen: Vandenhoeck & Ruprecht. 60–81.

Hinrichs, Lars 2016. Modular repertoires in English-using social networks: a study of language choice in the networks of adult Facebook users. In L. Squires (ed.), *English in Computer-Mediated Communication: Variation, Representation, and Change*. (Topics in English Linguistics 93). Berlin: Mouton de Gruyter. 17–42.

Hinrichs, Lars, this volume. The language of diasporic blogs: a framework for the study of rhetoricity in written online code-switching. In Cecelia Cutler and Unn Røyneland (eds.), *Multilingual Youth Language in Computer Mediated Communication*. Cambridge: Cambridge University Press.

Hinrichs, Lars and Joseph T. Farquharson (eds.) 2011. *Variation in the Caribbean: From Creole Continua to Individual Agency.* (Creole Language Library 37.) Amsterdam: John Benjamins.

Hinrichs, Lars and Jessica White-Sustaíta 2011. Global Englishes and the sociolinguistics of spelling: A study of Jamaican blog and email writing. *English World-Wide* 32 (1): 46–73.

Holmes, Janet 2013. *An Introduction to Sociolinguistics.* Fourth edition. New York: Routledge.

hooks, bell 1989. *Talking Back: Thinking Feminist, Thinking Black.* Cambridge, MA: South End.

Hornberger, Nancy H. and Karl F. Swinehart 2012. Bilingual intercultural education and Andean hip-hop: Transnational sites for indigenous language and identity. *Language in Society* 41(4): 499–525.

Huat, Chua B. and Koichi Iwabuchi 2008. Introduction: East Asian dramas. In Chua B. Huat and Koichi Iwabuchi (eds.), *East Asian Pop Culture.* Hong Kong: Hong Kong University Press. 1–12.

Hurst, Ellen 2008. Structure, style and function in Cape Town Tsotsitaal. PhD dissertation. University of Cape Town.

Hurst, Ellen 2013. Youth shape the way we communicate. *Mail and Guardian, Education.* http://mgco.za/article/2013-07-02-youth-shape-the-way-we-communicate.

Hymes, Dell 1974. Ways of speaking. In R. Bauman and J. Sherzer (eds.), *Explorations in the Ethnography of Speaking.* Cambridge: Cambridge University Press. 433–452.

Iedema, Rick 2003. Multimodality, resemiotization: Extending the analysis of discourse as multi-semiotic practice. *Visual Communication* 2(1): 29–57.

Ims, Ingunn Indrebø 2014. "Alle snakker norsk." Språkideologi og språklig differensiering i mediene. ["Everyone speaks Norwegian." Language ideology and linguistic differentiation in the media.] *NOA – Norsk som andrespråk [Norwegian as a Second Language]* 30(1): 5–40.

INSEE and INED 2010. Trajectoires et Origines: Enquête sur la diversité des populations en France. *Documents de travail,* 168.

International Telecommunication Union (ITU) 2015. Statistics: global ICT developments. www.itu.int/en/ITU-D/Statistics/Pages/stat/default.aspx

Introna, Lucas D. and Helen Nissenbaum 2000. Shaping the web: Why the politics of search engines matters. *The Information Society* 16(3): 169–185.

Iorio, Josh 2009. Effects of audience on orthographic variation. In M. Garley and B. Slade (eds.), *Studies in the Linguistic Sciences: Illinois Working Papers.* 127–140. www.ideals.illinois.edu/bitstream/handle/2142/14815/SLS2009-07Iorio.pdf?sequence=2

Irvine, Judith T. and Susan Gal 2000. Language ideology and linguistic differentiation. In Paul Kroskrity (ed.), *Regimes of Language: Ideologies, Polities, and Identities.* Oxford: James Currey. 35–83.

Ivkovic, Dejan and Heather Lotherington 2009. Multilingualism in cyberspace: Conceptualising the virtual linguistic landscape. *International Journal of Multilingualism* 6(1): 17–36.

Jaffe, Alexandra 2007. Codeswitching and stance: Issues in interpretation. *Journal of Language, Identity, and Education* 6(1): 53–77.

Jaffe, Alexandra and Shana Walton 2000. The voices people read: Orthography and the representation of non-standard speech. *Journal of Sociolinguistics* 4(4): 561–587.

Jahr, Ernst Håkon 2014. *Language Planning as a Sociolinguistic Experiment: The Case of Modern Norwegian*. Edinburgh: Edinburgh University Press.

Jahr, Ernst Håkon and Brit Mæhlum (eds.) 2009. Standardtalemål? [Oral standard?] Special issue of *Norsk Lingvistisk Tidsskrift* 27(1): 3–6.

Jakobson, Roman 1957. Shifters and verbal categories. In Linda R. Waugh and Monique Monville-Burston (eds.), *On Language*. Cambridge, MA: Harvard University Press. 386–392.

Jenkins, Henry 2006. *Convergence Culture: Where Old and New Media Collide*. New York University Press.

Jenkins, Henry 2012. "Cultural acupuncture": Fan activism and the Harry Potter Alliance. *Transformative Works and Cultures* 10. http://dx.doi.org/10.3983/twc.2012.0305

Jenkins Henry, Sam Ford, and Joshua Green 2013. *Spreadable Media: Creating Value and Meaning in a Networked Culture*. New York: New York University Press.

Jin, Dal Young and Kyong Yoon 2014. The social mediascape of transnational Korean pop culture: Hallyu 2.0 as spreadable media practice. *New Media & Society* 18(7): 1277–1292.

Jones, Graham M. and Bambi M. Schieffelin 2009. Talking text and talking back: "My BFF Jill" from boob tube to YouTube. *Journal of Computer-Mediated Communication* 14(4): 1050–1079.

Jones, Rodney, Alice Chik, and Christopher Hafner 2015. *Discourse and Digital Practices: Doing Discourse Analysis in the Digital Age*. Oxford: Routledge.

Jonsson, Carla and Anu Muhonen 2014. Multilingual repertoires and the relocalization of manga in digital media. *Discourse, Context & Media* 5: 87–100.

Jørgensen, Jens N. 2008. Polylingual languaging. Evidence from Turkish-speaking youth. *Multilingualism and Identities Across Contexts. Copenhagen Studies in Bilingualism* 45: 129–150.

Jørgensen, J. Normann, Martha Karrebæk, Lian M. Madsen, and Janus S. Møller 2011. Polylanguaging in superdiversity. *Diversities* 13(2): 23–37.

Jørgensen, Jens Normann, Martha Sif Karrebæk, Lian Malai Madsen, and Janus Spindler Møller 2015. Polylanguaging in superdiversity. In Jan Blommaert, Karel Arnaut, Ben Rampton, and Massimiliano Spotti (eds.), *Language and Superdiversity*. New York: Routledge. 137–154.

Jung, Sun 2011. K-pop, Indonesian fandom, and social media. *Transformative Works and Cultures* 8. http://journal.transformativeworks.org/index.php/twc/article/view/289/219

Kearse, Randy "Mo Betta" 2006. *Street Talk: Da Official Guide to Hip Hop and Urban Slanguage*. Fort Lee, NJ: Barricade Books.

Kébé, Abou Bakry 2009. La wolofisation du discours journalistique au Sénégal. In Alpha O. Barry (éd.), *Discours d'Afrique vol. I Pour un rhétorique des identités postcoloniales de l'Afrique subsaharienne*. Besançon: Presses Universitaires de Franche-Comté. 253–266.

Kelly-Holmes, Helen 2015. Analyzing language policies in new media. In F.M. Hult and D.C. Johnson (eds.), *Research Methods in Language Policy and Planning: A Practical Guide*. Hoboken, NJ: Wiley Blackwell. 130–139.

Kent, David B. 1999. Speaking in tongues: Chinglish, Japalish and Konglish. *KOTESOL proceedings of pac2* (the second Pan Asian conference). 197–209.

Kgositsile, Keorapetse 1968. A poet's credo. The impulse is personal. *Negro Digest* 17 (9): 42–43.

Kibora, Ludovic 2009. Téléphonie mobile: l'appropriation du SMS par une "société d'oralité". In Mirjam de Bruijn, Francis Nyamnjoh, and Inge Brinkman (eds.), *Mobile Phones: The New Talking Drums of Everyday Africa*. Bamenda (Cameroun)/Leiden: LANGAA/Africa Studies Centre. 110–124.

Kiessling, Roland and Maarten Mous 2004. Urban youth languages in Africa. *Anthropological Linguistics* 46(3): 303–341.

Kosofsky, David 1990. Exploring Korean culture through Korean English. *Korea Journal* 30(11): 69–83.

Koutsogiannis, Dimitris and Bessie Mitsikopoulou 2007. Greeklish and Greekness: trends and discourses of "glocalness". In Brenda Danet and Susan C. Herring (eds.), *The Multilingual Internet. Language, Culture and Communication Online*. Oxford: Oxford University Press. 142–160.

Kreutz, C. 2010. Mobile activism in Africa. Future trends and software developments. In Sokari Ekine (ed.), *Sms Uprising: Mobile Phone Activism in Africa*. Cape Town: Pambazuka Press. 17–31.

Kropf, Albert 1899. *A Kaffir–English Dictionary*. Lovedale: Lovedale Mission Press.

Kytölä, Samu 2012. Researching the multilingualism of web discussion forums: theoretical, practical and methodological issues. In M. Sebba, S. Mahootian, and C. Jonsson (eds.), *Language Mixing and Code-Switching in Writing: Approaches to Mixed-Language Written Discourse*. (Routledge Critical Studies in Multilingualism 2.) New York: Routledge. 106–127.

Kytölä, Samu and Elina Westinen 2015. "I be da reel gansta"– a Finnish footballer's Twitter writing and metapragmatic evaluations of authenticity. *Discourse, Context & Media* 8: 6–19.

Landert, Daniela and Andreas H. Jucker 2011. Private and public in mass media communication: From letters to the editor to online commentaries. *Journal of Pragmatics* 43(5): 1422–1434.

Lane, Pia 2011. The birth of the Kven language in Norway: Emancipation through state recognition. *International Journal of the Sociology of Language* 209: 57–74.

Lauzière, Henri 2010. The construction of Salafiyya: Reconsidering Salafism from the perspective of conceptual history. *International Journal of Middle East Studies* 42(3): 369–389.

Le Page, Robert 1997. Political and economic aspects of vernacular literacy. In Andrée Tabouret-Keller, Robert B. Le Page, Penelope Gardner-Chloros, and Gabrielle Varro (eds.), *Vernacular Literacy. A Re-Evaluation*. Oxford: Clarendon Press. 23–81.

Lee, Carmen 2017. *Multilingualism Online*. London: Routledge.

Lee, Jamie Shinhee 2014. English on Korean television. *World Englishes* 33(1): 33–49.

Lee, Jamie Shinhee, this volume. The Korean wave, K-pop fandom, and multilingual microblogging. In Cecelia Cutler and Unn Røyneland (eds.), *Multilingual Youth Language in Computer Mediated Communication*. Cambridge: Cambridge University Press.

Lee, Jamie Shinhee forthcoming. English in Korea. In Kingsley Bolton and Thomas A. Kirkpatrick (eds.), *The Handbook of Asian Englishes*. New York: Wiley-Blackwell.

Lee, Seung-Ah 2012. Learn Korean the fun way. www.korea.net/NewsFocus/Society/view?articleId=102228

Lee, Seung-Ah 2015. Of the fans, by the fans, for the fans: The JYP Republic. In Sangjoon Lee and Abé Marcus Nornes (eds.), *Hallyu 2.0: The Korean Wave in the Age of Social Media*. Ann Arbor: University of Michigan Press. 108–131.

Leland, John 2012. Adventures of a teenage polyglot. *New York Times*. March 9, 2012. www.nytimes.com/2012/03/11/nyregion/a-teenage-master-of-languages-finds-online-fellowship.html?_r=0

Leppänen, Sirpa, Anne Pitkänen-Huhta, Arja Piirainen-Marsh, Tarja Nikula and Saija Peuronen 2009. Young people's translocal new media uses: A multiperspective analysis of language choice and heteroglossia. *Journal of Computer-Mediated Communication* 14(4): 1080–1107.

Lewin, Beverly A. and Yonatan Donner 2002. Communication in Internet message boards: A quantitative analysis of usage in Computer-Mediated Conversation (CMC). *English Today* 18(3): 29–37.

Lexander, Kristin V. 2007. Langues et SMS au Sénégal. Le cas des étudiants de Dakar. In Jeannine Gerbault (ed.), *La langue du cyberespace: de la diversité aux normes*. Paris: l'Harmattan. 59–67.

Lexander, Kristin V. 2010. Le wolof et la communication personnelle médiatisée par Internet à Dakar. *Glottopol* 14: 90–103.

Lexander, Kristin V. 2011a. Voeux plurilingues électroniques – nouvelles pratiques, nouvelles fonctions pour les langues africaines? Journal of Language Contact, *THEMA* 3: 228–246.

Lexander, Kristin V. 2011b. Texting and African languages literacy. *New Media and Society* 13(3): 427–443.

Lexander, Kristin V. 2012. Multilingual texting in Senegal – A model for the study of mixed-language SMS, in Mark Sebba, Shahrzad Mahootian, and Carla Jonsson (eds.), *Language Mixing and Code-Switching in Writing. Approaches to Mixed-Language Written Discourse*. London: Routledge. 146–169.

Lexander, Kristin V. 2014. Le SMS amoureux. *Journal des Africanistes* 83(1): 70–91.

Lexander, Kristin, this volume. Nuancing the jaxase: Young and urban texting in Senegal. In Cecelia Cutler and Unn Røyneland (eds.), *Multilingual Youth Language in Computer Mediated Communication*. Cambridge: Cambridge University Press.

Library of Congress. American Library Association. www.loc.gov/catdir/cpso/romanization/arabic.pdf

Lillis, Theresa and Carolyn McKinney 2013. The sociolinguistics of writing in a global context: Objects, lenses, consequences. *Journal of Sociolinguistics* 17(4): 415–439.

Linell, Per 2009. *Rethinking Language, Mind, and World Dialogically: Interactional and Contextual Theories of Human Sense-Making*. Charlotte, NC: Information Age Publishing.

Ling, Rich and Naomi Baron 2013. Mobile phone communication. In Susan C. Herring, Dieter Stein, and Tuija Virtanen (eds.), *Pragmatics of Computer-Mediated Communication. Handbooks of Pragmatics (HoPs) Vol. IX*. Berlin: Walter de Gruyter. 191–216.

Livermon, Xavier 2012. Representations of Sophiatown in kwaito music: Mafikizolo and musical memory. In T. Falola and T. Fleming (eds.), *Music, Performance and African Identities*. London: Routledge. 169–190.

Livingstone, Sonia, Kjartan Ólafsson, and Elisabeth Staksrud 2013. Risky social networking practices among "underage" users: Lessons for evidence-based policy. *Journal of Computer-Mediated Communication* 18(3): 303–320.

Macnamara, John 1967. The bilingual's linguistic performance – a psychological overview. *Journal of Social Issues* 23(2): 58–77.

Madsen, Lian M., Janus S. Møller, and Jens N. Jørgensen 2010. "Street language" and "integrated": Language use and enregisterment among late modern urban girls. In Lian M. Madsen, Janus S. Møller, and Jens N. Jørgensen (eds.), *Ideological Constructions and Enregisterment of Linguistic Youth Styles*. Copenhagen Studies in Bilingualism. Copenhagen: University of Copenhagen, Faculty of Humanities. 81–113.

Mæhlum, Brit 1996. Codeswitching in Hemnesberget – myth or reality? *Journal of Pragmatics* 25(6): 749–761.

Mæhlum, Brit and Unn Røyneland 2012. *Det norske Dialektlandskapet [The Norwegian Dialect Landscape.]* Oslo: Cappelen Damm.

Makhudu, Kekethi D. P. 2002. An introduction to Flaaitaal. In R. Mesthrie (ed.), *Language in South Africa*. Cambridge: Cambridge University Press. 398–406

Manaka, Matsemela 1981. The babalaz people. *Staffrider* 4(3): 32–40.

Manus, Vicky B. 2011. *Emerging Traditions: Towards a Postcolonial Stylistics of Black South African Fiction in English*. Lanham, MD: Lexington Books.

Markham, Annette and Elizabeth Buchanan with contributions from the AoIR Ethics Working Committee 2012. *Ethical Decision-making and Internet Research 2.0: Recommendations from the AOIR Ethics Working Committee*. www.aoir.org/report s/ethics2.pdf

Martinez-Carter, Karina 2013. What does "American" actually mean? *The Atlantic Monthly*. www.theatlantic.com/national/archive/2013/06/what-does-american-actually-mean/276999/

McCormick, Kay 2002. *Language in Cape Town's District Six*. Oxford: Oxford University Press.

McIntosh, Janet 2010. Mobile phones and Mipoho's prophecy: The powers and dangers of flying language. *American Ethnologist* 37(2): 337–353.

McLaughlin, Fiona 2001. Dakar Wolof and the configuration of an urban identity. *Journal of African Cultural Studies* 14(2): 153–172.

McLaughlin, Fiona 2008a. On the origins of urban Wolof: Evidence from Louis Decemet's 1864 Phrase Book. *Language in Society* 37(5): 713–735.

McLaughlin, Fiona 2008b. Senegal: the emergence of a national lingua franca. In Andrew Simpson (ed.), *Language & National Identity in Africa*. Oxford: Oxford University Press. 79–97.

McLaughlin, Fiona 2014. Senegalese digital repertoires in superdiversity: A case study from Seneweb. *Discourse, Context and Media* 4–5: 29–37.

McSweeney, Michelle 2016. Literacies of bilingual youth: a profile of bilingual academic, social, and txt literacies. Doctoral dissertation, The Graduate Center at the City University of New York.

McWhorter, John 2013. TED talk. Txtng is killing language. JK!!! www.ted.com/talks/john_mcwhorter_txtng_is_killing_language_jk

Mendoza-Denton, Norma 1999. Sociolinguistics and linguistic anthropology of US Latinos. *Annual Review of Anthropology* 28(1): 375–395.

Mendoza-Denton, Norma 2014. *Homegirls: Language and Cultural Practice among Latina Youth Gangs*. New York: John Wiley and Sons.

Mesthrie, Raj 2008. 'I've been speaking Tsotsitaal all my life without knowning it'. Towards a unified account of Tsotsitaals in South Africa. In M. Meyerhoff and N. Nagy (eds.), *Social Lives in Language – Sociolinguistic and Multilingual Speech Communities. Celebrating the Work of Gillian Sankoff*. Amsterdam: John Benjamins. 95–110.

Mesthrie, Raj and Ellen Hurst 2013. Slang registers, code-switching and restructured urban varieties in South Africa: An analytic overview of tsotsitaals with special reference to the Cape Town variety. *Journal of Pidgin and Creole Languages* 28 (1): 103–130.

Meyer, Peter 1961. *Townsmen or Tribesmen. Conservatism and the Process of Urbanization in a South African City*. (With contributions by Iona Mayer.) Cape Town: Oxford University Press.

Molamu, Louis 1995. Wietie: the emergence and development of Tsotsitaal in South Africa. *Alternation* 2: 139–158.

Molamu, Louis 2003. *Tsotsitaal: A Dictionary of the Language of Sophiatown*. Pretoria: Unisa Press.

Moll, Luis and Richard Ruiz 2008. The schooling of Latino children. In Marcelo M. Suárez-Orozco and Mariela Páez (eds.), *Latinos: Remaking America*. Berkeley, CA: University of California Press. 362–374.

Morgan, Marcyliena 2001. Nuthin' but a G thang: grammar and language ideology in hip hop identity. In Sonja Lanehart (ed.), *Sociocultural and Historical Contexts of African American English*. Philadelphia, PA: John Benjamins. 187–210.

Morris, Rosalind C. 2010. Style, Tsotsi-style, and Tsotsitaal. The Histories, Aesthetics, and Politics of a South African Figure. *Social Text* 28(2): 85–112.

Mufwene, Salikoko 1996. The founder principle in creole genesis. *Diachronica* 13(1): 83–134.

Mufwene, Salikoko 1997. Jargons, pidgins, creoles, and koines: what are they? In A. Spears and D. Winford (eds.) *The Structure and Status of Pidgins and Creoles*. (Creole Language Library 16). Amsterdam: John Benjamins. 35–70.

Muñoz, Carlos 1989. *Youth, Identity, Power: The Chicano Movement*. New York: Verso.

Mybroadband 2012. Latest BlackBerry vs Android vs iPhone stats. mybroadband.co.za /news/cellular/55531-latest-blackberry-vs-android-vs-iphone-stats.html

Mybroadband 2014. BlackBerry shock in South Africa. mybroadband.co.za/news/smart phones/102947-blackberry-shock-in-south-africa.html

Nam, Siho 2013. The cultural political economy of the Korean Wave in East Asia: Implications for cultural globalization theories. *Asian Perspective* 37(2): 209–231.

Namba, Kazuhiko 2010. Formulaicity in code-switching: criteria for identifying formulaic sequences. In D. Wood (ed.), *Perspectives on Formulaic Language: Acquisition and Communication*. London: Continuum. 129–150.

Nesse, Agnete 2015. Bruk av dialekt og standardtalemål i offentligheten i Norge etter 1800. [The use of dialect and oral standard in the public in Norway after 1800.] In Helge Sandøy (ed.), *Talemål etter 1800. Norsk i jamføring med andre nordiske språk. [Spoken language after 1800. Norwegian in comparison with other Nordic languages.]* Oslo: Novus. 89–111.

Ngee Ann Polytech, School of Interdisciplinary Studies (Foreign Language Enhancement Programme). www.np.edu.sg/is/foreignlanguage/korean/Pages/Korean.aspx

Nortier, Jacomine 2008. Ethnolects? The emergence of new varieties among adolescents. *International Journal of Bilingualism* 12(1–2): 1–5.

Nortier, Jacomine and Bente Ailin Svendsen (eds.) 2015. *Language, Youth and Identity in the 21st Century. Linguistic Practices across Urban Spaces*. Cambridge: Cambridge University Press.

O'Brien, Donal Cruise 1998. The shadow-politics of wolofisation. *The Journal of Modern African Studies*, 36(1): 25–46.

Oh, Ingyu and Gil-Sung Park 2012. From B2C to B2B: Selling Korean pop music in the age of new social media. *Korean Observer* 43(3): 365–397.

Opsahl, Toril 2009. "Egentlig alle kan bidra!" – en samling sosiolingvistiske studier av strukturelle trekk ved norsk i multietniske ungdomsmiljøer i Oslo. ["Actually, anyone can contribute!" – A collection of sociolinguistic studies of structural features of Norwegian in multiethnic youth communities in Oslo.] PhD dissertation. University of Oslo.

Opsahl, Toril and Unn Røyneland 2016. Reality rhymes – recognition of rap in multicultural Norway. In C. Aliagas, M. R. Garrido, and E. Moore (eds.), *Hip Hop, language and Identity: Bridging Organic Learning and Institutional Learning Spaces*. Special Issue of *Linguistics and Education* 36: 45–54.

Orlikowski, Wanda 2007. Sociomaterial practices: Exploring technology at work. *Organization Studies* 28(9): 1435–1448.

Osiris 2014. Chiffres clés. Principaux indicateurs: téléphonie. http://osiris.sn/Telephonie.html

Otmazgin, Nissim and Irina Lyan 2013. Hallyu across the desert: K-pop Fandom in Israel and Palestine. *Cross-Currents: East Asian History and Cultural Review* 9: 68–89.

Otsuji, Emi and Alastair Pennycook 2010. Metrolingualism: Fixity, fluidity and language in flux. *International Journal of Multilingualism* 7(3): 240–254.

Pakir, Anne 2014. Glocal English in Singapore? A re-exploration of the localization of English. In Neil Murray and Angela Scarino (eds.), *Dynamic Ecologies*. New York: Springer. 49–57.

Palfreyman, David and Muhamed al Khalil. 2007. "A funky language for teenzz to use:" Representing Gulf Arabic inilnstant messaging. In B. Danet and S. C. Herring (eds.), *The Multilingual Internet: Language, Culture, and Communication Online*. New York: Oxford University Press. 43–63.

Paolillo, John 2001. Language variation on Internet Relay Chat: A social network approach. *Journal of Sociolinguistics* 5(2): 180–213.

Papacharissi, Zizi (ed.) 2011. *A Networked Self: Identity, Community, and Culture on Social Network Sites*. New York: Routledge.

Park, Jaram, Vladimir Barash, Clay Fink, and Miyoung Cha 2013. Emotion style: interpreting differences in emotions across cultures. *Proceedings of the Seventh International AAAI Conference on Weblogs and Social Media*. 466–475.

Park, So Young 2010. Transnational adoption, Hallyu, and the politics of Korean popular culture. *Biography* 33(1): 151–166.

Pascoe, C. J. 2012. Studying young people's new media use: Methodological shifts and educational innovations. *Theory Into Practice* 51(2): 76–82.

Paunonen, Heikki, Jani Vuolteenaho, and Terhi Ainiala 2009. Industrial Urbanization, working-class lads and slang toponyms in twentieth-century Helsinki. *Urban History* 36(3): 449–472.

Pennycook, Alastair 2007a. *Global Englishes and Transcultural Flows*. New York/London: Routledge.

Pennycook, Alastair 2007b. 'The rotation gets thick. The constraints get thin': Creativity, recontextualization, and difference. *Applied Linguistics* 28(4): 579–596.

Peuronen, Saija 2011. Ride hard, live forever: translocal identities in an online community of extreme sports Christians. In Crispin Thurlow and Kristine Mroczek (eds.), *Digital Discourse. Language in the New Media*. Oxford: Oxford University Press. 154–176.

Pew Research 2016a. Smartphone ownership and internet usage continues to climb in emerging economies. www.pewglobal.org/2016/02/22/smartphone-ownership-and-Internet-usage-continues-to-climb-in-emerging-economies/

Pew Research 2016b. Cell phones in Africa: communication lifeline. www.pewglobal.org/2015/04/15/cell-phones-in-africa-communication-lifeline/

Pew Research 2016c. Social networking very popular among adult internet users in emerging and developing nations. www.pewglobal.org/2016/02/22/social-networking-very-popular-among-adult-Internet-users-in-emerging-and-developing-nations/

Plester, Beverly, Clare Wood, and Puja Joshi 2009. Exploring the relationship between children's knowledge of text message abbreviations and school literacy outcomes. *British Journal of Developmental Psychology* 27(1): 145–161.

Pollard, Velma 1980. Dread Talk – the speech of the Rastafarian in Jamaica. *Caribbean Quarterly* 26(4): 32–41.

Pollard, Velma 1986. Innovation in Jamaican Creole: The speech of Rastafari. In M. Görlach and J. Holm (eds.), *Focus on the Caribbean*. Amsterdam/Philadelphia: John Benjamins. 157–166.

Porter, Gina 2012. Mobile phones, livelihoods and the poor in Sub-Saharan Africa: Review and prospect. *Geography Compass* 6(5): 241–259.

Preisler, Bent 1999. Functions and forms of English in a European EFL country. In Tony Bex and Richard Watts (eds.), *Standard English: The Widening Debate*. New York/London: Routledge. 239–267.

Preston, Dennis R. 1985. The Li'l Abner syndrome: Written representations of speech. *American Speech* 60(4): 328–336.

Quist, Pia 2008. Sociolinguistic approaches to multiethnolect: Language variety and stylistic practice. *International Journal of Bilingualism*, 12(1–2): 43–61.

Quist, Pia 2018. Alternative place naming in the diverse margins of an ideologically mono-lingual society. In Leonie Cornips and Vincent de Rooij (eds.), *The Sociolinguistics of Place and Belonging Perspectives from the Margins*. Amsterdam: John Benjamins.

Quist, Pia and Bente Ailin Svendsen (eds.) 2010. *Multilingual Urban Scandinavia: New Linguistic Practices*. Bristol: Multilingual Matters.

Rainie, Lee and Barry Wellman 2012. *Networked. The New Social Operating System*. Cambridge, MA: The MIT Press.

Ramirez, Catherine S. 2006. Saying "nothin'": Pachucas and the languages of resistance. *Frontiers: A Journal of Women Studies* 27(3): 1–33.

Rampton, Ben 1995. *Crossing: Language and Ethnicity among adolescents*. London/New York: Longman.

Rampton, Ben 1998. Language crossing and the redefinition of reality. In P. Auer (ed.), *Code-Switching in Conversation: Language, Interaction and Identity*. London: Routledge. 290–320.

Rampton, Ben 2011. From "multi-ethnic adolescent heteroglossia" to "contemporary urban vernaculars". *Language and Communication* 31(4): 276–294.

Rampton, Ben 2014. *Crossing: Language & Ethnicity among Adolescents* (Second edition). London: Routledge.

Rickford, John R. and Russell J. Rickford 2000. *Spoken Soul: The Story of Black English*. New York: John Wiley and Sons.

Rindal, Ulrikke E. 2015. Who owns English in Norway? L2 attitudes and choices among learners. In A. Linn, N. Bernard, and G. Ferguson (eds.), *Attitudes towards English in Europe. Part III: Attitudes towards English in Schools*. Berlin/Boston: Walter de Gruyter. 241–270.

Roberts, Beth Ellen 2005. W.H. Auden and the Jews. *Journal of Modern Literature* 28 (3): 87–108.

Robertson, Roland 1995. Glocalization: time-space and homogeneity-heterogeneity. In Mike Featherstone, Scott M. Lash, and Roland Robertson (eds.), *Global Modernities*. London: Sage. 25–44.

Rodriguez, Richard 1983. *Hunger of Memory: The Education of Richard Rodriguez: An Autobiography*. New York: Bantam.

Rotevatn, Audhild G. 2014. Språk i spagaten. Facebook-språket. Om normert språk og dialekt blant vestlandselevar [Language doing the splits. Facebook language. On standard language and dialect among pupils in Western Norway.] MA dissertation. Volda University College.

Røyneland, Unn 2009. Dialects in Norway: Catching up with the rest of Europe? *International Journal of the Sociology of Language* 196/197: 7–31.

Røyneland, Unn 2016. Revision of the Nynorsk standard: Deliberation, decision and legitimisation. In Sue Wright, Unn Røyneland, and Pia Lane (eds.), *Language Standardisation: Theory and Practice*. Special issue of *Sociolinguistica* 30: 83–105.

Røyneland, Unn 2017. Hva skal til for å høres ut som du hører til? Forestillinger om dialektale identiteter i det senmoderne Norge. [What should you sound like to sound like you belong? Conceptions of dialectal identities in late modern Norway.] *Nordica Helsingiensia* 48: 91–106.

Røyneland, Unn, this volume. Virtually Norwegian: negotiating language and identity on YouTube. In Cecelia Cutler and Unn Røyneland (eds.), *Multilingual Youth Language in Computer Mediated Communication*. Cambridge: Cambridge University Press.

Rubin, Uri 2010. Muḥammad's message in Mecca: warnings, signs, and miracles. In J. Brockopp (ed.), *The Cambridge Companion to Muḥammad*. Cambridge/New York: Cambridge University Press. 39–60.

Rudwick, Stephanie 2005. Township language dynamics: IsiZulu and isiTsotsi in Umlazi. *Southern African Linguistics and Applied Language Studies* 23(3): 305–317.

Ryan, Camille 2013. Language use in the United States: 2011. *American community survey reports* 22: 1–16.

Sabaté i Dalmau, Maria 2012. A sociolinguistic analysis of transnational SMS practices: Non-elite multilingualism, grassroots literacy and social agency among migrant populations in Barcelona. *Lingvisticae Investigationes* 35(2): 318–340.

Sacks, Harvey 1992. *Lectures on Conversations*. Oxford and Cambridge, MA: Blackwell.

Saleh, Walid. 2010. The Arabian context of Muḥammad's life. In J. Brockopp (ed.), *The Cambridge Companion to Muḥammad*. Cambridge/New York: Cambridge University Press. 21–38.

Sandøy, Helge 2011. Language culture in Norway: A tradition of questioning language standard norms. In T. Kristiansen and N. Coupland (eds.), *Standard languages and language standards in a changing Europe*. Oslo: Novus. 119–126.

Santa Ana, Otto 1993. The nature of the Chicano language setting and definition of Chicano English. *Hispanic Journal of the Behavioral Sciences* 15(1): 3–35.

Sapir, Edward 1951 [1931]. Communication. In Edwin Seligman and Alvin Johnson (eds.), *Encyclopaedia of the Social Sciences vol. III*. New York: Macmillan. 78–80.

Saville-Troike, Muriel 2003. *The Ethnography of Communication: An Introduction*. Malden, MA: Blackwell.

Schegloff, Emanuel A. 2007. A tutorial on membership categorization. *Journal of Pragmatics* 39(3): 462–482.

Schieffelin, Bambi B. and Rachelle C. Doucet 1994. The "real" Haitian Creole: Ideology, metalinguistics, and orthographic choice. *American ethnologist* 21(1): 176–200.

Schuring, G. K. 1979. Leksikologiese kenmerke van Tsotsitaal. *Taalfasette* 26(2): 59–71.

Sebba, Mark 2003. Spelling rebellion. In Jannis Androutsopoulos and Alexandra Georgakopoulou (eds.), *Discourse Constructions of Youth Identities*. Amsterdam/Philadelphia: John Benjamins. 151–172.

Sebba, Mark 2007. *Spelling and Society: The Culture and Politics of Orthography around the World*. Cambridge: Cambridge University Press.

Sebba, Mark 2012. Researching and theorising multilingual texts. In Mark Sebba, Shahrzad Mahootian, and Carla Jonsson (eds.), *Language Mixing and Code-Switching in Writing. Approaches to Mixed-Language Written Discourse*. London: Routledge. 1–26.

Sebba, Mark 2015. Iconicity, attribution, and branding in orthography. *Written Language and Literacy* 18(2): 208–227.

Sebba, Mark and Tony Wootton 1998. We, they and identity: sequential versus identity-related explanation in code-switching. In P. Auer (ed.), *Code-Switching in Conversation: Language, Interaction and Identity*. London: Routledge. 262–286.

Sharma, Bal Krishna 2014. On high horses: transnational Nepalis and language ideologies on YouTube. *Discourse, Context and Media* 4–5: 19–28. http://dx.doi.org/10.1016/j.dcm.2014.04.001

Shaw, Philip 2008. Spelling, accent and identity in computer-mediated communication. *English Today* 24(2): 42–49.

Shiohata, Mariko 2012. Language use along the urban street in Senegal: Perspectives from proprietors of commercial signs. *Journal of Multilingual and Multicultural Development* 33(3): 269–285.

Silverstein, Michael 1976. Shifters, linguistic categories and cultural description. In Keith Basso and Henry Selby (eds.), *Meaning and Anthropology*. New York: Harper and Row. 11–55.

Silverstein, Michael 1979. Language structure and linguistic ideology. In R. Clyne, W. Hanks, and C. Hofbauer (eds.), *The Elements: Parasession on Linguistic Units and Levels*. Chicago Linguistic Society. 193–247.

Silverstein, Michael 1993. Metapragmatic discourse and metapragmatic function. In John Lucy (ed.), *Reflexive language: Reported Speech and Metapragmatics*. Cambridge: Cambridge University Press. 33–58.

Silverstein, Michael 2005. Axes of evals: Token versus type interdiscursivity. *Journal of Linguistic Anthropology* 15(1): 6–22.

Slabbert, Sarah and Carol Myers-Scotton 1996. The structure of Tsotsitaal and Iscamtho: Code-switching and in-group identity in South African townships. *Linguistics* 35(2): 317–342.

Slade, Benjamin 2014. Overstanding Idren: Special features of Rastafari English morphology. In Rastafari Studies Unit (ed.), *Proceedings of the 2nd Rastafari Studies Conference & General Assembly 2013: Rastafari, Coral Gardens and African redemption. Challenges and opportunities. Commemorating the 50th anniversary of the Coral Gardens massacre (August 12–16, 2013)*, forthcoming. Mona, Jamaica: The University of the West Indies.

Smitherman, Geneva 2006. *Word from the Mother: Language and African Americans*. New York/London: Routledge.

Soffer, Oren 2010. "Silent orality": Toward a conceptualization of the digital oral features in CMC and SMS texts. *Communication Theory* 20(4): 387–404.

Soffer, Oren 2012. Liquid language? On the personalization of discourse in the digital era. *New Media & Society* 14(7): 1092–1110.

Sotirova, Irina 2014. *Hallyu* and student's motivation in studying Korean. In Valentina Merinescu (ed.), *Global Impact of South Korean Popular Culture: Hallyu Unbond*. London: Lexington Books. 75–79.

SouthAfrica.info 2011. SA mobile adspend "to double by 2012". www.southafrica.info /business/trends/newbusiness/mobileads-270511.htm#.VrNSLEA6w-g

Spilioti, Tereza 2011. Beyond genre: Closings and relational work in text messaging. In Crispin Thurlow and Kristine Mroczek (eds.), *Digital Discourse: Language in the New Media*. New York: Oxford University Press. 67–128.

Spilioti, Tereza and Alexandra Georgakopoulou (eds.) 2015. *The Routledge Handbook of Language and Digital Communication*. Abingdon/New York: Routledge.

Squires, Lauren 2014. Class and productive avoidance in The Real Housewives reunions. *Discourse, Context & Media* 6: 33–44.

Sridhar, Kamal K. 1996. Societal multilingualism. In Sandra Lee McKay and Nancy H. Hornberger (eds.), *Sociolinguistics and Language Teaching*. Cambridge: Cambridge University Press. 47–70.

Stæhr, Andreas 2014. Social media and everyday language use among Copenhagen youth. PhD dissertation. Copenhagen: University of Copenhagen. Faculty of Humanities.

Stæhr, Andreas 2015. Reflexivity in Facebook interaction – enregisterment across written and spoken language practices. *Discourse, Context & Media* 8: 30–45.

Staksrud, Elisabeth 2016. *Children in the Online World: Risk, Regulation, Rights*. Abingdon/New York: Routledge.

Statistics Norway 2015. www.ssb.no/forside/_attachment/269027?_ts=15533e71088

Statistics Norway 2017. Nøkkeltall for innvandring og innvandrere [Key figures for immigration and immigrants]. www.ssb.no/innvandring-og-innvandrere/nokkeltall/innvandring-og-innvandrere

Stokoe, Elisabeth 2012. Moving forward with membership categorization analysis: Methods for systematic analysis. *Discourse Studies* 14(3): 277–303.

Storch, Anne 2011. *Secret Manipulations. Language and Context in Africa*. Oxford: Oxford University Press.

Storch, Anne 2013. Doing things with words. In: Frederike Lüpke and A. Storch (eds.), *Repertoires and Choices in African Language*. Berlin: Mouton de Gruyter. 77–122.

Strømmen, Nils Petter 2017. Medietrender. [Media trends.] Kantar TNS.

Stroud, Christopher and Lionel Wee 2012. *Style, Identity and Literacy: English in Singapore*. Clevedon: Multilingual Matters.

Suchman, Lucy 2005. Affiliative objects. *Organization* 12(3): 379–399.

Suleiman, Yasir 2012. Ideology and the standardization of Arabic. In R. Bassiouney and E.G. Katz (eds.), *Arabic language and linguistics*. Georgetown University Roundtable on Languages and Linguistics Series. Washington, D.C.: Georgetown University Press. 201–213.

Svendsen, Bente Ailin and Stephania Marzo 2015. A “new” speech style is born. The omnipresence of structure and agency in the life of semiotic registers in heterogeneous urban spaces. *European Journal of Applied Linguistics* 3(1): 47–85.

Svendsen, Bente Ailin and Unn Røyneland 2008. Multiethnolectal facts and functions in Oslo, Norway. *International Journal of Bilingualism* 12(1–2): 63–83.

Swigart, Leigh 1992. Two codes or one? The insider’s view and the description of codeswitching in Dakar. In Carol M. Eastman (ed.), *Codeswitching*. Clevedon/Philadelphia/Adelaide: Multilingual Matters Ltd. 83–102.

Swigart, Leigh 1994. Cultural creolisation and language use in post-colonial Africa: The case of Senegal. *Africa* 64(2): 175–189.

Swinehart, Karl F. 2008. The mass mediated chronotope, radical counterpublics, and dialect in 1970s Norway: The case of Vømmølspellmanslag. *Journal of Linguistic Anthropology* 18(2): 290–301.

Swinehart, Karl F. 2012a. The Enregisterment of Colla in a Bolivian (Camba) Comedy. *Social Text* 30(4): 81–102.

Swinehart, Karl F. 2012b. Ayllu on the airwaves: rap, reform, and redemption on Aymara national radio. PhD dissertation. University of Pennsylvania.

Swinehart, Karl F. 2012c. Metadiscursive regime and register formation on Aymara radio. *Language & Communication* 32(2): 102–113.

Swinehart, Karl F. 2012d. Tupac in their veins: Hip-hop Alteño and the semiotics of urban indigeneity. *Arizona Journal of Hispanic Cultural Studies* 16(16): 79–96.

Swinehart, Karl F., this volume. Footing and role alignment online: Andean, indigenous or hip-hop nations? In Cecelia Cutler and Unn Røyneland (eds.), *Multilingual Youth Language in Computer Mediated Communication*. Cambridge: Cambridge University Press.

Tannen, Deborah and Anna M. Trester (eds.) 2013. *Discourse 2.0: Language and New Media*. Washington D.C.: Georgetown University Press.

Terkourafi, Marina (ed.) 2010. *The Language(s) of Global Hip-hop*. London: Continuum.

The Office of Ethnic Communities of the New Zealand Government 2013. *Korean Wave motivates Kiwis to learn English*. http://ethniccommunities.govt.nz/story/%E2%80%9Ckorean-wave%E2%80%9D-motivates-kiwis-learn-korean

Thiam, Ndiassé 1994. La variation sociolinguistique du code mixte wolof-français à Dakar, une première approche. *Langage et société* 68(1): 11–33.

Thompson, Dominic and Ruth Filik 2016. Sarcasm in written communication: Emoticons are efficient markers of intention. *Journal of Computer-Mediated Communication* 21(2): 105–120.

Thompson, Miché 2013. Cybersocialising: the variability of genre and register norms in Smartphone chatting. Unpublished Honours paper. Linguistics Department, University of the Western Cape.

Thurlow, Crispin 2003. Generation Txt? The sociolinguistics of young people's text-messaging. *Discourse Analysis Online* 1(1). www.researchgate.net/publication/251852851_Generation_Txt_The_sociolinguistics_of_young_people%27s_text-messaging

Thurlow, Crispin 2011. Determined creativity: Language play in new media discourse. In R. Jones (ed.), *Discourse and Creativity*. London: Pearson. 169–190.

Thurlow, Crispin and Kristine Mroczek (eds.) 2011a. *Digital Discourse: Language in the New Media*. Oxford: Oxford University Press.

Thurlow, Crispin and Kristine Mroczek 2011b. Introduction. In Crispin Thurlow and Kristine Mroczek (eds.), *Digital Discourse: Language in the New Media*. Oxford: Oxford University Press. xix-xliv.

Thurlow, Crispin and Michelle Poff 2013. Text messaging. In Susan Herring, Dieter Stein, and Tuija Virtanen (eds.), *Pragmatics of Computer-Mediated Communication*. Berlin: De Gruyter Mouton. 163–189.

Tolson, Andrew 2010. A new authenticity? Communicative practices on YouTube. *Critical Discourse Studies* 7(4): 277–289.

Trudgill, Peter 2000. *Sociolinguistics: An Introduction to Language and Society*. Fourth edition. London: Penguin Books.

Turkle, Sherry 2005. [1984]. *The Second Self: Computers and the Human Spirit*. Massachusetts Institute of Technology Press.

Turkle, Sherry 2007. *Evocative Objects: The Things We Think With*. Massachusetts Institute of Technology Press.

Uricchio, William 2004. Cultural citizenship in the age of P2P networks. In Ib Bondebjerg and Peter Golding (eds.), *European Culture and the Media*. Bristol: Intellect Books. 139–63.

Vassenden, Kåre 2012. Hvor stor er egentlig innvandringen til Norge – nå, før og internasjonalt? [How large is really the immigration to Norway – currently, previously and internationally?] *Samfunnsspeilet* 13: 7–12.

Vermeulen, Jan 2011. Smartphone usage stats: SA versus the world. November 11. Mybroadband. https://mybroadband.co.za/news/gadgets/38101-smartphone-usage-stats-sa-versus-the-world.html

Vertovec, Steven 2007. Super-diversity and its implications. *Ethnic and Racial Studies* 30(6). 1024–1054.

Vigouroux, Cécile B. 2015. Genre, heteroglossic performances, and new identity: Stand-up comedy in modern French society. *Language in Society* 44(2): 243–272.

Wagemakers, Joas 2012a. The enduring legacy of the second Saudi State: Quietist and radical Wahhabi contestations of Al-Walāʿ wa-l-Barāʿ. *Journal of Middle East Studies* 44(1): 93–110.

Wagemakers, Joas 2012b. *A Quietist Jihadi: The Ideology and Influence of Abu Muhammad al-Maqdisi*. New York: Cambridge University Press.

Watson, G. Llewellyn 1991. *Jamaican Sayings: With Notes on Folklore, Aesthetics, and Social Control*. Gainsville, FL: University Press of Florida.

Weinreich, Uriel 1953. *Languages in Contact. Findings and Problems*. Publications of the Linguistic Circle of New York, 1.

Wiedner, Jacob A. P. 2016. (De)mystifying Norwegian Romani – the discursive construction of a minority language. PhD dissertation. MultiLing, University of Oslo.

Wilhelmsen, Marit, Bjørn Are Holth, Øyvin Kleven, and Terje Risberg 2013. Minoritetsspråk i Norge [Minority Language in Norway]. www.ssb.no/utdanning/artikler-og-publikasjoner/_attachment/100940?_ts=13d3a8c3cf0

Williams, Quentin and Christopher Stroud 2014. Battling the race: Stylizing language and coproducing Whiteness and colouredness in a freestyle rap performance. *Journal of Linguistic Anthropology* 24(3): 277–293.

Wodak, Ruth and Scott Wright 2004. The European Union in cyberspace: democratic participation via online multilingual discussion boards? Unpublished.

Woolard, Kathryn 1999. Simultaneity and bivalency as strategies in bilingualism. *Journal of Linguistic Anthropology* 8(1): 3–29.

Wright, Scott 2004. A Comparative analysis of government-run discussion boards at the local, national and European Union levels. Unpublished PhD dissertation. University of East Anglia, Norwich.

Wronski, Michal and Arthur Goldstuck 2011. *Social media goes mainstream in South Africa*. tech4africa.com/blog/tags/world-wide-worx

Yang, Guobin 2009. *The Power of the Internet in China: Citizen Activism Online*. New York: Columbia University Press.

Zentella, Ana Celia 2007. 'Dime con Quién Hablas, y Te Dire Quién Eres': Linguistic (in)security and Latina/o identity. In Juan Flores and Renato Rosaldo (eds.), *A Companion to Latina/o Studies*. Maiden, MA: Blackwell. 25–38.

Zentella, Ana Celia 2009. Latin@ languages and identities. In Marcelo M. Súarez-Orozco and Mariela M. Páez (eds.), *Latinos: Remaking America*. Berkeley, CA: University of California Press. 21–35.

Index